# SOCIETAL GROWTH

# Other Joint Publications of The Free Press and The American Sociological Association

**Peter M. Blau,** ***Approaches to the Study of Social Structure***

The most concise and definitive statement of sociological conceptions of social structure. It dramatically illustrates the parallel as well as contrasting features of diverse theoretical conceptions of structural analysis. Contributors include: Robert K. Merton, George C. Homans, William J. Goode, James S. Coleman, Talcott Parsons, Walter L. Wallace, Gerhard E. Lenski, Robert S. Bierstedt, Tom Bottomore, Seymour Martin Lipset, Lewis A. Coser, and Peter M. Blau.

The 1974 meeting in Montreal

**Lewis A. Coser and Otto N. Larsen,** ***The Uses of Controversy in Sociology***

A critical assessment of some of the major controversies in sociology today. Twenty-three distinguished sociologists examine several areas of concern: trends in American society, cleavages in the social structure, individual and societal modernity, conflict and revolution, the resurgence of ethnicity, labeling theory, the links between knowledge and policy, and theoretical and methodological problems. The selections represent a wide range of issues but each is a probing of the tools or the results of the sociological enterprise.

The 1975 meeting in San Francisco

**J. Milton Yinger and Stephen J. Cutler,** ***Major Social Issues: A Multidisciplinary View***

Authorities from the fields of sociology, economics, psychology, anthropology, history, philosophy, law, and biology present different approaches to critical issues of our time that are currently the subject of active multidisciplinary research. This sharing of ideas is a rare event among today's scholars and provides the basis for a useful synthesis of social scientific ideas.

The 1977 meeting in Chicago

# Societal Growth

Processes and Implications

Edited by

**Amos H. Hawley**

A Publication of
The American
Sociological Association

THE FREE PRESS
*A Division of Macmillan Publishing Co., Inc.*
NEW YORK

Collier Macmillan Publishers
LONDON

The Free Press
A Division of Macmillan Publishing Co., Inc.
866 Third Avenue, New York, N. Y. 10022

Collier Macmillan Canada, Ltd.

Library of Congress Catalog Card Number: 79-7339

Printed in the United States of America

printing number

1 2 3 4 5 6 7 8 9 10

**Library of Congress Cataloging in Publication Data**
Main entry under title:

Societal growth.

"A publication of the American Sociological Association."
Papers presented at the annual meeting of the American Sociological Association held Sept. 4-8, 1978 in San Francisco.
Includes bibliographical references and indexes.
1. Social systems--Growth--Congresses. 2. Social evolution--Congresses. 3. Social change--Congresses. I. Hawley, Amos Henry. II. American Sociological Association.
HN3.S6 1979 301.4 79-7339
ISBN 0-02-914200-8

# Contents

# About the Contributors

JUDITH BLAKE received her Ph.D. degree from Columbia University in 1961. She was formerly Professor of Demography and Chair of the Department of Demography, University of California, Berkeley, and is now Bixby Professor of Population Policy, School of Public Health, University of California, Los Angeles. In 1976–77 she held a Guggenheim Fellowship. She is a member of the Assembly of Social and Behavioral Sciences, National Academy of Sciences. Her publications include *Family Structure in Jamaica, Western European Censuses,* and papers in numerous professional journals.

KENNETH E. BOULDING concluded his graduate education at Oxford University in 1941 and is presently Distinguished Professor of Economics at the University of Colorado. He has been president of the American Economics Association and the American Association for the Advancement of Science. He is a Fellow in the American Academy of Arts and Sciences and a member of the American Philosophical Society. Among the thirty books he has authored are *The Reconstruction of Economics, The Image, The Organizational Revolution, A Primer on Social Dynamics,* and *Ecodynamics.*

JAMES S. COLEMAN, Professor of Sociology at the University of Chicago, received his Ph.D. degree from Columbia University in 1955. He is a member of the American Philosophical Society and of the National Academy of Sciences and a Fellow in the American Academy of Arts and Sciences. Among his published volumes are *Adolescent Society, Introduction to Mathematical Sociology, Resources for Social Change,* and *Youth: Transition to Adulthood.*

PHILIP E. CONVERSE obtained his Ph.D. at the University of Michigan in 1958 and is currently Robert C. Angell Professor of Political Science and Sociology at the University of Michigan, and Program Director at the Institute for Social Research. He was coauthor of *The American Voter* (1960) and wrote the essay "The Nature of Belief Systems in Mass Publics" (1964). More recently he has been involved with Angus Campbell in a program of studies on the perceived quality of life, and a coauthor of *The Quality of American Life* (1976). He is a member of the National Academy of Science and a Fellow in the American Academy of Arts and Sciences.

SCOTT GREER earned his Ph.D. from the University of California at Los Angeles in 1952 and is now Professor of Sociology at the Milwaukee Campus of the University of Wisconsin. He was chief sociologist of the Metropolitan St. Louis Survey and formerly a member of the faculty of Northwestern University. In addition to two volumes of poetry, he has authored *Exploring the Metropolitan Community* (with others), *The Emerging City, Governing the Metropolis, Metropolitics, Urban Renewal and American Cities, The Logic of Social Enquiry,* and *The Urbane View.*

JOSEPH GUSFIELD, Professor of Sociology at the University of California, San Diego, received his undergraduate and graduate education at the University of Chicago, concluding with the Ph.D. in 1954. His area of current research is the sociology of knowledge and law. Among his publications are *Symbolic Crusade: Status Politics in the American Temperance Movement, Community: Critical Response, Academic Values in Mass Education* (with David Riesman and Zelda Gamson), and *The Illusion of Authority: Rhetoric, Ritual and Metaphor in Public Actions.*

AMOS H. HAWLEY received his Ph.D. degree from the University of Michigan in 1941 and is now Kenan Professor Emeritus at the University of North Carolina. He has been President of the Population Association of America (1971) and of the American Sociological Association (1978). He is a Fellow in the American Academy of Arts and Sciences. His publications include *Human Ecology: A Theory of Community Structure, The Changing Shape of Metropolitan America,* and *Urban Society: An Ecological Approach.*

ROBERT W. HODGE, since obtaining his Ph.D. degree at the University of Chicago in 1967, has taught at the universities of Chicago, Michigan, and California, and he is now Professor of Sociology at the State University of New York at Stony Brook. He has also served as a Senior Simon Research Fellow at the Victoria University of Manchester (England) and as a Visiting Professor at the Hebrew University of Jerusalem. He is a contributor of research papers to numerous professional journals and has recently coedited a special issue of *Social Forces* dealing with Social Stratification.

IRVING LOUIS HOROWITZ, Professor of Sociology and Political Science and Director of Studies in Comparative International Development at Rutgers University, after receiving his Ph.D. from Buenos Aires University in 1957, served on the faculty of Washington University until 1969 and held visiting professorships in a number of institutions both in the United States and abroad. Among his publications are *Social Science and Public Policy in the United States; The Rise and Fall of Project Camelot: Studies in the Relationship between Social Science and Practical Politics; The Use and Abuse of Social Science: Behavioral Science and National Decision Making; Ideology and Utopia in the United States: 1975–1976.*

MORRIS JANOWITZ, Distinguished Service Professor at the University of Chicago, received his Ph.D. degree from that institution in 1948. His work has long been concerned with the normative and political dimensions of urban institutions. Currently his research is addressed to a comparative analysis of citizenship and its transformation under advanced industrialism. He is a Fellow in the American Academy of Arts and Sciences.

NATHAN KEYFITZ, Andelot Professor of Sociology and Demography and Chairman of the Department of Sociology at Harvard University, received his Ph.D. from the University of Chicago in 1952. His most recent book is *Applied Mathematical Demography*. During 1978 he has lectured at the universities of Moscow and Costa Rica. He is a member of the National Academy of Sciences and a Fellow in the American Academy of Arts and Sciences.

ANNE T. LAWRENCE is a doctoral candidate in sociology and a research assistant at the Institute of Industrial Relations, University of California, Berkeley. She received her B.A. from Swarthmore College in 1974.

GERHARD LENSKI, Alumni Distinguished Professor of Sociology at the University of North Carolina and Fellow in the American Academy of Arts and Sciences, received his Ph.D. from Yale University in 1950. He is author of *The Religious Factor, Power and Privilege,* and *Human Societies.* He is currently at work on a book designed to provide a systematic statement of the new materialist evolutionary theory.

JUDAH MATRAS is currently Visiting Professor of Sociology at Carleton University in Ottawa, Canada. Born in the United States in 1934, he has been at the Hebrew University of Jerusalem since 1958 and associated with the Brookdale Institute in Jerusalem since 1976. He received his Ph.D. from the University of Chicago, has had visiting appointments at the universities of Chicago, Wisconsin, and Washington, and has done research and written extensively on population, social stratification, and their intersection as well as on Israeli society and population.

GARRY S. MEYER is completing his doctoral work in sociology at the State University of New York at Stony Brook, while serving on the professional staff of the Computation Center of the Stony Brook campus. His research interests embrace mobility and fertility, ethnic prestige, demographic change and mobility in academia, Markov models as causal chains, applications of multidimensional scaling and stratification, and urban systems.

J. JOHN PALEN received his Ph.D. from the University of Wisconsin in 1965 and now is Professor of Sociology at the University of Wisconsin, Milwaukee. He has published works on various urban-related topics, including *Urban America, The Urban World, City Scenes,* and *Social Problems.*

GERALD SUTTLES obtained his Ph.D. at the University of Illinois in 1966 and is now Professor of Sociology at the University of Chicago. He has worked extensively on local community formation in a metropolitan context. He is author of *The Social Order of the Slum* and coauthor, with Kirsten Gronbjerg and David Street, of *Poverty and Social Change*. His current research deals with the role of citizen activism in urban redevelopment.

STANLEY H. UDY, JR., Professor of Sociology at Dartmouth College, received his Ph.D. from Princeton University and, before moving to his present position, was a faculty member at Yale University. His principal publications include *The Organization of Work* and *Work in Traditional and Modern Society.*

IMMANUEL WALLERSTEIN received his Ph.D. from Columbia University in 1959. He is now Distinguished Professor and Chair, Department of Sociology, and Director, Fernand Braudel Center for Study of Economies, Historical Systems and Civilizations of the State University of New York at Binghamton. He is President of the African Studies Association and Vice-President of the Research Commission on National Movements and Imperialism, International Sociological Association. He has authored *The Modern World-System*, for which he received the Sorokin Award of the American Sociological Association, and *The Capitalist World Economy.*

HAROLD L. WILENSKY, Professor of Sociology and Research Sociologist in the Institutes of Industrial Relations and International Studies at the University of California, Berkeley, holds a Ph.D. from the University of Chicago (1955). He has served on the Councils of the American Sociological Association and the Industrial Relations Research Association and was a Fellow at the Center for Advanced Study in the Behavioral Sciences. His several books include *Intellectuals in the Labor Unions, Organizational Intelligence: Knowledge and Policy in Government and Industry,* and *The Welfare State and Equality.*

# Preface

The history of humankind is a record of the growth, convergence, conflict and accommodation of social systems. The general rejection of nineteenth century evolutionism and theories of progress drew attention away from phenomena of cumulative change or societal growth. Yet the fact remained that social systems increased in complexity, in energy consumed, in the numbers of people involved, and in the territories encompassed. That growth in this sense has often been followed by stagnation and decline does not contravene the historic experience, for the process has always been resumed again in another time and place.

Increase in scale is associated as cause and effect with profound internal transformations. No aspect of life, private or public, is unaffected by the reorganizations that are necessary to sustain system growth. Of equal significance are the impingements of growing systems upon other systems and upon the physical world at large. External ramifications multiply exponentially, thereby involving neighboring systems more and more deeply in each other's affairs. In a very real sense, then, societal growth is the most engrossing fact of history. It is, moreover, the source of virtually all of the problems addressed by the social sciences.

It was with these thoughts in mind that the 1978 Program Committee of the American Sociological Association* decided to adopt "Societal Growth: Processes and Implications" as the theme of the annual meeting of the Association, convened in San Francisco, September 4–8, 1978. This

*Stephen J. Cutler, William H. Form, John Kasarda, Otto N. Larsen, Edward O. Laumann, Albert J. Reiss, Jr., Alice S. Rossi, James F. Short, Jr., Andrea Tyree, Amos H. Hawley, Chairman.

called for as comprehensive an examination of the large and intricate phenomenon as time and resources afforded. The committee approached the matter with no hidden agenda, no belief that growth is good or bad, no preferred perspective. What was sought was a searching exploration of as many facets of the question as could be accommodated. The objective was analysis. The attainment of anything resembling a synthesis was not anticipated. Indeed it would have been presumptuous. Yet it is not unreasonable to expect that competent analysis might lay the groundwork for theoretical advances in the treatment of cumulative change. I think the papers brought together in this symposium do contribute to that end.

The committee was fortunate in being able to attract a group of distinguished scholars to a presentation of their views on various aspects of the phenomenon. A topic and a few guidelines were the only advice given each author. Accordingly, they speak not with one voice. Strong endorsements of an evolutionary view are accompanied by expressions of skepticism of the utility of that theory; long-standing hypotheses are argued pro and con; growth is seen as beneficial by some, detrimental by others; and ideological positions stand opposed on one or more issues. Still, as will be apparent to the reader, the papers are interwoven with many recurring ideas. These point to a greater-than-expected degree of consensus on what are the salient considerations in the study of growth. They also make any classification of the papers, such as that represented in the order of their appearance in this volume, more than a little arbitrary.

Omitted from the volume, much to our regret, are the many fine discussions offered by panel members of the several sessions. But since a large number of the papers included herein have been revised to take into account the criticisms and suggestions expressed by the discussants, their contributions are not lost.

Amos H. Hawley

# I

## The Forms of Societal Growth

1

# Introduction

*Amos H. Hawley*

A FIRST QUESTION to be considered in any attempt at a systematic treatment of societal growth is what conception of the process is most appropriate to the phenomenon under investigation. Use of the term "conception" is fitting, for the kaleidoscope of history offers many patterns for selection by observers. That any one pattern is sufficiently generic to subsume all of the others is an issue without a final solution. We are not prepared to say that history can be transposed as natural history. But we continue to try many conceptual models for their goodness of fit to the historic process.

The chapters of part 1, although addressed to the formal properties of growth, fall on a rough continuum from the very general to the relatively specific. Gerhard Lenski, the author of chapter 2, is largely responsible for the revival of evolutionary thought in sociology. His concern here is with outlying the long sweep of change in the collective life of human population without pausing to disaggregate, as it were, that life course into its short-term patterns. Evolutionary change is presented as a complex function of three historical parameters—population growth and distribution, technological accumulation, and organizational development—concepts that will reappear in many of the papers to follow. Lenski also anticipates another recurring observation, namely, the fortuitous character of change. The emergence of new biological or social forms, the acquisition of missing items of information, the availability of an unoccupied niche, or the outcome of competition for power among nations is unpredictable in other than probabilistic terms. It is at that point that the uses of history become problematical.

In the third chapter, I deal with the growth phase that intervenes between evolutionary stages, corresponding to what Lenski calls specific in contrast to general evolution. In my view, growth is a process of expansion which follows from an accumulation of information. Evolution is suspended during an expansion phase and is not resumed until after a growth potential is exhausted.

The expansion concept is developed in considerably greater detail by Judah Matras. Increases in population and in knowledge, the driving forces of the expansion process, lead to differentiation on two axes, one represented by the organization for production of amenities of all kinds, and the other by the organization for the distribution of awards and opportunities as well as of sustenance. As differentiation progresses the salience of the two organizational axes is altered with uneven consequences for the various facets of society. So devious and subtle are the ramifications of growth that measurement attempts are confronted by many dimensions that have thus far resisted their reduction to units on appropriate scales.

Whereas Matras considers the problem of measuring change substantively, James Coleman examines the matter from a technical standpoint. He makes it clear, however, that the approach to measurement must be contingent on the conception of change one brings to bear on the task. He, too, elects to use as his model of growth that of expansion in which there is a cumulative interplay between structural complexity and territorial scope. Each of the parameters poses a measurement problem. The first may be managed by observing changes in the numbers of active units comprising a social system; the second by noting shifts in the distances over which chains of interactions extend and in the number of links in the chains.

Nathan Keyfitz, a mathematician-demographer-sociologist, is less than sanguine about the independent causal powers of population in social change. In this respect he stands apart from those who accept the conventional wisdom concerning the role of population as cause. Like Coleman, Keyfitz is acutely aware of the strategic importance of the conceptual model employed for purposes of explanation. Population is no less subject to that constraint than is any other variable. He demonstrates his argument by displaying and examining an assortment of models involving population used in various disciplines and within disciplines. In view of that state of affairs the serious scholar is advised to juxtapose competing population models and attempt to assess the amount of variation explained by each.

These several chapters lay bare the anatomy of current conceptions of societal growth. In doing so they provide a useful introduction to further explorations into the process. As a by-product they also offer a convincing lesson in the mutual dependence of theory and method.

2

# Directions and Continuities in Societal Growth

*Gerhard Lenski*

IN CHOOSING SOCIETAL GROWTH as the theme for this year's convention, Amos Hawley calls us back to renewed consideration of one of the classic concerns of our discipline. For it is no exaggeration to say that throughout the eighteenth and nineteenth centuries, and even into the early years of the present century, sociologists, and anthropologists as well, made the growth, development, or evolution of human societies their primary concern. As Marvin Harris (1968) reminds us, the chief aim of the founders of sociology and anthropology was to create a new science of history.

It is no accident that the founders of modern sociology made so much greater use of historical and comparative materials than most of us today. They realized, as many today apparently do not, that when we limit ourselves to materials drawn largely from a single society, and, worse yet, from a single brief segment of that society's history, we make it impossible to build a true science of human societies. By limiting ourselves in this way, we not only exclude essential data, we also close off important questions, problems, and perspectives.

What we exclude, among other things, are the basic patterns and processes of history, including the patterns of societal growth and development. Yet, if there is any one feature of the human record that cries out for attention today, it is this process of societal growth which has so revolutionized the conditions of human life in the last ten thousand years.

Before turning to this, however, let me say a few words about the concept of societal growth itself. Growth is a more complex concept than it may initially seem. When we study *Webster's New Third International Dictionary*, we find that there are three distinct ideas embedded in the meaning of the word. First, it may refer to simple quantitative increase (*e.g.*, our bank account grows by 30 percent). Second, it may also refer to development or evolution, that is, to transformations that involve increased structural or organizational complexity. Finally, the word may mean progress, or positively valued transformations, especially intellectual or moral advance.

These definitions are important, not only because they serve as a reminder that growth means more than simple numerical increase, but also because they provide a clue to why the course of sociological theorizing and research came to be deflected from its original concern with societal growth. By the early decades of the twentieth century, it had become clear that this three-fold conception of growth could no longer be sustained. Societal growth, in the sense of moral advance, had become a very dubious concept.

Thus, in the early years of this century, leading scholars in both sociology and anthropology felt it necessary to free themselves and their disciplines from the burden of an idea which their own research as well as modern history had brought into disrepute. But in the effort to free themselves from this one idea, they abandoned much of the precious heritage of scholarship accumulated earlier. Above all, they abandoned the quest for a science of history, and in sociology, they allowed our discipline to degenerate into the analysis of a single society at a single moment in its history (Hughes, 1961).

Now, at last, in recent years this radical surgery is being brought into question and more and more sociologists are venturing out again into historical and comparative studies. And as this happens, interest in the classic issues of macrosociology is reviving, and not least among them those relating to societal growth.

My assignment, as defined by Amos Hawley, is to explore the directions and continuities in societal growth and the reasons for them. In this analysis, it will also be necessary to consider the question of the limits to societal growth. In my discussion of directions and continuities, I will draw on a somewhat wider range of data than is customary in contemporary sociology, but I make no apology for this. For if I understand the nature of science, it rests on the foundation of the comparative method, and it is a fundamental principle of the comparative method that one arbitrarily restricts the range of variation in his subject matter only at his own peril. This is not to say that we are called on to compare everything with everything, but if our goal is to understand the growth of human societies, it is dangerous to exclude data from any of them—especially from those which are *least* like the societies which are most familiar to us.

## A New Time Perspective

If we take this principle seriously, we find ourselves confronted with a radically new time perspective. For human societies have been around for a long time. No one can say with any precision just how long this has been, but the most conservative estimates today put the point of speciation (i.e., the point at which our remote ancestors ceased to interbreed with other primates and became a distinct species in their own right) not less than two million years ago, while more generally accepted estimates set this date somewhere between four and five million years in the past (Washburn, 1978).

These are figures we don't often discuss in sociology today, but they are absolutely essential as starting points for theory building about societal growth. Unless we are prepared to assume that the societies which exist in the world today, or in the recent past, are a representative sample of the universe of societies throughout history (an absurd assumption), it is ridiculous to try to use these societies alone as the basis for constructing theories about human societies as a whole and their processes of growth. Yet, if I am not badly mistaken, this is precisely what most sociologists have attempted to do for more than half a century.

Once we accept the longer view of history, we come to realize how grossly distorted our perspective on societal growth has been. For example, all the time since Columbus's discovery of America and since the Protestant Reformation constitutes less than one four-thousandth of the span of human history, taking even the most conservative estimate of the point of speciation. By the same standard, all of recorded history (i.e., since the invention of writing in the Middle East 5,000 years ago) constitutes only one-quarter of one percent of the total span of our species's history. Or, finally, if you take the whole of the period since farming, or plant cultivation, first began, you are still talking about only the last one-half of one percent of human history—the barest tip of the iceberg.

I mention these facts not to belittle the study of modern societies, but only to suggest that in studying them we need to develop a better perspective. When we compare our societies today with those of a more distant past, the essential features of modern societies stand out in sharper contrast, and the differences among these modern societies, important though they may be, appear more as variations on a common theme than as the fundamental and essential differences they otherwise seem to be.

By taking this longer view of history, we also come to see more clearly the biological foundations on which modern social systems rest. For in the beginning, hominid societies almost certainly lacked culture, in the sense of information transmitted by means of symbol systems. This was something that only gradually evolved, and there is good reason to believe that it is only in the last 35,000 years or so that culture has replaced genetics as the *primary* mechanism of adaptation in human societies.

Another important benefit that can be derived from this longer view of history is a new sensitivity to the essential unity of the entire process of societal change and development. We come to realize that the process of modernization and social change in the nineteenth and twentieth centuries is not something totally new and without precedent. Far from it. Our modern social revolution is the continuation of developments that began long ago in the prehistoric past. The thing that is really unprecedented is the current *rate* of change, which has been accelerating for thousands of years. But the forces responsible for the accelerating rate of change today are essentially the same as those responsible for the accelerating rate of change five thousand, or fifteen thousand, years ago.

And, finally, this new time perspective for which I am arguing helps us see more clearly the revolutionary role of technology in human societies, past and present alike. With this broader perspective we can begin to see that technology constitutes a critical new form of information which complements and interacts with the information we carry in our genes. Like the older mode of information, it is an expandable resource which not only pushes out the limits of the possible, but also structures the cost-benefit curves for all the options that fall within those limits, thereby exercising a powerful influence over our choices among them. Like the older mode of information which is the basis of biological evolution, technological information cumulates.

## Directions of Societal Growth

Having set the stage, let me turn to the first of our concerns, the directions of societal growth.

Probably the most obvious directional component in societal growth is the simple increase in numbers of the human population. Recent calculations indicate that 10,000 years ago, at the end of Paleolithic times and just before the beginnings of plant cultivation and animal domestication, the entire human population numbered no more than five to ten million (Dumond, 1975: 717; Pfeiffer, 1972: 349). By the time of Christ, numbers had increased to 300 million, and by the eve of the Industrial Revolution to approximately 700 million (Grauman, 1968). Today the figure stands at four billion; a striking 400- to 800-fold increase over the 10,000-year period.

A second trend of equally long duration is the expansion of the human population into new environmental niches. According to the evidence currently available, our species seems to have originated somewhere in East Africa, and from there gradually spread out until human societies came to occupy all of the continents except Antarctica (and even there temporary settlements have now been established). Equally important, however, over the years, with the aid of new technologies, human populations have gradually invaded formerly uninhabitable territories, such as deserts, mountains, rivers, lakes, oceans, and skies, and at least a brief landing on the moon has been achieved.

These trends are both closely linked to a third trend, the advance in the store of technological information. There is, of course, no simple measure of this advance, but recent research indicates that the rate of energy consumption correlates more highly with the other key components of the technological factor than any other readily available measure (Frisbie and Clarke, 1979) and, fortunately, it is not too difficult to calculate the change that has occurred in energy consumption during the last 10,000 years. Before the beginnings of plant cultivation and animal domestication, human energy consumption was chiefly in the form of food, supplemented to some extent by the use of wood for fire. Using the most generous possible estimates for both population size and for per capita energy use at the time,[1] the entire human population could not have consumed more than 30 billion calories per day. By contrast, we now consume 6,000 times this amount![2]

This same figure is probably also a fairly reliable measure of the increased production and consumption of goods and services in human societies. Translated into per capita terms, this represents a fifteenfold increase at the global level, and, in the case of the most industrialized societies, the increase ranges up to ninetyfold.

The growth of technology is also closely linked to basic changes in social structure. Since the end of the Paleolithic, both societies and communities have experienced explosive growth. During the millions of years of the Paleolithic, the largest human settlement of which we have any knowledge had a population of only 400 to 600 (Pfeiffer, 1972: 240), and the average size, judging from observations of modern hunters and gatherers, was apparently in the neighborhood of 25 to 40 (Pfeiffer, 1972: 375–76; Lenski, 1970: 131). Today, by contrast, the upper limit of the range of population for communities is approximately 15 million, and for societies, 800 million. The average size of communities today is impossible to calculate, but the median for the independent nation-state societies of the world is roughly five million—more than a 100,000-fold increase over societies of the late Paleolithic.

[1]Specifically, I am assuming a population of 10,000,000 and energy consumption of 3,000 calories per person per day.

[2]My calculations are based on UN data for 1973, as reported in *The Statistical Abstract of the U.S., 1975*, table 1403, with a modest 10 percent allowance for the increase in energy consumption between 1973 and 1978.

Paralleling these developments there has been an equally dramatic growth in organizational complexity. On the basis of what we have learned from observations of the hundred or so hunting and gathering societies that survived long enough into the modern era to permit careful study, it would appear that the only prevalent forms of structural differentiation within societies during the Paleolithic were age and sex specialization and differentiation along family lines. In some societies these were probably supplemented by part-time occupational specialization involving the roles of headman and shaman. Beyond this, however, there was apparently nothing. Thus, as recently as 10,000 years ago, human societies were only a bit more complex organizationally than the chimpanzee societies studied by Jane van Lawick-Goodall (1971) and others.

The situation began to change only with the beginnings of plant cultivation and animal domestication. These developments made possible for the first time the formation of a stable economic surplus, which is the necessary precondition for any substantial growth in organizational complexity. There is no need to trace all the details of the process, but it is important to note that the first multicommunity societies were apparently established sometime between 8000 and 3000 B.C., and this development led later to the creation of more far-flung kingdoms and empires. During this same period, there were the beginnings of both full-time occupational and associational specialization. Religious and political associations were formed as specialized entities staffed by full-time priests and officials. There is also evidence in this period of the beginnings of full-time craft specialization and full-time mercantile activity. This trend toward an increased division of labor has, of course, continued down to the present day, with the result that from an organizational standpoint, modern industrial societies bear little resemblance to human societies of just 10,000 years ago.

With the growth of larger and more complex organizations, property and wealth have accumulated and the need for records and record keeping has grown exponentially. The earliest responses to this took the form of three-dimensional clay tokens of various shapes and designs (Schmandt-Besserat, 1978), which later evolved into two-dimensional symbols that we recognize as writing. These early inventions laid a foundation for a succession of others, culminating in the invention of computers, copying machines, typewriters, telephones, and all the other paraphernalia of modern bureaucracies, and they have also been linked to the steady expansion of bureaucracies, both governmental and nongovernmental.

All of these developments—the creation of an economic surplus, the beginnings and expansion of full-time occupational specialization, and the growth of bureaucracies—contributed to another important pattern, the growth of urbanization. Urban communities, by definition, are communities whose residents are largely or wholly freed from the necessity of providing their own food and fibers. Until recently, however, the growth of urban populations was much slower than we often imagine. In fact, as recently as the eighteenth century, not more than 10 percent of the population of any agrarian society lived in truly urban settlements. Today, by contrast, 90 percent or more live in urban centers in a number of societies.

The great growth in specialized occupations and organizations has carried with it as a correlate an increase in the interdependence of human populations. And this, in turn, has necessitated major advances in the technologies of both transportation and communication. Few of these advances occurred, however, before the last 5,000 years, a fact which tells us much about the slow rate of growth in organizational complexity during the early millennia following the end of the Paleolithic.

The increased economic interdependence of human populations has also necessitated increasing use of standardized media of exchange, or monetary systems. In the earliest of these, the basic measure of value was simply some commodity in common use, such as grain or nails or cattle. However, as the volume of economic transactions increased, these proved to be too bulky, and rare metals were gradually substituted. In more recent times, paper currency and even electronic computer impulses have been substituted in an effort to keep abreast of the growing flood of economic transactions.

During this same period of time, there has been a more or less steady growth in the degree of political and economic inequality in human societies. In the absence of a sustainable economic surplus, there was no opportunity in Paleolithic societies for the few to acquire power and privilege at the expense of the many. Plant cultivation and animal domestication, and later, metallurgy, changed all this and opened the door to the growth of both political and economic inequality. At the global level, the range of inequality has steadily increased and is today, almost certainly, greater than it has ever been before. More than that, societal systems of stratification today are more complex than in the past (e.g., Slomczynski and Wesolowski, 1978).

One could easily increase this list of directional trends several-fold, but I will limit myself to mentioning briefly just three others which are too important to ignore. First, as the productive power of human societies has grown, so has their destructive power. The engines of war, like the engines of peace, have steadily grown more powerful. In fact, it is probably now possible for the first time in history for a handful of humans to destroy all of humanity and perhaps all of the higher forms of animal life as well. Second, another corollary of the growth in productive power is the growth in the impact of human societies on the biophysical environment. During the Paleolithic, human societies largely adapted to the environment, but with technological advance we have come more and more to adapt the environment to the needs and desires of human societies. Thus, increasingly we clear forests, dam up rivers, level mountains, and in a thousand other ways transform the world around us.

Finally, we have to include on our list of major directional trends the striking acceleration in the rates of technological innovation and social change. During the last several hundred years, innovation and change have occurred so rapidly that we have almost come to take this for granted. Most of us have real difficulty comprehending how different the situation today is from that which prevailed throughout most of history. But listen to one writer's description of the first million years of human history: "The most extraordinary thing about early man is his astonishing slowness in cultural development. . . . For a million years or so man evolved nothing more elaborate in the way of stone tools than flaked pebbles, hand axes, cleavers, rough scrapers, points and blades. It is not until later Pleistocene times that there were any marked improvements in workmanship or more elaborate inventions." (Cole, 1965: 123–24). From the standpoint of technology, there are less than half a dozen noteworthy innovations identified for the whole of human history down to 100,000 B.C., but in the brief span of 3,000 years between 10,000 and 7000 B.C. there were three times as many (Lenski, 1970: 162). Today, a comparable number of major innovations occurs in a few decades at most.

## Curvilinear Trends and Nonpatterned Aspects of Life

One criticism that has often been directed at evolutionists is that in their enthusiasm for identifying the patterns of growth of human societies, they either ignore those aspects of human life which fail to fit their preconceived notions or, worse yet, they force the facts to fit the theory. Personally, I believe this is untrue. Most evolutionists have been well aware of both the nonpatterned aspects of human existence and those which show curvilinear trends or reversals in direction. Taking the latter first, there are a number of examples which come readily to mind. Several years ago, Blumberg and Winch published a paper providing evidence of a curvilinear relationship between familial complexity and societal complexity. Somewhat earlier (Lenski, 1966), I argued the case for a similar relation between the level of intrasocietal inequality and the level of technological advance. Recently we have begun to witness a downturn in the rate of world population increase, reversing a trend of at least two centuries' duration, and some thousands of years ago the historic increase in the number of human societies came to an end and a decline set in as the era of empire building and societal consolidation began.

Beyond this, we recognize that there are many features of human life in which there seem to be no clearly defined trends or directions. For example, it is hard to see much evidence of persistent trends in art. One finds striking examples of both realistic and abstract art in both Paleolithic and modern eras. Similarly, in sexual mores there is no very obvious relationship between the level of technological or organizational complexity of a society and the restrictiveness or laxity of prevailing moral codes. And, finally, as noted earlier, it is hard to find any basis for belief in the view that moral progress is a correlate of societal growth.

It is important to keep these examples clearly in mind if we are to avoid an oversimplified view of both the historical process itself and evolutionary theory, which seeks to describe and explain that process. Clearly, there is more to history than growth. But having said that, we need to beware of the logical *non sequitur* that denies growth simply because it is not totally pervasive.

## The Paradox of General vs. Specific Evolution

Another major source of confusion in thinking about the directions of societal growth stems from the paradoxical fact that the dominant patterns of general evolution are not the same as the dominant patterns of specific evolution. In other words, the patterns which we observe for the world-system as a whole are not the same as the patterns we observe for the majority of individual societies.

Let me give a simple example. From the standpoint of general evolution, the dominant pattern is that with the passage of time human societies have, on the average, grown larger and more complex. But from the standpoint of specific evolution, the modal pattern has been extinction: Few, if any, of the societies that existed 10,000 years ago are still around today. Ironically, if any of them survived, they are probably among the handful of tiny hunting and gathering groups that have managed to hang on in remote and isolated areas scattered around the world. Most of the societies that existed at the end of the Paleolithic either were destroyed or combined with neighboring groups to form new societies.

Thus, the propositions of general evolution and of specific evolution often appear to contradict one another. In reality, however, one implies the other. The fact that the majority of societies of the past have vanished has been a necessary precondition for the massive expansion of those that have replaced them, given the finite limits of our planet. Ten thousand years ago, there were apparently between 100,000 and 400,000 tiny hunting and gathering societies occupying most of the earth's habitable land mass. Had all or most of them survived, the patterns of general evolution which I described earlier could not have occurred. While some movement in the directions indicated would certainly have been possible, it would have been only a small fraction of what took place.

Some will undoubtedly say, "Wouldn't it have been better if that had happened?" But that is another question. My point is simply that while the patterns of general evolution and the patterns of specific evolution are necessarily different, they are logically consistent.

## Sources of Societal Growth: The Underlying Continuities

It is one thing to document the changes that have occurred, but something else again to explain them. In fact, some have argued (e.g., Harris, 1968) that the greatest failure of the nineteenth-century evolutionists was their inability to do just this. Today, however, I think it may be possible for us to do what they were unable to do. Building on the foundations of the new synthetic theory developed in the biological sciences in the last forty years, and mixing in elements of neo-Malthusian theory, Marx's historical materialism, and modern systems theory, I think we can develop an explanation of the growth patterns of human societies that fits the evidence rather well.

The basic explanation of all the patterns evident in human life seems to be the same as the basic explanation of all the patterns in every other form of life—namely, the interaction of the species's genetic heritage with its environment. As biologists put it, it is the interaction of a species's gene pool and its environment which gives rise to the actual physical and behavioral properties of that species.

This is, of course, a very general statement and therefore not terribly enlightening. Nevertheless, it is the starting point, the foundation on which we have to build. Our job is simply one of adding specification to the terms of this basic relationship.

This brings us to the crucial concept of *information*. The oldest and most basic form of information is that found in the chemical molecule DNA, which is the foundation of all genetic systems. DNA-based genetic systems perform two essential functions: They store information and they transmit it. The information they store is a record of the past experience of their hosts' ancestors and it determines both the morphological and the behavioral potentialities of the organism which possesses it. Environmental influences determine the degree to which those potentialities are realized.

For members of the plant kingdom, genetic systems are the only mechanism available for storing and transmitting information. In the animal kingdom, however, genetic systems were supplemented at an early date, apparently, by the mechanism of individual learning. Modern research has shown that some very simple forms of animal life are capable of this and modify their behavior accordingly. But learned information is stored separately from genetic information and thus is usually lost at the death of each organism unless some mechanism of transmission is developed. Eventually, such a mechanism evolved in the form of genetically determined signals, such as specific sounds, motions, odors, or colors, which convey specific meanings—for example, a warning of danger, an indication of a state of sexual readiness, and the like. More recently, our own prehistoric ancestors developed the first symbol systems, which provided them with a far more flexible means of transmitting information (since symbols are not genetically fixed as signals are) and also a marvelous new system for storing it. The end result of all this has been that the characteristics of human societies are shaped by *three* components—our species's genetic heritage, the environment, and our various symbol-based cultures.

This leads us, then, to ask what each contributes to the end product and, in the present instance, to the phenomenon of societal growth. This is not an easy question to answer, but it is one that deserves considerably more attention than we have given it to date. Without pretending to have the final answer to this question, I shall try to sketch the broad outlines as they appear to me.

To begin with, our genetic heritage provides an inborn expansive tendency. This tendency is not unique to humans, of course. Rather, it is a component of all life and takes several forms. First, all species appear to have a capacity to produce more offspring than are necessary merely to maintain their numbers. In some species, this reaches fantastic proportions, with mature adults producing a million or more eggs or seeds in a given year. The higher mammals have a much smaller reproductive capacity, but even humans have a genetic potential for multiplying several-fold in a single generation under ideal conditions. Second, our genetic heritage motivates us to struggle to preserve life—our own life in the first instance, but also the lives of others on whom we depend or to whom we become emotionally attached, especially our children, who so easily become a kind of extension of our own ego. Then, finally, our genetic heritage provides us with a powerful predisposition, once survival is assured, to increase our input of rewards and satisfactions. Collectively, these elements of our genetic heritage lay the foundation for growth in numbers, in organizational size, and in productivity, as well as all their concomitants.

Turning to the environment, it has a dual function. On the one hand, it is the source from which we derive our energy and all the other material resources on which we depend for most of our rewards and satisfactions. On the other hand, however, it serves as a check and constraint on our expansive tendencies. Most resources are in short supply: There are not enough to satisfy all of our desires. In addition, most resources carry a price tag: We have to expend some of our current resources in order to acquire others. Thus, these factors of scarcity and cost tend to structure our patterns of action. We avoid those patterns of activity that carry a high price tag and yield a small return, and we gravitate toward others that offer big returns at small cost.

By adding culture to the mix, we complicate matters enormously. By means of culture, we supplement the store of information provided by our genetic heritage and individual learning. This process of supplementation is especially important where the acquisition and utilization of energy is concerned because the availability of energy is one of the primary constraints on human activity. Thus, energy-related technology (and this includes the tools and machines that determine the efficiency with which we use available energy as well as those which increase the available supply) is a key element in any explanation of the process of human societal growth.

Culture is also important because it can modify to some degree, which we still cannot accurately measure, the expansionist drive, the self-seeking tendency, and the other motivations with which we are endowed by our genetic heritage. For example, cultural information has led some societies to recognize that rapid population growth is not in their best interests. But culture has also inflamed the passions of countless political leaders, causing them to embark on ruthless programs of conquest. If I am not mistaken, these cultural influences should be thought of as variables in the equation which modify the effects of the constant, represented by our genetic heritage, but which never remove the constant itself.

Put together these three factors—our genetic heritage, the biophysical environment, and culture—and you have all the essential elements you need to account for the basic directions of societal growth I described earlier. For you have here the basic expansionistic force inherent in life itself; you have also the constraints imposed by the environment; and you have technology and the other elements of culture which modify the effects of both our genetic heritage and the environment. More than that, you have an explanation for the pattern of acceleration, which is such a striking and important feature of the process. As William Ogburn (1922: chap. 6) pointed out more than a generation ago, technological invention is essentially a process of combining existing elements of information, so that the rate of innovation tends to rise as the store of technological information increases. Moreover, this increase takes the form of an exponential curve, since the possibility of new combinations increases more than twice as fast as the number of elements of basic information. Also, the growth of technology leads to the growth of population and to the ease of communication, which increases the number of minds available to work on problems and the store of information available to them, both developments which further accelerate the process.

## The Limits of Growth

I would be derelict in my responsibilities, however, if I ended at this point. For recent developments have raised the question of whether there are not limits to the growth of human societies—limits set by the finite nature of our planet, and limits set also by the interaction of the old genetics and the new technology (e.g., Meadows, 1972; Heilbroner, 1974). With respect to the former, most of us would have been quick to agree twenty or twenty-five years ago. The possibility of utilizing the resources of other planets seemed then to be something suited more to the realm of science fiction than to serious scholarship. Today, the obstacles still seem enormous, but if one compares the technological distance our species has traveled in the last 10,000 years with the additional distance still required, it would be foolhardy to insist that they can never be overcome.

For me, the other barrier seems more imposing. When you put the new atom in the hands of the Old Adam, then you have real reason for concern. For though we dress ourselves in the latest of fashions, the underlying biological and psychological realities have not altered much. Greed, ambition, rage, and hatred are parts of human nature no less today than in the past, and today they can be served by vastly more destructive tools and weapons. It is not pleasant to contemplate, for example, what might have happened if World War II had occurred a decade or two later.

But let us assume for the moment that we can avoid such disasters and let us also assume, as seems likely, that it will be centuries before humans can begin to exploit profitably the resources of other planets. We must, then *still* expect some reversals in our historic patterns of growth, since our own planet cannot absorb much longer the kind of exponential growth in population and in the consumption of raw materials which has characterized the modern era.

Already, in fact, we seem to be witnessing the beginnings of several such reversals. According to United Nations data, the rate of world population growth peaked between 1960 and 1965 and has been gradually declining since that time. Also, the World Bank issued a report not long ago which suggested that the more industrialized nations of the world may be entering into an extended period of little or no economic growth.

Building on such developments, one could easily postulate the end of the era of growth. I believe, however, that this would be not only premature, but fundamentally mistaken. For if we can avoid an atomic holocaust or other man-made disaster, I think we can reasonably expect the process of societal growth, *in its most basic sense*, to continue. The changes will come in certain secondary aspects of the process.

As I have already indicated, the key element responsible for most of the growth in human societies in the last 10,000 years has been the expansion of the cultural store of useful information about the material world, namely, technology. I see no reason to expect *this* trend to end. While it may be difficult to continue to expand the store of energy in the next few hundred years (though even this is not certain), it is quite likely that major advances will be made in the creation of machines that utilize our energy resources more efficiently. The computer may prove to be the prototype of a whole new generation of machines that provide substantial benefits at little cost in terms of energy. More than that, modern technology creates capital-intensive industries, by and large, and so we no longer need huge work forces to produce a cornucopia of goods and services. Human populations can be substantially reduced, especially in technologically advanced nations, thereby reducing considerably the demand for goods and services without at the same time reducing their supply. Thus, the higher standards of living most people desire can be achieved without any increase in production.

Admittedly, all this is highly speculative, but I believe it is grounded in good theory and a considerable body of compatible evidence. If I am correct in my assumptions, the scenario for the future might turn out to be rather different from that projected either by the optimists who see simply a continuation of recent growth trends, or by the pessimists who see only doomsday ahead.

This third scenario envisions the possibility of continued growth in various directions, especially in the store of information available and probably also in living standards, but it anticipates an end to growth in certain other directions, especially in numbers and in the consumption of most raw materials. I would not claim that this third alternative is inevitable or even probable, but I do see it as a viable option and one that is more attractive than either of the others. It is an option that could well be overlooked, however, not only because of the ignorance or indifference of political elites and decision makers, but also because of the inattention of sociologists and other social scientists to the complex set of interrelated problems inherent in the process of societal growth.

3

# Cumulative Change in Theory and History

*Amos H. Hawley*

A COMPREHENSIVE OVERVIEW of the literature on social change would almost certainly bewilder the uninitiated person, should that individual have the patience to undertake so arduous a task. The observer would find that the spectrum ranges from Robert Nisbet's denial of change, there being only a "finely-graded, logically continuous series of 'stills,' as in a movie film" (1969:197), to Wilbert Moore's assertion that change is ubiquitous (1963:11–12). Running the gamut, it seems that change covers any difference between before and after states, regardless of the units affected, the magnitude of the differences, the time interval involved, or the repetitiveness of the difference. What is true in the aggregate, of course, is not true of individual scholars. Each has employed a definition designed for a particular purpose. I shall do likewise. By social change I mean any nonrecurrent alteration of a social system considered as a whole. The term "nonrecurrence" in the definition is intended to exclude rhythmic events, such as the waking-eating-sleeping round of the diurnal cycle, daily trips to and from work or school, the annual cycle of holiday festivities, the succession of generations, and other such pulsations. These are the means by which a given pattern of relationships is sustained rather than altered. A more difficult exclusion concerns short-term variations around a central tendency, inasmuch as they usually are recognized as such only in retrospect. Although we have tried diligently, we have perfected no way of recognizing such variations for what they are at the time of their occurrence.

Nonrecurrent alterations appear in many forms. Of these the most significant, if least dramatic, is what may be called cumulative change. This may occur as a single increment to the content of a social system, or it may be composed of a series of increments, each of which prepares the way for the next. In either case it constitutes growth of the system, a movement from small and simple to large and complex.

Why, it is reasonable to inquire, should one expect to find growth or cumulative change in social systems? Various answers suggest themselves. One rests upon an analogy with change in biological organisms. That the organism begins with a fertilized cell which, under appropriate conditions, subdivides repeatedly to produce increasing size and structural elaboration is common knowledge. Whether the processes involved in that phenomenon have counterparts in the growth of the human social system is too debatable to occupy us here. A second kind of answer to the question "Why cumulative change?" may be found in an argument from history. The historical record enumerates many instances of the rise of empires and of civilizations from small and simple beginnings. The fact that many have declined and disappeared does not gainsay the tendency to cumulative change. It merely poses another problem. Lessons from history are most convincing, however, when they can be shown to conform to a pattern that can be stated as a set of principles. That, if it can be demonstrated, would constitute a third and most satisfactory answer to the question.

The issue, then, may be stated this way: Is there a pattern in cumulative change? To pose the question in this manner may seem to minimize the part decision processes play in change. No one can deny that individuals calculate means to ends. But whether purposefulness in the individual has any necessary outcome in the aggregate is moot. In any event, I do not wish to be mired in an attempt to distinguish intended from unintended effects. The question to be considered here is simply: Are there kinds of events or circumstances which lead inexorably toward cumulative change? In the following remarks I shall treat this question by exploring the implications of three ideas current in much of our thinking, namely, irreversibility, evolution, and expansion.

## Irreversibility

The notion of directionality in change rests upon the assumption of irreversibility. This assumption is also basic to a holistic or social system approach to the treatment of change. Irreversibility may be due, as A. J. Lotka (1924: chap. 3)has pointed out, to the mere improbability that elements, after having been moved about randomly, can be immediately restored to their original order. The experience of picking up a deck of cards that has been dropped to the floor illustrates the point. That may seem to have a parallel in instances in which a major catastrophe so disorders the relationships in a social system that they cannot be reconstituted in the prior pattern. Such a situation, however, bears a closer resemblance to an omelet than to a disordered deck of cards: In neither case can the new arrangement of substances be unscrambled. But there is a third circumstance producing irreversibility. That occurs with the creation or emergence of new properties when previously separated organic units are brought into interaction with one another. The relationship thus formed is not inherent in any of the individuals.[1] While some relationships may be terminated, others may not, for interdependence is a survival imperative. The Hobbesian contract is not one that can be readily broken. Irreversibility is thus a condition of structural accumulation as well as of structural rearrangement. As applied to system change, irreversibility does not preclude the possibility of decline and even disappearance. It means rather that the succession of events by which a system was brought to a given state cannot be followed backward to a starting point. A different path must be followed in decline and it, too, moves through a nonreversible sequence.

Perhaps all of this is familiar enough, but an implication often overlooked, binding though it may be, is that the explanatory principles developed at one level of integration are not applicable to another level. To declare with Professor Homans (1964) that this conclusion is false because no satisfactory principles of explanation for higher levels of social integration have been demonstrated begs the question. What is at issue is how problems are stated, the selection of variables, and the modes of operationalization of variables. Nor has it been convincingly shown, contrary to the arguments of methodological individualists (e.g., Watkins, 1953:929ff.) that attitudes, perceptions, and other such conceptualizations are any more palpable than are relationships and combinations of relationships. No one, to my knowledge, has yet reassembled the whole human being from the many analytical abstractions employed in the pursuit of generalizations.

The reductionist is usually misled by a methodological tactic which the holist uses when engaged in quantification. To describe a population as consisting of so many individuals is no more a confession that the ultimate reality is the individual than is the measurement of a farm in acres of land an admission that only an acre is real. Similarly, while a single birth is an individual experience, a birth rate is a structural feature, and the explanations of the two facts may have little in common. The aggregate, the reductionist's conception of social reality, may be just an aggregate if composed of units thrown together simply because they conform to a given definition. But, if the aggregate is not the product of a statistician's convenience, then an explanation of its existence must lie elsewhere. Pursuit of the elsewhere takes one to a social structure.

It seems, then, that a theory of social change cannot be designed to explain both individual variations and social system variations, as Gudmund Hernes (1976) would have it. The individual life cycle has no counterpart in the duration of a social system. Functional positions can remain constant

[1]"Whenever certain elements combine and thereby produce, by the fact of their combination, new phenomena, it is plain that these new phenomena reside not in the original elements but in the totality formed by their union" (Durkheim, 1938).

despite the turnover of incumbents. That the converse is true seems very unlikely. Change in a social system alters the life conditions of all participants, and they must adapt in order to remain in the system. Irreversibility is the bridge linking levels of integration, the similarities among which lie mainly, if not exclusively, in analogy.

## Evolution

Irreversibility is an elemental assumption in the theory of evolution. Whether that concept is transferable from biotic to social levels of analysis depends a great deal on how it is interpreted. Certainly attempts to draw very close parallels between levels risk falling into the reductionist fallacy. The principle of irreversibility tells us there can be no general law of evolution operating across all system levels (Jacob, 1977). The properties distinguishing one level of integration serve as postulates for the next higher level. But the hypotheses designed to account for phenomena at the higher level must be cast in terms of the peculiar constraints that operate in and upon that level. Yet there are two respects in which the evolution concept has a generic meaning. Substantively it implies a change from simple to complex forms.[2] Analytically, change is viewed as proceeding through variation of units and natural or fortuitous selection. A necessary caveat in this latter respect is that the selection hypothesis is a tautology, albeit a highly useful one, but like all tautologies it suffers from a two-way causation. A point too little stressed is that societal evolution appears to be a Lamarckian rather than a Darwinian phenomenon.

One of the characteristics of traditional thought on evolution is the notion of discontinuity in change, or of change as moving through a stagelike progression. The simplicity of the stage concept is beguiling, despite the precariousness of the implied equilibrium assumption. It is doubtful, however, that an equilibrium assumption can be escaped, even by those who argue that change is imminent, for change can only be imminent when there is not-change. Equilibrium waits in the wings of the mind to move to center stage at every recognition of unit character. And, without the supposition of unit character, order in the universe would not be conceivable. More to the point of this discussion is the need for some means whereby historical time can be converted to analytical time. The stage concept serves that purpose for better or for worse. Despite its many detractors, the concept has shown remarkable vitality. It is an essential ingredient in the bio-ecologist's concept of the ecosystem, which has been its emulators in social science, and it lives on in the social evolutionist's chronology of societal types.

[2]G. E. Swanson uses the term "evolution" to mean "capacity to exploit environment" (1971:3).

It is noteworthy that biologists have turned from typological to probability models when the concern is with the phylogenetic problem, but they employ an equilibrium model when the ecological problem arises. The difference is more than a matter of preference; it points to a distinction between evolution and growth. Evolution deals with the appearance of new species or forms of whatever kind, while growth pertains to the maturation of a form to a point at which, presumably, the form is capable of reproducing progeny which are then subject to natural selection. In contrast to the variation-selection model of evolution, the growth model is best represented by the logistic curve. There is relatively little consensus, however, on what takes place in the passage along the curve. If we can resolve that difficulty, we may be in a position to determine how the two concepts accord with the history of societal development.

## Expansion

What is meant by cumulative change requires a definition of a social system. That term, as used here, denotes an arrangement of routine activities or roles and relationships by which a population sustains itself in a given environment. Cumulative change, then, refers to increase in the number and variety of roles and relationships. Such increase, however, cannot proceed far without increases in population and in territory. Population increments are needed, not just for the augmented variation it brings, but also to staff the growing structure of roles and relationships. Added population is needed also to provide a clientele, i.e., a market, for any increases in productivity that might occur. Differentiation without a market is like a building without a foundation. Increases in structural complexity also make demands for access to an enlarging territory from which to obtain food and raw materials and in which to find room for the conduct of activities. Complexity and scale are intimately linked, though the linkage may not always be superficially evident, hence, the use of the term "expansion" to characterize societal growth.

So far as I am aware, the Lenskis are among the few students of evolution to give even casual reference to expansion (1978). Otis Dudley Duncan, who shares the interest in evolution, suggested that expansion may be the key to the transition from one major level of social evolution to another (1964:57).[3] But very little systematic work on the concept has been forthcoming. The term has been commonplace in the historical literature for many years, but it has been used merely to describe particular series of events, instances of which crowd the historical record (Gras, 1922; Wood-

[3] "Social Organization and the Eco-System," in *Handbook of Modern Sociology*, ed. by R. E. L. Faris (Chicago: Rand-McNally, 1964), p. 57. See also S. N. Eisenstadt (1964:375).

ruff, 1966). Braudel speaks of the "logical laws of expansion," but I have been unable to find them in his work (1966, Vol. II:660). Occasional efforts to generalize the historical experience have been made, but those have been incomplete (McKenzie, 1934; Hawley, 1950, 1971; Gutkind, 1953; Quigley, 1961). Empirical studies, of which there have been many, have dealt mainly with events at the margins of expanding systems (Wilson and Wilson, 1954; Gough, 1955; Rao, 1970; Vidich and Bensman, 1960). More recently, the growth of interest in world systems promises a use of historical materials in a systematic development of the expansion concept (Wallerstein, 1974; Choucri and North, 1974). Very little of this work has found evolution theory a helpful basis from which to proceed. That may be because a point is reached in the growth of social systems beyond which evolution theory is no longer helpful. I will want to return to this suggestion later in my remarks.

Whether the process of cumulative change leads to evolution or growth depends, other circumstances constant for the moment, on how concurrent are advances in complexity and scale. There have been many instances in the past in which population has increased significantly without corresponding increases in structures, as a result of reductions of enemies or of windfalls in the food supply. If the loss of proportion between the population-carrying capacity of the system and the number of people on hand is the only disturbance that has occurred, the effect is a budding-off of colonies. The colonies move off in search of niches in the environment in which they might settle. They may be likened to progeny possessed of a range of variability and subject, therefore, to selection by environment. Some survive, and in doing so adapt their structures to new circumstances. Others succumb as a result of their inability to come to terms with unfamiliar environments. In this way evolution of social systems may be conceived. That is, through a combination of happenstance and adaptive success, one or more complex or advanced social systems are produced (Simpson, 1967; Jacob, 1977).

On the other hand, when complexity and scale advance more or less together, the effect is growth or expansion rather than evolution. But now it is necessary to inquire into how that process is begun, for that it could have a spontaneous causation is most unlikely. The axiom that a thing cannot cause itself is as applicable here as elsewhere.

The normal, if not the necessary, condition for expansion arises from the colonization process described above. A spread of settlements over an area may, under appropriate conditions, create a social field, a universe of more or less frequent interactions among the settlement units (Lesser, 1961; K. Wilkinson; 1970). A field may be visualized as a territory over which the several settlements, or centers, each with a tributary area differing in scope and resource composition, are variously linked in a common transportation network. One or two of the centers are situated at the intersection of intra- and interregional routes of travel, a much larger number are located at the crossings of internal thoroughfares, and some are found at the extremities of interior routes. The field notion, it will be noticed, substitutes an assumption of independence in evolution theory.[4]

Social fields are a commonplace in historical experience. History describes a western succession of such interaction networks. One of the earliest recorded centered upon Babylon in the Euphrates Valley. It was followed by a field of greater dynamics in the Meditteranean region where Miletus, Athens, Alexandria, Rome, and Constantinople served successively as focal points. Still later, ascendancy shifted to northwestern Europe, from which subsequently the interaction network was extended more and more widely.

Within an interaction field disequilibrium, which is a requisite for system change, is a chronic condition.[5] Not only are there disturbances arising from the biophysical environment, but each center is exposed, unequally to be sure, to repeated challenges from the social enviornment. Travelers circulate through the network, bearing ideas, experiences, and artifacts, that is, information and misinformation, originating from local and extralocal sources. Information piles up, as it were, in the most accessible center and drifts outward to the less favorably located centers.

Of all the kinds of information that flow into and through the network, that which affects facility in movement is doubtless the most critical. As Joel Smith has pointed out, it determines the measure of accessibility, sets the terms of expansion, and ultimately, as we shall see, imposes limits to growth (1968, 16:128–34). If invention is a drama enacted on a crowded stage, as Michal Polanyi has said (1959:117), there must be means for bringing actors with diverse experiences together. And as inventions enter into use they call new relationships into being, every one of which involves a transportation of some kind. Technical accumulation begins in mobility and is sustained by mobility.

As a general proposition it may be stated that the complexity and scale of a social system are a joint function of the efficiency of its techniques for the movement of people, materials, and information. Efficiency is measured most cogently by the number of activities that can be articulated per unit of time and cost. It derives partly from the tools for movement which, together with the knowledge for their fabrication and use, comprise what is ordinarily regarded as technology. But efficiency rests also on the less obvious, though no less important, organizational arrangements essential to the application of the tools. The relays of messengers employed for the integration of ancient empires was an organizational device. So also are the freight-forwarding agency, the commercial bank, and the insurance firm of a much later period. A more subtle member of this class is standardization of the

[4]This distinction has also been recognized by Donald Campbell (1965:30).

[5]According to Goster Carlsson (1968), the rate of change varies with the extent of disequilibrium.

terms of discourse, including language to be sure, but also weights and measures, coinage, units of time, rules of the road, standards of judgment, and, above all, forms of organization. The technology for movement is in no sense peculiar in its composition. Tools and organization are two sides of the same coin. Technology is nothing more nor less than the instrumental aspect of culture (Boulding, 1969).

These distinguishable components of technology are often staggered in their development. In many instances it seems that the tool appears before an effective organization for its use has been devised and that happens before the many adjunctive behaviors have made their accomodations. Alfred Chandler describes how experience with the adminstration of the railroad had to accumulate before a solution was found in a hierarchical management structure some twenty years (in the late 1860s) after the steam railway was introduced. But another twenty years passed before a standardization of time and of track gauge were accomplished, in the 1880s (Chandler, 1977; and Taylor and Neu, 1956). One of the more time-consuming phases of standardization, especially where relationships are bridging cultural differences, is with reference to forms of organization and the procedures by which they operate. For that requires a resocialization of not just the few users of the imported tools but of large sectors of a population and eventually of the entire population. In the end the effect will occur if the relationship is uninterrupted and if it has gained vital significance.

The tool-organization-standardization sequence creates conditions out of which other, different sequences unfold. For example, the effects of standardization as a facilitator of movement are not confined to one range of events. The standardization of railroad track gauge in the United States opened wider the gates to interregional flows of information and thus increased opportunities for invention. Similarly, an organizational form developed in connection with the application of one mechanical contrivance is often transferable to others. Chandler (1977) makes a point of how the management structure devised for the dispersed operations of the railroad became a model for other large-scale enterprises. An exogenous influence rarely ends with a single response in a system; rather it produces a concatenation of effects that terminates only when the system has completed its absorption of the new element. The process, comprising numerous feedback loops, gives to cumulative change a helical pattern of progression.

In the context of the interactive field the cumulative process is most rapid in the strategically located center. Accordingly, it gains an increasing capacity to mediate and coordinate a diversity of activities scattered over a widening area. The expansion process, as McKenzie observed some time ago (1934), involves coutervailing currents of redistribution. A centripetal movement of selected specialists and ancillary workers parallels the centralization of information to develop the institutions through which a center grows in size and in administrative power. A centrifugal movement of explorers, raw material extractors, processors, and managers carries technical acquisitions into resource developments on a receding frontier. Thus the field becomes organized in a hierarchy of centers and local tributary zones with the result that a single expanded system replaces a number of localized and relatively independent systems.

This is a process that can work on any scale, limited only by the technology for movement. As a matter of fact, however, it generates what might be regarded as organizational equivalents of scale. On the one hand, it radically changes the significance of population in local areas. The merging of lesser units into a larger unit is also a pooling of demographic resources. Each subsystem gains the benefit of a much larger labor force and range of skills than it could muster within its original boundaries. This is by way of compensation for the loss of local autonomy. On the other hand, expansion alters the orientation to territory. In the early phases communications are hampered by organizational differences between center and periphery. In consequence expansion can only proceed by the imposition of the center's institutional forms and procedures upon outlying settlements and that called for political domination of territory. But in the long run sustained interaction proves an equally, if not more, effective and a much less costly means of producing structural convergence than political coercion. Political domination gives way before an increasing ease of access to territory.

It is true, of course, that in the past, processes of expansion have run their course and come to an end many times over. Various explanations of the conclusion of expansion phases have been proposed. Ralph Turner, the historian, contended that a system can reach only to the outer edge of the region to which its agricultural techniques are adapted (1941:2:1298). Neither colonization nor the supply of armies is possible on a sustained basis beyond that limit. Carroll Quigley (1961) finds the end of expansion in the natural decay that sets in when the uses of surplus wealth become institutionalized. As that occurs energies are directed from invention to maintenance of bureaucratic positions. A case in point might be the institutionalization of slavery in the Roman Empire, which, according to F. W. Walbank (1964:19), so impoverished the citizen population that the local market contracted, and invention lost its incentives. The sinologist Mark Elvin finds a different cause of the termination of expansion. He says that "empires tend to expand to the point at which their technological superiority over their neighbors is approximately counterbalanced by the burdens of size" (1973:19).

Each of these statements describes a conception of how a return to equilibrium comes about. The unspoken assumption in each account is that the possibilities for growth are contained in and limited by a given technology for movement. The limits are approached by virtue of the difference between the exponents of increase in scale and complexity. While numbers of people and of activities increase additively, relationships increase by multiplication. In consequence a rapidly mounting density of interaction generates steeply rising costs of movement of people, goods, and messages. A point is reached in the density curve beyond which the costs of movement are too high to support any further elaborations of structure. Any tendency to exceed that density, *ceteris paribus*, results in a return to scale, as Boulding has observed in his seminal paper on a theory of growth (1953). The return to scale in simple systems is manifested in the colonization process mentioned earlier. In more complex systems it may develop as a strain toward decentralization of authority, forming subsystems, and restoring limited degrees of autonomy to local groups.

The growth process can always be resumed, of course, when further improvements in the technology for movement are introduced. Since that is apt to occur in some systems before it affects others, the former tend to expand into the territories of the latter, thereby absorbing them into an enlarging system. Several major mobility revolutions have subdivided western history into expansion phases. Earliest among these was the transition from animal-powered to mechanically powered movement. That began with the reliance upon wind and sail to venture beyond coastal waters and reached a maximum scope with the application of steam power to over-land as well as to over-water movements. In that regime it was possible to extend systems far beyond localities, harnessing the resources and markets of distant peripheries to centers of expansion. It has been suggested that the potentialities of the steam power era were fully utilized by 1870 and that very little change took place in the next several decades (Landers, 1966). But that is to overlook the telegraph, which appeared in the 1840s and launched a second important transition, namely, a separation of communication from transportation. By this means a new dimension was added to the territorial organization of economic, political, and other activities. For the first time central offices could exercise control on a daily basis over widely scattered branch offices and producing sites. Close upon the heels of the communication revolution came dramatic improvements in the facility for short-distance movement. The telephone and the electric street railway in the third quarter of the nineteenth century and the motor vehicle at the turn of the century gave a new scope to the pattern of local relations which had received only minor alterations since the domestication of the horse. The last of the major turning points has been in the making for some time and is not yet concluded. This is an advancing substitution of communication for transportation. It was initiated with the telegraph and telephone, was carried further by radio, radar, and television, and has reached a present apogee in satellite and laser beam transmissions. Technical information, management instructions, credit, and foreign exchange can now move independently of transportation. Moreover, the reduction of time distances to near zero have all but eliminated the boundaries of systems.

An inference from the hypotheses which have guided this discussion is that efficiency in movement is an accurate indicator of the extent of cumulative change. That, admittedly, has not been fully demonstrated. There is, however, a mounting volume of evidence to support the argument that a measure of mobility can serve that purpose. Wilfred Owen (1964:14) has shown that freight and passenger mobility are sensitive indicators of the level of economic development. Numerous correlation studies of comparative data reveal measures of communication to be among the most indicative of the level of other measures of development (United Nations, 1968; Olsen, 1968; Cutright, 1963). And Henry Barbera (1978) has effectively predicted the extent of external relation from the assumption that the power of a system is measured by the degree to which internal communications are developed. Mobility measures rival energy production as indicators of complexity or growth. But they are not qualitatively equal. Energy produced and consumed may be highly concentrated in a few localities or economic sectors. Transportation and communication, on the other hand, constitute a more widely distributed feature of a system.

## Conclusion

In conclusion, it appears that the course of history has progressively reduced the utility of an evolution model in the explanation of cumulative change. Although social variation as represented in occupational and territorial specialization has been carried to an unprecedented degree, it does not satisfy the assumption of the model; instead of the required capacity for independence of action, the differentiated parts are inescapably caught up in a tightening web of interdependences. This does not mean an end to, or even a slowing of, change. The accumulation of information in storage facilities—a means of transportation through time—is so vast that generations will pass before its potential uses are exhausted. In the meantime the impetus to change may be expected to shift from center to center, further reduction of cultural differences will occur, and the density of organization on a world scale will continue to increase. But the disappearances of evolution as a mode of change in human social systems, if true, is not without risks. Whereas in the anarchy of a multiplicity of localized systems fatal errors could be made here or there without jeopardizing the survival chances of other systems, in today's world that can no longer be expected. The single-world system has a limited tolerance for error. It must either acquire methods of anticipating and compensating for significant errors or fail to survive. In that event the evolution process may once again take command of the course of change. The opportunities for speculation on this theme are inviting, but space does not permit me to pursue them.

4

# Mechanisms and Processes of Societal Growth

*Judah Matras*

## Introduction

IN THIS CHAPTER I wish to (1) propose a definition of societal growth and indicate how it is related to the topics of growth and change discussed in the current growth-versus-antigrowth debate and in recent sociological writing; (2) review the major mechanisms, central processes, frictions appearing in societal growth; and (3) conclude with some thoughts about an agenda for research in societal growth. In the view which I shall try to present, societal growth is broader, more encompassing, than economic growth or demographic-economic growth, which is the topic of the growth-versus-antigrowth debate; but at the same time, it is much more specific and more circumscribed than are concepts of societal development, societal evolution, tranformation, system change, or modernization, which have been topics of sociological and more general social scientific discussion and analysis. To be sure, we are interested in societal growth as it affects various aspects of the "magnitude," "volume," or "density" of a society per se; but even more we are interested in societal growth insofar as it induces or bounds change in social structure and social processes and is, in turn, itself constrained by social structural features.

☐ Helpful comments on an earlier draft were provided by Monica Boyd, Hugh McRoberts, and Allan Steeves, all of Carleton University, Ottawa, Canada.

## SOCIETAL GROWTH DEFINED

What should we understand by the concept "societal growth"? Whatever the particular definition of society we adopt, we can agree to view a society as comprising (1) a population with (2) institutionalized roles, rules, and relationships governing (a) reproduction and socialization; (b) production and (c) allocations of goods, services, and social rewards and resources; (d) determination and articulation of collective priorities, values, or standards; and (e) control of individual and group behavior. That there is both stability and change in a society and in each of its various facets is a truism, but we can note (along with Daniel Bell [1973] and others) that we may divide these into "qualitative" and "quantitative" changes (or stabilities). Clearly if societal growth is to mean something other than "societal change" it must be restricted to the realm of "quantitative" changes, and further restricted to those quantitative changes of quite diffuse impact. We cannot view change from hunting and gathering to cultivation, or change from absolutism to representative government, or change from particularism to universalism, or change from arranged marriages to free or romantic marriage, as constituting in themselves "societal growth" (though it may, of course, turn out that these are more or less closely related to the "quantitative" changes which we may ultimately wish to include under a definition of societal growth). On the other hand, neither would the quantitative changes characterizing particular social units—births or deaths in a family, changing membership of a church or voluntary organization, increased profits for a business, or even the growth of an individual community—constitute societal growth, since their impact would not be diffuse or "societal."

It is the number of differentiated social units and subsystems and the density of their interrelationships in a society, and the volume of sustenance and other social rewards and resources produced, allocated, and exchanged in a society, which undergo "quantitative" changes that are of general or diffuse impact; and it is the quantitative changes in these dimensions and characteristics of a society that we may denote by the term "societal growth." Thus we may define societal growth as the growth in the number of, and density of interrelationships among, social units and subsystems; and the increase in the volume of sustenance and other social rewards and resources produced, allocated, exchanged, and converted.

*Growth in the number of subsystems* in a society occurs both (1) by differentiation and division of labor and (2) by expansion of main subsystem and societal, territorial or other boundaries. Very familiar illustrations of differentiation and division of labor include what is sometimes called "erosion" or transfer of family functions and evolvement of separate and distinct production, socialization, recreation, or religious subsystems performing them; the proliferation of specialized units, departments, or agencies within government or private firms; and the specialization of medical or of educational facilities and "tracks." Expansion of boundaries occurs as populations grow or as societies or social units expand territorially, merge with other existing units, or absorb and incorporate previously external or previously competing subsystems, e.g., political incorporation of suburbs or satellite cities within a larger municipal or metropolitan unit, the merger of corporations, the nationalization of economic enterprises, education, research, or welfare services, or the exploration, conquest, or settlement of new areas.

*Growth in the density* of interrelations among subsystems follows in part from growth in their numbers and from specialization and division of labor. Moreover, the improvements in communications and transport technologies render subsystems' interrelations less costly and more frequent. Household and family decision making and activity—whether about seeking or changing employment, or about consumption, or about additional births, or about education, savings, or investment—are often noted to be powerfully affected and influenced by the current political, social, and economic conditions generally and by the activities and conditions of the specific social systems as well as by attributes of the family, household, or members themselves. Primary producers, fabricators, wholesalers, retailers, and producers of services plan and carry out their own activities in relation to their past, expected, or already contracted relationships both with specific clients, buyers, or consumers and with more general markets. Government bodies are involved daily in economic and social intervention, control, regulation, subsidy of the activites of other subsystems as well as in information gathering, dissemination, and analysis. Moreover, the various subsystems in a given society—whether economic, political, social, educational, religious, or recreational—very often are in competition with one another to attract the participation and involvement of members, clients, or consumers; and they operate in the shadow of accessibility of alternative, often competing, subsystems to "their" members. Thus they must take account on an ongoing basis both of the "needs" or wishes or social patterns of clients and adherents *and* of the activities of the competing subsystems.

Goods and services produced in the course of social interaction are "social rewards"; and for many we have familiar measures of the volume of "production"—tons of steel, numbers of automobiles, bushels of wheat, numbers of patients treated, admissions to concerts, minutes and hours of television advertising, or whatever. Any other valued product of social interaction—such as deference and prestige, health, power, love, or security—is also a social reward, although we are less able (perhaps entirely unable) to measure "production" of such rewards. To the extent that a given social reward may be converted or exchanged for another one—e.g., guns for butter, diamonds for love, power for property, food for obedience—we may view that social reward as a "social resource" as well. Most goods and services are products of social interaction, as are, by definition, all other social rewards and resources. The production of social rewards in a society varies, of course, with the population size and composition, and in addition it varies with the physical environment, with knowledge and technologies accessible to it, with the system of values and priorities adopted, and with the organizational arrangements. The same kinds of factors and, in addition, the volume of social rewards produced affect the allocation of social rewards and resources in the society as well as the rules and patterns of exchange and conversion of social resources.[1]

*Growth in the volume of social rewards and resources produced* can occur as a consequence of population growth or of expansion of the physical environment. But such growth can occur, also, in consequence of discovery or adoption of new technologies, organizational shifts, or changes in values and priorities. We have measured growth in all manner of goods and services; we can probably measure growth in other kinds of rewards, such as "health"; but the "growth" in output of social rewards such as prestige, power, security, obedience, and sense of social order have at best been "asserted" or "shown." Nonetheless, some "growth" in output of most of these nonmeasured social rewards may be presumed to follow simply from population growth; and additional growth may by hypothesized to be related to other changes.

## SOCIETAL GROWTH AND THE GROWTH-VERSUS-ANTIGROWTH DEBATE

Obviously we are not by any means the first to consider these elements of societal growth. Indeed we are in the midst of a growth-versus-antigrowth debate in which academicians, politicians, business people, and others have been discussing and analyzing population growth, growth in production and consumption of goods and services, growth or depletion of resources and environment, and, often, the growth of political and other social institutions. And they have been evaluating such growth from the standpoint of individual or collective survival or with reference to some explicit or implicit standard of individual or collective welfare. In these discussions, "growth" seems to be cast in terms akin to those invoked by our own definition and illustrations, though emphasis is most frequently on population growth and on "economic" growth.

In this debate the implications of growth for survival, welfare, or wellbeing are generally imputed in very direct ways, in terms of ratios of re-

[1]On the concepts of social rewards and resources and their production, allocation, and conversion, cf. Eisenstadt, 1971.

wards or resources to population or numbers of claimants, e.g., in terms of per capita income, longevity, caloric intake, or cultivable land, clean water, or fossil fuel energy per capita. Among the best known of the more apocalyptic treatments are Ehrlich's *The Population Bomb* (1968) and the Meadows' *The Limits to Growth* (1972). These share a mode of approach involving projection of the numbers of population and claimants of various categories alongside the projection of available rewards and resources under given assumptions. And they share a conclusion: In the not-so-distant future there won't be enough. But increasingly this discussion has incorporated explicit and implicit assertions, and sometimes analyses, of the intervention or mediation of social organizational factors in the relationship between growth and well-being. Thus, for example, to analyze the relationship between economic growth and the "good life," E. J. Mishan (1977) lists as "constituents of the good life" food and shelter, health, nature, leisure, instinctual enjoyment, love and trust, self-esteem, kith and kin, customs and mores, role and place, the moral code, the great myths, and personal freedom. And he argues that continued economic growth works against modern man's enjoying or benefiting from them. Rather, continued economic growth disturbs the social organization of these "constituents" in ways interferring with man's enjoying them or benefitting from them.

Now, at least some of these "constituents" and social organizational factors have been topics of sociological discussion, usually with some concern for rigorous or consistent definition, and observation and measurement of their variation, and with some attention to the logic or acceptable methods of inferring relationships with other phenomena or variables. But, although he reflects in rather more detail on the relationships between technology and freedom in general, it suffices for Mishan to reflect briefly on, and make assertions about, the relationships between growth and the social organizational or psychological factors to which he alerts his readers; and he does not acknowledge any need for more systematic, detailed, or convincing analysis.[2] But it is exactly such a need which sociologists *do* acknowledge. And it is exactly in the sense that we hypothesize that growth processes—whether in population, in production and consumption of goods and services, in sizes, numbers, and densities of social subsystems, or in time durations of central life processes—bear on family and community, on socialization, on small or large or formal or informal groups or organizations, on stratification and mobility, on political and religious organization, on social change and social persistence, and on other organizational and structural features of a society and affect the very bases of social organization itself that we may denote them collectively "societal growth."

[2]In fairness it must be acknowledged that other participants in the growth-versus-antigrowth debate have offered much more sociologically sophisticated discussions on the bearing of growth on social organizational features, e.g., Schumpeter (1942), Boulding (1965), and most recently Hirsch (1976). But in general these have also stopped short of drawing on research on social organizational consequences of growth, and it would probably be hard to claim that they have advanced such research greatly.

## SOCIETAL GROWTH IN SOCIOLOGICAL ANALYSIS

The elements of societal growth are certainly familiar topics in sociological conceptualizations and discussions of social change or social dynamics. The topics of structural differentiation of institutional systems and subsystems and the growth in production and consumption of goods and services have been raised and discussed in the early evolutionary theories of social development, in Marx's analyses of the transformation from feudalism to capitalism, in Durkheim's theory of the division of labor, in Weber's analyses of rationalization and bureaucratizaton, throughout the writings on social change in the structural-functional tradition, and more recently in the revival of evolutionary perspectives on social change and transformation.[3] Discussion of the growth in the number and density of social units, institutional systems, and subsystems appears in the writings of Durkheim and Simmel, throughout sociological treatment of communities, work and industry, organizations, and stratification, and particularly in the rural sociology and human ecology traditions.

It is fair to say that on the whole the discussion of system and subsystem differentiation tends to be cast in the context of analysis of sociohistorical change, transformation, or modernization and in broad generalizations. There is extensive use of illustrative examples but, with some important exceptions, very little systematic observation or measurement. Similarly, the discussion, in sociological treatments, of growth or change in the volume of goods and services produced or allocated tends also to be cast in broad terms with little use made of the extensive data available. In particular, analyses of the relationships between subsystem differentiation or growth in production and other changes in social behavior or structural features are frequently made; but these are only relatively infrequently based on systematic data or rigorous analytical procedures. By contrast, the discussion of growth in the number, size, and density of social units and institutional systems and subsystems has drawn extensively on systematic observation and data—mostly administrative social and demographic data provided by governments, but more recently also data obtained in sample surveys—and there has been systematic measurement and systematic comparison or analysis of relationships between various kinds of system growth. But analyses of relationships between subsystem growth and other social organizational changes (e.g, political, stratification, kinship) tend also be be based on assertion and simple illustration and comparison.

Except for those of the "human ecology school," all these analyses of societal growth elements occur in the context of discussions of "change," "modernization," "development," and the like. These discussions have almost universally (1) incorporated "nonquantitative" and "noncumulative"

[3]For reviews, see Bell, 1973: chap 1; W. Moore, 1960; Parsons, 1966; and Eisenstadt and Curelaru, 1976.

variables; (2) hypothesized changes in the "nonquantitative" variables which are not easily documented empirically, much less measured, e.g., in attitudes toward ruling elites, persistence of work norms, centrality of kinship relations, and (3) assumed or hypothesized causal factors which are supposed exogenous to the social structure and organization of the society, e.g., changing religious beliefs, invention or discovery.[4] But the elements of societal growth as defined in the previous section and its main causal factors are quantitative and cumulative; they have unambiguous empirical referents for the most part; and to a large extent they are already measurable. Moreover, what I shall cite as the major causal factors in societal growth, (1) population growth or transformation and (2) expansion of the volume and accessibility of knowledge, can be viewed and cast as endogenous to the social structure; and indeed there are important feedback processes by which societal growth in turn affects population and knowledge. Thus, it is possible to develop a self-contained theory of societal growth whose propositions about interrelationships of population, knowledge, institutionalized roles and subsystems, and the production, allocation, and flow of sustenance and social rewards and resources can be plotted, tested empirically, and accumulated.

These are strengths of a theory of societal growth; but its weakness may be in its very self-containment, in its disconnectedness from the rich qualitative concepts collected in the history of analysis of social dynamics and change—such as cohesion and solidarity, consensus and conflict, and so forth—and perhaps in its accounting-system-like abstraction and distance from the richness of social life itself. In my view it is possible to begin to build a rigorous self-contained theory of societal growth and at the same time avoid the danger of its "exile" by addressing at the outset some of the connections between societal growth and "qualitative" aspects of social change. I make some additional notes on this topic in the final section of this chapter.

## Causes, Mechanisms, Processes, and Frictions

### ECOLOGICAL EXPANSION, POPULATION PUSH, AND INVENTION PULL

Among the sociological perspectives on social change and transformation, it is the human ecology perspective which has encompassed an explicit analysis of societal growth, conceptualized as "ecological expansion." Ecological expansion, according to Duncan (1964), is (1) an increase in numbers

[4]Cf., for example, Eisenstadt, 1970b.

of the population, sustained by (2) increasing human resourcefulness in extracting the requisite supplies of energy and material from the environment, and (3) an elaboration of the patterns of organization of the human collective efforts involved in this activity. In Duncan's view, ecological expansion is a major explanatory principle in accounting for the evolutionary transitions from one "societal level" to the next (where "level" refers to the size, technology, residence, and political organization patterns characterizing the society). Thus the societal growth associated with ecological expansion is, in Duncan's view, associated simultaneously with (1) the shift in the society's technology—implying or allowing the shift in production and in economic units or boundary systems—and with (2) the shift in the scope of the local territorial unit (e.g., from nomadic bands through the various stages to large urban communities) and the change in political and social institutions associated with such shifts.

Elsewhere (Matras, 1977) I have rephrased this slightly to suggest that ecological expansion can be viewed as population growth and the economic, technological, and social organizational changes that are mutually required to sutstain one another, i.e., that in this complex of "growth" variables it is population growth that can be viewed as the main causal factor, though in turn it is itself affected by the other variables in a feedback loop (figure 1). This formulation is consistent with the view of population change and growth as being the "engine" of societal growth and of social change generally; and it is akin to what Julian Simon (1977) has called the "population push hypothesis."

But a different view, the Malthusian analysis, of the process is equally familiar: Technological and economic and social organizational changes leading to increased production and distribution of food give rise, in turn, to population growth (figure 2). Simon has called this the "invention pull hypothesis" and has shown that, far from being in opposition to each other, the two hypotheses are mutually complementary. Moreover, many students of social development, change, modernization, and the like assign causal prominence either to technology or to knowledge generally, where "knowledge" comprises (1) the volume of ideas, theoretical information, and techniques, (2) the accessibility to these ideas, information, and tech-

**Figure 1.** "Population Push Hypothesis"

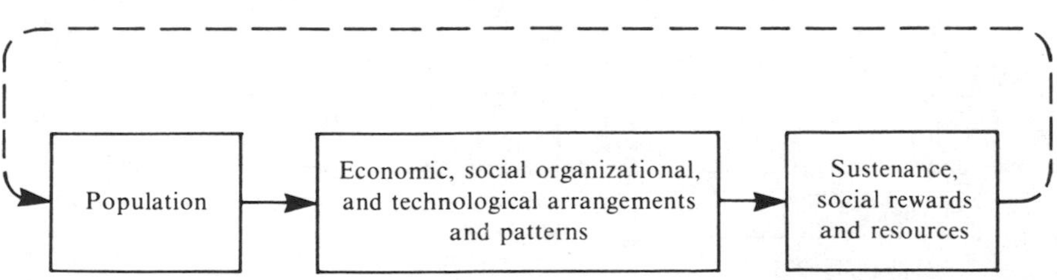

niques, and sometimes (3) the advantaged access to social positions and rewards of those possessing or with special access to knowledge.[5]

Thus, I would point as causal factors in societal growth to *both* population transformations (growth, change in distribution or composition, and turnover) and expansion of knowledge (stock of ideas and information, access to the stock of ideas and information, and role differentiation by differential possession of or access to the stocks of ideas and information). As we shall see below, it is also useful to partition the set of "economic and social organizational arrangements" variables into those associated with *production* of social rewards and resources and those associated with *claims* on, or *allocation* of rewards and resources. The set of relationships between population, knowledge, social structure, and the volume, composition and flows of sustenance and other social rewards and resources is represented schematically (and tentatively) in figure 3. It will be useful to indicate very cryptically the meaning of each of the boxes and arrows in figure 3 for a hypothetical "nongrowth" society.

We consider (A) size, distribution, and composition of a population, along with its "nongrowth" turnover of life cycles and generations and of migratory flows and counterflows; (B) the types and amounts of knowledge information, ideas, skills, and techniques, and their accessibility by institutionalized means—whether schooling, books, or other storage and retrieval; (C) the social structure governing the production of material and consumer goods and of social rewards generally (where social rewards are understood as any valued outcomes or outputs of social relationships and interaction)—including families, occupational positions and systems, formal organizations, hierarchically arranged groupings and the like; (D) the types and amounts of the various social rewards and resources produced—including material goods and services, esteem, social participation, leadership and followership, authority and influence, safety and health, and—as Eisenstadt (1971) has suggested—even a "sense of social order"; and finally (E) the social structure governing allocation, distribution, and rules of conversion of rewards and resources back to individuals and groups in the population.

**Figure 2.** "Invention Pull Hypothesis"

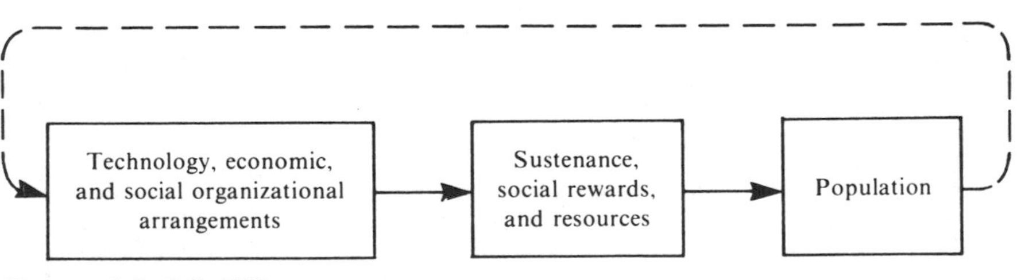


[5]See especially Bell, 1973.

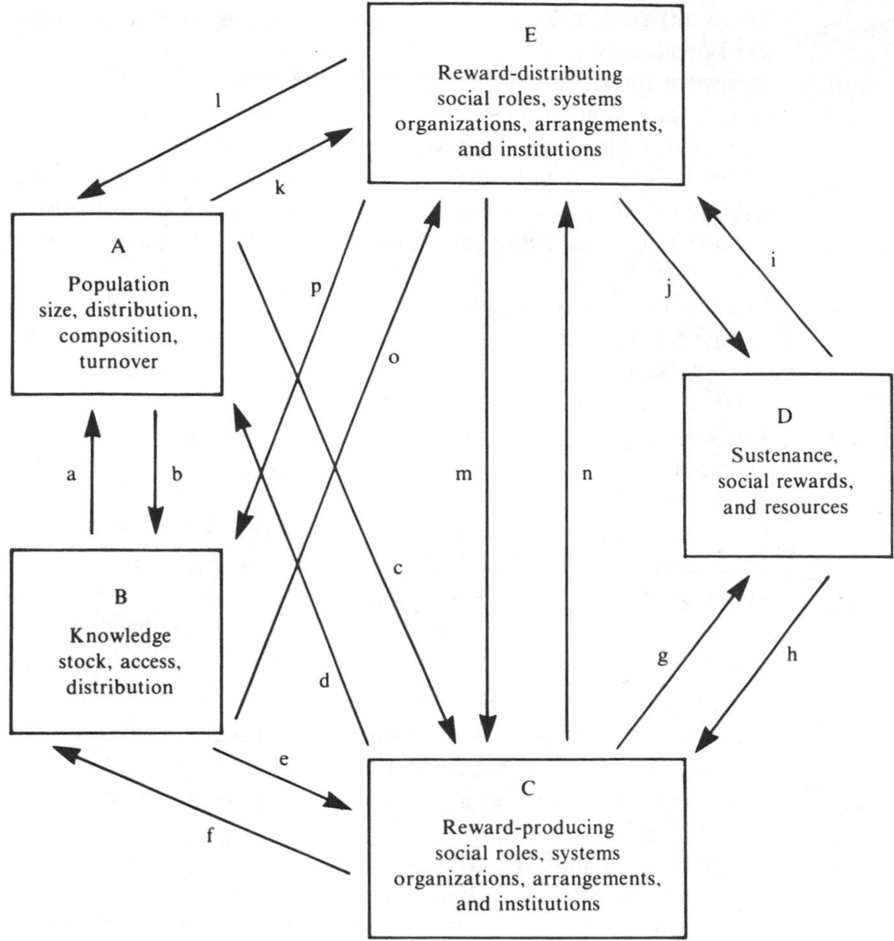


**Figure 3.** Population Social Structure—Rewards Regime

It is clear that any or all of these elements, (A), (B), (C), (D), or (E), can undergo change over time, and that changes in any one can induce changes in any or all of the others. But initially it is useful to consider some interrelationships in a nonchange, or in an equilibrium, state:

a. Arrow (a) represents socialization and acquisition of knowledge of all types by persons in the population, at the various ages and in various "social locations."

b. Arrow (b) represents the flow of information "into stock" concerning the population (or the society's human resources) itself: its size, distribution, locations, knowledge, skills, experience, consumption, behavior, etc.

c. Arrow (c) represents the attainment of roles or positions in reward-producing subsystems.

d. Arrow (d) represents the effects of reward-producing social structural arrangements on population distribution, composition, and turnover (and population growth in the "growth" situation).

e. Arrow (e) represents the use of knowledge, information, techniques, etc., in the production of social rewards (including the production of additional knowledge in the "growth" situation).

f. Arrow (f) represents the flow of information "into stock" concerning the (c) social structure (and, in the "growth" situation, the flow of knowledge, ideas, etc., from knowledge-producing subsystems).

g. Arrow (g) represents the output of sustenance and social rewards and resources of the various types, organized by the roles and subsystems of (C).

h. Arrow (h) represents feedback effects on the reward-producing structure of past output and of current stock of social rewards.

i. Arrow (i) represents the allocation or distribution of sustenance and social rewards of various types, with institutionalized claims organized by the roles and subsystems of (E).

j. Arrow (j) represents the demands, expectations, or relative values placed on the various types of sustenance and social rewards in the "stock," (D), organized in the (E) social structure.

k. Arrow (k) represents the attainment of roles or positions in reward-allocating subsystems.

l. Arrow (l) represents the effects of reward-allocating social structural arrangements on population.

m,n. Arrows (m) and (n) represent the overlaps and reciprocal effects of roles, positions and subsystems in the reward-producing and reward-allocating structures respectively, e.g., the extent to which position in the reward-producing structure is the basis for position and institutionalized claims on the reward-allocating structure.

o. Arrow (o) represents the use or effects of knowledge in determining claims in, or allocation or exchange of, social rewards and resources.

p. Arrow (p) represents the flow of information "into stock" concerning the (E) social structure.

We have some propositions and hypotheses, and we have some research findings about the relationships represented by arrows (a) through (p), but not nearly enough. Nonetheless, I propose that, by introducing (1) population growth and (2) growth and expansion of knowledge and trying to plot their consequences in the regime tentatively plotted in figure 3, we can begin to lay out the pieces of a theory of societal growth.

## MECHANISMS OF SOCIETAL GROWTH

Population growth and expansion of knowledge tend to disorganize and cause dislocations in ongoing social systems generally and, in our case, in the population—social structure—rewards regime. Aside from creating new demands and claims on available positions and rewards, population growth always occurs unevenly relative to the initial population and social structure; and inevitably it generates "squeezes" and imbalances (Moore, 1960; Matras, 1977). Similarly, the increase in knowledge disorganizes ongoing social systems and societal regimes because it allows new outputs of rewards and resources with new levels or combinations of inputs, affords new evaluation and ordering of existing rewards and resources, and changes the distribution of knowledge, and the role distribution generally, in the population (Bell, 1973). We can identify a number of mechanisms by which societies respond to these two types of growth. Of course, distinguishing among "mechanisms" is in large part artificial and for analytical purposes only: In fact, it is often impossible to isolate one from the rest.

### Expansion of Boundary Systems

Social units or systems are bounded in two senses: Individuals or subsystems or places are either "in" or else "outside" the unit or system by some boundary criterion; and the material and other rewards and resources flowing through the system are "bounded"—if not absolutely in volume, then by rules governing these types and volumes of inputs.[6] Expansion of boundary systems occurs when additional members are absorbed into the system or when the number of component subsystems within the boundary system is increased. Addition of new branches and departments to firms or organizations, incorporation of new territories into geopolitical units, takeovers, and conquests are all examples of expansion of boundary systems. An economy, a polity, a metropolitan hinterland, a mass social or religious movement, or a multi-university may have undergone expansion of boundary systems in its history.

Population growth is surely associated with expansion of boundary systems of all types and levels in a society; but it is probably neither necessary nor sufficient. Expansion of boundary systems probably *does* presuppose a minimum means of communicaton and control; and, because of division of

[6] On social boundary systems, see Parsons and Smelser, 1956, and Y. Cohen, 1969.

labor and economies of scale, it is typically presumed to be associated with higher (than pre-expansion of boundaries) productivity, whether of material or other rewards.

### INCREASED SCALE OF EVALUATION, PRODUCTION, DISTRIBUTION, AND EXCHANGE.[7]

The isolated self-sufficient household or subsistence-agriculture village produces sustenance to meet the needs or desires of persons linked in face-to-face relations, with largely shared priorities and evaluations. Expansion of knowledge, techniques, and communication permit both increased production and exchange over progressively larger populations and areas and, especially, production of standardized items for "anonymous" markets rather than fabrication to order for the individual consumer. Population growth reinforces and adds momentum to such increases in scale of communication, activity, and exchange. This mechanism complements the expansion of boundary systems or, indeed, may be viewed as a type of expansion of boundary systems.

Such expansion of the scale of production, distribution, and exchange can only occur alongside expansion of common symbols and evaluations, itself promoted by spread of education, communications, religious doctrines and symbols, and information media.

This concept is familiar enough with respect to material rewards and resources. What is less familiar is the parallel increased scale of production, allocation, and exchange of nonmaterial rewards. Work satisfaction, aesthetic pleasures, community participation, prestige, and deference are rewards which are sought in increasingly standardized forms by increasing numbers of individuals, and they are produced and rendered accessible in progressively larger social systems for increasing numbers of claimants. To be sure, many social rewards continue to be produced and obtained in social interaction organized on very small scale; but even small-group interaction, e.g., in families, in friendship groups, in groups, in committees, tends with growth to be increasingly standardized, with demands, expectations and actual rewards and trade-offs modeled on examples or images cast before larger and further-flung numbers of imitators.

Thus the *national* "selling" of Wheaties, Roots, the Kennedy family, CB radios, jogging, Richard Nixon, or electronic calculators is not only related to the production and physical distribution capabilities of the entrepreneurs and producers, plus the fundamental needs and demands of the growing and agglomerated population, but, also connected to nationally shared evaluations of health, fair play, convenience, glamour, patriotism, and good taste.

[7]For a recent review and analysis of scale and social relations, see Berreman, 1978.

## Multiplication and Differentiation of Formal Organizations

The distinguishing characteristic of formal organizations is very often held to be that they are purposive; they have explicit goals to which all members subscribe (Blau and Scott, 1962; Stinchcombe, 1965; Hall, 1972). In our terms, they are deliberately formed to be more efficient, more productive of social rewards—whether better mousetraps, more and higher education, salvation, systematic crime-busting or enemy-deterring, votes for John J. Candidate, or else prestige for their leaders and members—than would be possible without the formal organizations.[8] Population growth generates needs and pressures for enhanced ouput of sustenance and rewards; and expansion of knowledge offers new concepts, theories, information, techniques, and opportunities for enhancing output and evaluating it. It is the formal organization which is best equipped to exploit new knowledge and to mobilize knowledge and resources productively: whether the small business firm or bureaucracy, the Department of Health, Education, and Welfare or General Motors. Thus a characteristic response of society to growth of population or of knowledge is the formation of formal organizations, sometimes supplementing or replacing primordial groupings in the creation of certain rewards, sometimes assuming part of the tasks and functions of previous organizations, sometimes doing new tasks altogether.

Once formed, of course, organizations have their characteristic "life cycles" with growth characteristics, internal differentiation and hierarchies, and varieties of role relations. But the mechanism we are noting here is that by which increasing spheres of human interaction, all productive of social rewards of some type, shift from informal to formal organization. It is the need and desirability (or profitability) of enhancing output of some reward, occasioned by increased population or by changing information or values and the expected benefits of explicit formulation of objectives and the organization of activities directed for achieving them, which lead to shifting to formal organizational formats.

## Shifting Bases for Claims on Rewards

One of the important, yet obscure, mechanisms of societal growth is the shift in legitimate bases for claims on sustenance and other social rewards. In the simplest societies presumably all gather food and may eat what they gather; but even in this case there are some who by virtue of age or physical disabilities are unable to participate in the sustenance-producing activity but nonetheless have some claim on the sustenance obtained by others. In more differentiated societies claims on sustenance and other rewards, e.g., deference, have been based on a variety of activities or statuses. Aside from di-

[8]This point is made and developed in some detail by Stinchcombe (1965).

rect productive activities, other activities or achievements (e.g., in art, leadership, or courage), physical force, supernatural powers or "connections," superior knowledge, kinship, property ownership, or membership in some ascribed or achieved grouping may be variously taken as legitimate bases for claims on sustenance, rewards, and resources produced in or available to the society.[9]

In particular, the institutionalization of private landed property and the accompanying "rights" of ownership of property are frequently viewed as a key sociohistorical process, with implications for all of the rest of social organization. But the institutional meaning of property ownership has varied with the scarcity of land resources; and scarcity in turn is a function of the size and density of population. Thus it has probably been the case that land ownership has been more closely connected with social status and with formation of social strata in areas of high population density or relative scarcity of land (e.g., Western Europe or the northeastern United States) than in areas of low population density or relative abundance of land (frontier areas of North America).

Property rights over occupations, over types or sectors of trade and economic activity, and other specialized knowledge have also been institutionalized historically, and these were then associated with more or less well-defined entitlements. Expansion of knowledge and accessibility to it has worked to erode such entitlements and ultimately the rights themselves. Being literate or possessing generalized or specialized knowledge has long been closely connected with social status and with the formation of social strata. But the meaning of literacy, of educational attainment, or of specialized knowledge has also varied with the scarcity of knowledge resources. As population and knowledge grow, both demand for and supply of educational credentials change.

It is not yet clear whether the increasing correlation between educational attainment and measures of socioeconomic status—to the relative exclusion combined with a decline in the influence of other factors—is correctly judged a shift from "ascribed" or "achieved" or from "particularistic" to "universalistic" criteria of attainment of social status and social rewards (Blau and Duncan, 1967; Hauser and Featherman, 1977; Featherman and Hansen, 1978). In the first place, it remains to be seen if the connections between education and occupational status will be weakened in an almost universally highly educated population (just as the negative correlation between SES indicators and fertility is weakened in the universally contracepting society) or will remain as strong as now (cf. Freeman, 1976). Moreover, it is not clear whether "educational attainment" requirements have not become ascriptive screening devices in the labor market saturated with overcredentialism (Collins, 1971).

[9]The theme of variations and change in the bases of claims on social rewards is discussed by Eisenstadt (1963; 1971).

It is clear that as rewards are allocated, converted, and exchanged in a "market" situation, one set of institutions governs bases of claims on rewards; while allocation, conversion, and exchange in planned or "command" economies have different institutions governing claims on rewards. In particular, political positions often govern either control over reward distribution or claims on rewards, or both. One hypothesis of both Western and eastern European sociologists has been that those enjoying political control over rewards and resources in command economies by virtue of personal attainments and skills (1) form a solidary, ultimately relatively homogeneous social stratum and (2) seek and institutionalize means to pass on and preserve the rewards of their positions for their cronies, kin, and heirs.[10] This implies that class formation may have very little to do with the *particular* institutional bases of claims on rewards, e.g., property ownership or nonownership. Rather, it may be the formation of alliances and groups among those having privileged claims on rewards on whatever grounds, by virtue of social and political propinquity or common defense of their claims on the one hand, and among those lacking them on the other hand (cf. Eisenstadt, 1971: chaps. 6, 7; Matras, 1975: chap. 10).

If the propertyless were hierarchically undifferentiated in the past, the growth of knowledge works to differentiate them at present. The growth of knowledge and information, and the increasing dependence of production on knowledge and information, have put a great premium first and foremost on those "professionally" able to manage, control, and mobilize information and knowledge and their possessors and techniques and their practitioners for large-scale productive ends (cf. Bell, 1968, 1973: chap. 6). These are, of course, the "managers," who are widely acknowledged to be accorded status and other rewards, who in some societies have actually formed new ruling elites and in others have become at least part of the "recruitment stratum" from which ruling elites are recruited.[11]

## Tinkering with the Machine: Societal Analysis and Adoption of Innovations

An important consequence of growth and expansion of knowledge is the analysis of society and economy themselves, including description and analyses of production and distribution processes and systems. And an important response to the disorganization attending population growth is the adoption of some social or technological innovation. It is often the case that alternative ways of doing things are *known* in an organization or subsystem, but not adopted: Sheer inertia or normative prescription of current less effi-

[10] Aside from its well-known explication by Djilas (1957), this theme has been developed by Lane (1971) and by Bell (1973). For critical discussion see Parkin, 1971; Giddens, 1973; and Bauman, 1974.

[11] The concept of "recruitment stratum" and the changing composition of the recruitment stratum in Britain are discussed by Giddens (1972, 1973).

cient procedures may overcome purely instrumental criteria favoring the adoption of new ways of doing things. But population growth confronts the organization, the business, the church, the bureaucracy, and the state with a kind of crisis—and the social system must make adjustments in operating activities, and relationships. Moreover, if growth in knowledge is occurring as well, part of that represents growing capability of identifying and analyzing needs and opportunities, and willingness to introduce changes. These can include strictly technical improvements in such spheres as energy conversion, production, cultivation, and the development of new materials and crops and products, marketing, storage, and transportation. But they can extend also to spheres as systems of payment, work-sequence management, legal concepts, etc.

## PROCESSES OF SOCIETAL GROWTH

The processes of societal growth have already been identified, albeit quite cryptically, in the definition of the first section. In this section I try to illustrate them more fully and indicate how they are linked to the mechanisms of societal growth discussed above.

### INCREASE IN NUMBER OF SUBSYSTEMS, AND DENSITY OF INTERRELATIONS

As we have already noted, increase in the numbers of social units of certain kinds,—e.g., couples, families, households, friendship groups—follows directly from population growth itself. And increase in the number of subsystems "serving" these basic units, e.g., schools, stores, hospitals and the like, is also related, though not so directly, to population growth. Population composition itself comprises sociodemographic axes differentiating individuals and generating the formation of groupings and subsystems based both on similiarities and on differences: Sex, age, kinship, cultural origin, social origin, birthplace, race, religion, etc., are ascribed or primordial characteristics on the basis of which individuals are likely to associate with one another or else avoid association. Families comprise persons of both sexes and several ages, while age groupings exclude persons of other ages and often of the opposite sex. There are ethnic, language, and religion- or race-based associations as well as kinship and residence subgroups.

Further differentiation, and bases for association and formation of subsystems, derive from achieved characteristics: educational, occupational, artistic, military, political, etc. Certain groupings are formed by educated persons interacting with other educated persons; other groupings are formed by educated persons interacting with uneducated. Professionals associate with other professionals in some subsystems, with laymen in others; and so forth.

By generalizing this theme, we can see that the expansion of knowledge and accessibility of knowledge and information operates—from a socio-demographic point of view—first and foremost to *differentiate* the population along increasing numbers of *knowledge and information axes*. These may be occupational axes but are by no means restricted to occupation. Two or more individuals sharing knowledge or information of a given type or combination are obvious candidates for formation of a group, complete with institutionalized roles, interaction, rewards and gratifications, internal hierarchy, etc. Two or more individuals having interests, knowledge, or information of different types or combinations may also be candidates for formation of a group. It is important to note, for example, that persons reported in a census or survey as having, say, "completed four years of college" are (1) internally differentiated in terms of their knowledge, skills, information, interests, and access to information and to other persons, and (2) very much *more* differentiated in these ways than are those who, in the same census or survey, are reported as having, say, "completed elementary school" (even though "knowledge" is by no means indexed exclusively by school attainment). Thus, the growth of knowledge operates to differentiate population, quite independently of population trends themselves; and it generates new kinds of groupings and social subsystems.

Formation of formal organizations, the mechanism by which societies have been able to organize output and distribution of rewards and more efficiently, may be seen as involving primarily the sorting and choosing among the increasing number and variety of knowledge-combination (or, more often; ascribed-characteristic-knowledge-combination) subsystems and their mobilization and coordination in pursuit of the objectives at hand. This itself, of course, entails formation of subsystems for organizing communication and control within the organization, and evolvement of new hierarchies of subsystems and of individuals. Indeed it is the extension of the spheres of formal organizations accounting for greater proportions of the total volume of social rewards and resources which brings order to what might otherwise be the chaotic—or at least disordered—activity and interaction of the myriad combinations of groupings and subsystems formed and institutionalized in the high-knowledge, high-density society.

In the same vein, the extension of boundary systems and expansion of the scale of evaluation, production, and distribution of rewards, operate to order the myriad formal organizations and other small and large subsystems which, under conditions of expanding knowledge and information accessibility, are brought progressively into overlapping networks of communication and exchange. This idea is, of course, epitomized by the concept of the "world system" (Wallerstein, 1974), but concepts of neighborhoods, hinterlands, metropolitan area, or megalopolitan network also represent the idea of institutionalization of rules and conditions of exchange over large differentiated areas, large numbers and varieties or organizations and subsystems, or large populations. In all events, the very conduct of interaction, sustenance, and reward production and distribution and exchange across large populations and areas calls forth the formation of additional units or subsystems for provision of information, monitoring, coordination, and control.

The pressures to improve and increase production—whether originating in population growth or in the wish for increased consumption and rewards in a stationary population—combined with economies of scale rendered ever-more attainable in consequence of the expansion of knowledge and technique lend support to the growth in the size of organizations and subsystems. Supermarket chains, consolidated high schools, multi-universities, industrial conglomerates, port authorities, and interstate commissions once viewed as necessary or appropriate for producing goods or providing services more effectively and more efficiently than is possible on the part of similar but smaller subsystems may be perceived with much more distrust in the wake of antigrowth discussion and sentiment. And the "belief in bigness" as an American virtue is surely less secure than in the past. Nonetheless, even in societies not sharing a "belief in bigness," or perhaps even cultivating "smallness" and "independence" credos, the growth of knowledge and communication has been associated with "bigness" (cf. Servan-Schreiber, 1968) in size of subsystems and in scale of operations. It is not by any means a certainty that size implies "efficiency" or "profitability" in all circumstances or that there is a strictly economic basis for growth in the size of social units. The "payoff" to such growth may be primarily or entirely political or psychological in nature: It may be the case that organizations or subsystems which do not grow in size are unable to "keep up with" the growth in knowledge and its accessibility over time.

Two social subsystems may be related because (1) they have some or all members in common, (2) there are direct interchanges (exchanges of rewards or resources) between members of the two respective subsystems, or (3) there are indirect interchanges between the two subsystems. In a hypothetical situation of "complete isolation," a subsystem would have relationships with no other subsystem; and a "relatively isolated" subsystem would have interrelations with only one other or a few other subsystems. Conversely, in a very dense "subsystem space" each subsystem would have direct interrelations—of one or another of the three types—with a large number of other subsystems. And it would have indirect interrelations with many more, at least from the point of view of social propinquity and accessibility.

The large-population, high-knowledge society is usually also an urban society or a high-agglomeration society, so that typically its growing number of subsystems leads to very dense "subsystem space." A central problem for subsystems located in a dense subsystem space is the sorting of interrelationship options, assignment of priorities, and criteria for association and exchange with other accessible subsystems, or for avoiding or declining associations and exchange (cf. Hawley, 1950; Hauser, 1963). As with individuals, subsystems sharing "ascriptive" or "achievement" attributes, e.g., business firms of similar composition or producing similar products, may well be "candidates" for association or interaction; but they may also be highly competitive. Conversely, subsystems with quite different attributes, e.g., a family and a bank, may also be potentially in close cooperation or competitive, or mutually indifferent. There are probably many conceptual and research activities required ahead to enable us to understand inter-subsystem relations under societal growth conditions.

### Increase in Volume of Sustenance, Rewards, and Resources

Growth in population is associated with increase in the goods and services and other social rewards produced, allocated,and exchanged even if, as the classical Malthusian view holds, there are diminishing returns to population or labor increments. In fact, there does not seem to be much empirical or historical support for the operation of diminishing returns to population increments (Easterlin, 1967; Kelley, 1972); and if anything the burden of the evidence seems to support the "population-push hypothesis," i.e., the hypothesis that population growth enhances not only production, but also productivity (Simon, 1977). The "antigrowth" stance sometimes includes the view that the alleged "growth" in product which is due to improved techniques, information, or expanded knowledge is only nominal growth or "reckoned as growth" without actually contributing anything to well-being (cf. Mishan, 1977). But it is generally acknowledged that—by conventional standards of reckoning and measurement—growth in education, knowledge, and techniques is indeed associated with growth in production and consumption of goods, services, and other rewards, whether by savings in labor, by introduction of new goods or services or rewards, by more efficient marketing and distribution, or by some other direct source. Clearly the expansion of boundary systems and increased scale of production and distribution introduce economies which may, in turn, be translated into enhanced production of material and nonmaterial rewards.

The increase in the volume of resources produced in the society's various reward-production subsystems raises two major types of questions. The most important type of question concerns the distribution and disposition of the rewards (or the additional rewards) produced: Who gets what, and what is done with it? And a second type of question concerns the effect of increment of rewards on individual behavior, time and space budgets and horizons, life cycles and partial life cycles, and social relationships.

The first type of question may be partitioned and rephrased as follows:

1. Who, among direct participants in the production of sustenance and rewards, gets what parts of the output or product, and what can or do they do with it?
2. Who else (other than direct participants in production) receives or makes claim on (or "appropriates," "taxes," "skims off," or otherwise obtains or claims) what part of the product? On what grounds, with what bases of legitimacy? To do what?

The orthodox analysis of distribution and disposition of rewards and product is cast in terms of wages, rent, interest, dividends, and the like, and in terms of consumption, savings, and investment. This is well and good as far as it goes; but it assumes as fixed the social structural factors that sociological analysis—or, for that matter, economic history, "political economy," and other social scientific disciplines—recognize as variable in time or across societies.

The familiar, classical approach to this question is represented by the Marxian concept of "surplus value," the excess of total production of commodities (rewards) over that minimum quantity which must be consumed in the course of producing the amount produced. The control over surplus value, in the hands of the bourgeoisie by virtue of the private property institutions evolving in capitalist society, is crucial both to economic development and class division in capitalist society. An elaborate analysis of magnitude and disposition of surplus value (or simply "surplus" in their terminology) is a central topic of Baran and Sweezy's *Monopoly Capital* (1966), where the authors argue that the modern corporate system controls and channels the growing economic surplus to largely alienating and antihuman activities largely to preserve its own power. An opposite view—that surplus value has been widely distributed to the working class in the "successfully developing capitalist societies such as the United States, Western Europe and Japan"—has been advanced by Boulding (1970). In all these views, the analyses, of course, deal directly with distribution of material goods and services and not directly with other social rewards. Nevertheless, there is always reference, explicit or implicit, to related nonmaterial rewards and resources, especially power and influence. However, these analyses, though raising directly and explicitly the question of differing and conflicting claims on receipt or control of rewards produced, have not laid out the full range of possibilities for competing claims on output or its control.

A distinction (originated by Weber) between resources embedded in kinship, territorial, or other ascriptive units and "free-floating" resources has been drawn in some detail by Eisenstadt (1963, 1970b). It is by mobilization, control, and manipulation of free-floating resources that entrepreneurs, charismatic groups, or individuals can gain access to societal "centers," or themselves actually join or replace the centers as modernizing elites and thereby introduce societal changes, transformations, and modernization. The growth of free-floating resources is itself a form of societal differentiation. The question of who (i.e., what social groups) takes control of such resources under what circumstances, to what ends, and with what consequences for the society's internal structure is not only a historical problem concerning each society or several societies; rather, it is a central problem in the sociological analysis of societal change, transformation, development, or modernization.[12]

The point to note here is that, far from seeking the single social category to whom to impute "appropriation" or "control" of resources and rewards, it seems reasonable to presume variation in patterns and bases of claim and control over "surplus" or "nonembedded" or "free-floating" rewards and resources. The social unit exercising control over rewards in a society may be the state; a political party; a stratum or class based on property ownership, religious authority or piety, lineage or kinship grouping; a commune or local community; a formal organization, or some combination. These various social units may have similar or dissimilar images and purposes to address and promote in allocating, converting, investing, or consuming the resources and rewards in question: maintaining or expanding a cultural pattern, territorial unification, national independence, economic development, or whatever. Thus, the issue of distribution and disposition of growing rewards and resources produced is a major intersection between societal growth, as defined here, and the traditional sociological analysis of change and development.

The question of individual effects or responses to changing volume of rewards or resources is fairly obscure. Even the effects of increased income are far from being well documented or plotted. *Some* of the changes in nonincome rewards to individuals can be subsumed under the "social mobility" rubric—status and deference, access to various strata and social groupings, and the like—so that studies of attitudinal and behavioral consequences of mobility (or consequences of status inconsistency) bear on this question. So far, however, there is no clear demonstration of such effects independent of the main effects of the rank dimensions themselves (Jackson and Curtis, 1972). However, those "effects" studied have been largely those connected with occupational mobility, and it is possible that the more direct examination of changes in volumes of other rewards may reveal interesting or meaningful consequences.

## FRICTIONS IN SOCIETAL GROWTH

We can identify two very general types of frictions associated with societal growth: (1) competition for positions, rewards, or resources exacer-

[12] Compare the discussion of Lenski (1966) on this topic.

bated by uneven growth and by knowledge-induced changes in demands and expectations; and (2) population and resource "squeezes" which upset existing "sociometric" or mutual selection regimes and patterns and other exchange, market, or resource-conversion regimes and patterns. Competition for goods, services, rewards, or resources among individuals, groups, or strata is familiar enough in the nongrowth society. Under conditions of societal growth certain kinds of rewards, e.g., space or physical or social access to other persons, places, or subsystems, may be rendered more scarce, hence presumably more valuable or more competition-generating. The growth of different kinds of rewards may take place at rates differing sufficiently or in ways that generate problems and indeed social or physical dangers. For example, growth in the number of automobiles or aircraft with insufficient roads or airlines or traffic control arrangements and institutions is disruptive and dangerous. The growth of urban settlement faster than the growth of stable employment opportunities and educational, medical, sanitary, police, or other services is a familiar example of such frictions.

A different type of imbalanced growth is the growth of knowledge and information among disadvantaged individuals and groups and the absence of corresponding growth in their material welfare or social participation and power. Under conditions of expanding knowledge, information, and analyses concerning others in the same society, inequity is rendered intolerable.[13] In particular, whatever their histories and past ideologies, under conditions of societal growth all manners of social, demographic, or cultural "pluralisms" become increasingly anachronistic within the boundaries of any given society and correspondingly the source of conflicts seeking either assimilation-integration or separatist-type resolutions.

The "marriage squeeze" is the most familiar example of a population squeeze. In its simplest form, a marriage squeeze is a lagged result of an inflection in fertility in a mate-selection regime in which, say, males typically marry females two years their junior: If there is an upward inflection in fertility, the females of the enlarged birth cohort will—when reaching conventional ages for marriage—encounter a shortage of eligible males, i.e., males two years their senior. A familiar variant on the simple marriage squeeze is the squeeze generated by increasing educational attainment in a marriage regime wherein females typically marry males, say, two years their senior who have the same or higher educational attainment: If there is an upward shift in the distribution by educational attainment, females in the cohort first enjoying the improvement will be confronted by a shortage of two-years-older males with appropriate educational credentials. Resolutions of marriage squeezes involve either (1) delaying or forgoing marriage or else (2) changing the mate-selection rules; but we are far from having much understanding of how this takes place empirically.

[13] This point is developed by P. M. Hauser in his 1968 presidential address to the ASA, "The Chaotic Society" (Hauser, 1969).

The theme of "increased supply of X-category persons, but no takers," or of "increased demand for Y-category persons, but no candidates" recurs throughout the intersection of population studies and social organization and is characteristic of societal growth. Whatever the particular or general forms of resolution of such squeezes, it is clear that there must be changes in the "prices" or conditions of exchange or conversion of social resources and rewards. An increasingly familiar example is that of the status, income, and occupational returns to educational attainment: As average educational attainment has risen, the level of educational attainment characterizing *each* occupational category has risen as well, and average socioeconomic returns per year of educational attainment have diminished (cf. Freeman, 1976).

## Societal Growth and Social Change: On a Research Agenda

### MEASURING SOCIETAL GROWTH

I cannot write a textbook on measurement of societal growth; perhaps someone else can, or perhaps a collaborative effort could produce such a text. That would certainly be a significant and useful contribution. For the time being we must improvise and devise ways and procedures for measuring the causes, mechanisms, and processes of societal growth. I think that much can already be convincingly measured, and as talented students attack these problems, we are likely to see rapid progress in the near future.

We know a great deal about measuring population size, composition, distribution, and turnover; and we can measure change in population fairly accurately and in considerable detail for many societies. The attempt to measure the volume, composition, distribution, and accessibility of knowledge and information is much newer, but nevertheless quite promising. Certainly we are able to differentiate societies and subgroups in terms of knowledge, and we can obtain some measures of growth as well.[14]

We need to be able to measure boundaries of societies and of the most important subsystems and institutional spheres, and to be able to plot their growth and changes. Data on numbers of persons, areas, numbers of subunits at different levels composing the society or subsystem are indicative of boundaries and of expansion of boundaries. For certain kinds of units we are accustomed to thinking about and measuring boundaries: National societies and political units and regional economies and church membership and protest movements are discussed with explicit or implicit measures of their boundaries and changes in their boundaries; and we can extend and generalize these concepts and measurements. We can already measure the scale of

[14] This topic is treated at length in Bell, 1968, 1973.

production and of allocation or distribution of certain kinds of rewards. We can compare the proportions of sales of made-to-measure suits with those of ready-made garments, Wonder Bread with products of the corner bakery and with home-baked bread, reporter-reported news items with wire-service news dispatches, and messages of parish priests or congregation ministers and rabbis compared with those of Billy Graham or Oral Roberts. But it is hard to compare an SEI score with membership in one of the "social classes" of Yankee City, or for that matter to compare being in one of the middle classes in Yankee City with being in the middle class in Middletown. And it is even harder to measure or compare the "scales' of distribution of prestige, deference, or social standing in the 1930s and 1940s with those of the 1960s and 1970s, i.e., to compare the extent to which images, evaluations, and opinions are similar or dissimilar over large populations or across vast areas. It is hard to compare the satisfaction of viewing the local opera or dance group in the summer festival or the local park or high school with that of watching the Met or a famous ballet or dance company on national TV; and it is difficult to compare the "importance" of getting the neighbor elected to the town council with that of the national elections. But we do need to devise ways to extend the concepts of "scale" or production and distribution to nonmaterial rewards.

Similarly, we know how to measure and compare the proportion of total bread consumed which is baked at home and that baked and marketed by business organizations. Perhaps we could measure the proportion of the total volume of information and values learned in school, in the home, in the neighborhood, in the mass media respectively. But these are also concepts which need to be extended greatly: For all types of social rewards and resources, we must identify the subsystems—including formal organizations—in which they are produced and distributed, and try to measure the proportions produced within and outside of formal organizations respectively.

The description and measurement of bases and legitimation of claims on social rewards and resources, or of control over allocation of rewards and resources, seem conceptually and concretely much more difficult than measurement of the other factors and mechanisms mentioned so far.[15] Probably the empirical establishment of legitimation in general is very difficult, if indeed possible: It probably entails an anlysis of characteristics, qualities, and imputed attributes of persons in various positions of recognized authority, with claim on rewards, with actual control of resources, etc. (or positions characterized by their absence), combined with opinion and attitude data. This might permit assigning values of relative weight or importance of all factors on a list of potential bases or legitimation of claims or rewards which might include, say, *participation* in one of a variety

[15] But see the interesting and suggestive work of Laumann and Pappi (1976), who have tried to catalog and measure "influence resources" in the town in which they investigated stratification and networks of association, prestige, and influence.

of ways in the very production process and interaction; *ownership* of some resource used in the production process, e.g, property, techniques, part of market; *kin* relationship or inheritance of rights, claims, or entitlements; civil or religious *authority*; *power*; specialized or general *knowledge*; and so on. This is an area of research of measurement that awaits its very earliest development.

Finally, among societal growth mechanisms, the extent of analysis of society itself, and the attempts to introduce or adapt social (or economic or political) innovations, also seems to defy simple measurement. It is possible to measure the numbers of social scientists, their budgets, or their publications. Possibly, measuring the rates of *diffusion* of specific given innovations—e.g., employment of blacks in previously segregated occupations or industries, use of automated production lines, promotion or hiring of women to positions of authority, introduction of pass-fail options in the universities—is one approach to measurement of social innovation. Employment of "innovations" systems engineers, R&D organization or budget, may be an indication of the importance or even the rate of innovation. But the apparatus for measurement of innovation is distinctly in need of development.

Measurement and analysis of processes of societal growth are more familiar in some respects, but even more problematic in other respects. It is possible theoretically to identify, or at least to compute the number of possible two-person, three-person, . . . *n*-person relationships in a population of any given size. Also, it is possible to identify and count groupings and subsystems at different levels in the major institutional spheres: factories and banks and stores, line and management, bureaucratic divisions and sections and departments, work groups and sales teams, and the like. Procedures familiar in the study of organizations, small groups, bureaucracies, families, etc., can serve as well in measuring growth in number, size, and density of subsystems (Scott, 1965).

But what is problematic is the sorting of these groupings and determination of their salience or the salience of one or another axis of differentiation, for different facets of social organization.[16] For it is one of our central hypotheses that the salience or importance of the various axes of differentiation, bases for social participation, claims or rewards, or control of production and allocation of social rewards, *changes* or is transformed under societal growth.

The salience of axes of differentiation is indexed by the various patterns of exchange and conversion of rewards. A pioneer attempt to represent and measure the structure of group associations and their salience for patterns of influence, decision making, and production and exchange of rewards and resources for one community at one point in time is undertaken by Lau-

[16]For an excellent discussion and summary, see Stinchcome, 1965. This discussion offers but few clues to *measurement* of the weight or salience of groupings or axes of differentiation, but rather depends on insightful choice.

mann and Pappi (1976). They use especially network analysis and multidimensional scaling to describe social differentiation and informal relations in the community they studied, and they use distance-matrix analysis and correlation and regression techniques to analyze the structure of influence and influence resources. Similar approaches can be adapted to addressing problems of change induced by population growth and transformations and by expansion of knowledge.

The "familiar" in the measurement of the volume of sustenance and rewards is the elaborate apparatus of economic analysis. Production, distribution, flows, and price mechanisms can be measured and analyzed insofar as the conventional goods and services are concerned. Moreover, concepts of costs and utilities of decision making of all types, indeed of human behavior generally, are being introduced and subjected to the scrutiny of economic analysis—or at least analysis by economists (e.g., G.S. Becker, 1977). But rewards such as prestige, honor, authority, influence, love, social participation, and security have not yet received this treatment, and it remains to extend procedures for direct comparison, measurement, and analysis to these types of social rewards as well (rather than assume them as "exchanges" or "payoffs" for foregone production or income which *is* more readily measured, as economists sometimes do).

Finally, the *relationships* between the social structure, roles, subsystems organizing the *production* of rewards, and the actual volume and composition of rewards, and the social structure, roles, subsystems organizing *claims on* and *distribution* of rewards (arrows [m] and [n] in figure 3) must be measured. Obviously the body of research relating income, consumption, health, "prestige," social participation, or other reward distributions to occupational differences, family roles, residence, or group membership has important bearing here and establishes, for example, the importance of occupational positions in the reward-distribution regime. But it is widely acknowledged that both the range of social rewards whose distributions or allocation are studied (e.g., income, but rarely autonomy, authority, or dependency; consumption, but rarely influence or honor) and the categories of reward-production roles (occupations, but rarely friendship; marital status, but rarely extended family roles or relationships, neighborliness, or community participation) have been very limited. Again, the central hypothesis is that societal growth implies disorganization, and subsequent reorganization, of this product-distribution regime.

## SOCIETAL GROWTH AND SOCIAL ACCOUNTING

The attention being paid the elements of societal growth, and the methodological sophistication being brought to bear in these inquiries, seem to guarantee progress in the measurement of societal growth. In fact, we could view a number of societal models, or societal parts of "world-models"—especially those encompassing population, knowledge, and rewards jointly—as partial representations of societal growth. Some examples may be suggestive of both possibilities and pitfalls in the study of societal growth.

The social indicator concept has been of different purposes for different individuals, investigators, or groups. For some it is primarily an instrument for the quantification and analysis of social change and its causes and correlates. For others it has been intended as an instrument of formulation, monitoring, and evaluation of social policy and intervention (Bell, 1973: chap. 5). In a review of rationales for social indicators, Land (1975) lists the "social policy" rationale, a "social change" rationale and a "social reporting" rationale and goes on to elucidate the defining characteristics of social indicators and propose a paradigm for "social indicator models": including the (1) scope and content of indicators, and (2) provision of a guide to analysis of social change. Land reviews the history of the social indicator concept and problems of arriving at a satisfactory definition. He himself proposes three distinct types of social indicators:

1. Output descriptive indicators: measures of the end products of social processes and most directly related to the appraisal of social problems and social policy.
2. Other descriptive indicators: more general measures of the social conditions of human existence and the changes taking place therein.
3. Analytic indicators: components of explicit conceptual models of the social processes which result in values of the output indicators.

In actual practice, social indicators have been inclusive enough to comprehend practically every social statistical time series. In their important volume on social indicators, Sheldon and Moore (1968) included chapters dealing with trends in population; economic growth (output of goods and services); labor force and employment; knowledge and technology; government activity; family structure; religious institutions, membership, and activities; consumption; leisure activities; health, schooling; stratification and mobility; and welfare. The 1977 U.S. government publication devoted explicitly to social indicators has included data on population; the family; housing; Social Security and Welfare; health and nutrition; public safety; education and training; work; income, wealth and expenditures; culture, leisure, and use of time; and social mobility and participation. In each area, the data include objective indicators for the United States and international comparisons and, in addition, indicators of "public perceptions" concerning each topic (U.S. Dept. of Commerce, 1977).[17]

[17] This brief mention of the social indicator studies cannot do justice to the remarkable collection of materials in the U.S. government volume and to other work and publications on the recent social indicator and societal monitoring activity. Lists of references and other national social indicator reports as well as specific sources for the data presented are given in the *Social Indicators 1976* volume.

Two somewhat more specific approaches to modeling and measurement which also comprehend much of societal growth are social or demographic accounting models and econometric models of entire societies. One approach is essentially a population projection format that encompasses also changes in population composition due to life cycle changes, attrition, or mobility, e.g., to education, to movement into or through the labor force, to marriage and family-building, as well as the more familiar survival, aging, and migration. These models have had extensive application in analysis of growth, attrition, turnover, and changing composition in school populations, armies, etc. (Bartholomew, 1972; Stone, 1971, 1975). The other approach is that of the econometric model, comprising a set of simultaneous equations relating a set of measurable social factors, such as population, labor force, marriage, delinquency, income, schooling, migration, and suburbanization (Hodge and Klorman, 1975; Pampel, Land, and Felson, 1977).

These approaches and models all share a capability of incorporating the elements of societal growth. They can deal convincingly with quantitive and cumulative facets of social change; and it seems not too much to hope that societal growth can be measured and studied with the aid of such approaches. But these approaches—social indicators, sociodemographic accounting models, and econometric models—also share a distance from, and indeed a measure of indifference to, some of the major concerns and problems of both traditional and contemporary sociology and sociological study of social change. While attending to cataloging and "accounting" of social facts and events and to rigourous analysis of relationships among them, these approaches tended to ignore issues of order, value, solidarity, or the contrasts between society and community, power and autonomy, sacred and secular, conflict and consensus, in sociological analysis and to ignore their bearing on social change in particular. This is not an inherent failing (or strength, as many would no doubt have it) of the approaches or models themselves, but rather is a matter of the uses to which they are put and the questions and formulations to which they are addressed.

In my view, the study of societal growth can be pursued with rigor and on a strong empirical basis; and it can at the same time be integrated with traditional mainstream sociological concerns. I turn briefly to this issue in the concluding paragraphs.

## WEDDING SOCIETAL GROWTH AND SOCIAL CHANGE

The fact that we can observe and measure various facets of societal growth, and that we are likely to be able to measure additional dimensions in the near future, need not sentence the concepts and ideas of societal growth to the exile from the mainstream of sociological inquiry that has been the lot of many of the observation-and-measurement-based strands and traditions in sociology. Such exile has come about because of different traditions and concerns behind the very formulation of problems and issues (Sociological *Problemstellung*, as discussed by Eisenstadt and Curelaru, 1976) and perhaps a certain amount of mutual disinterest on the part of followers of "historical" and of "survey" methodologies respectively in the questions and concerns addressed by students of practitioners of the other approach. Thus sociologists interested in current social problems, styles of life, inequality and life chances, attitudes, role behavior, or group relations have often bypassed historical analysis and perhaps have not seen much importance in the problems which it has addressed. Sociologists interested in problems of order, solidarity, and cohesion, consensus and conflict, religion, power, authority, and rationality have often not been able to find interest or attraction in survey research, statistical analysis, or mathematical models. Of course, there have been many exceptions and there are many acknowledged intersections between "historical-comparative" sociology's topics and approaches and those of the "empirical-measurement" schools. But these intersections have often remained vague and badly in need of more direct attention.

If societal growth is a topic whose theoretical and research "home" is likely to be in the "empirical-measurement" school, it is nevertheless of sufficiently direct importance for the "historical-comparative" school to render promising the elucidation of its intersection with mainstream issues such as those concerning the bases of social order, and its regularities, the sources and mechanisms of legitimation or of individual acceptance of social order, and the varieties of harmonies and disharmonies in social life. To do so it is necessary to go beyond the very general hypotheses of the form: "Societal growth tends to upset and induce change in patterns of legitimation and authority" or "Societal growth tends to introduce competition and conflicts over positions, rewards, and resources." Rather, we need to work out propositions about directions of change related to societal growth. For example: Under societal growth, informal or less formal mechanisms of social control become inadequate to protect individuals or groups from the adverse consequences of the behavior, or indeed from the very diversity, of others. Accordingly government is called upon to regulate all manner of behavior and activity and to enforce agreed-upon rules and regulations. Governments have varying degrees of success in such enforcement, and societies may outgrow the capacities of the various governmental agencies of regulation and control. Under what conditions do consensus-based controls and sanctions suffice to maintain order? Under what conditions does societal growth induce coercive or repressive arrangements for preservation of order? What are the roles of population composition, of educational and skill levels, of value orientations, of degrees of equality or inequality in social participation and in distribution of rewards as mediators or determinants of the consequences of growth for modes of social control? For any given society, these are questions which have concrete answers, and they may be ascertained empirically. There are two basic kinds of requirements for doing so.

First, it is necessary to seek explicit and detailed formulations of the observed, hypothesized, or "guessed" relationships between societal growth variables—population and knowledge, social structure and social rewards variables—and the "mainstream" social organizational variables in question—whatever their levels of abstraction or generality, whether formation of strata or categories of social solidarity or pervasiveness of secularism; and to work out procedures for investigating such relationships empirically.

Second, it is of critical importance to have replicate, or approximately replicate, studies. This point is made frequently and eloquently (see, for example, Laumann, 1973: 210; Duncan, 1969 *b*, 1975); yet it is probably still not taken as seriously as it should be among researchers, granting agencies, journal and monograph editors, and dissertation committees alike. Replications of studies and analysis of changes in relation to societal growth are possible with "existing technology" and hold promise of building an understanding of the impact of societal growth on the very central dimensions of social life and social organizaton.

# 5

# The Measurement of Societal Growth

*James S. Coleman*

THE MEASUREMENT OF SOCIETAL GROWTH must wait upon conceptual development, for we must know what we mean by societal growth before we can begin to measure it. The matter would not be difficult if it were clear that societal growth consisted of growth in numbers of persons in a given well-defined "society," or of some other, equally simple change. But then the study of societal growth would be nothing more than the study of population growth, and thus would be no reason for any special concern. Until this conceptual development takes place, there are few useful things that can be said about measurement. One is to make some general statistical statements about time series, trend analysis, and other statistical techniques that are likely to be useful in the measurement of societal growth. A second is to attempt to anticipate possible directions of conceptual development and to indicate just how one might go about measurement, conditional upon the direction of conceptual development. I will attempt the second of these two tasks. This means I will provide little information about measurement per se, but will devote nearly all of my attention to speculation about the possible directions that conceptual development can take—interlarding these occasionally with comments on how one would carry out measurement if it were a particular kind of change we were after.

## Hints from Other Kinds of Systems

How to approach the general problem is not at all clear. Perhaps we are too much a part of what we are observing, too close to the phenomenon to see it in focus. There are other systems which change in certain ways with growth, and it may aid us in gaining a perspective if we look at some of these. Perhaps the most interesting is the physiological system, for there we can observe changes of several sorts. The simplest is the growth of an animal from birth—maintaining the same form, keeping the same organs, merely growing. Even here, there are peculiarities, for not all parts grow at the same rate. In human beings, for example, the brain stops growing in early childhood, while most of the rest of the body continues to grow through adolescence. In this kind of growth, where all elements are present from the beginning, where structures expand but do not change in character, the measurement of growth is simply that which most parents record of their children: a measurement of *size*. The measures may be of different attributes of size: height and weight, for example (or, less frequently measured in the case of physiological individuals, volume). They may be of the whole or of parts: the height of the person or the length of an arm or a leg, or a finger, the circumference of the head or the waist, bust, hips, thighs, or biceps. And the measures of size may be more esoteric: the calories burned per unit of work performed, for example. But whatever the measure, whatever the part being measured, the principal change that is recorded in such a case is a change in size. Furthermore, the changes in size that occur in lifetime growth are changes of a magnitude that is anticipated in the initial structural design. Thus the necessary structural elements for the adult individual are nearly all present from the beginning, and it is just a matter of expansion of scale.

A greater degree of complexity is introduced by those species that undergo a metamorphosis. A caterpillar becoming a butterfly is the most spectacular example. Here too there is a system of growth, but of a very different kind. It is growth which manifests itself in a total change of form. There is very little change, though some simple growth in size, of the individual while it remains in a given form. Then suddenly there is a total transformation, in which no parts are the same, and the metamorphosis has occurred. This kind of change is interesting to note and to observe. However, there is no "problem" of measurement of this change, because it is a full discontinuity. Now, it may be possible to go below this, to examine the processes through which the metamorphosis takes place and to trace by stages and slow changes what appeared to be a discontinuous change. Such observation is not straightforward, because, as with the caterpillar-butterfly, most species that undergo metamorphosis do so in some form of seclusion. And such observation is more likely to be of interest in the study of metamorphoses than in the study of "growth"; for just as Rip Van Winkle, who wakes up to find a transformed society, may be uninterested in the stages through which this transformation occurred, such total transformations may be in general less interesting than changes that are less encompassing.

A third kind of change found in physiological systems is the kind of change that occurs over a long period of time in the development of new species. There is an elaboration or extension of the structure of which the individual is composed, new types of structures develop (for example, a skeleton of bone is unnecessary for small creatures, but becomes necessary for larger ones, because of gravitational force), new organs develop to carry out new functions (for example, eyes developed as the individual became mobile), and other similarly extensive changes take place.[1] It is this third kind of change which corresponds to the kind of societal growth that should be our principal concern here. And it is this kind of change which is difficult to conceptualize and measure, for there are not clearly defined dimensions that allow one to specify some quantitative change. What I will do is discuss two approaches to conceptualizing this change and look at the implications of each of them for measurement.

## The Elements of Which a Society Is Composed

One approach to social theory is that of purposive action. Social philosophers like Kotarbinski and Von Mises have been action theorists, sociologists such as Talcott Parsons have been as well, and the whole body of economic theory is built upon a purposive theory of action, the conception of economic man. With such a theoretical approach, the fundamental elements of the conceptual system are actors. Thus one of the first questions that must be answered is: Who are the actors? The answer is not as simple as it seems, for if we look at the work of action theorists, it is not always true that persons are the sole, or even the principal, actors. Economics illustrates this best (since economics has gone furthest in the actual development of a theory of action), and in economic theory, there are a number of actors: persons, households, firms, governments. That is, in economic theory, persons are utility maximizers, households are also; firms are profit maximizers; and governments (particularly in the German school of economists) maximize the "utility for the state."

Although economists shift from one actor to another as a matter of practical convenience, the fact that the relevant actors in a society change over time is a matter not to be passed over lightly, if one is interested in charting the growth of society. For as society grows, actions that were once taken by persons as individuals come to be taken by corporate actors of various sorts. Indeed, the very emergence of modern purposive corporate actors which are incorporated under government statute is a relatively new phenomenon. The conception of a legal actor in society (which could sue and be sued, which had rights and obligations, an income and assets) over and above a single individual arose only with the end of the Middle Ages. The growth in the number of these corporate actors became explosive only

[1]See D'Arcy Thompson (1943) for an extended discussion of these changes.

in the second half of the nineteenth century; and in the twentieth century we have a society populated by large numbers and many types of corporate actors. Their growth in numbers cannot be easily tabulated, because nothing comparable for corporate actors to a population census for persons has been carried out. But some statistics have been assembled to show the growth in recent years in the population of corporate actors in society. Figure 1 shows this growth.

Measures such as those given in figure 1 give some indication of societal growth through the population growth of a new kind of actor. Such mea-

**Figure 1.** Growth of Corporations in the United States.

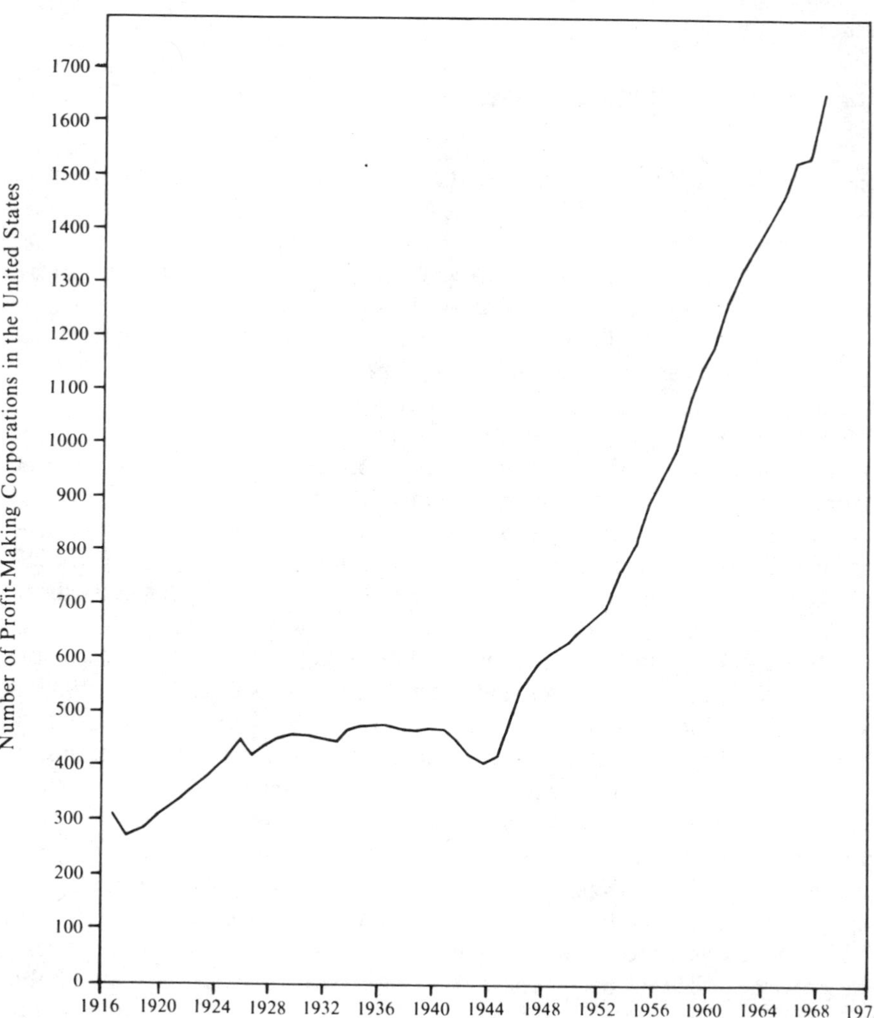


SOURCE: Adapted from Shi Chang Wu (1974).

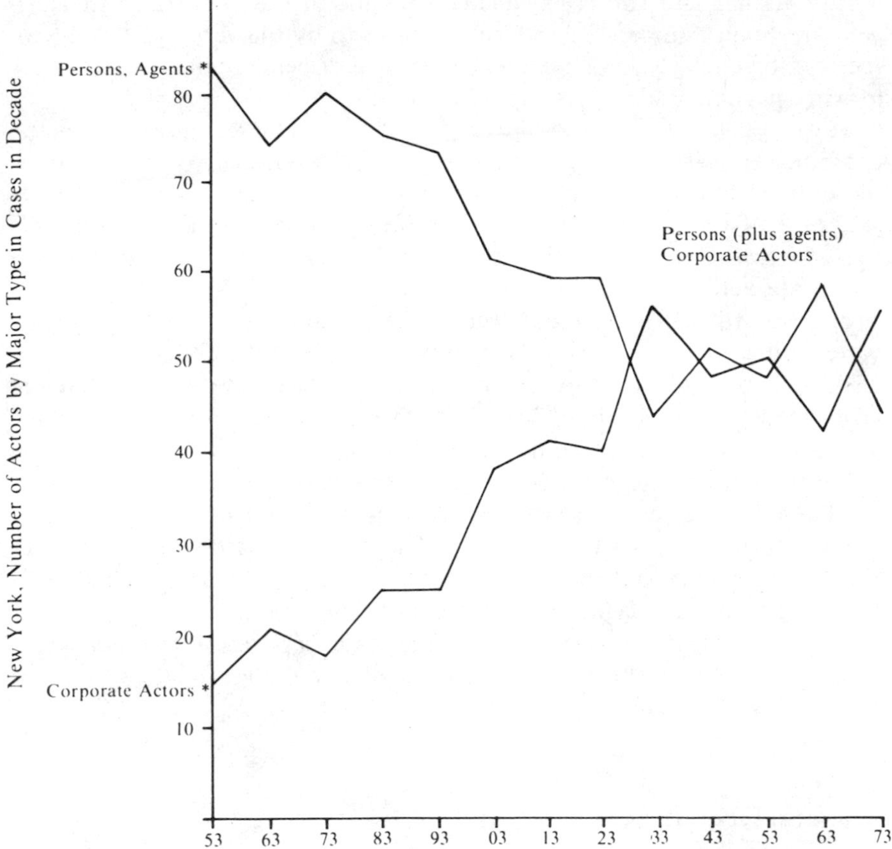


**Figure 2.** Participation of Persons and Corporate Actors in Court Cases, United States, 1853–1973

SOURCE: Adapted from Grossman (1974).

sures can be disaggregated for different types of corporate actors (for example, profit-making corporations, trade unions, professional associations, nonprofit associations of other types), providing information about the time of development of various corporate sectors. Beyond that, however, are measures of the role of corporate actors in social interactions of different kinds. For example, a measure of the societal importance of this new type of actor is its appearance as plaintiff or defendant in court cases. In a simple society in which all relevant actors other than government are persons, then the parties at court will all be persons, or else government. As corporate actors become relevant, this changes. Figure 2 shows, for example, changes that have occurred between 1853 and 1973 in the nature of the parties before the New York appelate court. The graph shows very well the growth, irregular but continuing, in the proportion of parties that are corporate actors, and the complementary decline in the proportion that are persons. Such a measure shows societal growth by the very functioning of society: the changes in the relative importance of persons and corporate actors in a particular kind of social interaction.

Legal proceedings are not the only form of social interaction that can be examined to learn of changes in the nature of the actors involved in that interaction. Another example is news events. Figure 3, based on content analyses of the front pages of the *New York Times* about the same hundred-year period, shows the proportions of actors mentioned in news events that are corporate actors, and the proportion that are persons. The increase in the proportion of corporate actors over this period does not mean that persons were acting less frequently in later years. It means rather that there was a relative increase in the newsworthy actions of corporate actors—that the structure of social action in the United States, as reported in the *New York Times* over this period of time, changed very greatly in the direction of a structure in which corporate actors rather than persons are the actors.

These illustrations, based on three sociologists' research, show the general strategy that I am suggesting here. The strategy is to determine the fundamental elements in theories of social systems and then to trace changes in those elements as they are recorded in the functioning of society. I have chosen theories of action, because this theoretical approach is both a promising one and one which illustrates especially well changes that have occurred in the fundamental elements.

## Societal Growth as the Length of Chains

One approach to societal growth begins with a listing of fundamental social processes which involve an individual person. For example, one of these is the process of acquiring the goods he consumes. Then for each such process, we can ask the distance from him that it originated. In the case of consumer goods, one extreme point of origination is with the person himself. For many persons in the nineteenth century, but for few now, nearly all of their foodstuffs, the major part of their clothing, and all the materials that went into their housing originated in the household itself. A farm household which grew its own food, spun its own wool or flax, and lived in a log house built by hand consumed few goods that it purchased from anyone else. Its money income and money expenditures were very small, because it produced nearly all it consumed.

The other extreme point of origination is halfway around the world. If all the goods that a New Yorker consumed were made in Japan, then this would be close to the other extreme. The more appropriate antithesis to home production, of course, is not the most distant point, but an equal likelihood for every point on earth, or a likelihood for each point proportional

**Figure 3.** Slopes of Continuous Trend and Moving Averages of Attention Given to Individual versus Corporate Entities over the Time Series.*

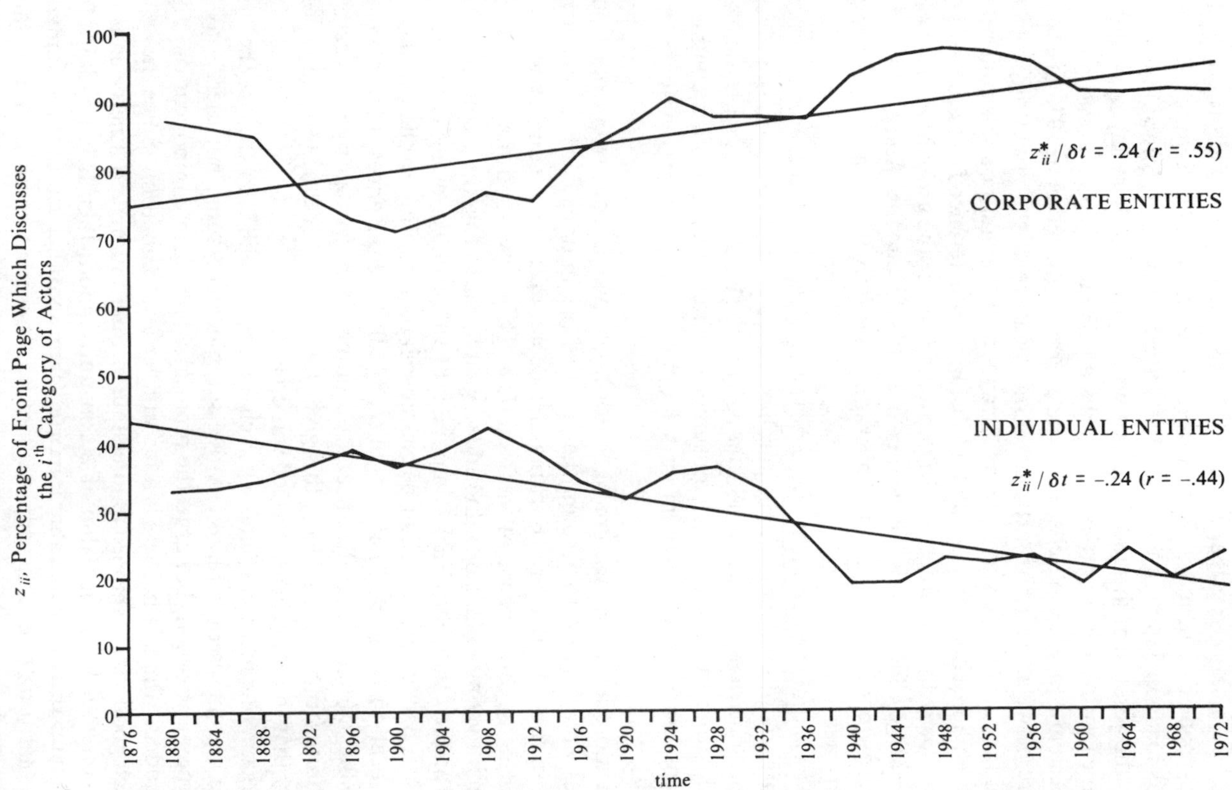


*Moving average of time $t$ is the arithmetic average of the four-year interval of $t$ with the four-year intervals before and after $t$.

SOURCE: Adapted from Burt (1975).

to the population of persons at that point. Thus if 7/4,000 of the world's population lives in the Chicago metropolitan area, 1/20 in the United States, 1/40 in Japan, and so on, a Chicagoan's consumption would be indifferent to national origin if 7/4,000 of his consumer expenditures were for goods made in Chicago, 1/20 for goods made in the United States, 1/40 for goods made in Japan, and so on. The criterion for indifference to distance (i.e., the absence of distance bias) is a weaker one, for here Japan would be grouped with other countries equally distant from Chicago.

Actual consumer purchases by the average Chicagoan in 1978 are somewhere between these two extremes. One measure of the growth of society, from the point of view of a given Chicagoan, is the point on this continuum between household production and distance-indifference for the set of purchases made by this Chicagoan. Then a measure of the growth of society for the average Chicagoan is the average over all Chicagoans. And a measure of the growth of society for the average American is the average over all Americans.

The actual measurement of the distance bias in consumer purchases can be carried out by examining the purchase of a sample of persons, but it need not be done that way. It can be obtained for the United States with some approximation by data on total consumer expenditures, interstate commerce for consumer goods, and imports from various countries of consumer goods.

A more accurate measure of the distance bias in consumer goods purchases would take into account the point of origin of each of the materials used in the manufacture. Fortunately, economics has a concept which is useful here, the concept of value added. Thus any good may be broken down into components of value added which, taken together, constitute the final price of the good. Each component of value added, at a given location, say, in a particular plant, can be characterized according to the distance of that location from the final consumer. If all these distances, multiplied by the value added at that distance, are summed and divided by the total expenditure (total value added), this gives the average distance from the consumer that the value he purchased was created.

Again, one method of making such a measurement is to analyze the consumer purchases of a representative sample of persons, not merely as to their point of origin, but as to the point at which each component of value was added. And again, there is a far simpler approximation. Since the value of each good that is shipped in interstate or international commerce ends up as a component of the value of a consumer good, then it is possible, for each state, to count, as value imported from another state, the shipments from that state minus the shipments of nonconsumer goods into that state, adding back in the shipments of nonconsumer goods into that state which were transformed into goods consumed in the state. In other words, the value imported by a given state which originated in another given state is the value the second state exported to the first minus the value contained in those exports which originated elsewhere. Then the value *consumed* by a given state that originated in a given other state is this quantity minus the value contained in those imports that were subsequently exported. Similar considerations hold at the levels of international commerce.

The matter can be treated by use of state or regional input-output techniques. With matrices that show industrial output by region to each other industry in each region, it is possible to calculate the desired quantity, the total value added in region X that is consumed in region Y. Fortunately, some work on regional input-output analyses has been carried out, so that the technical tools are available (Barno, 1967: 105–7; Carter and Brody, 1970: 143–82). Data also are available, though not as complete as might be desired. Altogether, in this case, both the conception of precisely what is to be measured and the data for measurement appear to be within our grasp. The result of such measurement, whether carried out only for consumer goods as discussed earlier, or for all value added, as discussed immediately above, would be to give a well-defined measure of the geographic growth of the production-consumption chains that are involved in economic activity. This is only one component of society, but an important one.

The case of economic goods began earlier as an illustration of a more general phenomenon of which these processes of economic production and consumption are only one case. It is useful, then, to turn to others. One of these is child socialization. We can ask the question, just as it was asked for consumer goods, What fraction of the socialization of, say, a six-year-old child, is carried out within the household, by the parents? And what fraction originates at the neighborhood level? What fraction originates, through the school, at the level of state or nation? What fraction originates, through the medium of television, radio, movies, or popular music, at the level of the nation? What fraction originates from other nations?

These questions may be more difficult to answer empirically than comparable ones in the economic sphere, because there is nothing comparable to interstate and international commerce data, and there is no natural unit of measurement such as price. Yet the other avenue of measurement, through dissection of the experiences of a population sample, remains available. It seems clear that there has been less rapid societal growth in socialization of children than in economic goods. Yet the growth is apparent, even before measurement. For example, an average six-year-old in America spends a fraction of every day watching television, most of which originates in California. This is time which before television the child would have spent in interaction with other children, or with his parents, or in some other activity with a local origin. The most striking changes, however, have occurred internationally. In several countries conflicts emerged over the use of the Sesame Street television program for teaching children to learn English. The controversies had to do with the implicit American values and style that were being imported through the socialization that occurred as part of Sesame Street.

Such a controversy could never have arisen some years ago, because Sesame Street is the first internationally diffused instrument of explicit socialization. Ever since some years before its existence, there have been implicit socialization instruments diffused internationally by television and movies. Thus the experience of an African child with access to a television set may include cowboys and Indians, space exploration, urban crime, and a variety of other programs that originated in America, far from his home.

The empirical answer to the socialization problem can possibly treat time in the same way that money is treated in consumer purchases, and count socialization experiences in terms of the time expended on them. The empirical use of time budgets has been developed, and it is quite possible to apply this approach for the study of distance bias in socialization.

There are, however, some problems of conceptualization that must be resolved before such measurement can be useful. If a mother follows the advice of Dr. Spock in deciding how to discipline her child, is this to be considered a socialization practice that originates in the household (because it was administered by the mother) or nationally (because it was based on something written by Dr. Benjamin Spock in New Haven, Connecticut)? If the point of origin is to be considered the household, then an important aspect of the expansion of socialization practices will have been missed, that is, the shift from a mother's using the experience of her mother or of neighbors to using a national source.

Similar problems exist in determining where socialization that takes place at school originates. There has been national textbook material since McGuffey's readers; clearly the point of origin of a textbook should play a part in determining the point of origin of school socialization. Here as in the case of parental socialization practices, a concept like that of value added in economic production is necessary. Any practice as delivered to the child contains components that had their origin at different points. In principle, it would be possible to construct an "input-output" matrix, showing for each element that finds some ultimate use in socialization what fraction of the input from which it came into being came from different sources, identified as to type of input and location. Despite its construction in principle, such a matrix could offer serious difficulties in practice; yet here, as elsewhere, some approximations and estimates from various data sources would be valuable in allowing such a matrix to be constructed and used for measuring distance bias in socialization and its change over time.

A third fundamental process that can be used in the same way as the production and consumption of private goods and child socialization is authoritative commands and other directives used in governance. At one extreme stands an independent householder, say, a farmer, of the nineteenth century, whose activities were very largely governed by his own will or by local community custom. At the other extreme would be a person of the future for whom governance of his work and consumption activities originates from a central source, say, the UN headquarters. Such an extreme would of course never be realized, because some aspects of governance, such as garbage collection and street repair are necessarily tied to the locality and depend on local conditions. But short of that extreme, one can see how societal growth can be manifest through increases in the distance between the point of origin of authoritative commands and the point of output or of execution. The major shift in recent years in the United States from local laws and regulations to federal laws and regulations would show up in such a measure of societal expansion. One of the most striking is the shift, in many localities, from locally determined school attendance patterns to federally determined ones, as a result of school desegregation. Another is the imposition of a national highway speed limit of fifty-five miles per hour, replacing statewide limits. Another is in the establishment of federal standards and inspection procedures for meat that is butchered for sale, replacing variable or nonexistent state standards.

Similarly, two sources of increased distance of authoritative commands in the workplace would have an impact on such a measure: the increase, throughout this century, of multiplant firms operated under the overall jurisdiction of a single corporate headquarters which establishes certain policies to be followed in local plants; and more recently, the entrance of federal regulations such as OSHA safety regulations, HEW affirmative action hiring programs, and EPA environmental regulations in plant location, construction, and operation.

A small amount of growth from a national to an international locus has taken place in recent years, particularly among Common Market countries and among East European countries subject to Soviet hegemony. Common Market parliamentary decisions have radically altered the prices paid by consumers and the policies with regard to farmers in Britain, for example.

It is clear that in the area of authoritative commands and governance there has been extensive societal growth in recent years, in the above ways and others. What is less clear is the best way to measure this growth. There is nothing comparable here to an expenditure budget or a time budget that was usable in one of the preceding areas; consequently, a population sample seems less valuable in this case. Many of the authoritative commands or laws or rulings are not ones which a citizen directly experiences and can thus report on. Rather, they are commands received and responded to by employer, city agency, school board, state agency. Thus the citizen receives them as commands from one of these local authorities; yet the local authorities in implementing these commands are no longer authorities; they are agents of a national authority.

Probably the best approach to measurement of the distance between origin and impact in authoritative commands is to use the existence of laws, regulations, and agencies. How this can best be done to provide an appropriate measure is a difficult question which goes beyond the scope of this chapter.

I have discussed three fundamental social processes which involve individual persons and illustrated how we can measure the distance from the person that the process originated. Changes in these distances become measures of societal growth in the particular process in question. Thus by this appoach it becomes possible not only to measure the rate of societal growth, but also to show how that rate of growth differs from one social process to another.

The processes discussed above, however, are not the only ones of interest (although an increase in the number of processes of interest increases the overlap between them). Another is that of *social responsibility* for a variety of individual problems, and the locus of that responsibility. Only a few generations ago, the locus of nearly all the social responsibility for problems of sickness, old age, infirmity, mental incapacity, loss of employment, and other types of dependency was held at the level of the family. The neighborhood or immediate community assumed a portion of the burden for some kinds of dependency; there developed the institution of the County Poorhouse, the County Home for the Aged, and the County Orphans Home. But steadily the locus of responsibility has moved to a higher level—first to the state, and more recently in the United States to the national level. Welfare and unemployment compensation contain a mixture of local, state, and national inputs; responsibility for the aged and disabled has increasingly moved to a national level with Social Security and Medicare. Responsibility for care of the handicapped has become increasingly a state and national matter, with legislation covering educational facilities, as well as access to buildings and other public places.

Measurement of the locus of responsibility for various kinds of problems is not as difficult as measurement of the locus of authoritative commands. First, it is easier to lay out a list of the various problems of dependency, and then it is possible for each to determine the locus of responsibility. This varies, of course, not only between nations but also somewhat between localities and between states in the United States. Yet the general procedure is clear.

I will not discuss other processes here which could be used to measure components of societal growth: social interaction, leisure entertainment, travel, and others. The general approach to measuring societal growth as a change in the distance between point of origin of a process and point of termination should be evident from the examples given above. For a number of types of processes, there are two general strategies of measurement, as exemplified in the production-consumption of private goods. One is to take a sample of persons as the starting point and trace the origins of those processes which terminate with them, and the other is to obtain transaction data that are location-specific. For different social processes, one or the other of these approaches will likely be more feasible. For example, for travel, there are origin-destination data for airline travel which can be used to measure changes over time in the average length of trip.[2] On the other hand, for determining changes in the locus of child socialization, data from population samples using time budgets may be more feasible.

## A Modification: Number of Links in the Chain

A conception of societal growth similar to that of the physical distance between origin and termination of a social process is the number of links in the process. This is not applicable to all processes (for example, not to travel), but is directly relevant to some. In economics, for example, the growth of an economic system is measured by the length of the chain of production from raw materials to final consumption. As an economic system develops, the number of transformations or operations that occur in the chain of production increases. What once consisted of two operations in food production-consumption—that is, harvesting and preparation for the table—now consists of many in the case of TV dinners, frozen pizza, and other prepared foods. And in production of manufacturing goods, the chain of production has lengthened even more.

Measurement of the number of links in the production chain (as can be carried out by use of the inverse of an input-output matrix, or by tracing backward from the consumption patterns of a sample of persons) provides one measure of the growth of society somewhat different from that of geographic distance discussed in the earlier section, but with a similar general orientation.[3] This is more nearly a direct measure of economic complexity, where the measure discussed in the preceding section was a measure of the geographic distance encompassed by this chain of production and consumption. The two measures would be correlated, but not perfectly.

A similar measure of the number of links in the chain can be carried out for communication of information. The situation here, however, is not so straightforward. If persons were attentive only to what went on in their households, nearly all information of interest to them would be obtained by

[2]This is, of course, confounded by the varying role that alternate means of transportation, such as automobiles and ship travel, play over time. However, there are also statistics for these other transportation means and it is possible to carry out measurement by drawing upon the several sources.

[3]The concept of a "chain of production" is somewhat less general than that of an input-output matrix, for it assumes an input-output matrix of triangular form, in which each intermediate product can be placed as following some and preceding others. An input-output matrix for a more general economic system allows for cycles in which A is not only an input to B, but B is an input to A as well. However, empirical input-output matrices characterizing real economics show roughly a triangular form.

direct experience or at only one remove. In a society consisting of self-contained villages, nearly all the information that persons attend to concerns other villagers and events in the village. The information is not all firsthand, but a large fraction is. There are items which circulate by rumor, and this together with the absence of a formal system of mass communication can mean that there are several steps in the communication of news of an event, despite the fact that it is close at hand.

In a more complex society in which persons' interests are in events that may be some distance from them, there are systematic media of news gathering and dissemination: newspapers, magazines, and the electronic media. In such media, there are several links between the event and the final consumer of information.[4] These are qualitively different from the interpersonal links in a village, but the difference would not be captured in a measure of the length of the communications chain, even if it turned out that the number of links was generally greater in the case of the mass media.

It is true, however, that a communications matrix would look very different for a society in which much of the information to which persons attended was channeled through the mass media and one in which most information of interest to persons was obtained from other persons. What seems likely is that some measure obtained from a communications matrix of this sort would allow characterization of societal growth and differentiation. The measure necessary is the degree to which information to which persons attended was received through a differentiated organ of mass media rather than interpersonally. This would require time budgets of a sample of persons in the society, showing with whom they were in communication or to what medium they were attending.

Another area in which there is a direct comparability to the chain of economic production is the chain of command in authority systems. Both in the authority system of government, to which the citizen is subject, and in the authority system of the employer, to which the employee is subject, growth and differentiation produce longer chains of command. Again taking the person-centered perspective, we can ask what fraction of the authoritative commands or directives to which he is subject originate at one, two, three, etc., levels of command from him. The matter may become complex in both government and employment, because a command or directive he receives may have a component that originated at several levels from him, together with components added at each intermediate level. For example, congressional legislation on industrial safety lays down general principles, and these are made more specific in the guidelines which created OSHA; then the OSHA central staff further specifies these guidelines, the regional inspectors make their own interpretations, and the firm to which they are applied

[4]Although communication of information was not mentioned in the discussion of distance measures for various social processes, it is an excellent candidate for such a measure, and one for which the measure would be straightforward, requiring only identification of the location of the event to which the person was attentive and the location of the person.

implements them in a particular way. The final impact upon the purchaser of a lawnmower, for example, is the combination of all these components originating at different levels. The matter is similar in the employer-employee authority system. But again, the general approach is clear, and although some empirical problems of identifying the point of origin of a directive, and some technical problems of creating the correct measure remain, the approach follows very much that of measuring the chain of economic production.

All of these measures of the length of chains in various social processes that terminate at the individual are much like those of geographic distance. Yet the two types of measures provide somewhat different information on the growth, differentiation, and expansion of society. They are not substitutes for each other, but complementary ways of capturing the sprawling and nebulous idea of societal growth and partitioning it in ways that allow one to study how its various components affect one another.

## Conclusion

I have attempted in this paper to illustrate two approaches to the measurement of societal growth. Both approaches are based on particular conceptualizations of what happens in societal growth. The first is based on a conceptualization in which social systems are composed of fundamental elements (in the illustration of action theory that I used, these elements are actors), and we ask the question: How have these elements changed over time? The second is based on a conceptualization in which social processes which terminate at the individual have an origin. It asks either of two questions in the two variations I presented: How distant geographically is the origin of the process from its termination at the individual? or How many operations or transformations or links in the chain of processes are there between origin and termination?

# 6

# Causes and Consequences of Population Change

*Nathan Keyfitz*

CAUSES, AS AMOS HAWLEY well knew when he assigned me this topic, are elusive entities. Relations, correlations, comparisons, measures of change we can establish by just working hard. And these are needed, because though they are not equivalent to causal knowledge they do provide evidence on causes. It has been shown a thousand times that more educated couples have fewer children, and this is an important fact; it nonetheless remains a mystery whether providing people with education and no other changes will cause them to have fewer children. If it does, we want to know what kind of education will have that effect; will it suffice merely to educate people to the means of contraception? What accompanying changes in other variables like income and urbanization are needed for the effect to show itself? The raw negative correlation between family size and education is a beginning of knowledge only; if that correlation did not exist, we would be less hopeful of finding causation in this direction.

That causes are elusive does not mean that they are scarce. They are very prominent in the literature of social science and even more so in journalistic writing. In fact, it is their abundance that makes trouble in the form of coexistence of arguments that both policy X and policy not-X will solve overpopulation (or inflation or anything else). The mutual contradictions among casual arguments will be a main theme of this chapter.

Causes and consequences, whatever their status in the real world, are clearly properties of models. Any model, whether verbal or mathematical, is like a set of interconnected levers and wheels and valves, such that when one of them is pressed or turned or opened something happens elsewhere in the system. And when the world is modeled in different ways, different levers appear to cause change in a given variable. The levers are policies, and my theme will be the indeterminacy of policy in the face of a multiplicity of models and uncertainty as to which model applies.

Once we fix people's attention on a particular model so that it fills their consciousness, it seems obvious in the light of that model what causes what, and from that it follows what should be done to change the variable in which change is sought. To say that someone is persuasive—whether he is a social scientist or a political leader—is to say that he has somehow the ability to fix our attention on a picture of how things work and to exclude from our thoughts other competing pictures. Models, whatever purer purpose they serve, are also powerful means of persuasion. To make the most use of this feature, it is customary to present the model first, and let it exercise its almost hypnotic effect, so that the policy conclusion will be readily accepted. Opponents who can resist the hypnotic effect suspect that the policy conclusion came first in the mind of the model maker, and the model followed after as a device of rhetoric.

All this and worse has been said of Malthus, on the one hand, and the demographic transition, on the other. What happens to the birth rate when income rises? The Malthusian says it goes up, and he can prove it from a carefully worked out model. The proponent of the demographic transition says it goes down, and he is equally convincing. We need not review the arguments here, except to say how wholesome it is to juxtapose one commonly believed model with another, and to see how in practice the decision between them is made. The real world, through the empirical data that it throws up or that can be coaxed out of it, in some degree constrains the choice of model, in some degree leaves the choice indeterminate. If facts do not decide between models, then the decision among them is relegated to fashion, to a prevailing ideology, or to the interest of the powerful.

Students have approached population in at least four different ways—from the viewpoints of engineering, biology, economics, and sociology. Each of these professions and disciplines is mature enough to provide a picture of the world that is complete, in the sense that every issue raised is taken care of and every question asked is answered within the system of the discipline. Yet each discipline is also inadequate in that it formulates a narrow set of questions and excludes from its view any part of the evidence that would unduly broaden its vision. Each loses its power to convince once the listener's attention strays to some other picture of the world into which the excluded evidence fits better.

## People as Nodes in an Energy Transfer System

Of the human as of other species the ecologist asks the question "Where does their food come from?" Food supplies determine how many can live. With Mexico City's 12 million or Cairo's 9 million in mind, we describe an ecological setting in which food energy circulates in a particularly simple way. Essentially this way of thinking is to be found in writers too numerous to cite; the following type of scenario is implicit in much current expression, though the details vary from writer to writer. It deals with the place in the sun that a large aggregation, say of ten million people, will require.

Ten million people on a cereal diet of about 1 1/4 pounds per day need one-fifth of a ton of grain each per year. Over any large stretch of country, allowing for houses, roads, and wooded patches, and without imported fertilizer, about one ton per hectare (2 1/2 acres) is the best that can be expected, so the 10 million people will require 10,000,000/5 hectares, or 20,000 square kilometers, which is a square 140 km. on a side, or less than 100 × 100 miles.

Think, then, of the sun's energy falling on a reasonably fertile temperate or tropical area measuring 100 x 100 miles, a small fraction of the energy converted into carbohydrate and stored in the form of dried grain. When transferred to people, the grain enables them to keep alive and do the work of each day, which is mostly tilling, planting, cultivating and harvesting grain. Woodland has been set aside to provide fuel for boiling rice or baking bread. With careful tending of the soil—making terraces where the land slopes so as to retain the water and also prevent soil from being washed away—the process can go on forever. Its limiting factor is soil minerals and nutrients rather than solar energy, and indeed only a small fraction of the incident solar energy is drawn on even in the most fertile farmland.

Now what about urbanization? Suppose that the ten million people are not scattered over the landscape but mostly concentrated in a great city. That increases the energy input required, for now most of the grain has to be transported an average of about sixty miles. With present technology the easy way to do that is with stored solar energy in the form of petroleum. But we cannot count on this if the system is to be permanent, and so some way must be found of using the current solar input for transport. One way is by a mirror field heating boilers which run turbines and produce electricity that suffices for electric railways. A 30 × 30 mile area would gather from the sun all the energy needed for transport as well as for a degree of mechanizing in the tilling, harvesting, and processing of the crop. Here we have a selfcontained energy transfer system that would use the solar electric generators now being designed for the 1980s. Such a system requires no rain and no soil, and so could be located in desert areas too dry for farming.

But good land is available; and even with the inefficient system here described, the United States would easily support half a billion people in even more concentrated cities than we now have. We have some 350 million acres of fertile land, so there would be room for fifty-five such city-hinterland systems, each of ten million people. The world as a whole could contain many hundreds of such systems. There is no trade-off between amenities and population growth, since desert land abounds, and more area devoted to the collection of sunlight for electricity will not mean less food. A trade-off between amenities and growth is to be found within agriculture: If people wish to eat meat, some of the grain will have to be fed to cows and population will be smaller.

Further details of this engineering utopia can easily be filled in if needed. But it is intended only to show how easily large populations can be permanently provided for on a pure energy calculus. Like many other utopias, this one is empty. It offers no reason why the human nodes in the sun-grain-people energy transfer system should submit to the arrangement. At best it sets some outside physical limits on what is socially possible. Social scientists ask about the human actors: How do they organize production? What economic incentives motivate the production of grain, or what political power compels it? The utopia tells how people relate to the landscape but not how they relate to one another. It omits an issue that has been implicit in the life of human settlements since the first Neolithic gardeners learned how to produce more than they required for their own sustenance. It was on that surplus that cities, armies, tax collectors, and civilization were able to come into existence, but not until someone did the organizing.

Omission of the social interrelations may well be significant. Indeed it arouses the sinister thought that would associate the large population and the technocratic utopia with a strong rule to guarantee efficiency and stability. Suspicion of such a hidden agenda in the engineering model, combined with deadly military applications, is turning many of the oncoming generation against science. The American Association for the Advancement of Science (AAAS) is disturbed by this and wants to change the image of science. The issue is deeper than any image, and the relation between science and technology on the one side and the political system on the other deserves the most serious attention.

## Biology

Biology finds it easier than engineering to admit the existence of human institutions, but it does so in a very long perspective. The family, for example, is rooted in the flattened sexual cycle of human beings; instead of the estrus cycle there is continuous attraction of the sexes to one another (E. O. Wilson, 1975: 548). Symbolism and language are dependent on the human globular head, with a cranial capacity of 1,500 or more cubic centimeters. The central nervous system executes the symbol-processing needed for language and the social organization based on language.

Yet the forms of the family, language, and social organization vary enormously, both among social groups and within any one group as it endures through time. How can there be so much variation? "The explanation," says Wilson, "may be lack of competition from other species, resulting in what biologists call ecological release. . . . Man has been so successful in dominating his environment that almost any kind of culture can succeed for a while, so long as it has internal consistency and does not shut off reproduction altogether. No species of ant or termite enjoys this freedom. The slightest inefficiency in constructing nests . . . could result in the quick extinction of the species by predation and competition from other social insects" (p. 550).

Economic activities and the way that these are tied to the family are of much interest to biologists. "The populace of an American city, no less than a band of hunter-gatherers in the Australian desert, is organized around this unit. . . . During the day the women and children remain in the residential area while the men forage for game or its symbolic equivalent in the form of barter and money" (p. 553).

Wilson is here pointing to one of the great universals of human social organization. But sociologists ask much more localized and specific questions. In particular, why do women today refuse to "remain in the residential area," leave their children in day schools, and themselves go out and forage for money in the same way as men? Of married women with children under six years of age nearly 40 percent forage now, while only a generation back the fraction was just over 10 percent.

Similarities between human and animal behavior appear in age and sex of migrants: "The dispersants of rodent populations, from mice or beavers, are almost invariably young adults, and their movements are precipitated by aggressive interactions with the more secure, generally older territorial residents. . . . In semi-enclosed mammalian societies, such as baboon troops and lion prides, the young males are the main dispersants. . . . There appears to be no overall strong sex bias in dispersal. In some species emigration is undertaken principally by the males, in others by the females, and in still others by both sexes equally" (Wilson, 1975: 104).

The continuity between the subhuman and the human in successively wider geographical dispersion is cited in the well-known textbook of N. J. Berrill (1966: 464). "As a whole, the vertebrates are animals that have had an extremely remote marine ancestry . . . have become highly structured swimmers, and have become progressively adapted to living out of water. Terrestrial vertebrates are outstanding in having become independent of the aquatic environment and independent of change in the environmental temperature. The present human effort to travel through space, possibly to reach other worlds, may be regarded as continuation of this general vertebrate trend." Sociologists take a less cosmic, more concrete and immediate view of the reaching into space. They are more inclined to see the conquest of outer space as a monument to President Kennedy, as related to cold-war rivalry with the Russians, as a way of developing technology that would be useful for defense—the whole, a context in which the aerospace lobby could advance its interest. A sociologist might be tempted to look back over a few centuries and say that the flight to the moon was a continuation of the series of explorations by Europeans that discovered America and the Pacific in the burst of curiosity that we call the Renaissance. But he would probably resist the temptation to say this, not on the grounds that it is not true, but rather because it is a perspective that helps little with the more immediate issues that he feels called upon to tackle.

Alice Rossi shows some of the present consequences of our prehuman ancestry. Hormonal change affects social intercourse, though the nature of the interaction is obscure. Shorter time intervals between births have been induced by the wish of mothers to economize their time for the labor market, and this could interfere with recovery from the biological stress of a previous birth, a recovery made easier in earlier times by lactation and other causes of delay. Shorter interbirth intervals could well contribute to postpartum depression .

Biology puts real constraints on social arrangements.

> Fetal exposure to hormones may lay down propensities for male, as opposed to female, behavior after birth. . . . A biosocial perspective argues that such propensities shape the parameters within which learning takes place and affect the ease with which males and females learn (or unlearn) socially defined appropriate gender behavior (Rossi, 1977: 12).

In its early days, and especially about the turn of the century, sociology was thoroughly biologized, a phase that evolved into ideas that can only be called racist. By the 1930s sociologists reacted to this by divorcing their subject from biology altogether. Many still think that seeking biological antecedents of human populations and societies is reactionary, a viewpoint that has even been expressed by some biologists. Wilson and Rossi show that we can apply biology without falling into racism.

Almost as repugnant as dividing mankind into races and attaching qualitative epithets to these is subordinating human population to requirements of sustenance. Malthus aimed to demonstrate the futility of revolutionary changes in human institutions by showing that it was our numbers that set the material level of our lives and that our numbers would tend to increase up to the limits of subsistence. Since the time of Malthus, technology—of food production and other things—has improved to the point where it makes less and less sense to impute numbers to exogenously determined food supplies.

Yet the determination by sustenance persists as at least part of the explanation of some population phenomena. That India became interested in birth control long before Burma cannot but be related to India's precarious grain balance and Burma's surplus. At something like three million exportable tons of rice about the time of World War II, this surplus could sustain fifteen million people, and that is about the number of people that have been added since that time. Now, having climbed up on its food supplies,

Burma is starting to take its problems seriously and is turning to birth control, which it could disregard while the surplus lasted. It is also reconsidering its economic problems; population pressure makes development unpostponable.

It is all very well to call this viewpoint Malthusian and thereby condemn it as accounting for population on biological grounds. Yet every writer who goes deeply into the questions of population sooner or later shows ambivalence toward Malthus. Marx persistently castigated Malthus, then conceded that population pressure was inevitable under capitalism, but asserted that it would be avoided under socialism (Petersen, 1970). Contemporary writers declare that economic growth and contraception will solve the population problem, but end by warning that unless prompt action is taken toward economic growth and contraception, population-induced poverty will intensify. Malthus is their fallback position.

Biology is useful for explaining population change, but only within some outside limits that are very wide. Economics considers questions that lie well within those limits.

## Economics

Economic explanations take the point of view of the individual decision maker, who assesses costs and benefits of a proposed action and moves positively if the latter exceed the former. Evolutionary and historical considerations are subordinated to a calculus of personal advantage by people choosing under scarcity. The test of such an approach is not the moral one—there are worse sins than selfishness—but whether it can explain current happenings and so lead to control.

Consider the loosening of the marriage bond that shows itself in the high divorce rates of the 1970s. Marriage is a part of the division of labor in society; it depends on different endowments of the spouses, in particular the apparent greater effectiveness of men in the work world and of women in the home (G. S. Becker, 1960). This difference of capacities provides the basis of exchange; with the restricted market for female labor of past times, a woman was better off sharing a man's income than with any income she could earn independently. When production was largely carried out within the family there were great benefits from the division of labor—men hunted, and women cooked and sewed. Only after production ceased to belong to the home and wages were in some degree equalized did a woman come to have the material possibility of rejecting an unsatisfactory husband to take a job of her own.

This economic approach enables one to say that the cause of the high divorce rate (as well as of the low birth rate) is the good state of the labor market. On this calculus of individual advantage, sexual equality weakens the division of labor that held the family together through long ages. That in the last decades women have had increasing access to jobs explains the long-term trend of divorce.

Yet the better position of women in the labor market can only be a partial explanation of divorce and the slackening of family ties. Divorce is partly a relief from the effects of low mortality. Married couples today stay together almost as long as they did a century ago; the change is mostly that marriages that would then have been dissolved by the death of one of the partners are now dissolved by divorce.

Moreover, if the family has become slack, so have other institutions. It is not only that wives leave their husbands; priests and nuns leave their church, soldiers desert their units, students quit school. Temporary or permanent dropping out is a feature of our age. While the institutions of religion, the military, and education may never have commanded the loyalty that nostalgia prompts us to believe, the increasing rate of desertion over the postwar period is a matter of statistical record.

If the general extension of individual freedom at the expense of institutions is a feature of our times, then increasing divorce must be seen as part of this extension. It is gratuitous to elaborate a theory for divorce based only on the choices women can make in the labor market. Some part of the explanation of increasing divorce must derive from the wider phenomenon of institutional change, and part also arises from improved mortality. Not one but at least three causes are operating, and the task is not so much to elaborate and refine a theory based on any one as to find what part each of the three causes plays and how it fits in with the others.

Abstract theory that presents itself as the total explanation is not confined to economics. "Divorce," says one textbook in sociology (Leslie, 1973: 443), "may be sought whenever the advantages in it appear to outweigh those involved in remaining married." This would be a useful statement if we had some independent way of measuring the advantages on the two sides. Without such measures it is merely vacuous, even comical.

The first-rate minds in economics who have turned their attention to fertility in recent years have produced explanations in terms of decision making within the family, on the assumption that the family is conscious of what it is doing and deliberately maximizes utility. At Lee puts it, "The new home economics . . . assumes that couples choose or demand the number of children that will maximize their expected utility, where utility is derived from numbers of surviving children, 'quality' of children, and consumption of other goods" (1977: 6).

Says T. W. Schultz:

> [T]he cost of children increases with the rise in price of human time. . . . [T]he reproductive behavior of parents is in large part a response to the un-

> derlying preferences of parents for children. . . .[But there are]sacrifices, measured in terms of opportunity costs, that parents must be prepared to make in acquiring the future satisfactions and productive service they expect to realize from children. . . . [P]arents equate the marginal sacrifices and satisfactions, including the productive services they expect from children, in arriving at the value of children to them. . . . [T]he analytical key . . . is in the interactions between the supply and demand factors that influence these family decisions (1973: 2–3).

In Leibenstein's (1967) analysis the productive usefulness of children goes down with the shift of production out of the home and into the factory; on the other hand, the cost of raising children goes up with compulsory schooling and higher standards of child upbringing. The historical trajectory summed up in the demographic transition can thereby in a certain sense be explained.

In the purely economic response of fertility to the market for women's labor, data on the secular trend show the opposite direction to that shown by cycles. As employment conditions have improved over the long term, childbearing has indeed diminished, but that does not mean that unemployment of women would be an effective pronatalist policy—aside from its other disadvantages. For people defer marriage, and especially defer childbearing, when things are bad in the labor market. Once the low birth rate has been established in a society, women avoid having children in prosperity because of the opportunity cost of their time and in depression because they cannot afford to have children. This irreversibility suggests a historic process of declining fertility not easily influenced by the usual policy instruments.

Any theory that is seriously advanced is supported by some data. Does women's employment reduce their fertility? Of course it does, and a regression can even seem to tell us by how many points per thousand the birth rate will go down for each rise of one percent in the female participation rate. Does women's having fewer children on the contrary cause them to seek work outside the home? The same data as before can be made to show that it does; the regression would just go the other way. What we need is data that will discriminate between the two directions of causation.

Sociology is less apt to adopt a single model than other disciplines, and I shall cite one example of this openness. Waite and Stolzenberg (1976) have gone a certain distance toward giving competing models a chance to reveal themselves. They summarize the literature on which determines which, as between fertility and labor-force participation of women, and report their own analysis of the intentions of women under twenty-five. They find reciprocal influences, with more effect of labor-force participation plans on fertility than the reverse. Their women seem to arrive at fertility expectations and labor-force participation plans at the same time—a simultaneous interdependence rather than sequential influence of one on the other. The authors hold constant age, education, race, and other variables that might affect both terms of the relation, but concede that other variables they have not thought of might be responsible for both fertility and participation. The difference between intentions and performance has still to be reckoned with, and so does the effect of labor-force conditions at the time (1973) the question was asked. The sample consisted of 4,500 women, which is large enough, but it contained just one set of labor-market conditions, which is not enough. Very different results would have been obtained in the 1930s, 1940s, and even the 1950s, when the participation rates of married women were much lower. Nonetheless their model does try to find what affects what, rather than taking the direction of causation for granted.

Can the causal direction be found by asking a sample of women whether they are working because they can't have children or don't want them, or whether working dominates and is the reason for their not having children? Probably not; we can have little faith in the answers to such a question, for other experience has shown that people's ability to interpret their own behavior is limited. Questions on childbearing intentions conspicuously failed to anticipate the turning points of the fertility curve; it is as though women reported what they and their neighbors had been doing with regard to childbearing, rather than what they would do in the future.

Not only must data be applied to discriminate between models, rather than just be fitted to one model, but we must be prepared for the answer to come out different in a different historical and institutional context.

## The Institutional Context of Fertility

The new home economics is specific enough to be checked against facts, not so much to find if it is true as to see in what historical circumstances it is applicable. The drop in fertility that occurred in times of bad crops and scarcity in preindustrial Europe usually came not from lower marital fertility rates, but rather from delay of marriage. It was as though a young couple would not marry until there was a farm for them to take over. On this inheritance hypothesis control of fertility is by age at marriage more than by restraint within marriage. But if the decision making of the couple itself does not help explain European population history, it can still help for those parts of the world where marriage is nearly universal and takes place at young ages.

In Java marriage does not typically require that the young couple be able to sustain themselves independently. If there is any general notion of such a matter in the peasant village it is, on the contrary, that the young couple are entitled to land, and the more children they have the more land they ought to get. Historical memories of land being redivided in each generation, always in proportion to need, are still retold in the Javanese village today, almost as though they were live institutions. Such redivision has not occurred for a long time, and yet as an ideal it influences current behavior.

For the peasant with this redivision at the back of his mind, the European notion of reproductive restraint is reversed: It is not access to land that sets the limit on one's family, but rather the number of children one has that governs the amount of land he should control. Evidently such a relationship could persist only with low densities, and was destroyed during the century and a half in which the population of Java rose from ten million to seventy million.

What evolved in place of land redivision was a system of wage labor on rented land, growing especially out of the colonial method of sugar production. When there is plentiful employment at miserable rates of wages rather than a fixed landholding, one gains little by postponing marriage; better marry early and have many children, for each of them will earn a little, and in the aggregate they will be able to support their parents. The earlier one marries, and the more children one has, the sooner and the more comfortably one will be able to retire. The logic of the system requires discipline within the family, which Javanese child-rearing strongly inculcates. The father and grandfather have a far more exalted status in Javanese than in American society. Adult sons would no sooner hide their parents away in an old people's home or a retirement colony than you and I would send our children to an orphanage because it is too much trouble to take care of them if they live with us. The Javanese treats his parents as well as he treats his children. Lack of family discipline among Americans is one of a hundred reasons why the Javanese system would not work in the United States.

We find then that Javanese parents have their old age security in the large number of children, and this has been given as an explanation of their high fertility. No objection, provided one sees it as institutionally limited. European security was based on a small but adequate family property. To have many children, and not turn most of them out as beggars, would have meant dividing up the property and so impoverishing the parents in their old age. Parents had their old age security in the fewness of their children.

## Economic Development and Childbearing

All this has come to life recently in a book edited by historian-sociologist Charles Tilly (1978) which looks in detail at Europe's fertility decline. Before opening the book, one could have safely bet that the demographic transition would not be able to stand up to the barrage of historical facts. Anyone who propounds a demographic transition starting in the nineteenth century, preceded by uniform high birth and death rates, the fall of deaths and of births in the smooth S-shaped curves of the textbook diagrams, may be asked, "But have you seen Blaschke's study of rural Saxony from the twelfth to the eighteenth century?" If one has not even heard of Blaschke's massive work (Tilly, 1978: 26) he probably does not know that in Saxony the peasants had relatively small numbers of children, but that the workers in handicrafts and incipient rural manufacturing had many children.

Tilly has this point (the difference between landowning and wage labor fertility) in mind when he suggests that such a hypothesis could help account for the gross regional differences in European fertility before the declines of the nineteenth century. "The relatively low premodern fertility levels of Italy, France, Spain, and Portugal could result from the high proportion of peasants to the total. The great block of high fertility in eastern Europe could be a consequence of the early proletarianization of the rural population on great estates." He warns that this needs confrontation with the evidence, but then goes on, "One more question raised by this line of reasoning is how fertility could ever have declined in the countryside. The answer is that the opportunities for rural wage labor declined" (1978: 37).

All policy analysis depends on the transfer of relations from one set of circumstances to another. What conclusions can be drawn from the study of nineteenth-century Europe for the Third World in the late twentieth-century? We know that the birth rates of Europe in the nineteenth-century were lower than those of Bangla Desh today; that marriage was much later; that dependency rates were much lower; that population was less dense; that landholding was much simpler, usually private ownership by the tiller, with rack-renting and share-tenancy relatively rare. We know also that Asia today has some very advanced industry of a kind that would have been inconceivable in the nineteenth-century, and that a much larger fraction of the population lives in cities. The list of differences is long, and yet without weighing them and striking a balance we cannot make any transfer of experience from one situation to the other.

Tilly comes close to making such a transfer in his second-to-last paragraph (p. 349), where he describes a possible series running from peasant society to proletarianization to embourgeoisement. Proletarianization tends to raise fertility, and in recent decades we have seen instances, including Jamaica, in which fertility has gone up with the first impact of economic advance. And then, says Tilly, the acquisition of property and the investment in children's futures among all classes of the population checks fertility more decisively than ever before.

Proletarianization in Tilly's sense is occurring in the Third World on an unheard-of scale, in the countryside as well as in the cities. The process includes detachment of individuals and of families from their villages of birth, and the shift from sustenance on the land to a marginal existence in large- or small-scale industry or to service. Apparently urbanization does not bring the automatic fall in the birth rate that one would expect from the

Western experience; some Third World countries show little difference in family size between city and countryside.

This by itself would make the prospects for early population control in the Third World very dim. But in many poor countries literacy is more widespread than it was in Europe at a corresponding stage. Does not education have an effect that would be superimposed on the other factors? And what about the clear and present interest of governments in cutting their population growth, quite the opposite of nineteenth-century Europe?

So it turns out that in order to draw conclusions from the past one has to take account of noncommensurable factors that are unlikely to offset one another. Asia today has more population separated from the soil and not yet middle class than Europe had two centuries ago, and this intermediate condition, this proletarianization, is a bad prospect for population control. On the other hand, Asia has more literacy, governmental pressure in the right direction, contraceptive techniques, and, above all, the example of the rich countries. How do these alter the relation between economic advance and the birth rate?

In the end we have to accept Tilly's warning "against the effort to derive a standard sequence for the demographic transition from the experience of single western countries and to apply it directly to the poor countries of today's world" (p. 52). When twenty years ago scholars were confident that the demographic transition gave a simple and complete account of the modern fall of fertility, that theory did not cause much stir in the world at large. Now that scholars have reservations about the theory, and find its simple form wholly inadequate, the world at large accepts it as literal truth and takes it as causally operative: Economic development is the best contraceptive.

## Evolution and Cross-sectional Analysis

Sociologists had their fling at evolutionism in the writings of Herbert Spencer and his followers. We now see that doctrine as quaint, even ludicrous. The long-term effect of our discipline's experience has been to inoculate us against the subtle forms in which the evolutionary assumption asserts itself. Alert to the bias that things are always going in the one direction called growth, we cannot easily accept some of the inferences that the evolutionary framework makes possible. Whether evolution takes the form of Rostow's Stages of Economic Development, or the increase of Gross National Product by a certain percentage year after year, sociologists find it suspect as a way of understanding social change. As Karl Polanyi said, "Change seems to happen so easily for the evolutionist."

More than one analyst proceeds from a scatter-diagram in which incomes of countries and their fertility are negatively correlated to the conclusion that a rise in income will lower fertility over time. This is a complete *non sequitur* unless one assumes that all are moving in the same direction. If they are, then in Marx's expression the advanced societies show those that are backward the image of their own future. One can accept enough of evolution to believe that all countries will go through the same trajectory, but this is a matter of faith not easily proven empirically.

## Detail Is Required for Policy

Mauldin and Berelson (1978) have provided the most extensive analysis of country data bearing on the fertility decline in the Third World at the present day. They consider twenty-four earlier studies of the past fifteen years and show the limitations of these. Their own comprehensive analysis is based on the decline in the crude birth rate (CBR) from 1965 to 1975. For ninty-four countries they present indexes of literacy, life expectancy, the nonagricultural labor force, GNP per capita, and other measures of modernization. They had started with over a hundred variables in all and eliminated most of them either on the basis of their low correlation with the CBR or their high correlation with some other independent variable, and came down to seven, which for some purposes were condensed down to one index of modernization.

The selection of variables can be decisive. Evenness of income distribution in the Mauldin-Berelson analysis was included in the hundred examined but dropped before the seven were selected for the regressions. Yet the World Bank has made the condition of the lower 40 percent pivotal, and Robert G. Repetto has show statistically, again by regressions among countries, that evenness of distribution is a bigger factor for fertility control than any other, including the absolute level of income per capita.

Mauldin and Berelson calculate zero-order correlations, multiple regressions using various combinations of the independent variables, path analysis, cross-classifications. Their most important conclusion is that family planning program effort does have an independent effect. Thus it appears that socioeconomic factors by themselves explain 66 percent of the variance of the decline in the CBR; program effort by itself explains 78 percent of the decline in the CBR; both together explain 83 percent. Conceding that some of the program effort is simply a concomitant of the modernization, there is still enough separate variation of program effort to infer its independent effect.

This is not absolute proof of the program effect, since there could always be other undiscovered variables that are correlated with it. One considered by the authors is the low fertility of island peoples. Most of the countries showing no fall are African. Yet the tireless effort to ascertain other variables and their not appearing makes the conclusion convincing. If cross-sectional passive observation can ever prove anything, then surely it has here proved that family planning programs do have an effect in reducing fertility.

And that is a policy-relevant conclusion. It shows that relatively small amounts of expenditure—a national program effort can be mounted for the cost of one cement plant—produce substantial results.

Yet one can wish that it would indicate more. If a country already has a strong family planning effort, would it gain by increasing that effort? The table of countries by program effort and social setting shows little difference between moderate and strong programs; in fact, if two countries—China and North Vietnam—were omitted there would be no difference. And virtually no difference appears between the weak program countries and those with no program at all. It is in the rise from a weak to a moderate program that the striking effect takes place. If my interpretation of a ceiling and a threshold is correct, it limits the countries that will benefit from further investment to those on the shoulder of the curve. Yet the small number of cases and the cross-sectional data make all this uncertain.

Even more important for those who determine policy is the kind of family planning effort rather than just the amount. What was correlated was a score on fifteen different measures, ranging from favorable public statements by political leaders, through substantial use of mass media, to serious and continuous evaluation effort. These are very different lines of effort, and, if there are important differences among them in respect to response, then it is not much use to be told broadly that it pays to make an effort. The techniques of Mauldin and Berelson will serve readily for such analysis, but we may have to wait another ten years until the present ongoing process generates more data.

Of the ninety-four less developed countries considered, only eight showed CBR increase between 1965 and 1975; fourteen showed no change; seventy-two showed declines. Yet virtually all were undergoing what Tilly calls proletarianization, and hence should have increased in fertility. Evidently the net effect of social differences between Europe on the one hand and Asia, Africa, and Latin America on the other, when they were in comparable phases of development, is favorable to the latter. But which of the numerous variables in which they differ is responsible remains a mystery.

## Resources as a Cause of Population Change

Resources are what populations depend on for their subsistence, so the numbers of people are controlled by resources. But resources—minerals under the ground or tillable land on the surface—are constant; how can constant resources account for population changes? The answer given by

Malthus is that the constant resources are a ceiling at which population growth will sooner or later be stopped, either by the fall of birth rates or the rise of death rates.

But that is a static view. Resources as objects in the ground may be the same, but knowledge changes and transforms those resources considered as economic entities. The ability to drill down through the seabed brings petroleum into use that previously did not exist as far as our lives were concerned; the petroleum can be made into fertilizer and directly increase food supplies, and so support population. Resources, plus the technology to extract and use them, are a dynamic and changing element in the population base and indeed a cause of population change. But applying this to policy presents a dilemma.

## Choosing Between Causal Schemes

When the citizen of the industrialized country burns more petroleum, or uses more copper or more cocoa, he directly and immediately adds to the money incomes of the producer country, so that Saudi Arabia, or Ghana, or Chile has more dollars or yen with which to buy the producer goods that will enable it to become industrialized in its turn. Our American high level of consumption is the means by which the development of the poor countries can be financed. It is virtually a duty for us to continue our high consumption, if we have any consideration for the poor countries. Their development depends on our rapid economic growth.

The above is the argument that was commonly used during the 1950s. But now, with not much more data, a wholly different argument has come to be heard, expressed not in money terms but in terms of supplies of essential resources. The United States, with 6 percent of the world's population, consumes 30 percent of the world's minerals. Bauxite from Jamaica, petroleum from Venezuela, coffee from Colombia flow into our industrial processes. If these are in fact necessary to industry in fixed proportions, and we use one-third of the world supply of them, then all the remaining countries of the world can have no more than twice as much industry as we have in total. Practically speaking, this would mean no development at all outside of Europe, Japan, and a few small countries already on the road. On this viewpoint we harm the poor countries by our profligacy; the way to help them is to economize in our use of materials. Their development depends on our slowing down and would be much aided by an economic depression on our side.

Thus, of the two arguments, fashionable respectively in the 1950s and 1970s, the one proved without any question or doubt that our purchases of their raw materials was what gave the poor countries the capital to industrialize themselves, the other that we are already using so much in the way of raw materials as to deprive the poor countries of these essential ingredients for their development. Both arguments are indeed policy-relevant, only they lead to opposed policies.

Unless there is a way to choose between them, no policy advice on how to help the poor countries can emerge. Plainly the facts must be consulted to see which view is right. Here the decisive fact is whether world supplies of materials are infinite or finite. Those who present the first model deride the talk of exhaustion of minerals and fuels; those favoring the second model see exhaustion as imminent. What makes the discussion long and the decision difficult is that it is not the static physical contents of the soil and subsoil that are in question so much as the prospective costs of extraction, whether future changes in technology will multiply resources or whether we will have to live with today's technology. Cheap and abundant energy will release all the materials mankind can ever need. Whether nuclear fusion will furnish cheap and safe energy by the year 2000 is one of the "empirical" questions that must be answered before we can decide whether we are helping or hurting the poor countries by importing half of our petroleum supplies and much of our minerals.

## Technical Innovation and Carrying Capacity

Directly concerned with the support of population, what is the effect of innovations like synthetic rubber and synthetic fibers? From an overall world viewpoint, they release land formerly producing latex, sisal, hemp, and jute for food production and so directly increase carrying capacity. But they also make the exports of Indonesia, Bangla Desh, and other poor countries less than they would be in the absence of the innovations. The producing country loses foreign exchange with which it could industrialize and so increase its carrying capacity. We have a distributional change between countries; the world may be able to carry more people, but we are richer and Bangla Desh is poorer. And there is an internal distribution aspect as well, since the rubber and sisal and jute plantations are taken over by peasants for rice cultivation. The returns from the plantations were in the control of the governments of the countries concerned, while the gains from more land to cultivate benefit the squatters and others who convert plantations to rice fields. The resultant effect of invention of synthetics on population-carrying capacity is obviously unfavorable if one takes the economic-development-through-sale-of-raw-materials model; it is just as obviously favorable if one takes a population-resources model.

The life of the researcher and policy consultant is made simpler if he has one single model of the phenomenon in question, from which he can draw a conclusion on what causes what and from this conclusion make a recommendation for policy to influence the phenomenon in the desired direction. The purpose of this chapter is to suggest that whatever the ease, clarity, and incisiveness of the procedure, it may come to a wrong conclusion and be worse than no analysis at all. This danger imposes on us as researchers and policy consultants the need to hold in our minds not one but a variety of models incorporating the phenomenon; to bring data to discriminate which is correct; among the subset of models that seem consistent with the data, to see what differences emerge in the conclusions to which they lead; and insofar as the data do not effectively discriminate, then to suspend judgement. About forty years ago statisticians discovered that a test of significance is incomplete unless it takes account not only of the hypothesis under test, but of the alternatives to that hypothesis. This may or may not be a satisfying methodology, but it is the best that we can honestly use. To concentrate attention on a single model serves more to convince an audience than to ascertain the truth.

Let us consider one final instance of the need to test competing models, reverting to the secular decline of the birth rate, which is perhaps the central problem of demography.

## Competing Theories of Fertility Decline

Children were long regarded as producer goods owned by their parents, and parental decisions to have children were determined accordingly. Once children could no longer be regarded as producer goods, it was natural to suggest that they might be consumer goods. They fitted well into the new household economics that provided, among other things, a framework for analysis of family-building decisions.

In either of these models the deciding agent is a person, a fixed self, the occupant of the skin of Mrs. A. The individual as so defined appropriates pleasing or useful objects outside of her skin and makes decisions on the basis of utility as to what to appropriate, or more strictly what to trade for what. But in reality the self is both more and less than the contents of someone's skin. Says a well-known textbook of social psychology (Boring et al., 1939: 84), "The self early comes to include more than the individual. Cherished toys grow to be a part of the child's personality. He comes to regard an injury to them as an injury to himself."

Thus rather than consider children as either producer or consumer goods, let us think of them as extensions of the selves of the parents. If parents have children in the measure in which they can consider them extensions of their selves, they will have more children when that kind of identification is more feasible. It is certainly more feasible when the children are bound to their parents, either by economic dependence or by family discipline. In the measure in which the dependence is decreased and the discipline relaxed, parents will be less able to identify with their children, will view them as less central to their selves, and so be less interested in having them. They will instead identify with automobiles, second homes, and other goods and put their resources into these.

On this way of looking at the matter, the inability of parents to identify with their children during the 1960s would have reacted on the willingness of couples to have further children. To check out how far this explains the declining birth rate of the 1960s and 1970s we need independent measures of child discipline, identification with children, and other variables that would seem perfectly feasible to attain. And we could also check the thesis cross-sectionally: Are the countries and cultures where children respect their parents, are most thoroughly under their control, and therefore can be considered part of their selves by the parents, the ones where fertility is highest?

Have I proved this theory as against the alternatives? Not on the amount of data that I or anyone else has so far assembled. Is it on its face less convincing than alternative explanations in terms of prices and qualities? I do not believe so.

## Conclusion

My intention in this treatment of Amos Hawley's theme is to draw attention to the strengths of the several disciplines, and in particular to see how sociology can add to its own virtues the long-range approach of biology and the incisiveness of economics. The latter is especially valuable for policy, but only where it takes account of the institutional context, gets the direction of causation straight, and effectively discriminates among competing models.

Until the genuine checking of theories against alternatives becomes part of the scientific mores, our policy relevance will be at best merely apparent and at worst downright misleading. For the foreseeable future we must be prepared to have competing theories on the social science market, with policy makers choosing among them according to their preferences. But meanwhile everyone will gain by awareness of the diversity of models, and by more rigorous specification of the institutional context within which model A, B, or C applies. There are real differences among human societies, so that the reasons for fertility decline in nineteenth-century England may be very different from those in late twentieth-century Java.

Aside from this, the essential facts may be difficult to ascertain. Is the world running out of foodstuffs? If it is, then synthetic fibers that release land for cultivation add to the world's carrying capacity and hence to its possible population. If it is not, then our use of synthetic fibers deprives Bangla Desh and Indonesia of export markets for jute and sisal and decreases their carrying capacity.

Below all of these issues is a difficulty, a deep and threatening abyss that is a nightmare for empirical social science. This is the danger not only that a theory selects which facts are relevant to its testing, but that the facts which it selects inevitably confirm the theory. Such a condition would make theories self-confirming on the basis of the only evidence suited for testing them. In the worst presentation of this danger the values of the investigator would determine what policies he wants to recommend; he would look for theory on which these would be based, and the facts by which the theory would be confirmed would be summoned up, as it were, by the theory. The whole of social science would be an emanation of the values of the scientists.

We must not avert our eyes from the danger that a theory can be self-confirming. Good social science escapes in the measure in which the investigator keeps the danger in mind.

Amos Hawley asked me to report on the causes and consequences of population change, and I have done that, perhaps more extensively than was wanted. Several disciplines provide inferences that accord with facts. The solar energy received by the planet sets an upper limit on the population—human and other—that can survive here. We are the continuation of a process of biological evolution, and that frames some of the conditions under which we operate as individuals and as societies. Truth is present in both the energy transfer and the biological model, but immediacy is lacking. Immediacy and policy relevance are to be found in economic models, along with incisive formulations. But the incisiveness is dulled when any of them is compared with competitors. Sociology and history show that relations can be genuinely different in different times and places. And yet out of inadequate and only partly tested models, whose application varies from place to place and time to time, comes the only knowledge that we have of the causes and consequences of population change.

# II

# Structural Ramifications of Societal Growth

7

# Introduction

*Amos H. Hawley*

IT IS NOT ENOUGH, of course, to outline the phenomenon of societal growth in broad strokes. One needs to know specifically what takes place within a society as it grows larger. It will be recalled that in the preceding section the argument was made that increase in scale is severely limited without changes in structure. The chapters in this section deal with that relationship from a variety of perspectives.

In chapter 8 Stanley Udy tests with anthropological data the hypothesis that increase of complexity results in loss of efficiency unless there is an intervention of some type of managerial strategy. In other words, differentiation without coordination is unproductive and might even be a survival risk. Thus a development of hierarchy is necessary to maintain the viability of a growing system.

Hierarchy has its roots, as Robert Hodge and Garry Meyer point out, in the inequalities built into the division of labor. They observe the presence of hierarchy in sets of urban places, i.e., in the territorial organization of population, in the prestige rankings of firms which correlates with their reliance on advanced technology, and in the stratification of individuals. A unique feature of the Hodge and Meyer chapter is the demonstrated relationship among the various kinds of hierarchies.

How a partitioning of functions leads to a hierarchical structure might not be uniform in all instances. It could, for example, create an incompletely integrated system such as Udy describes in which a delegation of responsibilities from a central authority is necessary to make the system work. Or it could result from excessive centralization and a consequent tendency in a system to return to a more manageable scale. We do not understand the full import of the urban deconcentration described by John Palen. It could be a fleshing out of an urban hierarchy through a delegation of urban functions scaled to sizes of places. If so, it would be indicative of a movement toward a more complete integration of territorially distributed activities in the urban system. On the other hand, the decentralization of administrative functions to local communities in metropolitan areas, as conceptualized by Gerald Suttles and Morris Janowitz, would seem to be a solution to an initial overcentralization. The process, in their view, promises to revitalize an overly bureaucratized democracy.

The democratization process has also been working at other levels. That, as Judith Blake shows, is taking the form of a long-delayed relaxation of nineteenth-century domestic norms to permit women and children to participate more fully in societal institutions. The transition from a reliance upon ascription to achievement criteria promises a fuller utilization of the capabilities of these two significant categories of the population. One cannot but wonder why the progress of increasing complexity was so long in extending its effects to these groups.

But Harold Wilensky and Anne Lawrence are not entirely persuaded that achievement has completely replaced ascriptive criteria in the allocation of persons to roles in a complex society. They contend that the two sets of criteria are not independent of one another. Rather does achievement tend to be recognized within categories of ascribed status. Thus does continuity persist in the face of change.

Nevertheless, societal growth has manifestly multiplied the options available to individuals. This might well be the meaning of individualism as the term is currently used. But, as Philip Converse analyzes the trend, it is not at all certain that the number of options is a measure of life quality. Many options may have noxious consequences, immediately or in the future, for the individual or for society. Our inability to anticipate consequences prevents an easy conclusion that the quality of life is enhanced by societal growth. The balancing of costs and benefits poses yet another measurement problem. The result of that computation might cast light on the extent to which the structural development of the social system has realized its full potential.

8

# Societal Growth and Organizational Complexity

*Stanley H. Udy, Jr.*

THIS CHAPTER WILL DEAL with the effects of societal growth on the structural complexity of work organization and its consequences. My basic hypothesis is that unless certain managerial strategies intervene, societal growth results in increased organizational complexity, which, in turn, results in progressively *declining* levels of organizational performance.[1]

If this is true, the social history of organizations in a growing society emerges as either a history of progressive inefficiency resulting from passive adaptation, or a continuing battle to sustain performance in the face of inexorable pressures making for its deterioration.

We must admit that, on the face of the matter, the world certainly looks this way at times. Furthermore, the suspicion that this battle is currently being lost has, at least in America, recently become a matter of some public concern. Modern industrial society often appears to be growing into so many differentiated, interdependent segments that organizations not only have genuine difficulties effectively relating to their social environments, but in the process of trying to do so are apt to become so hopelessly complex internally that they can no longer accomplish anything. In short, it often seems as if "nothing works anymore," at least nothing that is very highly organized. This accusation is leveled equally against "big government,"

[1]In previous work (Udy 1959:70; 1970: 128–29) I have alluded to an apparent decline in organizational performance in the course of economic development. A recent commentary on this work by Norr and Norr (1977) raised many interesting questions, and I am grateful to them for motivating me to look at this particular matter in more detail.

"big business," small farms, local schools, plumbing contractors, and delicatessens, and its levelers seem, on the whole, to run the entire gamut of political, class, and ethnic complexions.[2]

Although I do not consider myself a pessimist, I am nevertheless convinced that there is something to this "nothing works anymore" theory. However, unlike many contemporary social commentators, I believe this theory has always been true—that it reflects a very general human social condition going far beyond our current historical situation. There is, I think, a general case to be made, and I believe it begins with the effects of societal growth on organizational complexity.

This chapter represents a search for such a general case. The first and most important step will be to examine the effects of societal growth on organizational complexity and performance, and the intervening effects of managerial strategy, in a sample of 369 work organizations distributed over 125 nonindustrial societies.[3] Then, using as a backdrop the general tendencies uncovered by this examination, I shall comment on certain critical developments in nineteenth- and early-twentieth-century American industrial management, and their impact on the contemporary organizational scene.

## Societal Growth

There are many ways of viewing societal growth, and I shall not dwell on them here since this paper is mainly about the organizational consequences of societal growth, rather than societal growth itself. For the purpose at hand, I find it most useful to define *societal growth* in a basically Spencerian sense as an increase in the number of concretely differentiated yet interdependent institutional sectors in the society concerned (Spencer, 1880: 347–72; cf. White, 1959; Chodak, 1973; Emery and Trist, 1972: 156–81; Parsons, 1966). An "institutional sector" is a set of related activities or aspects thereof distinctively conceptualized in the culture, as revealed by typical descriptions of members of the society. In addition merely to being distinctively conceptualized, an institutional sector may also be "concretely differentiated," to the degree that its activities are embodied in specialized organizations culturally defined as predominantly oriented to the

[2] Apart from various journalistic commentaries, Elgin and Bushnell (1977) provide a rather elaborate recent example of this theme in social criticism, and I am indebted to my colleague Professor David K. Miller for calling it to my attention.

[3] The sample of societies was drawn according to criteria first set forth by G. Murdock (1957) and is described in Udy (1970: 131–34). The 369 work organizations constitute all those found reported for those societies, on the basis of a review of the Human Relations Area Files and other related literature (see Udy, 1959), in sufficient detail. Neither all 369 organizations nor all 125 societies were described in sufficient detail to be used in all parts of the analysis.

sector in question. Finally, sectors whose respective activities affect one another are "interdependent."

We do not need to develop a general theory of societal growth to pursue our particular problem, and we shall not try to do so. We need only to identify a very few institutional sectors that are especially relevant in their effects on work organizations, and to be able to argue that they can be ordered in such a way as to reflect progressive institutional differentiation in social structure. This we can do. It proved possible to array the 125 societies in our sample on a scale which measures, by rank order, increasing differentiation of institutional sectors. These sectors are: organized work itself (which we find differentiated as an institutional sector in every society we have studied); a system of exclusive proprietorship in land and/or capital equipment; a centralized political system; a complex stratification system; and a generalized technological system. The cumulative scale is summarized in table 1. Though it is hard to believe there are none anywhere, no exceptional cases appeared in the sample.[4]

Lest it appear that this is a more grand enterprise than we are actually engaged in, I must at this point enter a few caveats. This scale alleges nothing more than a cumulative series of structural requisites (Levy, Jr., 1952:63), and is not an evolutionary scheme. The causes of movement from one "stage" to the next must therefore be sought in the arrival, at the propitious time, of some external event or development, for example, sedentary agriculture, industrialization, or commercial capitalism. Furthermore, since this scale is based on cross-sectional data, it in itself technically shows no sequence of growth at all. Nevertheless, the fact that we do have here a series

**TABLE 1. Growth in Preindustrial Society**

| Growth "Stage" | Differentiated Institutional Sectors Cumulatively Present | Cumulative Frequency |
|---|---|---|
| I | Organized work | 125 |
| II | Exclusive proprietorship | 101 |
| III | Centralized political system | 59 |
| IV | Complex stratification | 25 |
| V | Generalized technological system | 3 |

[4]This is a revised version of the same scale used in Udy, 1970. Essentially, "sedentary agriculture" has been removed from the scale, since it is more properly a technological innovation than an institutional sector, and "generalized technological system" has been added. *Exclusive proprietorship* is the vesting of exclusive rights of use or disposition of specified territories or essentially immovable objects in specified parties. A *centralized political system* exists if a specified group exerts general authority over two or more communities, and *stratification* is *complex* if three or more stable social classes are reported. A *generalized technogical system* is present if technology as such is conceptualized in the culture as a general system of knowledge and reflected in that form in the activities of at least one differentiated group.

of theoretically arguable requisite structures into which one can sensibly interpolate external causal events, coupled with the existence of a few historical examples of societies actually moving from one alleged scale type to the next in the order indicated, provides some basis for accepting this scale as portraying actual stages of growth. I shall thus do so here, and proceed to use it to examine the effects of societal growth on organizational complexity and performance.

## Growth, Organizational Complexity, and Performance

Every known human society contains *organizations*; i.e., social systems defining the interactions of people in specified groups purposefully directed toward the achievement of specific, announced objectives. Organizations are perhaps relatively more important in some types of societies than others, but in all societies they represent the major vehicle through which concentrated goal-directed effort takes place. Among the most important kinds of organizations are *work* organizations, which have among their major objectives the physical alteration of the material environment. Since material on work organizations is relatively easy to deal with, I have generally used such organizations in preference to other possibilities in comparative organizational analysis, and use them here.

We shall be concerned with both the *performance* and *complexity* of organizations. From the available ethnographic descriptions, two rough, dichotomous measures of performance were developed. The first purports to indicate "efficiency of personnel allocation." Any organization with a way of adjusting its size to conform to changes in work load through time was deemed "efficient" in this respect, while organizations without a way of doing so were deemed "inefficient." Of the organizations in the sample, 328 could be so classified, of which 253 were deemed "efficient." Our second performance indicator alleges the presence or absence of "rational administration." If the organization involved either specifically defined jobs or recruitment on the basis of demonstrated achievement, or both, it was classified as exhibiting at least some "rational administration." Of the 290 organizations where this determination could be made, 104 proved to involve "rational administration" in this sense.

Our hypothesis alleges organizational complexity as a variable intervening between societal growth and organizational performance. The *complexity* of an organization was measured by the number of distinct behavioral subsystems in the organization oriented to or controlled by different respective institutional sectors in the social setting. It was possible to assign varying degrees of complexity in this way to 365 organizations in the sample, and degree of complexity observed varied from 1 through 4. The institutional sectors to which the organizational subsystems were related included, in one case or another, all of those appearing on the scale in table 1, but also often included others as well, such as kinship, religion, and, in a few societies, a market economy.

Since complexity purports, in our hypothesis, to be an intervening variable, it is thus allegedly important in two ways. First, complexity involves a proliferation of subsystems, each oriented to a different institutional sector, but with no guarantee of integration among the institutional sectors themselves. We would therefore expect increasing complexity to be damaging to performance by virtue of both diffusion of effort and possible dissipation of energy through conflict among subsystems. Second, since any organization is perforce oriented to its social setting, we would expect societal growth in the form of an increasing number of differentiated institutional sectors to cause an increase in organizational complexity, particularly in the absence of any mechanism partially "insulating" the organization from society by restricting the scope of its orientation. These two expectations, when combined, lead us further to expect societal growth to have an adverse effect on organizational performance, again assuming that no "tinkering" is going on anywhere that effectively "insulates" the organization or its members from the broader social environment.

Table 2 shows the overall effect of societal growth on complexity, and its relationship to both efficiency of personnel allocation and rational administration. As society grows, organizations indeed do consistently become increasingly complex, and consistently decline in efficiency of personnel allocation. Neither trend, however, is so marked as our theoretical argument might anticipate, and we are thus led to believe that a certain amount of "tinkering" is indeed going on, especially in the case of rational administration, where there is an actual reversal of the trend we would expect in the absence of any intervening strategy.

**TABLE 2. Relationship of Growth to Organizational Complexity and Performance***

| Stage of Societal Growth | Percentage Complex† | Percentage with Efficient Personnel Allocation | Percentage with Rational Administration |
|---|---|---|---|
| I | 4.9% (81) | 92.2% (77) | 75.9% (54) |
| II | 12.6 (95) | 76.4 (89) | 13.4 (82) |
| III | 28.3 (106) | 74.7 (99) | 30.5 (82) |
| IV–V | 44.6 (83) | 63.5 (63) | 37.5 (72) |

*Numbers in parentheses are total *n*'s of organizations, here and in the tables following.

†Here, and in tables 4 and 5, organizations with 3 or 4 degrees of complexity are "complex"; those with 1 or 2 degrees are not.

Before considering the "tinkering" question, we should comment on the apparently very high performance levels of organizations in "primitive societies (stage 1 on the growth scale), and the precipitous drop that evidently occurs, particularly in rational administration, between stages I and II. No immediate *causal* explanation for the primitive situation is at hand, but it is not difficult at least to explain our data by a "survival value" argument. Almost no stage I societies possess sedentary agriculture or any alternative food-producing technology of comparable effectiveness. Essentially all stage II societies do. One can argue, therefore, that given exclusive reliance on hunting, gathering, or small-scale fishing for food production, no stage I society is likely to survive unless a consistent pattern of very high organizational performance has developed in it for whatever reason. The effect of this situation is a generally very high initial level of organizational performance in societies that survive long enough to start growing at all. A further implication, specifically of the advent of sedentary agriculture or the like at or around stage II, is that, at least until some Malthusian or similar mechanism has time to develop, a consistently high performance level in food production is no longer essential to societal survival. There is thus "room" for the mechanisms alleged in our model to operate. They can proceed to damage organizational performance quite severely, not only without destroying the society, but conceivably even while the standard of living is actually improving.

Despite these considerations, the amount of "tinkering" implied by table 2 suggests the presence of a significant effort to avoid or even reverse the apparent effects of growth on performance. Table 3 shows the direct effect we have hypothesized of organizational complexity on each of our indicators of performance, and with rather striking force. Organizations that become complex really "go to hell in a hand basket" very rapidly, particularly insofar as rational administration is concerned. It appears that any effective "tinkering" is best directed toward reduction of complexity, which reduction, in turn, will then presumably affect performance positively. However, it is conceivable that once complexity has been reduced, one might additionally "tinker" with performance directly, and, as we shall see, there is evidence that this happens.

**TABLE 3. Organizational Complexity and Performance**

| Degree of Complexity | Percentage with Efficient Personnel Allocation | | Percentage with Rational Administration | |
|---|---|---|---|---|
| 1 | 93.0% | (100) | 85.3% | (75) |
| 2 | 81.6 | (158) | 21.3 | (150) |
| 3 | 52.6 | (38) | 12.5 | (32) |
| 4 | 27.6 | (29) | 10.0 | (30) |

**TABLE 4. Relationship of Growth to Organizational Complexity and Performance, *with* Managerial Strategy**

| Stage of Societal Growth | Percentage Complex | Percentage with Efficient Personnel Allocation | Percentage with Rational Administration |
|---|---|---|---|
| I | 0.0% (13) | 83.3% (12) | 37.5% (8) |
| II | 1.8 (55) | 86.3 (51) | 16.7 (48) |
| III | 1.9 (52) | 87.8 (49) | 31.0 (42) |
| IV–V | 16.3 (49) | 82.5 (40) | 57.8 (45) |

## Managerial Strategy

Such "tinkering" takes the form of what we shall call "managerial strategy." Every organization, being purposive, generates decisions about its structure and operations. The locus of such decisions, wherever it may be—and it varies greatly in different kinds of organizations—we call "management." Insofar as such decisions exhibit a consistent pattern through time impacting on complexity or performance, the organization will be said to have *managerial strategy*. Table 4 shows the relationship of complexity and performance to societal growth under conditions of managerial strategy.

We see that such strategy is, on the whole, quite successful in staving off the effects of societal growth. With managerial strategy, almost no organizations become very complex until stage IV, and only a few do even then. Personnel allocation is held to an essentially constant, high level of efficiency. And rational administration, after stage II, *increases* markedly with managerial strategy. In contrast, table 5 shows what happens in the absence of managerial strategy. The situation is notably different, and, with one exception (which we cannot immediately explain), strongly conforms to our initial hypothesis.

We can distinguish two broad forms of managerial strategy in the sample: reciprocity and contract. Both forms are based on an explicit understanding among the parties involved to behave in specified ways for a

**TABLE 5. Relationship of Growth to Organizational Complexity and Performance, *Without* Managerial Strategy**

| Stage of Societal Growth | Percentage Complex | Percentage with Efficient Personnel Allocation | Percentage with Rational Administration |
|---|---|---|---|
| I | 5.9% (68) | 93.8% (65) | 82.6% (46) |
| II | 27.5 (40) | 61.1 (36) | 6.2 (32) |
| III | 53.7 (54) | 61.2 (49) | 30.8 (39) |
| IV–V | 85.3 (34) | 30.4 (23) | 3.7 (27) |

specified time in the future (K. Davis, 1949:470). Both reciprocity and contract have the potentiality of restricting the scope of orientation of the work organization and thus reducing its potential complexity, as table 6 shows. (Table 6 eliminates organizations in stage I societies, where complexity is not expected in the first place.)

Reciprocity and contract are thus almost equally effective in reducing organizational complexity, and are also of approximately equal effectiveness in eventually bringing about efficient personnel allocation. Administrative rationality, however, is another story, and on this score reciprocity is not very effective at all. Probably this is because it involves no mechanism that can operate directly on individual jobs. Under a strategy of *reciprocity*, the actual products of labor are not pooled or exchanged for something else (such as money) that is redistributed in any way; rather, work is simply returned for work. Two or more groups mutually assist one another such that over an extended time period all groups involved respectively do similar amounts of work, with the product simply accruing to the particular group for which the work is being done at the time. In contrast, *contractual strategy* offers an opportunity for direct control over the structure and performance of individual jobs. The products of labor are pooled, and they themselves, or something in exchange, are redistributed in some way that can be controlled and directly related to work. It is thus only with contractual strategy that anything approaching "primitive" rationality is achieved at "higher" growth stages. Most of these effects operate via reductions in complexity, but both strategies also have slight independent effects on efficiency of personnel allocation. Furthermore, as we would expect, contract has a substantial independent effect on rationality, while reciprocity has none at all (I spare you the tables).

Contract thus emerges as the stronger of the two strategies in the long run. The advent of money as a general medium of exchange, furthermore, greatly enhances the advantages of contractual strategy. Similarly, reciprocity is not well adapted to a social structure with highly ramified exchange patterns. Table 7 reflects these considerations, and shows a gradual demise, with societal growth, of reciprocity in favor of contractual strategy.

**TABLE 6. Relationship of Type of Strategy to Complexity and Performance***

| | Percentage Complex | Percentage with Efficient Personnel Allocation | Percentage with Rational Administration |
|---|---|---|---|
| No strategy | 53.9% (128) | 54.6% (108) | 15.3% (98) |
| Reciprocity | 0.0 (64) | 90.2 (61) | 5.1 (50) |
| Contract | 10.9 (92) | 82.3 (79) | 57.9 (76) |

*Growth stages II–V only.

**TABLE 7. Societal Growth and Type of Strategy**

| STAGE OF SOCIETAL GROWTH | NONE | RECIPROCITY | CONTRACT | *n* |
|---|---|---|---|---|
| I | 84.0% | 0.0% | 16.0% | (81) |
| II | 42.1 | 30.5 | 27.4 | (95) |
| III | 50.9 | 21.7 | 27.4 | (106) |
| IV–V | 41.0 | 14.5 | 44.6 | (83) |

## The Nonindustrial Situation: Summary

Our nonindustrial data thus support our initial hypothesis. Societal growth produces organizational complexity, which in turn reduces organizational performance. In the face of this situation, reciprocity and contract emerge as managerial strategies, which—when they are present—stave off the adverse consequences of growth for performance quite effectively. Our data further show certain correlates of societal growth that perhaps run counter to certain popular beliefs. They clearly indicate that modern industrial society has no monopoly on organizational efficiency and administrative rationality. On the contrary, it appears that organizations under "primitive" conditions are highly efficient and very rationally administered. From that point on, however, it is downhill all the way, insofar as efficiency and rational administration are concerned, unless people do something about it. And the evidence is that in "traditional" preindustrial society beyond the "primitive" stage, at least some people do indeed do something about it almost half the time. Efficiency and rationality are by no means absent there either.

The next question to be faced is whether these basic patterns extend to modern industrial society, and, if so, how. To lay the groundwork for addressing this question, we must first ask why some preindustrial organizations have managerial strategies and others do not. Organizations in highly "primitive" settings present a special "survival value" case, which we have already discussed, and we have suggested also that the advent of sedentary agriculture at least temporarily relieves survival pressures such that organizational performance could viably decline, which it does. Yet at the same time, in at least some parts of the societies concerned, managerial strategies do appear, and presumably in the interest of sustaining or improving organizational performance. Perhaps they are, in part, responses to increased population pressure on food supply, as we suggested they might be earlier, but they seem more importantly to be connected with shifts in distribution of wealth. On this score, it is instructive to compare organizations with and without managerial strategy at growth stage III and beyond, where really marked inequalities first begin to appear in such distribution. In such societies, 84.4 percent of the ninety-six relatively small organizations rooted in local families and in the local community involved managerial strategies, while only 21.5 percent of the ninety-three relatively large organizations rooted in the overall political system or the upper reaches of the class structure did. The implication is that as wealth is appropriated by those in power, efficient organizational performance becomes essentially a localized lower-class concern, in the interests of survival. This situation is further reflected in the emergence of two broad types of contractual strategy. The first results in a mutual, cooperative association among equals and is typically directed toward such concerns as cooperative plowing of fields, maintenance of local irrigation works, communal fishing enterprises, and local construction projects. Until growth stage IV is reached, this type is almost the only form of contractual strategy observed, aside from a few hired hands on family farms and the like. With complex stratification, however, a second form of contractual strategy (actually an extension of the "hired hands" situation) emerges in the form of large proprietary interests or comprehensive centralized political units hiring people to work for pay. Only ten such cases appear in our sample, but they are essentially all alike in their deviant character. Eight of them comprise all of the cases in the lower left-hand cell of table 4, for example, where contractual strategy notably fails to reduce their compleixty. Furthermore, none of them exhibits rational administration, and only one is efficient with respect to personnel allocation. They actually begin to shade over into certain politically based organizational forms without managerial strategies, such as peonage, and two or three of them are rather borderline in this respect.

There is thus some preindustrial evidence that as differences in power and wealth emerge, particularly in company with large-scale operations apparently directed toward capital accumulation, contractual strategy declines in effectiveness and becomes relegated to small-scale local operations more readily "insulated" from broader political structures (cf. Norr and Norr, 1977). Contract alone cannot seem to withstand massive doses of political power, and in the process the essential "manageability" of large-scale organizations involving ramified internal political power differences is called into question. The scene for another possible battle against the forces of societal growth in the interest of organizational performance seems to be taking shape. It does not, however, become fully developed until well into the industrial revolution.

## The Industrial Situation: An Interpretation

It is our thesis that this demise of the performance-maintaining effectiveness of classical contractual strategy, in the face of large-scale operations rooted in the political and class structure, lies at the base of an "organizational crisis" in late-nineteenth-century American industry. Technologically, the industrial revolution extends well back into the eighteenth century, and socially it began to be evident in the nineteenth. But it was not until almost the start of the twentieth century that many of its important organizatonal and managerial implications became truly evident, and it is with these implications, as they relate to our model, that we shall be concerned. They appear to derive, not only from industrial technology per se, but from its historical conjunction with capitalism as well.

While the advent of sedentary agriculture creates a situation conducive to the *devaluation* of organizational performance, the advent of machine technology does just the opposite. By virtue of its sheer productive capacity, machine technology greatly increases the potential marginal value of even the smallest increments of efficiency. In short, with industrialism, organizational performance really starts to make a difference, and when this potentiality is combined with capitalist goals of accumulation, the result is a set of truly formidable pressures to sustain and improve technical efficiency. The difficulty is that the same stress on capital accumulation simultaneously favors the development of large, hierarchically organized enterprises strongly implicated in the political and class structures of the social order—precisely the kind of organizational form that we have found to be *destructive* to the effectiveness of classical contractual managerial strategy. There is considerable evidence that by the end of the nineteenth century, American industry was in fact becoming seriously caught between relentless pressures to increase productive efficiency and equally relentless organizational trends of the kind we have just described and that led in the opposite direction. In essence, further elaboration of the subcontracing systems in common use by large enterprises of the day made for dissolution of the production system, while the alternative of centralization by straight-line authority hierarchies led to inefficiency through introduction of institutional political complexities (Nelson, 1975). The problem, therefore, was to devise a new managerial strategy that rendered large-scale hierarchical organization compatible with a high performance level. Here again we must remind ourselves of the historicity of industrial capitalism. It is at least conceivable that with a different system of political economy, this problem could have been posed in quite a different form. For example, at least technically, one could have searched for a mangagerial strategy that would render industrial efficiency compatible with small organizations connected in some kind of network. Or one might have searched for a way to improve the performance of decentralized subcontracting systems. But the major entrepreneurs of the day can, on the whole, hardly be said to have been very interested in keeping their organizations small or in delegating truly large amounts of authority to their subordinates. Clearly, from the viewpoint of the people who were paying to have the problem solved, the most attractive solution had somehow to achieve high performance while still retaining large-scale hierarchical organizations—something never before accomplished at "higher" stages of societal growth.

What came to be called "scientific management," however, did accomplish just that. By the device of separating planning from execution and assigning the former to higher authority levels, lower levels of the organization could effectively—if somewhat uneasily—be "insulated" from external social structure and thus, in our terms, rendered less complex. Furthermore, through the authority structure itself, both job specificity and rewards for performance could be rigorously controlled by management, which by now occupies a solid, definite locus in the upper reaches of the hierarchy. In this way, the "scientific managers" not only rendered large-scale hierarchical organization *compatible* with high performance, but actually succeeded in finding a way to make politically involved hierarchies positively *conducive* to efficiency, thereby effectively reversing an age-old relationship (Taylor, 1911; Babcock, 1918). Viewed in this way, the new "classical" managerial strategy, as it was developed from early scientific management and related efforts shortly after the turn of the century, must be regarded as a truly brilliant tour de force.[5] Only recently is scientific management beginning to be recognized as a truly significant victory in an important battle against the organizational depredations of societal growth. It has, of course, long and quite properly been recognized as a battle fought by the front office against considerable popular resistance, and won at no little human cost.

I am inclined to agree with Braverman (1974) that "scientific management" is the last major managerial strategy to have developed, and that it still stands as the fundamental industrial solution to the age-old problem of maintaining organizatonal performance in the face of societal growth. For a short period, something called "human relations" made some claims to being a new, alternative strategy, but in the end "human relations" turned out to be not really too much different from scientific management, to pertain to different aspects of the organization, or simply not to exist at all (Perrow, 1972:97–143). Yet there are signs that scientific management is creaking seriously at the joints, and these signs are quite different from the ones alleged by the "human relators." Quite apart from the possibility that scientific management may suffer from being a peculiarly capitalist solution—and really a nineteenth century one at that—as a strategy it seems to operate much less effectively in reducing complexity at higher levels in the organization than at lower levels. Perhaps it was never meant to do otherwise, but this is nonetheless a critical difficulty even under capitalistic conditions, because it means that with further societal growth involving systemic interdependence, organizations will become increasingly difficult to manage, de-

[5]For an excellent summary of the essentials of the "classical strategy," as they termed it, see March and Simon (1959:12–33). Similarly, one of the best discussions of scientific management is found in Braverman (1974: 85–137).

spite an ideological facade of lower level efficiency. And the problem is exacerbated if indeed such observers as Daniel Bell (1976) are correct in contending that the current path of institutional differentiation in the growth of industrial capitalism is toward genuinely contradictory demands among increasingly interdependent sectors.

In short, it appears that a new managerial strategy is in order, but it is not clear exactly what is should be. Its most likely direction would seem to be toward an application of what Lawrence and Lorsch (1967) proposed some time ago as "contingency theory," and there have indeed been some applied forays in that direction. Our position, however, would be that nothing definitive has developed as yet. The problem is to absorb the effects of multiple conflicting institutional pressures as society increases in scale, such that organizations remain simple enough to function in relevant ways. Neither scientific management nor its various offshoots seem equal to this task, and a good part of the organizational morass in which we seem increasingly to find ourselves today is, I think, a reflection of this fact.

## General Conclusions

In a way, our basic conclusion is that, organizationally speaking, it is true not only that "nothing works anymore," but also that in a very real sense nothing ever has "worked anymore." The process of societal growth induces complexity in organization, which in turn makes it difficult for organizations to perform well technically. This matters more in some types of cultures than in others. In certain "traditional" cultures it matters very little; organizations adapt well to societal growth and, as a result, perform technically rather badly, but with no serious consequences. In no culture, however, does performance matter not at all; managerial strategies thus develop which, in effect, prevent organizations from adapting thoroughly to societal growth and thereby enable them to sustain higher performance levels. Organizational performance currently seems to matter quite a bit in industrial society—perhaps too much—and current managerial strategies do not seem quite equal to the task of sustaining it in the face of effects of societal growth. Although this situation may appear at times to have crisis proportions, it is neither unique nor new.

John Calvin once admonished people to attack human tasks with great joy despite the fact that every human enterprise was ultimately doomed to failure. Such advice may seem today to be difficult to stomach, if not indeed a bit ridiculous. Yet we have seen here that people involved in organizations must surely have taken this admonition to heart, for though it is true that nothing in organizations ever works anymore, people have always kept trying to get it to work, perhaps not always with great joy, but not infrequently with unaccountable optimism.

9

# Social Stratification, the Division of Labor, and the Urban System

*Robert W. Hodge and Garry S. Meyer*

ACCORDING TO THE FUNCTIONAL THEORY of stratification, the unequal distribution of resources which is observed in all known societies may be traced to the division of labor within them. Because different men and women do different things, the possibility is engendered that they will be differentially rewarded for doing them. Specialization is therefore seen as the root cause of stratification in the functional theory. Our purpose in this essay is threefold. First, we examine three major facets of the division of labor and indicate in selected ways both the extent and persistence of their stratification. These are the divisions of labor in space, in purpose or goals, and in means—in other words, what are commonly known as the divisions of labor according to cities, industries, and occupations. Second, we examine some relationships between the city systems of nations and characteristics of their systems of socioeconomic stratification. Finally, we speculate about some of the ways in which individual firms serve to link the urban, industrial, and occupational divisions of labor, while at the same time complicating the rather elegant notion of their interconnection which is embodied in central place theory.

□ We are indebted to Sui-Ying Wat for directing our attention to some fugitive materials on income distribution and to Angela V. Lane for sharing with us her unpublished research on the socioeconomic status of industries. Portions of the research reported here were initially supported by the National Science Foundation (NSF #G-85, NSF #GS-725, and NSF #GS-1397), whose support is gratefully acknowledged. Needless to say, neither the National Science Foundation nor the individuals mentioned above necessarily share the views expressed here or are responsible for any errors contained in this manuscript.

## The Territorial Division of Labor

Although the functional theory of stratification (Davis and Moore, 1945) reminds us that the division of labor is a potential engine which drives social stratification it provides no clue to what promotes the division of labor itself. However, it is readily apparent that the unequal territorial distribution of natural resources is one important source of the division of labor: You can't fish where there is no water or go logging where there are no trees. While we would be the first to acknowledge that environmental constraints do little more than limit the possibilities, in the sense of Alexander Goldenweiser (1942), for the elaboration of the territorial division of labor, that observation is no reason for dismissing the environment as a factor affecting territorial and other forms of the division of labor.

Central place theory (Christaller, 1966; Lösch, 1954) provides us with one coherent basis for expecting a division of labor between different places in territories with similar natural resources. Different goods have different ranges and can be marketed over territories of varying size depending upon the costs of transporting them and the economies of scales realized in manufacturing them. Milk, for example, is a good with a small range relative to beer, since it is subject to spoilage and must be kept under refrigeration while being transported. By way of comparison, Coors is the only beer that we know of which must be kept under refrigeration while in transit. Since a lot of people think it is the best beer in the United States, many an easterner would gleefully return from an excursion West with a case of Coors in tow. A few years ago, Coors figured that, despite the prohibitively high costs of transportation, they could market it in the East. We can't imagine they did very well because the beer having been refrigerated from Golden, Colorado, all the way to Long Island, the local merchants promptly took it from the fridge and put it on the shelf with all the rest of their beer. So much for that; back to our discussion.

According to central place theory, then, the economics of marketing and manufacturing conspires to generate a series of interlocking, overlapping trading areas, each with its own trading center whose size depends upon the ranges of the goods produced and marketed there. These central places form a hierarchical system of cities, with larger places being characterized by a greater variety of services available and goods produced. The size distribution of central places spans the full range from a crossroads service station selling bread and beer on the side to major metropolises like Chicago and Atlanta whose hinterlands encompass entire economic regions. In areas where the spatial distribution of towns obeys central place theory, places in the same size class are spaced evenly across a region and their hexagonally shaped trading areas form a grid which completely covers the region.

The size distribution of cities in a region organized according to central place theory follows the well known rank–size rule, a theorem which has been established by Beckmann (1958; also see Losch, 1954: pp. 108–220). According to the rank–size rule, the product of the size of the ith city ($=S_i$) and its rank ($=R_i$) is equal to a constant, $C$. We have, then,

$$R_iS_i=C, \tag{1}$$

Since the rank of the largest city is unity, we have, on substituting $R_1=1$ for $R_1$ in equation 1,

$$C=S_1, \tag{2}$$

so that the constant is equivalent to the size of the largest place in the region. Substituting equation 2 in equation 1 and dividing by $R_i$, we find that

$$S_i=S_1R_i^{-1}, \tag{3}$$

which is the usual form of stating the rank–size rule.

No known economic region *perfectly* conforms to central place theory, though many come very close to doing so. Distortions of the topography created by mountains, rivers, and large bodies of water suffice to account for deviations from the ideal type. These features may also affect transportation costs and operating expenses, so that the size distribution of cities is also likely to depart from the rank–size rule. Consequently, most of those who have investigated the rank–size rule have studied its general form (see, e.g., Duncan and Reiss, 1956). This may be obtained from equation 3 by replacing the size of the largest city ($=S_1$) by an unknown constant ($=K$) and letting the exponent of $R_1$ also be an unknown parameter ($=a$). Allowing for the fact that even the generalized rank–size rule may not perfectly fit an actual distribution of cities by size, the generalized rank–size rule is given by

$$S_i=kR_i^{-a}(e_i), \tag{4}$$

where $e_i$ is an error term assumed to be randomly distributed with mean zero in its logarithm. Ordinary least-squares estimates of the parameters $k$ and $a$ can be obtained by taking the logarithm of both sides of Eq. 4 and computing the regression of log city size on the log of its rank.

Using the estimates constructed by Kingsley Davis (1971), we have fitted the generalized rank–size rule to the size distribution of cities for every country with five or more cities with populations of 100,000 or more. Separate estimates were made for 1950, 1960, and 1970. The intercorrelations across countries between the estimates of $k$ and $a$ are shown in table 1, which also shows the intercorrelations of these parameters with the coefficient of determination associated wtih the regressions for estimating the parameters.

Before inspecting the results shown in table 1, we should remark that the generalized rank–size rule provides a remarkably good fit to the city size distributions of most countries included in the present analysis. The worst fit observed in the data set occurs for the Philippines in 1950, where the coefficient of determination was a mere .7671. This case, however, is based on only seven cities of 100,000 or more. Among countries with ten or more cities of 100,000 or more, the worst fit is observed for the United Arab Republic (Egypt) in 1970, when the observed coefficient of determination, based on fifteen cities, was .8656. The best fit of all, believe it or not, was observed for the United States in 1950, the value of the coefficient of determination being an astronomical .9975. Most of the coefficients of determination are well in excess of .9, an observation which holds for the developed as well as the developing countries.

That the city-size distributions for most countries are described rather well by the generalized rank–size rule is all the more remarkable in light of the fact that we are working only with the upper tail of the full size distribution of cities. Smaller cities typically function as retail, wholesale, and/or light manufacturing centers, the major special function of cities under 100,000 in population most likely being that served by resort towns. Consequently, one would expect the theory of central places and, hence, the rank–size rule to hold best among cities toward the lower end of the size range. This is perhaps even more the case in the developing nations, where not only may large cities take on special functions such as centers of government and culture, but where a single large, primate city often dominates the urban scene.

We may now turn to the inspection of table 1. For purposes of constructing this table, the sign of $a$ (all the estimated values of which were negative) was ignored. If one wished to keep the sign of $a$ in this matrix as it was estimated, then one should change the sign of any correlation involving one, but only one of the $a$'s. (The reason for this complication was simply to keep all of the numbers entered on the data tapes positive in sign.) The most obvious feature of table 1 is self-evident upon inspecting the correlations enclosed in triangles just above the diagonal of the table. These represent the correlations across countries of the same parameter of their city-size distribution as estimated in 1950, 1960, and 1970. In general, these associations are substantial and suggest that there is appreciable relative stability in the parameters of the city size distributions of nations. Countries whose city-size distributions were well fit by a generalized rank–size rule in 1950 continue to have distributions which are well fit by this model in both 1960 and

**TABLE 1. Intercorrelations Across Countries of Estimated Parameters of City Size Distributions, 1950–1970**
(Number of Cases Shown Below Diagonal)

| Parameter and Year | $k$ 1950 | $k$ 1960 | $k$ 1970 | $a$ 1950 | $a$ 1960 | $a$ 1970 | Coefficient of Determination 1950 | Coefficient of Determination 1960 | Coefficient of Determination 1970 |
|---|---|---|---|---|---|---|---|---|---|
| $k$(1950) | . . . | .9403 | .8645 | −.0665 | −.0420 | .0045 | .3613 | .3058 | .2552 |
| $k$(1960) | 36 | . . . | .9801 | −.1153 | −.0382 | .0100 | .3723 | .2725 | .2227 |
| $k$(1970) | 36 | 40 | . . . | −.1234 | −.0596 | −.0839 | .3687 | .2820 | .2180 |
| $a$(1950) | 36 | 36 | 36 | . . . | .7764 | .6662 | −.3829 | −.4963 | −.5585 |
| $a$(1960) | 36 | 41 | 40 | 36 | . . . | .9358 | −.1902 | −.1138 | −.1853 |
| $a$(1970) | 36 | 40 | 53 | 36 | 40 | . . . | .0023 | .0514 | −.1827 |
| $R^2$(1950) | 36 | 36 | 36 | 36 | 36 | 36 | . . . | .9281 | .8448 |
| $R^2$(1960) | 36 | 41 | 40 | 36 | 41 | 40 | 36 | . . . | .8902 |
| $R^2$(1970) | 36 | 40 | 53 | 36 | 40 | 53 | 36 | 40 | . . . |

All estimated values of $a$ are negative; for purposes of making these computations, the sign of $a$ was ignored.

1970, despite real changes in their levels of urbanization. However, while the stability is certainly pronounced, the relevant correlations are in many instances considerably less than unity. Insofar as this is the case, real, relative change was taking place; the analysis of these changes, which goes beyond the scope of this chapter, would doubtless prove informative.

Another point worthy of note in table 1 follows from inspection of the correlations in the square matrix—set off by a box—in the upper right hand corner of the table. These represent all the associations—lagged and cross-sectional—between the estimated value of $k$ and the coefficients of determination. Since $k$ reflects the size of the largest city in each country, these correlations imply that the generalized rank-size rule tends to fit slightly better in those countries with supermetropolises for their population centers. No causal import can, however, be attached to this association without further analysis, because there is reason to believe that the connection between these variables may only be a reflection of the relationship that both have to economic development.

Because many of the teeming metropolises of the developing world may be considered primate cities whose economic base is insufficient to support their populations, one might expect the rank-size rule to fit slightly less well in developing countries. However, despite the existence of primate cities in the developing nations, the supermetropolises of the world—Tokyo, London, New York, and perhaps Paris—are largely in the captivity of the developed nations. For example, in 1950 there was a correlation of .4771 between gross national product per capita and the estimated value of $k$. In the same year, a correlation of .4507 was found across countries between the actual size of the largest city and gross national product per capita.

The results in the foregoing paragraph at least suggest that the associations between the estimated values of $k$ and the goodness of fit of the generalized rank-size distributions may be spurious. However, in 1950, we find upon controlling for gross national product per capita, that the partial association between the estimates of $k$ and the coefficients of determination is .3066, a figure which implies that $(100)](1)-(.3066)^2/(.3613)^2]=28.0$ percent of the covariance between the fit of the rank-size rule and the estimated size of the largest city can be traced to their respective associations with gross national product per capita. The corresponding partial correlations for 1960 and 1970 are .2444 and .2056, respectively, which imply that in 1960 about 20 percent and in 1970 about 11 percent of the covariance between $k$ and the goodness of fit of the rank-size rule could be attributed to the level of economic development.

The above calculations yield three tentative conclusions. First, such connection as exists between the goodness of fit of the rank-size rule and the estimated size of the largest city in a nation cannot be explained away by gross national product per capita. Second, the fraction of the covariance between these variables which is accounted for by the level of economic development itself declines monotonically between 1950 and 1970. Finally, both the gross association and the net association, controlling for gross national product per capita, between the estimate of *k* and the goodness of fit of the rank–size rule declines over the period at hand.

Since the seemingly most obvious interpretation of the relationship between the estimates of *k* and the goodness of fits of the rank–size rule fails to explain the association away, one may at least speculate about the possible relations between these factors. Since to the best of our knowledge we are at this juncture exploring new turf, the sociological imagination necessarily comes into play. What occurs to us, and we would not put much faith in it, is that countries with large population centers are perhaps also more likely to have a centralization in the center of corporate headquarters and planning activities, a feature which ought to facilitate the coordination of development in the hinterland. Countries without a large and well-established center of population may well experience some competition between alternative centers, a feature which would certainly contribute to a relatively poor fit of the rank–size rule. Speculations such as this cannot, of course, be established with the data at hand or even with those currently available; in addition, they must be qualified both by the fact that the association in question is not large to begin with and by the possibility that it might disappear altogether with more adequate controls for the level of economic development.

There is little else of interest in table 1, save an intriguing line of correlations beneath the upper right-hand corner of associations we have just been discussing. For present purposes, let us ignore these and reiterate that the main conclusion to be drawn from table 1 is that there is substantial relative stability through time in the parameters of the city size distributions of nations. Given this stability, we regard it as appropriate to build a typology of them, in order to indicate the substantial variety in city-size distributions of the nations of the world.

Any effort to construct a typology must begin with a reference point, and the obvious reference point for construction of a typology of city-size distributions is the rank–size rule itself. We have here been dealing with a generalized rank–size rule, in which the assumption that the product of a city's rank and its size is not a constant. Consequently, we may take the rank–size rule, without generalization, as a standard for classifying the observed distributions. Evidently, any typology constructed in this way can have but two dimensions, since there are only two variable parameters—*a* and *k*—at stake. According to the rank–size rule without generalization, the parameter *a* should be close to unity in absolute value. Tolerating a 5 cent margin of error on each side of this figure, we can first classify nations according to whether or not the estimated value of *a* for their city-size distribution falls above, below, or within the bounds set by $.95 \leqq a \leqq 1.05$. *The second dimension of the typology at hand comes from the estimate of k*. Inspection of equation 4 reveals that $k$ is in fact the value of the size of the largest city in a country expected on the basis of the fitted, generalized rank–size rule for that country. The rank of the largest city is evidently one, and unity raised to any power is still unity. Consequently, we have from equation 4 that

$$(5) \qquad S_1 = k,$$

where $S_1$ refers to the expected size of the largest city. One may consider the ratio $(S_1)/(k)$, therefore, as a plausible indicator of whether or not the largest city in a country is a primate one, where $S_1$ is the actual size of the largest city in a country. This ratio forms the second dimension of the typology at hand. Again tolerating 5 percent margin of error, we can classify countries according to whether the population of their largest city, relative to that expected from the fit of a generalized rank-size rule, falls above, below, or within the limits $.95 \leq (S_1)/(k) \leq 1.05$. This forms the second dimension of the typology at hand.

The resulting typology of city size distributions is shown in table 2. As can be seen, the city-size distributions for most countries are rather more steep than would be the case if the product of the rank of a city and its size were a constant. About equal numbers of countries have largest cities which are either 5 percent smaller or 5 percent larger than expected on the basis of the fit of a generalized rank–size rule to their city size distribution. Only one country, West Malaysia, can be thought—according to the criteria employed here—to have a city size distribution which corresponds to the rank–size rule without generalization. For the remaining countries either the city-size distribution is steeper or flatter than that expected by the rank–size rule without generalization or their largest city is smaller or larger than expected by the same ungeneralized rule.

As Berry (1961) observed some years ago, there is appreciable variety in the city size distributions of the nations on this planet. This is amply confirmed by the distribution of countries in the present typology. The most frequent type, and the one characteristic of many developing nations, exhibits a distribution of cities which is relatively steep but is dominated by a single metropolis considerably larger than predicted on the basis of the generalized rank–size rule. With the exception of four Central and Eastern European nations—Austria, Bulgaria, Czechoslovakia, and Hungary—all of the countries falling in this type are representatives of the less developed world.

The second most frequent type and the one characteristic of the most developed of the Western nations also involves a relatively steep distribution of cities, but with an urban center rather less in size than one would expect even from such a relatively precipitous distribution. Australia, Canada, Sweden, the United States, and West Germany fall into this type, but it is

**TABLE 2. A Typology of City-Size Distributions, 1970**

| RATIO OF SIZE OF LARGEST CITY TO ESTIMATE OF *K* | ABSOLUTE VALUE OF *a* | | |
|---|---|---|---|
| | *<.95* | *.95 to 1.05* | *>1.05* |
| | | *COUNTRIES* | |
| <.95 | Netherlands<br>Nigeria<br>Saudi Arabia<br>Switzerland | East Germany<br>Italy | Australia<br>Belgium<br>Brazil<br>Canada<br>China<br>German Federal Republic<br>Ghana<br>Pakistan<br>Poland<br>South Africa<br>Sweden<br>Syria<br>U.S.A. |
| .95 to 1.05 | India<br>U.S.S.R. | West Malaysia | Algeria<br>Indonesia<br>New Zealand<br>North Vietnam |
| >1.05 | France<br>Japan<br>North Korea<br>Romania<br>Spain<br>Yugoslavia | Colombia<br>Congo Democratic Republic<br>Mexico<br>Morocco<br>United Kingdom | Argentina<br>Austria<br>Bulgaria<br>Burma<br>Cuba<br>Czechoslovakia<br>Hungary<br>Iran<br>Iraq<br>Peru<br>Philippines<br>South Korea<br>Taiwan<br>Turkey<br>United Arab Republic<br>Venezuela |

not under the sole proprietorship of the developed nations. Brazil, China, Ghana, Pakistan, and Syria also appear in this corner of the typology. Four nations fall in the intermediate type between the first two, i.e., their city-size distributions are rather steep and the size of their largest city is appropriate to this distribution.

At the extremum of the typology where the city-size distribution is flat and the largest city too small for such a distribution, there are but four cases—two developed nations, Switzerland and the Netherlands, and two developing ones, Nigeria and Saudi Arabia. At the final extrema of the typology, Belgrade, Bucharest, Madrid, Paris, Pyongyang, and Tokyo reign over city-size distributions which are both relatively flat and for which they are too large. If one regards the ratio of the size of the largest city to that expected on the basis of the generalized rank-size rule for its country as a measure of urban primacy, then, we are very pleased to report, Paris is the most primate city in the world. By this criterion, Paris, in 1970, was 2.9 times larger than it should be—a size roughly proportional to its prices and the egos of its denizens.

The remaining cells of the typology are intermediate ones between the cases discussed above. Relatively few countries lie in these cells, and there is no apparent pattern to the allocation of countries to them. What emerges, then, from this exercise is the documentation of the considerable variance in the city-size distributions of nations. Evidently, the two major types are, to a considerable degree, differentiated along the axis of economic development. However, across the board it is clear that both developed and developing nations exhibit city-size distributions of most types. The result is that neither of the dimensions used to create the typology is closely associated with economic development, the correlation of the estimate of $a$ with gross national product per capita being $-.0254$ and the correlation of the ratio of the actual to the expected size of the largest city being $-.1332$ with the same variable.

The relative sizes of cities are, of course, no certain indicator of their position in the urban hierarchy. In a system of cities, smaller places may occupy functional niches disproportionately important relative to their size. Typically, such cities serve special functions such as seats of government or centers of culture. Nonetheless, size and size alone remains a significant dimension of city systems and is correlated, albeit imperfectly, with most classifications of cities. The variety in the city-size distributions of nations may well reflect, then, a similar variety in the urban systems of countries. Needless to say, we cannot be certain about this conjecture without undertaking a comprehensive investigation of the city systems of the world's nations and economic regions. Short of undertaking such an inquiry, the rather simple characteristics of city-size distributions that we have analyzed herein remain among the few available indicators of the urban systems of nations. And, as we shall see below, the features of city-size distributions investigated here appear to provide some clues to patterns of social stratification as well.

## Stratification and the Industrial Division of Labor

The observed distribution of cities by size within a country can be regarded as the outcome of two factors which are not necessarily in equilibrium at any fixed point in time. These are, of course, the aggregate decisions of thousands of firms about plant location, relocation, and expansion which determines the spatial distribution of the demand for labor and the aggregate decisions of thousands of actual and potential workers about their choice of residential location which determines the spatial distribution of the supply of labor. In general, organizational decisions about industrial development and expansion have been regarded as the engine which drives the migration of laborers, but, in fact, industry probably has as much propensity to migrate to workers as workers have to migrate to industry; this is especially the case in a world like ours where workers are protected by state and national insurance schemes from short-run unemployment.

Quite apart from how the migration of industrial firms and workers can affect the urban system, it can also bring about significant changes in the way the systems of labor and stratification interpenetrate wtih each other. For example, through the 1940s and 1950s there was both a significant migration of American blacks from the South to northern cities and a substantial expansion of southern industry as northern firms relocated and built new plants accessible to the relatively cheap labor available in southern states (see, e.g., Heberle, 1948). The result of these movements was a substantial change in the racial composition of American industries. For sixty-one industrial groups which could be matched between the censuses of 1940, 1950, and 1960, we have decomposed the impact of their regional composition upon their racial concentration.

The decompositions were effected using a technique suggested by the economist Borts (1957) and elaborated by Duncan and his associates (Duncan, 1959; Duncan, Cuzzort, and Duncan, 1961: pp. 120ff.). The results are displayed in table 3, where it can be seen that the regional distribution of industries accounted for 9.6 percent of the interindustry differences in the concentration of blacks in 1940. However, as the industries drifted toward the South and as blacks moved in increasing numbers into northern cities, this figure fell to 6.1 percent by 1950 and continued to drift downward through the 1950s to a scant 3.7 percent by 1960. Here, then, is a clear example of how the joint movement of posts to persons and of persons to posts has changed a significant feature of industrial stratification. From a period in which the racial concentration of industries was clearly related to their regional distribution, we have entered a period in which region plays a much less substantial role in explaining the industrial pursuits of black workers.

The industrial division of labor has never occupied center stage among students of social stratification and mobility, who have focused their attention primarily upon the occupational division of labor. Consequently, what we know about the stratification of industries is considerably less well established than what we know about occupational and class stratification. However, a number of significant points begin to emerge from some hitherto unpublished investigations.

**TABLE 3. Variance Decompositions of the Percentage of Black Workers in 61 Industries, United States, 1940–1960**

| VARIANCE COMPONENT | YEAR 1940 | 1950 | 1960 |
|---|---|---|---|
| | MEAN SQUARE DEVIATIONS | | |
| Total variance | 51.31 | 44.44 | 38.70 |
| Explained by regression | 17.44 | 8.99 | 5.18 |
| A. Net effect of regional composition | 4.91 | 2.71 | 1.45 |
| B. Joint effect of regional composition and associated variables | 8.69 | 4.45 | 2.58 |
| C. Net effect of variables associated with regional composition | 3.84 | 1.83 | 1.15 |
| Unexplained by regression | 33.87 | 35.45 | 33.52 |
| | PERCENT | | |
| Total variance | 100.0 | 100.0 | 100.0 |
| Explained by regression | 34.0 | 20.2 | 13.4 |
| A. Net effect of regional composition | 9.6 | 6.1 | 3.7 |
| B. Joint effect of regional composition and associated variables | 16.9 | 10.0 | 6.7 |
| C. Net effect of variables associated with regional composition | 7.5 | 4.1 | 3.0 |
| Unexplained by regression | 66.0 | 79.8 | 86.6 |

Computed from published tabulations of the 1940, 1950, and 1960 censuses of population. See Duncan, Cuzzort, and Duncan (1961:127) for method.

A comprehensive investigation of the public's perception of industrial prestige has never been undertaken. About fifteen years ago, however, Hodge and his associates did solicit prestige ratings for a limited number of industries from a national probability sample of 458 adults. The ratings for the seventy-one industries, which have never been published, were obtained by requesting respondents to sort small cards bearing industrial stimuli into a nine-step ladder of social standing—the same techniques used by Siegel to devise the vast majority of ratings employed in his well known prestige scale for all occupations (Siegel, 1971).

Our analysis of these industrial prestige ratings contained no surprises and their behavior is roughly parallel to that of occupational prestige ratings. First, there is appreciable consensus between groups of raters, themselves located in different niches of the socieconomic order, in their assessment of industrial prestige. For example, we intercorrelated the ratings obtained from respondents who themselves differed according to the major occupational group of their family's main earner. Without exception these associations between groups of raters differing in their own occupational level were in excess of .9, often falling closer to unity than to the indicated value. Industrial prestige seems in this regard to work like occupational prestige; when one is discussing the prestige of an industry, one is discussing a phenomenon about which there is appreciable, albeit less than perfect, agreement between significant groups in the society. Second, the actual prestige ratings of the industries reveal that the highest ratings are accorded to those industries which are involved in the manufacture or use of the most advanced technologies or technological products, while the lowest ratings are attributed to those industries which remain labor-intensive. Among the highest ratings are received, for example, by the "aircraft industry," "drug manufacturing," and "medical clinics," with the highest rating being reserved for the "electronics industry." Among the industries receiving the lowest ratings are "coal mining," "crop harvesting," and "commercial fishing," the lowest rating of all being captured by a "laundry." Industries like "newspaper publishing," "ship building," and "retail business" fall in the middle of the spectrum. These observations are consonant with the idea that the prestige scores of industries can in large measure be predicated on their occupational composition. Finally, although the seventy-one industries included in our survey cover the full spectrum of industrial activities, the prestige scores attributed to industries are attenuated relative to those observed in our investigations of occupational prestige. The highest prestige score achieved by any industrial title included in our survey was 77.5, on a possible scale from 0 to 100. The lowest rating was 26.8. By way of contrast, the occupational ratings we solicited with a similar method covered nearly the full, logically possible range of scores. Siegel records (1971: 69–91, table 2) the prestige ratings of a "member of the President's Cabinet" at 88.9 and that of a "migrant worker" at 13.7, again on a scale ranging between 0 and 100.[1] The evidence is necessarily tentative, owing to differences in the coverage in the investigations of industrial and occupational prestige, but these results are again consistent with the view that the prestige of industries is in large measure derivative from the prestige attached to the occupational posts within them. Most occupational skills are required in most industries, so the range in industrial prestige ratings should be attenuated relative to the range in occupational prestige ratings if the latter are, in fact, the basis upon which the public assesses the social standing of the former. That we have found to be the case in our inquiry.

Earlier investigations of industrial prestige (Brayfield, Kennedy, and Kendall, 1954; R. E. Campbell, 1960) were based on small and unrepresentative samples and provided assessments of only a handful of industries.

[1]The title "migrant worker" does not have the lowest score of all occupations in Siegel's list, but it is the lowest score recorded by any occupation in the major study around which Siegel's scale is developed.

Consequently, little can be said about the temporal stability of popular conceptions of the social standing of industries. Recent, unpublished work by Angela V. Lane leaves no doubt, however, that objective indicators of the socioeconomic status of industries are very stable in the short run. Using the method of principal components, Lane has constructed socioeconomic status scores for all industries from census data bearing upon the income, occupational, and educational distributions of their male labor force. These scores are available for both 1960 and 1970. The correlation between them is a healthy .8551, which is as low as it is only because there were substantial changes between 1960 and 1970 in the actual job content of the detailed industrial titles of the U.S. Bureau of the Census. When the analysis is restricted only to those titles with near-perfect matches between the censuses, the correlation between their 1960 and 1970 socioeconomic status scores rises to .9674. Thus, like the parameters of the city-size distributions of nations, the socioeconomic location of industries within the United States appears to be quite stable through at least short periods of time.

## Stratification and the Occupational Division of Labor

In central place theory, the industrial division of labor between cities or centers of population gives rise to the distribution of cities by size which we have previously studied. Knowing that cities are industrially differentiated is sufficient reason for stating that they are occupationally differentiated as well. While most broad types of occupational pursuit are required by every industry, the occupational mix of industries varies considerably. The occupation-specific demand for labor by various industries is not constant, and cities which differ in their industrial composition may be expected, *ceteris paribus*, to differ in their occupational composition as well.

The point we have just made doubtless seems trivial. On analysis it is less obvious, however, than it superficially seems. First, at the individual level, the connection between one's occupation and one's industry is far from perfect—a fact which flows from the elementary consideration that most industries require most types of occupational labor, broadly defined. Thus, when one assumes that the industrial division of labor between cities perfectly mirrors the occupational division of labor which also exists between them, one is basing that conclusion on a very loose, individual-level connection between one's industrial and occupational affiliation. Second, it does not require much sociological imagination at all to see that there are a variety of factors which could easily distort, from one place to another, the industry specific demand for labor. Chief among these factors are technology and bureaucratization. New technologies introduced into old industries typically bring about substantial change in the occupational specific demand for labor in those industries. Since the technology does not diffuse instantaneously, at any moment in time different firms in different places, producing the same goods, will require varying occupational mixes. Likewise, home office cities which house the administrative centers of multilocational firms will, even though their *industrial* composition may be similar to other places, exhibit a greater demand for white-collar labor. Consequently, for these and other reasons, one cannot assume that the relationship between occupation and industry will be the same everywhere; at least to the extent this relationship varies, one cannot perfectly reproduce the occupational division of labor between cities by knowing the industrial division of labor between them.

Owing in part, perhaps, to a curious division of labor between the social sciences, wherein "industry" belongs largely to economics, "occupation" to sociology, and the spatial distribution of both to geography, there are surprisingly few inquiries which focus upon the ways in which occupation and industry are interpenetrated with each other and both are interpenetrated with the urban system and the process of status attainment. For example, an important but seldom cited paper by Galle remains one of the few exercises in the sociological literature which simultaneously deal with occupation, industry, and the urban system. His conclusion "that the differing occupational structures of large metropolitan communities are accounted for in large part by the specialized tasks these communities perform in the national economy" (Galle, 1963; 267) is not surprising, but even he does not provide an estimate of the covariance between the industrial and occupational divisions of labor in metropolitan communities. In addition, his analysis—owing to limitations in the census data available to him—rests on rather broad and heterogeneous occupational clusters. And despite the virtual explosion of research bearing on processes of status attainment subsequent to the publication of Blau and Duncan's seminal work *The American Occupational Structure* (1967), we know very little about how these processes are shaped by the industrial contexts in which they occur and virtually nothing about their connection, if any, with the urban system.

We do, of course, know a considerable amount about occupational stratification as such, if not about how it is intertwined with the urban system and modes of economic production. Indeed, we are prepared to venture seven generalizations about occupational stratification which, at this juncture, seem beyond reasonable dispute. First, the stratification of occupations appears to be well grounded in the cognitive and/or evaluative structures of national populations. There are three important pieces of evidence which bear upon this point. (1) Although literally hundreds of investigations of popular evaluations of occupations have been undertaken, there is not a single report in the published literature of any difficulty in obtaining such assessments, despite the fact that the tasks involved in collecting such information are usually quite complex relative to the items included on a typical survey questionnaire. This is certainly consistent with the view that invidious comparisons between occupations are a part of ordinary, day-to-day life. (2) Analyses of occupational prestige studies leave little doubt that different categoric groups within a society share quite similar views of the occupational order (see, e.g., Reiss et al., 1961; Svalastoga, 1959; Tiryakian, 1958). (3) Even when respondents are given no explicit instructions about the criterion for assessing occupations, but are left free to group them according to any criteria they want, they form occupational clusters from which a dimension closely related to the more usual occupational prestige ratings can be extracted via multidimensional scaling (see, e.g., Burton, 1972; Kraus, Schild, and Hodge, 1978). The combined evidence from these three sources leaves scant doubt that occupational evaluations reside in the common value systems of, at least, industrialized societies.

A second generalization concerns the convergence of alternative strategies for soliciting occupational assessments. In the literature on occupational prestige a tremendous variety of stimulus questions have been utilized to solicit occupational evaluations. These range from rather straightforward inquiries about the social standing of occupations (Siegel, 1971) to assessments of the social class position—upper, middle, working, or lower—of their incumbents (Centers, 1953). The relative standing of occupations observed in inquiries as diverse as these is remarkably consistent. Correlations within the same country between inquiries invoking alternative, *but plainly evaluative* dimensions of occupational status are typically well in excess of .9. The upshot of this generalization is clear: Popular *evaluations* of occupations are for all practical purposes methodologically independent. Invoke any evaluative dimension and what comes back is approximately the same thing, whether you call it occupational prestige, occupational status, the Benjamin Franklin score, or whatever.

A third generalization about occupational stratification concerns the similarity in occupational prestige scores between nations. Despite the diversity in their socioeconomic and political orders, the evaluations of occupations in most countries are remarkably similar, a point well documented in Treiman's definitive study *Occupational Prestige in Comparative Perspective* (1977). The only major exception to this generalization is a tendency for skilled workers to be evaluated somewhat more highly, relative to lower echelon white collar personnel, in Eastern European Communist bloc nations than in the industrialized, more capitalistic nations of Western Europe and North America (see Treiman, 1977, on this point).

A fourth generalization concerns the temporal stability of occupational prestige ratings. In the United States we have accumulated forty years of experience with popular evaluations of occupations, dating from Counts's study in the early 1920s to Siegel's comprehensive investigation in the mid-1960s. Without exception these studies reveal that there has been little change at all in the prestige standing of occupations, despite the massive changes in the occupational distribution which were underway during this same period. The correlation between the ratings of occupations in the 1947 North-Hatt study (National Opinion Research Center, 1947) and its replication in 1963 (Hodge, Siegel, and Rossi, 1964) was .99. Furthermore, the socioeconomic location of occupations appears to be no less stable than their prestige standing. In describing his socioeconomic index for all occupations (Duncan, 1961*a*), Duncan (1961*b*) showed that there was appreciable short-run stability in its components, to wit, the educational and income levels of occupations. Subsequent work in both Great Britain (Routh, 1965) and the United States (Duncan, 1968) has verified the substantial stability in the economic position of occupations. Most recently, Tyree and Smith (1978) have reported an astounding correlation of .850 between an indicator of the wealth of the incumbents of occupations in Philadelphia in 1789 and the median income of incumbents of the same forty-two occupations in 1969. Results such as these leave little doubt that the pattern of occupational stratification is a relatively permanent fixture of the social order.

The determinants of occupational prestige ratings form the subject of the fifth generalization concerning occupational stratification. In constructing his socioeconomic index, Duncan showed that roughly four-fifths of the variance in a summary measure of an occupation's prestige could be explained by indicators of the income and educational levels of its incumbents (Duncan, 1961*a*). This result referred to only forty-five titles which could be matched between the 1947 North-Hatt inquiry and the detailed occupational classificaiton of the U.S. Bureau of the Census. Siegel (1971) was subsequently able to demonstrate that this result could be generalized to the full range of occupations. Investigations of other factors affecting the prestige accorded to occupations has failed to uncover any further determinant of occupational prestige which even approaches the importance of the income and educational levels of an occupation's incumbents. This is not to say that other factors such as the racial and sexual composition of occupations (cf. Siegel, 1970; Meyer, 1978) do not affect their prestige grading. The effects of factors such as these are, however, small and add little—if one invokes the criterion of "explained variance"—to what is already known about an occupation's prestige once one has ascertained the education and income levels of its incumbents. Similar results have recently been obtained in comprehensive inquiries of occupational prestige in Israel (Hartman, 1975; Kraus, 1976), so there is a basis, albeit a limited one, for generalizing this result beyond the confines of the United States. We conclude, then, that (1) education and income are most likely the main determinants of an occupation's prestige and that (2) they explain roughly four-fifths of the variance in prestige ratings between occupations.

A sixth generalization about occupational stratification flows from the fifth. Once Siegel's prestige scores for all occupations became available, it was possible to compare their performance with that of socioeconomic indices of occupational status in studies of status attainment. The results of these exercises are unambiguous: Whatever feature of occupations accounts for the associaton between the occupations held by fathers and their sons, it is better captured by indicators of occupational SES than by indicators of occupational prestige. Correlations between the occupations of fathers and sons based on their prestige grading are not only less than those based on their socioeconomic level, but their pattern is consistent with the thesis that prestige scores—at least in this context—are little more than error prone indicators of an occupation's socioeconomic status (cf. Duncan, Featherman, and Duncan, 1972; Featherman and Hauser, 1976). This generalization has an important implication, so long as one buys the assumption that prestige gradings of occupations are legitimate reflections of the public's conception of occupational stratification. Given the results and this assumption, one may conclude that the process of intergenerational occupational mobility—which is far from closed by any criterion—is viewed as even more open by the public than it in fact is in socioeconomic terms. Correlations between the occupations of fathers and sons based on the prestige of their occupations run on the order of .3, while those based on the socioeconomic level of their occupations are typically in excess of .4; thus, roughly speaking, the public sees the process of intergenerational occupational transmission as nearly half again $(= [100]\ [.3]^2/[.4]^2 = 56.25)$ as open as it proves to be when the socioeconomic status of occupations is the measure of the occupational attainment.

The final generalization we are willing to venture about occupational stratification simply asserts that the socioeconomic level of an occupation is conditioned by its industrial affiliation. In the detailed occupational classification of the U.S. Bureau of the Census, there are a number of large residual categories which are simply designated, within a major occupational level, as "not elsewhere classified." These include (1) salaried and (2) self-employed managers, officials, and proprietors, (3) foremen, (4) operatives and kindred workers, and (5) laborers. In published tabulations involving detailed occupations, the census typically subdivides these residual categories of workers within a major occupation group according to their industrial affiliation. The income and education levels of workers so divided—despite the fact that their general occupational level is the same—are by no means identical. This alone suffices to document that the socioeconomic level of an occupation is contingent upon the industrial context in which it is performed. However, Hodge (1962) has in addition shown that the industrial differences so observed are themselves reasonably consistent from one occupational level to another. Consequently, one may not only surmise that the socioeconomic level of an occupation depends, in part, upon its industrial context, but may also conjecture that the impact of industrial context is, in relative terms, roughly the same from one occupational level to the next.

The foregoing generalizations leave little doubt that we have learned a great deal about the stratification of occupations in the past two decades or so. However, they also make clear that we still know very little about how the system of occupational stratification is intertwined with the system of industrial stratification. Indeed, our understanding of how the occupational and industrial divisions of labor are interrelated is far from complete. While something is known about the way the industrial and, to a lesser extent, the occupational *divisions of labor* are linked to the urban system, virtually nothing is known about how industrial and occupational *stratification* are connected to city systems, a topic to which we now turn.

## Social Stratification and the Distribution of Cities by Size

We now return to the subject with which we began this excursion, namely, the distributions of cities by size. Here we seek to propose, in a preliminary way, some of the connections which might obtain between social stratification and some parameters of the system of cities. We begin by examining the relationship between the dominance of the largest city in a country and the extent of income inequality.

When a national economy is dominated by a single metropolitan complex, one can reasonably expect that the cultural and social core of the society will be concentrated there. Furthermore, it is not unreasonable to presume that such a center, by virtue of the fact that much of the society's goods, services, information, and foreign exchange will either originate from it or be channeled through it, will extract an implicit tax from the residue of the society for the central role it plays in the national economy. This is, of course, just so much pious sociological cant to justify studying what we propose to investigate here, to wit, the relationship between the primacy of a nation's distribution of cities by size and its level of income inequality.

A recent United Nations compilation (1978) of international statistics on income inequality provides estimates of the income shares of the upper 5 percent of households for twenty-one nations for which we have fitted the generalized rank–size rule to their distribution of cities by size. For seven of these twenty-one countries, we find that the largest city is at least 1.5 times larger than expected on the basis of the city size distribution of that country. The largest cities of these countries are Buenos Aires, Cairo, Manila, Mexico City, Paris, Tehran, and Tokyo. In six out of seven, or 85.7 percent, of these countries the five percent of households with the highest incomes hold 20 percent or more of total income, the mean share for the seven countries combined being 25.1 percent. For another seven countries, the largest city is larger than expected, but less than 1.5 times larger than expected on the basis of the fit of the generalized rank–size rule to the city-size distribution for that country. In three out of seven, or 42.9 percent, of these countries the income share of the top 5 percent of households is 20 percent or more, the average for the seven countries combined being 21.6 percent. Finally, in the remaining seven countries, the largest city is always smaller than expected given the fit of the generalized rank–size rule to the distribution of cities by size in those countries. In not a single one of these seven countries does the upper 5 percent of households capture as much as 20 percent of income, the mean share for these seven countries being a relatively paltry 15 percent, or slightly less than 60 percent of income captured by the top 5 percent in countries dominated by a large, primate metropolis.

The relationship we have just described is surprisingly regular and statistically quite significant. Contrasting the countries whose largest city is at least 1.5 times larger than expected with all the rest yields .913 for the value of Yule's Q. The associated chi-square, corrected for continuity, is 5.469, which is clearly significant well beyond the conventional .05 level (Pr[ $\chi^2_c \triangleq 5.412$ d.f. = 1] = .02). The evidence in hand, then, points to a linkage between the dominance of the urban hierarchy by a primate metropolis and the level of income inequality.

This relationship is not undone by simple statistical controls. Here we make reference to another data set pertaining to income inequality which provides us with Gini coefficients. This set (Jain, 1975) is more extensive than that compiled by the United Nations. However, the materials are based on somewhat different populations. For present purposes, we converted Gini coefficients based on "workers" into Gini coefficients based on households by means of a linear transformation established by regressing the household measures on the worker measures over the countries for which both were available (see Semyonov, Hodge, and Tyree, 1978, for details). Over fifty countries for which both the percentage living in cities of 100,000 or more (= *U*) and gross national product per capita (= *G*) are also available, we find correlations of -.581 and -.585, respectively, between the level of income inequality (= *E*) and these indicators. The Gini coefficients are available for twenty-six countries for which we also have the ratio of the actual to the expected size of the largest city (= *P*). Over these countries, a correlation of .375 is found between the level of inequality and the present index of the primacy of the largest city. All of these zero-order correlations are significant at least at the .05 level. Since the index of primacy is virtually uncorrelated with either gross national product per capita or urbanization, its net effect is not much changed when these factors are controlled. The standardized regression of $E$ on $P$, $U$, and $G$, computed from the zero-order, pairwise present correlations, is given by

$$E^* = .36(P^*) - .29(G^*).44(U^*), \tag{6}$$

with all the coefficients significant at least by a one-tailed test and the associated multiple correlation being a relatively healthy .749. We conclude that among the nations of the world both economic development and urbanization are associated with increased levels of income equality. However, population concentration in the largest city, which one can reasonably imagine cements the power of those in power, is positively associated with the concentration of income.

Income equality is not the only feature of the stratification systems of nations which is related to characteristics of their city-size distributions. We postulated, for example, that the fit of the generalized rank-size rule to the size distribution of cities within a country was a plausible indicator of the spatial rationality of the economy. A good fit of this distribution would indicate, for example, that city functions were dispersed throughout the urban hierarchy, rather than being irrationally and often inaccessibly concentrated in one or two dominant centers. Spatial rationality of this kind can only serve to bring the general population into contact with modern industrial and business enterprise, if only in a superficial way. Consequently, one might suppose, under these conditions, that the occupational value system of the populace would converge to that characteristic of the developed nations of the world. Thus, we sought to determine the relationship between the conformity of a nation's city-size distribution to the generalized rank-size rule and the similarity of its occupational prestige ratings to the worldwide standard established in Treiman's international prestige scale for all occupations (1977). Since Treiman's scale is predominantly based on ratings of occupations obtained in developed nations, the dependent variable in this analysis essentially reflects the similarity between a nation's occupational prestige grading and that characteristic of the developed world.

There are thirty-one countries for which we have fitted the generalized rank--size rule to their distibution of cities by size and for which a correlation is available between national assessments of occupational prestige and the scores of the same occupations in Treiman's scale. In studying the relationship between these two variables we have proceeded qualitatively, rather than quantitatively for the simple reason that it is very clear upon inspection, the correlations of the country ratings to Treiman's occupational scores that there are a few extreme outliers which are quite likely to distort any effort to establish linear relationships between the variables at hand. Furthermore, we have qualitatively categorized these logically continuous variables so as to effect what appeared to be more nearly natural divisions in the data, rather than the necessarily arbitrary ones which would have produced equal marginal frequencies in both directions. We find that the coefficient of determination reflecting the fit of the generalized rank–size rule to the city-size distributions is in excess of .96 for sixteen of the thirty-one nations under consideration here. Of these, ten, or 62.5 percent, have a correlation between their own occupational prestige ratings and the scores of Treiman's scale in excess of .9125. For the remaining fifteen nations, where the generalized rank–size rule fits less well, we find that four, or 26.7 percent, have an association this high or higher between Treiman's scores and their own prestige gradings of occupations. The association we have just described amounts to a Yule's Q of .642, which is associated with a chi-square of 4.01 ($\Pr[\chi_c^2 \doteq 3.84 \text{ d.f.} = 1] = .05$). Hence, we conclude that there is at least tentative evidence for a connection between the orderliness of nation's cities by size and the convergence of its occupational prestige system to those characteristic of the developed world. Finding this association is doubtless as surprising to the reader as it was to us, especially in view of the crudeness of the indicators at hand. Nonetheless, for the reasons mentioned above, we do not believe the association is without meaning; to the contrary it is just one more indication of the possible ways in which the city systems of nations may be profoundly interpenetrated with their systems of stratification. The few relationships discussed herein are only suggestive of these linkages, and a great deal of work remains to be done before our understanding of them is even reasonably complete.

## Discussion

We have now completed our tour through the worlds of cities, industries, and occupations. The sights we have seen are not unlike the wonders of the world in the eyes of an ordinary tourist: Spectacular though they may be, the connections between them are not clear. Although we have drawn a few, largely speculative links between city systems and the social stratification of nations, the main theme that emerges from our excursion is that the patterns in the worlds we have visited have not much changed, despite the massive turnovers in the populations which inhabit them. The parameters of the city-size distributions of nations and the general shape of industrial and occupational stratification in the United States are much the same now as they were a few decades ago. Had we undertaken our voyage ten, twenty, or perhaps even more years ago, we would have encountered much the same scenario. That societies can withstand substantial demographic and economic expansion without incurring massive structural changes in the basic shape of their schemes of urban, industrial, and occupational stratification is, in our judgment, well documented by the materials herein, for virtually every society we have mentioned has been on a course of population growth and industrial expansion over the time horizon of this chapter. But why this is the case remains a puzzle to which we neither have nor can see an obvious answer.

There is, however, one point about which we can be quite clear. Although our visits to the worlds of cities, industries, and occupations have been more like separate trips than an integrated tour, we can state with some clarity the basis upon which they are linked together. That what we have been able to say about these linkages is limited testifies more to our ignorance about how they work than to our ignorance about what they are. The most apparent institutional link between cities, industries, and occupations is the multilocational firm. Such firms exert control at a distance over jobs in cities where they are not headquartered, and together with thousands of unilocational firms they establish the industrial profiles of cities, their occupation-specific demands for labor, and the ways in which industry and occupation are laced together, city by city, into a socioeconomic order.

At least in the United States, the significance of multilocational firms as an integrating force is plainly on the upswing. Everyone knows that the largest firm in the nation is a public concern, namely, the federal government. Its appetite for expansion seems without bound. But even in the private sector, multilocational firms are controlling an increasing proportion of jobs. The geographer Allen Pred observes:

> In Great Britain, for example, the proportion of assets in the sectors of manufacturing and distribution held by the 100 largest organizations burgeoned from roughly 44 per cent in 1953 to about 63 per cent in 1963. In Sweden, between 1966 and 1970 alone, multilocational organizations increased their share of total office employment in the manufacturing and wholesaling sectors from 60 to 70 per cent. By 1974, 150 multilocational business enterprises answered for 88 per cent of Sweden's total exports. And, partly as a result of foreign operations, the country's 200 largest domestically-headquartered business organizations had aggregate revenues that exceeded the gross national product. As another case in point, between 1960 and 1973 the number of domestic and foreign jobs controlled by the 500 largest multilocational industrial organizations in the United States grew from 9.2 to over 15.5 million, or in excess of 68 per cent. (By comparison, total U.S. non-agricultural employment grew by only about 36 per cent during the same period.) . . . In summary, the situation in the U.S., as well as in other advanced economies, has reached the stage where a clear majority of private-sector employment is directly associated with domestically headquartered multilocational corporations and firms, and where virtually the entire remainder of private-sector employment is tied to one of three work-place categories: first, the single establishment business organizations supplying goods and services to multilocational business and *government* organizations; secondly, the single-establishment businesses providing goods and services to members of the household sector, most of whom de-

> rive their income from private-and public-sector multilocational organizations; and, finally, multilocational business organizations with foreign headquarters. [1977: 98–99].

George Orwell was wrong! It's only 1979 and we're almost there, five years ahead of schedule. Oh, and he's called Big Mac, not Big Brother.

Not a great deal is known about the stratification of specific firms or processes of status attainment within them. It is, of course, possible that individual firms and specific posts within them—rather than industries and occupations in the generic sense—are the units of stratification. Some indication of this can be found in the study of industrial prestige reported above. We included in our investigation the names of a few large, specific firms, as well as the industries in which the activities of these firms are concentrated. Thus, we find that the "General Electric Company" receives a prestige score of 72.1, well above "lightbulb manufacturing" and a bit below the "electronics industry." The "IBM Corporation" comes in with a score of 70.3, substantially above "accounting machine manufacturing" at 54.9, but still less than the "electronics industry" as a whole. The remaining contrasts are more nearly exact ones: The "General Motors Corporation" obtained a prestige score of 76.2, while the "automobile industry" stood at 67.8; the "Standard Oil Company" was, at 70.0, well above the ratings of both "oil refining" at 55.3 and "oil fields" at 54.9, and, finally, the "steel industry" at 70.2 was behind the "United States Steel Corporation" at 77.1—the highest rating of any specific firm and the second highest rating on the entire list. Results such as these certainly make clear that the public does not view the prestige of specific firms as simply derivative from the prestige they attribute to the industries of which they are a part. Industrial prestige ratings evidently gloss over significant differences in the evaluation the public makes of specific firms within an industry. If this is true for industries, it most likely is also true for occupations as well. To better understand the division of labor and the stratification of it, we may well have to tune our instruments of measurement more finely so that we can speak about specific posts in specific firms, rather than about generic clusters of jobs according to their industrial use and their occupational skills.

The locational decisions of firms shapes the economic bases of our cities and the locational decisions of multilocational corporations gives concrete substance to the connectivity of cities. These decisions, as Pred has noted (1977; p. 111), also distort the urban hierarchy, so that the system of cities is typically more complicated than one would predicate on the basis of central place theory alone. According to central place theory, not only should nationally functioning organizations be headquartered in the dominant metropolitan complex, but, perhaps more important, the development of such firms should be symmetrical in the sense that regional- and local-level units of such national corporations should be present in identical city subsets.

This plainly is not the case and, consequently, the urban hierarchy is considerably more complex than the simple chain of dominance presumed, say, by fitting the rank–size rule to the size distribution of cities.

As a case in point, we can consider the regional level headquarters of Standard Oil of California and of Safeway Stores, Inc., both of which have their national headquarters in the Bay Area metropolitan complex. Allen Pred has developed a scheme of sixty-six metropolitan complexes for the United States which differs from the Standard Metropolitan Statistical Areas (SMSA's) of the U.S. Bureau of the Census in two ways. First, not all SMSA'S are included in Pred's scheme, which refers only to the largest metropolitan areas, and, second, some SMSA's have been combined in Pred's classification to form a single metropolitan complex (for details, see Pred, 1977; 134–137). Of the thirty-four regional-level headquarters of Standard Oil of California, twenty-five, or 73.5 percent are located in one of Pred's sixty-six metropolitan complexes. Of the twenty regional headquarters of Safeway Stores, Inc., sixteen, or 80. percent, are in one of these metropolitan complexes. That any of these headquarters are located outside these major metropolitan centers is itself indicative of how multilocational firms' choices of location can create perturbations of the expectations of central place theory. Although we will not pursue the matter here, the location of regional headquarters outside of major population centers, by both Safeway Stores and Standard Oil of California, is obviously related to their penetration of markets with sparse populations and no major metropolitan areas. There is no instance where either has located a regional center outside, but adjacent to a major metropolitan area, such as putting a regional headquarters in Rockford, Illinois, next door to Chicago. Instead, the regional headquarters of these firms which lie outside of the major metropolitan complexes identified in Pred's scheme tend to be located in the major center of population concentration in the subregions they serve. With these remarks, we restrict the remainder of our attention to the regional headquarters of these firms which are located in one of the sixty-six U.S. metropolitan complexes identified in Pred's classification.

The most obvious point emerges from an analysis of the interpenetration of the regional level operations of these two firms. Of the twenty-five metropolitan complexes with regional-level headquarters of Standard Oil of California, nine or 36 percent, also have regional-level headquarters for Safeway Stores, Inc. Of the forty-one metropolitan complexes without a regional center of Standard Oil, seven, or 17.1 percent, do have a regional center of Safeway Stores. The association we have just described is far from perfect; it amounts to a Yule's Q of .464 and it is not significant at the conventional level of .05. According to central place theory, the regional headquarters of Safeway Stores, Inc., ought to be nested wtihin the subset of cities that have regional headquarters for Standard Oil of California, but this is not even approximately the case: Nearly half—seven out of sixteen, or 43.8 percent—of the regional-level headquarters of Safeway are in places without regional headquarters for Standard Oil of California.

A rather different picture emerges when we control the analysis for region. Twelve of Pred's sixty-six metropolitan complexes are located in the western or Rocky Mountain states. Within this broad region, the regional headquarters of Safeway Stores, Inc., are *perfectly* nested within the subset of metropolitan complexes containing regional headquarters of Standard Oil of California. In fact, all of the nine metropolitan complexes which contain both a regional center for Safeway and one for Standard Oil are located in the West or Rocky Mountain areas. In addition, these nine metropolitan complexes with regional centers for both firms are among the ten largest of the twelve western and Rocky Mountain metropolitan complexes. Only the Riverside–San Bernardino complex, which is the sixth largest in the region, is without regional headquarters for both companies, this anomaly doubtless being attributable to the fact that both firms have regional centers in nearby Los Angeles.

Outside the West and Rocky Mountain areas, fourteen of the fifty-four metropolitan complexes in Pred's scheme have captured a regional headquarters for Standard Oil of California and seven have a regional headquarters for Safeway Stores. None has regional headquarters for both firms. The disassociation is perfect and complete. Furthermore, the locations of the eastern regional headquarters of these firms is far from perfectly related to city size. Of the fourteen largest eastern metropolitan complexes, six, or 42.9 percent, have a regional headquarters for Standard Oil of California. The remaining eight Eastern regional headquarters of this firm are located in the forty smaller metropolises of the East, Midwest, and South. This amounts to a Yule's Q of but .478 between city size and the location of regional headquarters for Standard Oil of California. The picture for Safeway Stores outside the West and Rocky Mountain regions is much the same. Of the seven largest metropolitan complexes in the East, Midwest, and South, only one has a regional center for this firm.

The picture which emerges from this example is quite clear. *Within the region* in which they are nationally headquartered, the regional centers of these two firms are almost perfectly interpenetrated both with each other and with the size distribution of cities. *Interregionally*, that is, outside the regional hinterland of their national headquarters, the regional headquarters of these firms are not only disassociated from each other but also are only weakly connected with the size distribution of cities. This case is, of course, only an illustrative one, but it does indicate how the locational decisions of multilocational firms can produce gross distortions from the pattern postulated in central place theory. Such distortions not only produce complexities in the urban system, perhaps especially at the level of interregional connections, but also doubtless engender variations in the patterns of the industrial and occupational division of labor and the stratification of them.

The only fitting conclusion that we can draw from the diverse materials surveyed herein returns us to the point from which we departed. The functional theory of stratification informs us that the division of labor suffices to establish the stratification of labor. Nothing we have viewed here does anything but confirm that conjecture: On the turf we have covered labor is divided and it is stratified. But why is it stratified in the way and to the extent it is? And, especially, why are the patterns of stratification so persistent from one period to the next, even though the division of labor itself is undergoing substantial change? The functional theory neither provides us with any clues to the answers to questions such as these nor gives us any specific instruction about how and to what extent the urban, industrial, and occupational divisions of labor are intertwined with each other. In this chapter, we have at least suggested that unraveling the knits which link these systems together will require us to pay rather more attention to the behavior of specific firms and organizations than has been common in the past. Doing that, even if it provides no firm conclusions, may well have the salutary consequence of drawing the literatures bearing upon organizations, social stratification, and human ecology more closely together.

10

# The Urban Nexus: Toward the Year 2000

*J. John Palen*

FROM MESOPOTAMIA TO THE MATURE industrial urban centers of the nineteenth and twentieth centuries, the city has served as both the disseminator and the generator of change. Urbanization has become *the* way of life in developed nations in general and the United States in particular. This chapter will discuss some of the spatial and social consequences that have accompanied the urbanization of North America, and speculate on some of the potential developments that will affect the nature of the urban world we live in for the remainder of this century.

## The Concentrated City

The nineteenth-century American city was a city of concentration. With a radius rarely extending beyond three miles, most cities in the first half of the century were walking cities. Initial industrialization fostered centripetal rather than centrifugal forces. Since steam power, which was the energy base of nineteenth-century industrialization, could not be transferred over long distances, the American industrial city emphasized concentration and centralization. Factories based on steam power clustered in a core surrounding the central business district (CBD) near rail lines and water power. This in turn led to the concentration of wholesale distributing activities. Population densities were further augmented by the necessity for workers in an era of limited transportation, low pay, and long hours, to live in close proximity to the manufacturing plant in which they worked under exploitive conditions. The consequence was an inner core of factories and tenements surrounding the CBD.

Technological developments of the late nineteenth century further accelerated CBD concentration and dominance. Office buildings grew ever higher due to the Otis elevator, while Jenney's steel frame ended the era of thousands of years in which buildings had to be supported by their massive outer walls. Now steel framing walls could be hung from the steel skeleton and soar to any height the foundation and building codes would permit.

Despite the attention and emphasis Turner and others gave to the frontier, the real growth was not in the hinterland but in the cities. The growth of city population paralleled the growth of city power. Large cities grew at the expense of smaller places, the rate of city population growth during the last half of the nineteenth century being at least twice the rural rate. The urban growth was fueled by rural-to-urban migration, but more importantly by massive foreign immigration and natural increase. Chicago, the archetypical industrial city, doubled its population every decade between 1850 and 1890. Our imagery of the city is often frozen on this cross-sectional frame in the development of the metropolis. The resulting depiction equates urbanization with a tightly contoured, high-density city where commercial, industrial, and residential space is at a premium and intensively used.

## Emerging Metropolitanism

A new era of limited urban dispersion began in the 1890s with the rapid adoption of electric street railways which effectively doubled the distance one could commute to work. By the turn of the century, every city of note had electrified its streetcar lines. New tract developments and streetcar suburbs developed along the expanding streetcar lines (Warner, 1962).

Perhaps those most benefiting from the new electric street railways were the middle class, who could now effectively separate place of work from place of residence. By the beginning of the twentieth century, commuter lines had given the city a star shape (Hurd, 1903). Commuting to work from outlying, territorially differentiated residential areas—whether or not they were yet legally defined suburbs—thus became the pattern of choice. Population deconcentration went well beyond city limits. Smaller, once independent outlying communities eventually became bedroom suburbs or satellite towns (Schnore, 1957).

The convergence of the public transit lines on the CBD graphically illustrated the social and economic importance of the central business district as the generator of societal change. The work of early Chicago school ecologists and the Burgess concentric zonal hypothesis in particular documented this reality (Burgess, 1924).

Burgess's model of urban growth assumed a concentrated and compact city with a laissez-faire economic system and rural inmigration, where the major means of locomotion were still foot and street railway. Because manufacturing and industry were concentrated in the zone surrounding the CBD where rail lines—and sometimes water lines—converged, it was assumed that this was the "natural" point of entry for urban newcomers. Thus, each incoming immigrant group would first settle in the densely packed tenements of the zone of transition—usually in socially, religiously, and ethnically segregated enclaves. With passage of time, accompanied by some economic mobility and/or assimilation, the more fortunate of the group would then migrate out to more desirable areas of less intense land usage (Wirth, 1928).

Thus there evolved a city of divergent and distinct spatial and social zones with the mainspring producing, the pattern being economic competition for prime space. The internal structure of the city thus evolved through competition, which produced invasion, succession, and segregation of new groups and usages. (The Darwinian ancestry in the concepts and terminology are apparent.)

## Metropolitan Ascendancy

During the 1920s, technological innovations, particularly radical advances in both communication and transportation, wrought profound demographic and social organizational changes in urban form. The city, which was increasingly territorially based, extended demographic, economic, and social dominance over an ever-expanding hinterland. The consequence was the development of the metropolitan area as the most meaningful urban unit.

In addition, by 1920 the nation was for the first time over half urban. During the 1920s the mobility of persons, goods, and ideas was greatly enhanced by transportation and communication advances. The automobile and truck dramatically improved the level of short-distance transportation. Now it was no longer mandatory for the factory to be on the rail line or the residential area near a streetcar line or commuter railroad station.

The automobile dramatically accelerated the pattern of metropolitan development and ascendancy. Between 1915 and 1930 alone, automobile registration jumped from 2.5 million to 26.5 million: Urban expansion now extended beyond legally fixed city boundaries and residential suburbs increasingly bordered the central cities. Once independent and self-contained crossroads, markets and outlying towns found themselves engulfed by the expanding urban nexus as suburbs and satellite cities, the latter serving as specialized employing, as well as residential, areas (Schnore, 1957).

What the motor vehicle did for transportation, the telephone did for communication. By the 1920s the telephone had become a common adjunct of local business, and long-distance telephone communication was a practical—if expensive—reality. Over half of all residences also had telephones by the 1920s. A consequence was the liberation first of residences and then of factories and offices from central locations. An increasingly diversified metropolitan area became possible.

The census first officially recognized this new reality in 1910 by establishing forty-four ad hoc "Metropolitan Districts," which at that point already housed one-third of the nation's population. The awareness that cities were now part of a larger urban complex was reflected in the pioneer works of perceptive writers such as Gras and McKenzie (Gras, 1922; McKenzie, 1933). Half a century ago, they foresaw that the city per se had yielded its influence in the generation of change to a larger unit, the metropolitan unit, and that beyond the metropolitan unit a system of cities was emerging.

The half-century from 1920 to 1970 was the era of the metropolitan unit. For every decade within that period, the metropolitan sector—core or fringe—grew, while rural areas consistently lost population. For example, during the 1960s the mean annual rate of net change was 1.8 percent for metropolitan counties, but only 0.02 percent for nonmetropolitan counties. Solely rural counties had a 0.4 percent annual decline (McCarthy and Morrison, 1978).

Currently three-quarters of the nation's population resides within metropolitan areas. Within metropolitan areas the pattern has been centrifugal, from central core to suburban periphery. Since 1920 and throughout the twentieth century, if annexation is controlled, suburban growth has outpaced that of central cities (Zimmer, 1976). Moreover, the highest rate of growth in nonmetropolitan counties during this period was found in those counties having metropolitan-type characteristics and/or experiencing overspill. The latter areas, commonly referred to as "exurbs," simply confirmed the pattern of metropolitan dominance.

Following World War II, retail trade, manufacturing industries and service establishments followed residential population to the suburbs. Suburban shopping malls—virtually nonexistent thirty years ago—now number in excess of 15,000 and account for over half the nation's retail sales. With over three-quarters of employed suburbanites working in suburbs, old patterns of commuting between central city employment and suburban residence break down. Redistribution of population, commerce, and industry to once peripheral locations has resulted in the emergence of an integrated and diffuse metropolitan community. Within this metropolitan community, the central city remains the first among equals, but the central city no longer controls and dominates the metropolitan area. The city has been superseded by the metropolitan area as the nation's basic unit of population concentration and organization.

## URBAN DISPERSION

Dynamic transformations, however, remain a ubiquitous characteristic of the urban scene. As recently as three decades ago, the central city was apparently at its zenith; the CBD still undisputedly dominated the metropolitan area; urban and interstate expressway systems were virtually unknown; outlying shopping malls hardly existed; and mass suburbanization was still in the future.

Now the pattern of metropolitan dominance is being challenged by an emerging pattern of increased dispersion and deconcentration. Metropolitan areas are no longer even semi-independent. Communication and transportation advances such as WATS lines and commuter air shuttles have further reduced the friction of space. The commuter railroad line of the turn of the century made it possible for a vanguard of businessmen to separate their residential locations from the city. Commuter air travel now puts a premium on accessibility to an airport as much as to a central city. The question of distance is increasingly measured not in miles or kilometers, but in time. Even with terrestrial travel, the question "How far is it?" commonly anticipates a temporal rather than spatial response. Increased mobility of goods, persons, and ideas suggest that a new urban phase, one of a national urban unit, is in a formative stage.

The emerging pattern of a national urban society forces us to rethink traditional assumptions. A score of years ago, Otis Dudley Duncan suggested that the concept of a "rural-urban continuum," while perhaps having heuristic value, had little empirical validity (Duncan, 1957). Emerging nonmetropolitan growth patterns strongly suggest that the concept of rural-urban continuum has now lost even heuristic utility. The demographic and economic growth of counties, several counties removed from Standard Metropolitan Statistical Area (SMSA), increasingly suggest that any rural-urban division has lost the shards of meaning that it may have still possessed even a score of years ago. New patterns also contradict the long-held assumption that the degree to which one is affected by the social and economic conditions of urbanization is a consequence of the distance from the point of population concentration. This change has yet to be fully reflected in policy or research. The Department of Agriculture, for example, still divides nonmetropolitan counties into six types which "describe a dimension of urban influence in which each succeeding group is affected to a lesser degree by the social and economic conditions of urban areas. This includes the influence of urban areas at a distance as well as within the counties themselves" (U.S. Department of Agriculture, 1974).

As rural-urban divisions have lost even nominal utility, so contemporary distinctions between metropolitan and nonmetropolitan are losing empirical utility. Metropolitan growth increasingly comes from territorial expansion of existing SMSA's and/or the designation of new SMSA's. (Thirty-four SMSA's have been added since the 1970 census.) Between 1950 and 1970, the Houston SMSA increased by 5,071 square miles and elsewhere, outlying counties are also being rapidly absorbed into SMSA's—more than 200 between 1960 and 1975 alone (Berry and Kasarda, 1977). This expansion, coupled with nonmetropolitan growth, suggests that events have outpaced our explanatory concepts. Forty years ago, Louis Wirth noted that urbanism—that is, urban behavior patterns—had become the American way of life. Now, urbanization, or the living in urban-defined places, has also become ubiquitous. As we continue to expand into a national metropolitan society, distinctions between metropolitan and nonmetropolitan will become ever more blurred. With the number of SMSA's approaching 300 and the boundaries of existing metropolitan areas progressively expanding, it becomes increasingly difficult to distinguish between metropolitan and developing nonmetropolitan counties. The urban versus nonurban characteristics that played such a powerful role in the sociology of an earlier era have for decades been bereft of explanatory power. As we enter an era of national metropolitan society, the metropolitan-versus-nonmetropolitan dichotomy similarly loses its empirical and explanatory utility.

## Evolving Developments on the National Metropolitan Scene

Our emotional and policy adjustment to the urban organizational change from the metropolitan unit to the urban society will not be without trauma. Whether we can comfortably surrender obsolete rhetoric and concepts remains to be seen. Our rhetoric still glorifies small-town life styles while bemoaning the vices of the big city—long after both, in the stereotypical form, have ceased to exist. Acceptance of the implications of a national urban policy reflecting present realities remains problematical.

Such a policy would have to consider developing trends that will modify the national urban scene for the remainder of this century. We have already noted the end of the era of metropolitan concentration; other developments of note are the shift of population and power from the northern heartland to the developing southern rimland, the limited resurgence of central cities' CBDs and residential areas, and the acceleration of black suburbanization.

## A NATION OF CITIES

The historic shift of population from the industrial North to the developing cities of the South has received belated, if generous, professional and popular attention. Some 40 percent of the thirteen million population growth occurring between 1970 and 1976 occurred in the three "Sunbelt" states of California, Florida, and Texas. Urban areas in the North, since 1970, have generally either lost population or made only marginal gains. The only northeastern states with population increases exceeding the national average of 7 percent were states better known for recreational advantages than industrial might: Maine, Vermont, and New Hampshire.

Northern urban areas that have been the nation's centers of population and power for a century or more are suddenly finding themselves on the defensive. The dramatic statements from some northern mayors could lead one to postulate that they fear that at the turn of the century the North will be thought of by many, not as a place to work and reside, but rather as a recreational area for prosperous southerners.

Census Bureau estimates are that industries in the South will continue to diversify and expand at a rate half again as fast as the national average (*New York Times*, Feb. 8, 1976, p. 42). Improvement in personal income levels also can be expected in the Sunbelt, as can a shift of political power. The change in the universities of the region can already be seen, with once-parochial institutions growing in status and scholarship. The issue is not whether the South will rise again—it has. (For a dissenting view, see Jusenius and Ledebur, 1976.)

The reaction of officials and officeholders within the old industrial heartland to southern ascendancy has gone from initial disbelief to profound panic. Congressional legislation has been introduced to rework federal distribution to favor older, i.e., northern, cities. The implicit assumption is that if all older cities are not to become like the South Bronx, massive federal subsidies are mandatory. An underlying assumption is that the growing Sunbelt cities and the declining cities of the traditional northern heartland are becoming ever more dissimilar.

Such stereotypical analysis by focusing on the momentary and dramatic, overlooks the longer-term implications and consequences. The southern shift, rather than confirming the doom of Detroit and Baltimore, signifies a move toward a national urban system. While population has been moving south, federal dollars are now moving north. Houston and Detroit, for example, both have populations about 1.3 million, but Detroit in 1976 received \$56.6 million in federal housing and urban development aid, while Houston received \$23.5 million. Similarly, Cleveland, with a population of 638,000, received \$34 million, while Dallas, with a larger population of 872,000, received only \$15 million.

As of fall 1978, supposedly declining Snowbelt cities such as St. Louis and Baltimore had lower unemployment rates (6.6 percent and 6.5 percent) than the Sunbelt cities of Atlanta and Los Angeles (7.0 percent and 8.3 percent).

The consequence is not that New York and Houston are becoming radically dissimilar, but that they are becoming more similar. A score of years ago, these two cities would not have been compared, much less confused, with each other; twenty years hence, a businessman may find Houston a narcistic version of New York.

## CENTRAL CITY REVITALIZATION

Descriptions of American cities often read like contemporary renditions of Dante's *Inferno*, where it is inscribed over the gate of hell:

> Through me the way into the doleful city,
> Through me the way into eternal grief,
> Through me a people forsaken.
> (Canto III, lines 1–3)

Throughout the 1960s and 1970s, the constant refrain was that central cities were in a critical state. The term "urban crisis" was not only encased in the lexicon, it became accepted as a state of fact. The liturgy of business pullouts, decreasing tax revenues, increasing poverty and crime has been endless, and the consequences have been clear; in Newark is written the future of central cities (Sternlieb, 1971). Cities supposedly are dying, their vital signs maintained by external life-support systems, with the federal government making the judgment whether or not to pull the plug. Without consciousness of hyperbole, a conference of large city mayors in 1977 proclaimed that what was at stake was not only "the survival of our cities," but "the survival of the American way of life as we have known it." (For two of the better discussions of the financial plight of cities, see Kasarda, 1978, and Herman and DuBoff, 1977.)

Not surprisingly, most discussions regarding the future of urban areas focus not on what will occur, but rather on the degree and timing of the collapse. This view is reflected in Philip Hauser's 1977 statement that "the stark facts indicate that the worst still lies ahead. The urban crisis will grow worse before it grows better. . . ." On the assumption that all else has failed, a Marshall Plan for the cities has even been proposed (Porter, 1976).

Cassandras seeking harbingers of the decline of the city frequently point to the declining employment opportunities and high proportion of unemployed in central cities. Within central cities, the percentage of residents without adequate educational or on-the-job training has been increasing, while the blue-collar jobs that could provide training and employment have been suburbanizing; the so-called mismatch hypothesis (Downs, 1973; Gold, 1972; Harrison, 1974).

While the employment base of cities may not continue to decline, there is an obvious pattern of systemic redistribution of manufacturing, services, and retail trade. The numbers of "For Rent" signs plastered on older multistoried factory and warehouse buildings surrounding central business districts testifies to the evacuation of blue-collar positions to suburban locations. The central city remains the repository for workers with lower skill and education levels, while the factories that could provide employment relocate in newer, single-story facilities abutting the major radial routes and interstate highways.

City employment data show a mixed pattern, though, for while blue-collar employment in cities has been decreasing, white-collar employment opportunities are increasing. While from 1960 to 1970 there was a 12.7 percent reduction in blue-collar jobs, there was a concurrent 7.2 percent *increase* in city white-collar employment (Kasarda, 1976). Suburbs had a higher rate of white-collar growth, but the city's increases occurred in spite of declines in overall city population.

The assumption that overall city employment will inevitably decrease has been largely taken for granted. Between 1970 and 1974, for example, Detroit lost 18.5 percent of its jobs; St. Louis, 18.3 percent; Philadelphia, 12.1 percent; Chicago, 8.4 percent; and New York, 6.4 percent (U.S. Department of Labor, 1976). Such figures are usually quoted in a manner that implicitly at least suggests a long term, secular trend. However, most recent data show a different pattern. Since 1976, the number of persons employed in cities has been increasing—in the North as well as the South. For example, between 1976 and 1978, St. Louis *increased* employment by 16,343 jobs; Detroit by 31,622 jobs; and New York by 108,270 jobs (U.S. Department of Labor, 1977*a*). Unemployment in 1978 was worse in Los Angeles and Atlanta (8.3 percent and 7.0 percent) than in St. Louis and Cleveland (6.6 percent and 6.8 percent).

This is not to suggest that the cities' employment crisis is over, but only that it is equally fallacious to automatically project past patterns into the future.

One oft-noted visible symptom of central city decline is retail sales, and sales in CBD's have been declining, both in absolute terms and as a percentage of metropolitan area sales (Hawley, 1971). Aging downtown stores' losses have been the gain of suburban shopping malls, some 15,000 of which have been erected in the last twenty or so years. Today, shopping centers account for over half of all sales in personal and household items.

Again, though, the lineal decline of recent decades may not be an accurate harbinger of the city to come. Downtown stores will never again have the dominance or retail trade they exercised during the centralizing era of the streetcar and subway, but so long as the downtown is a major white-collar employment center, the CBD will be a solidly profitable location for retail sales. And downtown remains the location of choice for insurance firms, financial and legal services, and administrative headquarters of all sorts. Central business districts are experiencing considerable new business construction. From the mid-1960s to the early 1970s, there was more than a 50 percent *increase* in office space in older cities such as New York and Chicago, while Houston doubled its office space (Manners, 1974).

The emerging possibility is that for CBD's, the worst may be over. The dominance of the presuburban era will not return, but most cities are in the process of stabilizing at a moderate but reasonable level of economic activity.

Cities certainly are not reentering their days of wine and roses, but I would also contend that the facts do *not* indicate that "the worst still lies ahead" and that "the urban crisis will grow worse before it grows better." It appears that all-but-universal acceptance of the thesis of inevitable and irreversible urban decay has come just as the data indicate renewed urban vitality and regeneration.

## NEIGHBORHOOD REVIVAL

Economic stability, however, does not necessarily mean a revival of interest in the city as a place of residence. What, then, of the city as a place to live? A 1972 Gallup Poll indicated that only 13 percent of those interviewed preferred living in a city to suburban or small-town alternatives. Thus, it is not surprising that residential neighborhoods have been considered in substantial part irrelevant to the urban future. Compared with massive urban renewal programs of the 1950s and 1960s or attempts to revive the CBD, community residential areas have attracted only marginal attention. The automatic assumption has been that those having a choice, i.e., white middle-class home buyers, will shun the central city for suburban locations (B. J. Friedan, 1964).

In the past, only three exceptions to this process of city residential area decline were commonly noted: first, luxury high-rise apartment areas; second, "unique neighborhoods" (e.g., Soho in New York, Capitol Hill in Washington, D.C., Hyde Park–Kenwood in Chicago); and third, a few surviving ethnic neighborhoods.

However, none of the above provides much encouragement for a substantial "back to the city" movement; and if such is to occur, the city must again become a place of choice for middle-class residence. Some two decades ago, Philip Hauser predicted such a possible return flow of migrants into the central city:

> The combination of urban renewal in the inner zones of central cities and blight and urban sprawl in the suburbs is tending to disrupt the pattern of

> population distribution which has placed the higher income groups farthest out from the center of the city. Should these trends continue, the residential land use pattern in metropolitan areas would be turned inside out, with the newer and more desirable areas located in the rebuilt inner city zones as well as in the most desirable parts of suburbia. (Hauser, 1960)

At that junction, migration into the city proved to be more vision than substance, but there is currently a limited but symbolic countermovement toward central city residence. Ironically, though, the present cityward movement is not to new, cleared and rebuilt sites, but to neighborhoods of older residences in greater or lesser states of decay which are now recycling. Middle-class whites and blacks are migrating into central city neighborhoods that according to the classical Burgess model or the filter-down economic model should be abandoned to the economically marginal. Interestingly, the move of industry and manufacturing from the city to suburbs has resulted in more diversified low-intensity patterns of city land usage. In the original Burgess growth model, central city residential property is vacated for commercial industrial usage. Today the pattern is more often the reverse with, in some cities, once-commercial buildings being rehabilitated as residences. For example, the Soho section of New York contains numerous older commercial structures which have been transformed into homes (Hudson, 1978).

While the transformations of neighborhoods from commercial to residential might become more common during the next decade, the great bulk of residential regeneration will be in residential neighborhoods. Neighborhoods such as New Town in Chicago, Ansley Park in Atlanta, the Fan in Richmond, Five Points in Denver, and the Mission District in San Francisco are physically more robust than a decade ago. Moreover, this resurgence has occurred largely without substantial federal, state, or municipal assistance. In fact, many neighborhoods have been organized by the residents expressly to contest local government disinvestment in services, maintenance, and interest.

Recycling neighborhoods usually possess residences that were originally constructed to standards generally unavailable in new suburban housing. Revitalizing neighborhoods also generally are well located in terms of accessibility, transportation routes, and overall physical location.

Young adults with families were in the vanguard of the suburban push of the 1950s, and young adults—now more often childless—are in the vanguard of the return to the central city. Demographically, migrants into the city are generally young, childless, married adults, white, urban bred, well educated, employed in professional or managerial positions, and earning middle- to upper-middle-class incomes (Bradley, 1977). Newcomers also tend to be socially active and have an intense commitment to "their" neighborhood.

Whether revitalization will spread beyond areas meeting the construction and accessibility criteria of the upper-middle class should become apparent by the mid-1980s. Many inner-city areas were originally constructed to house a working-class population, and such neighborhoods built for the nineteenth-century hoi polloi have limited appeal to the late-twentieth-century middle class. Also, even the most successful upgrading neighborhoods have liabilities, particularly for single-income families with school-age children.

Ironically, the very success of non-government-sponsored neighborhood revitalization is spawning a new generation of problem definers who now express concern, not that the city is decaying, but that it is regenerating too rapidly. Rapid renovation, they fear, will result in the expulsion of those current residents unable to absorb the increasing rents and property taxes of an upgrading neighborhood. Thus, a gentrification of inner-city neighborhoods will occur, with the poor becoming "urban nomads," priced or pushed out of their neighborhoods (National Urban Coalition, 1978).

One of the newest funding fashions at HUD is the plight of inner-city residents residing in upgrading neighborhoods. (Concern over those living in *decaying* inner-core areas, however, remains passé.) However, the belief that upgrading speeds residential mobility and creates a special class of "urban nomads" has yet to be supported by empirical evidence. High urban residential mobility has long been one of the many liabilities of urban poverty. According to Bureau of Census data assembled by the author, during 1975–1977, almost half (48 percent) of all poor householders (incomes under $5,000) in metropolitan areas moved. Among poor householders under age forty-five, the probability of having moved during the past two years is considerably greater than the probability of having remained in the same residence. Whether the revitalizing areas have higher- or lower-than-average rates of mobility than comparable nonrevitalizing areas isn't known. There is some suggestion, however, that those leaving central city neighborhoods, either because the ties to the neighborhood are weak or the cost of maintaining them is too high, may be moving to older, inner-city suburban communities (National Urban Coalition, 1978).

One of the consequences of neighborhood revitalization, then, could be greater suburban and central city heterogeneity—at least on an aggregate level. Another consequence should be some improvement in the cities' tax bases and real property—a development central city mayors have long and earnestly desired.

## RACIAL CHANGE IN SUBURBS

As noted previously, the demographic and ecological patterns of the first three quarters of this century document centrifugal movement within metropolitan areas of both populations and commercial-industrial enterprises from core to periphery (Kasarda and Redfearn, 1975). Census data suggest that this trend accelerated after World War II while the population of large central cities generally absolutely declined during the 1960s and 1970s. This commonly was due to black population increases being overshadowed by heavy migration of whites out of the cities. Reynolds Farley indicates that the fifteen largest cities in the nation typically gained some 62,000 nonwhites, but lost 189,000 whites (Farley, 1976). Black migration into cities tapered off during the 1970s, but black fertility rates, though decreasing, remain in excess of those of whites. Whites also tend to be somewhat older than blacks, and thus have higher mortality rates. Consequently, central cities experience aggregate population declines and increases in the proportion of nonwhite residents. The black population of central cities is still increasing, but only 0.9 percent a year. It was a much higher 2.9 percent a year during the 1960s (U.S. Bureau of the Census, 1977*c*).

Suburban areas, by contrast, continue to grow both in absolute numbers and as a proportion of the metropolitan area, and maintain their image as all-white enclaves. As of 1950, one-quarter of the nation's population (24 percent) lived in suburban rings; this increased to a third (33 percent in 1960 and 37 percent in 1970). Currently there are four suburbanites for every three city dwellers. Within metropolitan areas virtually all population growth during the 1960s and 1970s was suburban growth. Metropolitan ascendancy for the past score of years thus has been suburban ascendancy.

Blacks in suburbs, on the other hand, have been noticeable by their absence. The general conclusion of researchers appears to be that black suburbanization is increasing, but only marginally (Schnore, Andre, and Sharp, 1976; Farley, 1970; Taeuber, 1975). While the rate of black suburbanization during the first seven years of this decade exceeded that for whites (a 34.5 percent black increase, compared with a 9.8 percent white increase), these rates in part reflect a limited black population base. This, however, is in the process of changing. Between 1970 and 1977, some 1.2 million blacks became new suburbanites, raising the total number of black suburbanites from 3.4 million to 4.6 million (U.S. Bureau of the Census, 1978*b*). Currently, almost three-fifths of all blacks (58 percent) live in central cities and one-sixth (17 percent) live in urban rings of SMSA's (U.S. Bureau of the Census, 1977*e*).

That one-sixth of all blacks are suburbanites does not mean, however, that the black proportion of suburban residents is substantially increasing. Blacks still comprise only 5.6 percent of all suburbanites, and this will not change dramatically as long as whites also are suburbanizing. Between 1960 and 1977, there were 21.9 million new white suburban residents. Suburbs as a whole will retain their pale complexion so long as white suburbanization continues.

However, the very magnitude of the suburban drive in recent decades suggests some diminution of the movement during the 1980s. Upper- and middle-class whites desiring to suburbanize have in substantial part done so.

Remaining central city whites are increasingly those who either by choice or lack of a suburban down payment will remain city folk. Middle-class suburbanization also is no longer automatically lily-white. In the case of Washington, D.C., the majority of current movers from city to suburb are black. The 1980s will show whether this is an exception or the vanguard of a new urban pattern.

There is some question, though, just how "suburban" some of the suburbs that blacks are entering are in basic characteristics. The social and economic character of some of the areas entered by suburbanizing blacks during the 1970s could be better typified as older working-class, industrial towns rather than stereotypical suburbs.

Also, older ring suburbs particularly in the Northeast and Midwest often differ little in character and housing quality from central city neighborhoods. Such suburbs increasingly serve as a point of suburban entry for blacks and other minorities. In such cases, suburbanization occurs as a consequence of the extremities of the black ghetto extending across city-suburban legal boundaries. In such cases, black suburbanization can hardly be equated with racial integration.

While middle-class blacks are no longer economically excluded from suburban residence and white prejudice appears to be decreasing, after two decades of court cases and civil rights legislation we remain a racially divided society (National Opinion Research Center, 1972; Sorensen, Taeuber, and Hollingsworth, 1975). Whites still opt for segregated neighborhoods. Reynolds Farley reports that over a quarter of the whites surveyed said they were unwilling to move into a neighborhood that had one black family; half were unwilling to move into a neighborhood that was one-fifth black; and three-quarters were unwilling to move into a neighborhood that was one-third black (Farley et al., 1977).

Since virtually all blacks say they are willing to move into a neighborhood that has one or two black families, there is a high probability that once a neighborhood becomes integrated, blacks but not whites will move in. As Molotch has illustrated, all that is necessary for racial changeover is that black housing demands on an area exceed white demands (Molotch, 1973). Thus, even in the absence of specific "white flight," market turnover will produce a predominantly black area within a few years.

Is this, then, the future of black suburbanization? Is black suburbanization nothing but chimera? Perhaps not. Even with all the caveats and reservations, black suburbanization—if not integrative per se—is at least increasing. Nor are the absolute numbers of increases always insignificant. Black suburbanization accounted for 59 percent of the growth of Washington, D.C.'s suburbs during the first four years of this decade. This amounted to 100,000 persons, a greater gain in four years than in the previous twenty. Today, there is a higher proportion of blacks in Washington area suburbs than in the national population.

Of course, one city—even the nation's capital—does not make a national pattern, but past experience may not be the best predictor of future change. Three decades ago, racial segregation in schools, transportation, and restaurants was constitutionally sanctioned, and anyone predicting that the major constitutional issue of the late 1970s would be whether or not special-admission programs for blacks illegally discriminated against whites would have been considered a candidate for St. Elizabeth's. In studying American urban processes, the implicit assumption that the future will replicate the past is especially dubious.

So long as blacks constitute only one-eighth of the population, it is demographically impossible for suburbia as a whole to develop a dark pigmentation. Nonetheless, the 1980 census will, I suspect, reveal a greater increase in black suburbanization than the generally pessimistic research based upon the last census would lead one to expect. If I am correct, academic research of half a decade from now may be documenting a "surprising" upturn in black suburbanization.

## Some Final Comments

This chapter suggests that urban-nonurban differences are differences that have ceased to make a difference. The metropolitan-nonmetropolitan distinction is also disappearing, and a national urban system is upon us, in the South as well as the North. Within central cities, the glory days of domination are no more, but neither are CBD's and residential neighborhoods on the verge of total collapse. "Urban crisis" has become embedded in the lexicon, as it ceases—at least in academic terms—to have meaning.

Economically, cities are now largely solvent, but at the price of becoming part of a national system. The federal contribution to the local budget of Newark went from 1.7 percent of the city's general revenue in 1967 to 11.4 percent in 1976 and jumped to 55.2 percent in 1978. Other cities showed a similar pattern, and in terms of opening the federal coffers, once the central city has broken the path, the suburbs have been quick to follow. The myth of local independence may become mere gossamer under the reality of external sources of budget maintenance. Whether this change is for good or ill is still debatable, but it suggests that in the future, the federal piper will call the tune. The question is, what tune will be chosen? Noncompliance with federal guidelines already has become a luxury in which few communities can afford to indulge.

At the same time that an urban system is evolving at the national level, there is increasing concern for and emphasis on local neighborhoods within urban areas. While living in an urban world, attention is increasingly being redirected to the physically, socially, and perhaps psychologically manageable unit of the neighborhood. Selected areas of central cities are again becoming places of residential choice for the middle and upper-middle classes who may think and work nationally but prefer to live locally. During coming decades, neighborhood revitalization may well go from a fad to a national movement. The profound changes under way owe little to the activities of sociologists. As social scientists, we have not even been particularly astute in observing new urban trends until they are well established.

Our images of suburbia also remain remarkably resistant to modification. Suburbs are becoming increasingly heterogeneous racially as well as socially. While we remain a racially polarized society, the suburban wall of exclusivity has been cracked. Black suburbanization, no longer an exception to the rule, may become the pattern of the 1980s. Whether suburbanization can be equated with integration is more problematical.

Whatever the direction of future urban patterns, the generators of change are increasingly crystallizing at the national level. If coherent and cogent urban policies are to develop, they must reflect cognizance of the emerging national urban nexus.

# 11

# Metropolitan Growth and Democratic Participation

*Gerald Suttles and Morris Janowitz*

COMMUNITY CHANGE HAS BEEN examined persistently within an evolutionary framework that stresses the replacement of old social forms by new ones. Indeed the notion of social change itself has often been reserved for such dramatic replacements. The frequent juxtaposition of paired terms *(Gemeinschaft-Gesellschaft,* preindustrial-industrial, mechanical-organic, folk-urban) is one example of this type of formulation. A large body of literature on the "decline of community" fleshes out for some investigators the dominant theme that preoccupies community analysis and social change in general. Despite its well recognized weaknesses, the heritage of Toennies appears in one guise after another in both popular and academic works on the local community.

The alternative approach is a more differentiated conception of social change, one that is more accommodative of cumulative patterns of change and attuned to contemporary empirical findings. One explicit and general statement along these lines is that proposed by Julian Steward (1955), who saw social change in terms of new levels of sociocultural integration rather than discrete "stages," each defined so as to exclude the social forms of its predecessor. The key processes in Steward's conception of social change were structural differentiation and a cumulative pattern of social innovation. New social forms emerge without necessarily dislodging old ones, and the central question is the articulation of the existing and emerging forms.

□ This chapter has profited from the comments of Sylvia Fava, Robert Gutman, and Albert Hunter. The authors would like to express their appreciation for these comments and the hope that they have responded effectively.

For Steward, as well as ourselves, the process by which this articulation occurs is problematic rather than the foregone conclusion of "evolutionary laws." The most frequent pattern of articulation seems to be one of increasing specialization with the associated construction of supportive linkages between older and newer social forms as well as the transformation of older social forms. The construction of these supportive linkages is problematic in that their emergence is often delayed and or incomplete. Their construction involves deliberate and thoughtful social action rather than relying only on an unintended process of selection and adaptation.

While we wish to emphasize the problematic character of articulating new and older social forms, there are certainly a number of cases which seem to fit this roughly drawn paradigm. Thus, although the family has lost many of its economic functions, it has become increasingly important in providing the incentives for economic activity (Schumpeter, 1942) and education attainment. In turn the family itself seems to have undergone a transformation, making it a more flexible unit so that, for example, it can be disassembled and reassembled so as to better assist its members to respond to the external demands placed upon them. Moreover, the family is experiencing yet another transformation in accommodating itself to the expansion of women's rights and a less sexist division of labor. Of course, a number of scholars have forecast for the nth time the "disappearance of the family." Those familiar with similar forecasts in the 1930s are apt to be more cautious.

One could pursue this form of analysis for a variety of social institutions which at one time or another have been waived to the grave by one sociologist only to be resurrected by another. Although the simple evolutionary idea of Toennies dominates much of the literature of the territorial community, the history of sociological research includes the continuous documentation of points of view compatible with Steward's emphasis on a more complex conception of social change rooted in structural specialization and the cumulative pattern of social response. This tradition of research has many intellectual sources, but there is a direct continuity in the analysis of urban life in Mayhew, Booth, Thomas, Park, and Burgess and the post-World War II community studies.

Our intent is to focus on the local community. Our purpose, however, is not simply to affirm its existence but to examine the much more stubborn problem of the articulation between the local community and other institutions of the wider society. The forecasts of sociologists have not only confused intellectual work on the local community, they are part of the popular folklore that has impeded our management of public affairs, particularly our ideology guiding the organization of partisan politics. Images of detached self-sufficiency, sentimental attachment, and mutual aid have been so prevalent that they have crowded out considerations of the local community as one of the settings in which public opinion is mobilized and organized. In its most romantic form, this conception of the local community almost ensures that contemporary communities will show a "decline" from their idealized "origin." On the other hand, instrumental conception of the local community tends to define its role narrowly in terms of mutual aid, informal social control, and therapeutic assistance.

Both the romantic and instrumental conceptions of local communities tend to omit the construction of bridges to integrate them into existing institutions of the wider society, especially partisan politics. Empirical accounts of the 1970s (Hunter, 1974; Warren, 1975; Kornblum, 1974) repeatedly find that the local community is undergoing a process of internal differentiation or a transformation from a relatively isolated, self-centered unit into a multitiered one in which the separate functions of the wider society are associated with territorial aggregations that produce more than one level of the local community. This paper distinguishes four levels of the local community; the *social bloc,* which is essentially the community of sentiment identified in past analysis; the *organizational community,* which adopts explicit goals and formal organizational procedures; the *aggregated metropolitan community,* which attempts to consolidate community groups so as to relate them to the growing scale of metropolitan organization; and *national neighborhood lobbies,* which seek to balance the demands of people as residents and consumers against those demands which frequently the same people support as members of their workplace. Ingrained habit might lead some observers to regard the "higher" stages of this tier of local communities as replacements for the lower ones. But this is exactly the sort of thinking that has been so fruitless in the past. Our own effort is to examine this nested hierarchy of community associations as an instance of social differentiation and the partial articulation of community groups with broader social institutions, particularly those which grow out of the division of labor. This orientation toward community organization rests on our concepts of the local community not as a residue but rather as a social construction, as a voluntaristic adaptation to urbanization. These categories are derived from the prior formulation of local community as that of "the community of limited liability" and "the defended community" with its distinctive urban character (Janowitz, 1967; Suttles, 1972).[1]

We are not the only ones who have singled out some of these levels of community organization (Greer, 1962; Hunter, 1974). No new research findings are presented here and, indeed, much of our argument is compatible with Burgess's attempt to single out a particular level of community for

[1] We see the present work as extending and combining the analytic approaches developed in the concepts "the community of limited liability" and "defended community." The former anticipates the voluntarism and organizational flexibility which seem to characterize emerging community structures, while the latter places the needed emphasis on the changing context within which community structures must respond to changes in the wider society.

analyses.[2] This does not mean to say that we can identify a new and completed level of sociocultural integration between the local community and wider social institutions. At best, we do see nascent movements in that direction and, therefore, a new conceptual effort is necessary to put them in context.

## Community Organization and the Quality of Life

The nation-state has become the dominant social form in the contemporary societies of Western Europe and the United States. It has been frequently pointed out, however, that the articulation of the diverse interests of those societies requires the persistence of subnational groupings. Industrial societies are exceedingly diverse, and the problem of developing an effective or working consensus relies upon a political process of representation and debate. As it is increasingly evident, even very small extremist groups can hobble the effective management of complex societies unless such societies can achieve popular and decisive political regimes. The very complexity of industrial societies makes this working consensus more difficult to achieve.

This process of representation and debate is hardly contained within the political party structures. It extends as well to an enormous number of subgroups which in many instances are only marginally related to one another and only episodically drawn into partisan politics. For parliamentary democracies, it is essential that this conglomeration of groups and their interests be aggregated and balanced so as to ensure workable majorities and effective political leadership. The most obvious way in which this aggregation is partially achieved in modern industrial societies is through the occupational structure and its linkage to political parties. To a considerable extent, political analysts have proceeded as if this were the sole way of aggregating public opinion in the modern industrial state. Class structure in this view provides either the existing or emerging means of forming public opinion into disciplined constituencies. In Marxist theory, of course, social classes are seen as the ultimate and exclusive means of mobilizing publics within industrial society. Most mass society theorists and functionalists (Kornhauser, 1959; Fischer, 1976) recognize the persistence of primordial groups alongside occupational strata in the formation of public opinion, although there

[2] Burgess's papers reveal that he and his co-workers were fully aware that the community areas they defined in Chicago included many subareas and that the community areas themselves were often included in larger, well-recognized territorial units (e.g., Bronzeville). Rather, Burgess seems to have intended to identify areas that were (1) widely recognized, (2) sufficiently large for the purposes of service delivery and political mobilization, and (3) in possession of a complement of institutions for day-to-day self-sufficiency. Indeed, it seems apparent that Burgess saw these community areas as units within which citizens could be aggregated and mobilized rather than natural areas within which this had already taken place through an exclusively natural process.

is still a strong tendency to regard the primordial groups as fragile "survivals" which are not rooted in the contemporary process of social differentiation in industrial societies.

None of these interpretations, however, seems to be adequate as a basis for understanding modern industrial societies or in developing an effective democratic theory of citizen participation. There has been a persistent decline in the linkage between economic or occupational groups and the political parties in the United States. Moreover, the interests of occupational groups are usually very specialized and narrow, and it is quite misleading to think of them as representing the broad interests that individuals have in their various capacities. Viewed analytically, occupational groups can be aggregated only on issues of incomes and profit—those are the only interests they share. Real individuals, however, often have strong interests as consumers, taxpayers, parents, or the outraged victims of crime and disorder. While the organizations of the workplace specialize in guarding citizen interests in income, it appears to us that the local community is becoming increasingly distinct as the defender of a more diffuse set of interests indicated in the phrase "quality of life."

Widespread concern over the "quality of life" has become especially prominent during the last fifteen years and has given rise to a variety of social movements: environmentalism, consumer protection, no growth, local community control and taxpayer revolts, for example. These citizen movements reflect a real concern with territorially based or locational decisions made by regulatory, administrative, and public service agencies that affect both public finances and the "quality of life" in the broadest sense. Existing political party organization has been particularly ineffective in capturing these emergent constituencies and enrolling them in the old "workplace" coalitions of the Republican and Democratic parties. Political leaders have made strenuous and repeated, but unsuccessful efforts to deal with these political dilemmas. The urban agenda of the Kennedy administration, the Great Society programs of the Johnson administration, the New Federalism of the Nixon administration, and most recently Carter's "Urban Plan" all represent more than token efforts to respond to the various expressions of dissatisfaction. The novel aspect of such expressions is their vociforous quality and the inability to house them within the "regular political process" simply by adding to the inventory of federal, state, and local programs—"more of the same."

At the local level, especially among suburbanites and low-income minority subcommunities, these social movements indicate a chronic dissatisfaction with governmental forms themselves; with their remoteness, their bureaucratic structure, and their imputed coerciveness. Opposition is generated when the federal government has sought to regulate local efforts at social control, self-help, and ethnic or parochial solidarity. Public reaction has been aroused by the intrusion of government into local organizations, particularly the schools but also most other welfare organizations at the front line of service delivery. Therefore, new social programs reinforce the call for "less government," especially "big government."

At still a broader level, the unevenness of the distribution of public resources among different local communities has been a source of outspoken dissatisfaction. The imbalance between the suburbs and central city is only the most striking among a host of programs that differentially benefit "have" and "have not" communities. Despite expanding employment opportunities and welfare services as well as revenue sharing, governmental decisions seem to increase rather than redress the perceived difference between "have" and "have not" communities. Because of the wide variety of such programs, realistic comparisons are actually quite difficult, but the sheer growth of governmental programs has heightened awareness of these disparities. When it is most responsive, federal intervention frequently increases both the reality and appearance of differences between the advantaged and the disadvantaged.

These discontents seem increasingly to focus most heavily on the federal government. According to a 1973 Harris survey (Subcommittee on Intergovernmental Relations, 1973), the public expresses no more enthusiasm for Congress and the presidency than it does for local government—an abysmal showing of between 18 and 30 percent on the positive side, about the same as those saying that they would take part in a demonstration "even if someone gets hurt" (27 percent). These levels of public confidence in the federal government represent a dramatic decline in public confidence in the federal government relative to local government.

It is clear from these observations that there has been the development of a distinctive and new set of social interests which demand attention but which do not fit readily within the existing framework of partisan politics: a reassertion of a parochialism, discontent with the intrusion of government into local service institutions, a mindfulness of the inequities of public choice, and a belief that the highest levels of government respond to "special interest" rather than to the "public interest." The dimensions of this social discontent are extremely diffuse, even contradictory.[3]

Conflicting and poorly expressed interests are an intrinsic and inevitable feature of modern industrial societies. Articulating them often requires that they be brought into relief, be organized and aggregated, and experience the

[3]Thus, some analysts (Bish and Ostrum, 1973) have taken the step of recommending an extension of the municipal fragmentation of the suburbs into the central city, the central idea being that each person could seek out an optimal "mix" of public services by shopping among communities. Public choice models of this sort, however, seem only to aggravate the problems of aggregating public opinion and also to widen the differences between communities which are the source of so much dissatisfaction. The formula "every man his own community" is utopian not only because such residential movement is impossible, but because public policies are often a package deal and cannot be parceled out simply by the process of residential segregation even if one is willing to make the totally unrealistic assumption of free residential choice.

fate of compromise, concession, bargaining and political debate. According to democratic theory, one seldom gets exactly what one wants—that is part of the reason why it is so hard to maintain a social democracy in modern industrial societies. The effectiveness of social democracy, however, is enhanced when all parties to the dispute have what they consider a fair voice in the determination of the outcome. It seems clear by now that the sponsors and representatives of the local community have become progressively differentiated from those of the workplace and that nothing short of a new level of sociocultural integration—the modernization of community organization—can effectively include their demands.

## Systemic Patterns of the Metropolis

The root causes for this differentiation of residential and workplace interests are to be found in three broad trends which have been present in the United States over the long term but which have reached threshold levels since World War II. First, the increasing separation of place of work and place of residence has reached the point where the interests vested in each of these sites cannot be represented by a single organizational form. Second, the scale of metropolitan organizations has grown to where an effective interface between them and the local community requires an increase in the scale of the local community. Third, the fragmentation of metropolitan areas is so pronounced that existing links between local government and the federal government are inadequate.

## Place of Work and Place of Residence

The Great Depression and the New Deal produced a new and enlarged interdependence and coalition of workplace groups which achieved a pervasive influence in American political life. The economic crisis of that period effectively established a national coalition that gave the Democratic party dominance over policy making for over twenty years. Both at the national and the local level political leaders tended to be attentive and responsive to the economy and to the emerging workplace interest groups; labor and higher wages, big businesses and economic growth, minority groups and welfare benefits, regional groups and economic development. Party competition worked largely within these goals, and the parties differed largely in their claims at being more or less effective in bringing them about.

Thus business groups, labor unions, and professional associations became both highly pyramided and national in scope by the end of the 1950s with the result that their leadership often had continuous access to the highest levels of political decision making. Indeed, as Lowi (1969) points out, many of the federal control agencies or departments (labor, agriculture, commerce, welfare, etc.) were essentially the public counterparts to each of these interest groups. In that period, the mobilizaton of groups primarily in the workplace was a viable strategy for organizing public opinion not only because of the consensus on the goal of economic development, but also because the workplace and the residential unit were not that separate from one another. A very large proportion of the United States workforce was in manufacturing or in jobs where residence and place of work were located often in the same community and certainly in the same municipality. In part, the union "local" was able to represent both the residential and the occupational community. Ward political organization was typically an extention of occupational groups clustered around their factories, stores, schools, and public facilities. Occupational and residential interests could be articulated within either the same group or groups closely related to one another because of their common spatial boundaries.

In particular localities, these kinds of industrial working-class communities remain (Kornblum, 1974), but since World War II the overall trend has been toward pronounced deconcentration of population. Large numbers of blue-collar workers have moved to the suburbs or at least to areas less unattractive than those hovering about the factories and shops. White-collar and proprietorial groups have dispersed farther and earlier. In some of our larger metropolitan areas it can be estimated that as much as half of the work force may live in municipalities other than the one they work in. Such people actually have two local governments: one that makes decisions about the municipality within which they work and another which makes decisions about the municipality in which they reside. They vote in the local elections of their residential area but the most powerful group they belong to is often in another municipality. In the post-World War II polycentric, metropolitan region, the territorial bases for occupational and residential organization have become more spatially separated. In turn, the distinction and potential conflict between occupational and residential goals have become more visible. It is not just that residential groups increasingly have abandoned the old New Deal Coalition, but that occupational groups within this coalition seem to have narrowed their focus as well. For groups emerging out of the place of work, interests in wages, economic growth, and higher profits increasingly dominate. For groups emerging out of the place of residence, however, quality of life has become increasingly important. Thus, the articulation of these goals is progressively complex and fits uncomfortably within the political party coalitions developed in an earlier period.

To a large extent workplace associations continue to preempt the avenues of political influence and dominate public policy. Nonetheless, there have been marginal attempts to recognize the growing separation of place of residence and the distinctive interests expressed by each of its representatives. The urban agenda of the Kennedy administration launched limited initiatives in this direction. Johnson's War on Poverty made a much more ambitious effort to conciliate community interests, but ran aground on the opposition of incumbent urban leaders, political and professional. The New Federalism of the Nixon administration sought to decentralize governmental investment through increased revenue sharing, but this seems neither to have changed past patterns of local investment nor to have brought much visible relief to local taxpayers. These revenue transfers have grown under the Carter administration and have been joined to a proposed program which seeks to enlarge local initiative.

In all of these instances partisan political parties have been unequipped to mobilize public opinion within the existing political system to give shape and legitimacy to these new presidential efforts. The result has been a popular reaction of considerable disaffection. Undoubtedly, in part this dissatisfaction grows out of the increasing expense of government without sufficient visible increase in benefits. However, much of it is attributable to political incapacity to articulate the spatial and organizational separation of place of work and place of residence.

## The Increasing Scale of Metropolitan Organization

The disarticulation of economic and community interests has been enlarged by the growing scale of urban organization and its remoteness from citizen accountability. The scale of urban organization has not only become gargantuan by pre–World War II standards, it has progressively escaped the direct management of elected officials. Transportation, health and sanitation have crescively become the responsibility of regional authorities which encompass a number of municipalities. As the federal administration has extended outward and become an increasingly major arbiter of public goods, it has chosen its own administrative boundaries without respect for those of the central city or suburban municipalities. The level at which decision making takes place includes territories that are vastly larger than even the biggest of our central cities. Legislation and court orders for "community inputs" in such programs and administrative units must reckon with a public organized on a much more limited scale.

This growth of scale is no less marked among private businesses. The corporation has been succeeded by the conglomerate and now what are called the "internationals." Old department stores have become outlets for new chains, and whole industries have been joined by acronyms that do not seem to stand for any familiar enterprise. Old elites have become paid employees. Local business leadership may exist, but it loses its autonomy as it is engulfed in larger and larger organizations.

Such a massive assemblage of private and public organizations increases centralization without necessarily identifying some level at which one may seek to exert political influence. The number of organizations themselves has grown, and they increasingly lack any common territorial referent. At times the federal government uses the Standard Metropolitan Statistical Area (SMSA) as an administrative unit, but at other times it uses a larger regional unit or a smaller group of municipalities that conforms to no common territorial unit. A growing number of "metropolitan authorities" work with varying territorial units and member communities or counties.

Nor are these different levels of government independent from one another despite the careful wording of their titles and the rhetoric on the separation of national, state, and local government. The federal courts continuously monitor a host of local agencies and in the absence of compliances to federal law have had to take receivership of particular agencies to the point that the courts have become one-man administrators of entire school systems, housing authorities, and pollution-control bodies. Regional transportation authorities quickly intercede in local zoning and building programs. The transfer of state and federal funds routinely involves them in the review of the most parochial front-line service delivery agency: the schools, the local library, zoning boards, and hospitals. The federal-state-local arrangements in funding imply that every level of government is involved no matter what the territorial unit is in which implementation occurs. New provisions for citizen participation at public hearings provide a point of entry, but no one can seriously consider these hearings a final disposition. Cases regularly move up the chain of decision making and, of course, the ultimate judgment that may be sought is that of an overworked Supreme Court. And, of course, community groups are in the forefront of those keeping the Supreme Court overworked. Some of its most significant decisions of late have been to arbitrate local disputes; disputes over public housing site selection, over zoning ordinances, and over group housing.

The increasing scale and interconnectedness of public and private organizations have made decision making remote, but they may have also charted out a new path of public influence. As local or municipal politics become less isolated and decisive, the tendency among community groups seems to have been twofold. On the one hand, there is the tendency to seek access to higher authority, particularly the courts and federal control commissions. On the other hand, there appears to be a very diffuse pattern of activism which aims its efforts at almost every level or unit of government irrespective of their formal responsibilities. Popular disaffection does not produce political apathy. The all-purpose referendum has found increasing use. The ad hoc citizen lobby, temporary alliances among community groups, and the use of an assortment of public hearings have been intensified. Indeed, one cannot but be struck by the multiplicity of citizen strategies which seem to be initiated all at the same time; court appeals, public hearings, paid lobbyists, public demonstrations, and political campaigns.

## Metropolitan Fragmentation

In addition to the separation of place of work and residence and the growing scale of organization is the increasing fragmentation of the metropolitan area. At the end of World War II, the population of the central cities was about two and one-half times that of their surrounding suburbs. At present the population in metropolitan areas is about evenly split between the central cities and their suburbs despite substantial growth in both. Previously the dominance of the central cities allowed its mass media, its leaders, and its larger enterprises to give some direction both to the central city and its surrounding suburbs. Over time, however, most of our central cities have become "land locked" by incorporated suburbs. Neither the suburbs nor the central cities seem able to produce popular leaders or social initiatives that attract a popular following throughout the metropolitan area. Instead, central city governments are moving in the direction of the "toy governments" of suburbia which regularly throw themselves on the mercy of federal, state, or regional levels of taxation or governance. The case of New York City, once a leader in urban innovation, is a striking example of this growing incapacity of local authority.

The reduced capacity of local government has not been accompanied by the growth of broader political party structures to articulate the diverse demands of metropolitan regions. Nor has metropolitan government achieved an effective constituency. Instead the citizenry remains committed to their local forms of municipality with persistent and renewed vigor. There are even strong secessionist movements in some areas to fragment county governments (e.g., the northern tier of Cook county, the Peconic portion of Suffolk county) to form new counties. It would appear that in the absence of very effective regional political coalitions, there is an increasing political demand to retreat to even more parochial forms of local self-management. Local government has come to serve as a symbolic expression of dissatisfaction, even if it lacks the substance to deal effectively with the conflicts of interests that lead to this dissatisfaction.

The fragmentation of metropolitan areas is manifested in a deterioration of elite coalitions. In the pre-World War II urban center, the investments and interests of the business community were heavily concentrated in the central city, especially the central business district. These interests warranted a protective strategy toward its maintenance: the maintenance of its physical plant, support for its cultural institutions, preservation of its housing stock, and at least minimal services for its work force. Since World War II, however, the economic interests of business elites have become much more differentiated and diffuse. Many have followed the suburban population and have invested heavily in regional shopping centers and industrial parks. Some have left the central city altogether and concentrated their operations in the suburbs. Those with financial interests located solely within the central city are an increasingly narrow economic segment. As a result the local business community has become progressively fragmented in its capacity to support or oppose local political regimes. Leaders of firms which are still concentrated in the central city may continue to support the dominant political groups there, but their efforts are weakened by a growing number of business leaders who may be indifferent to, or even oppose, central city development or redevelopment.

## The Aggregation of Community Forms

The growing scale of organization, jurisdiction fragmentation, and increasing separation of place of work and place of residence are converging trends which weaken both our political party organization and local governmental forms. They are weakened, in part, because they are ill equipped to regard the metropolitan region as a single unit with a common economy and a shared physical plant. They are weakened as well by their inability to articulate public opinion with sufficient scope to respond to the diversity of demands and interests which exist. The scale of organization often thrusts decisions outside the boundaries of the local political party or administrative unit. Jurisdictional fragmentation also divides the interests of elites and encourages the short-run opportunism of one community at the expense of another. And the separation of place of residence and place of work brings into sharper relief the conflict between those stressing quality of life versus economic growth.

For most policy makers, the favored solution to this predicament has been metropolitan government. Metropolitan government, however, has proved to be extremely unpopular in the United States and has developed only under very special circumstances. Metropolitan government only looks like more government, rather than effective government. Aside from its unpopularity, however, it is our view that the proponents of metropolitan government focus too narrowly on the administrative forms of urban management without due attention to the development of an articulate infrastructure of citizen organization within which a working consensus can emerge. This is a serious omission, not only because it runs against the grain of democratic theory, but because it overlooks a significant move in this direction by community organization.

The most persistent and widely documented form of the local community is the *social bloc* (Keller, 1968; Hunter, 1974; Greer, 1962). This is a small face-to-face territorial group within which residents establish or assume a very diffuse and generalized set of normative expectations. In most instances it advances to include only a narrow grouping of residents: people who live on the same block, an ethnic enclave, a well-isolated part of the urban landscape, or a single high-rise building. It is a general-purpose group that seeks to handle all the residual reciprocities that people seek after the normative capacities of *Gesellschaft* are exhausted. It seems to be especially important in ensuring a sense of mutual safety and the countless favors that can be claimed on account of proximity. It is especially well developed among groups who feel themselves vulnerable to victimization and find in this diffuse form of community a needed assurance of security (Suttles, 1972). As Kasarda and Janowitz (1976) document, length of residence seems the most essential condition for its development. Usually the social bloc is not a purposive group—something foreseen and intentionally made —but it can be of this type (Hunter, 1975). It arises out of the cumulative efforts of separate households to reduce anonymity, especially where anonymity reduced one's sense of security. It exists because residents cause it to happen, not because there is a benign bureaucracy assisting those who settle near one another.

The social bloc is not the kinship community of peasant societies nor is it the residue of rural communities which have been transplanted to an urban metropolis. Residents may make use of primordial ties to help construct such social blocs, but they can be thought of as a thoroughly contemporary social form, a self-regulating group in which local opinion and interaction exert noncoercive social control. Its members furnish a form of mutual surveillance and a set of standards of physical maintenance and provide a sense for the interdependence of collective life. Within the confines of the social bloc, people can most readily internalize the costs and benefits of interdependent living.

The informal and diffuse character of the social bloc makes it ill suited for highly organized efforts. This character makes it resist broad-scale efforts at social change which originate in the wider society. Thus, much of the agitation of community groups against the intrusion of "big government," "big business," or "big labor" originates from this level of the local community. Understandably, members of a social bloc think that they know best what serves their own welfare and how to achieve their own ends. Land clearance, changes in police practice, changing school boundaries, and local traffic management are especially likely to provoke members of the social bloc. This is particularly true where, as is usually the practice, little or no effort is made to consult with those who make up the social bloc. Thus, one of the prime sources of social bloc discontent is simply the extensive bureaucratization of urban life and the remoteness of decision making in the expanded scale of organization of metropolitan government.

The demands arising out of the social bloc often take on an extremely parochial form since they tend to represent a narrow range of social interests. Frequently, social blocs are simply opposed to change and usually they are opposed to broad strategies that would more evenly distribute the costs of urban life—scatter-site public housing, school integration, mixed land usage, methadone clinics, etc. However, the social bloc is also a relatively powerless social group. Occasionally, its members have found the opportunity for expressing their discontent in particular social movements—taxpayers' revolts or antiredlining groups, for instance—but their participation is episodic and often ineffective.

Nonetheless, the social bloc seems to have been drawn progressively into more formal associations through the confederation of contiguous neighborhoods. Although the literature on the subject is quite uneven, these *organizational communities* have become especially widespread in American cities (Hunter 1974; Warren, 1975). Member social blocs obtain representation in a larger organization and, in return, help finance through their dues a small staff, office space, and some form of community news coverage. The need for member social blocs is quite explicitely recognized, and often an effort is made to identify them before attempting to develop the organizational community (Emmons, 1978). The confederational form is viewed as giving legitimacy to the organizational community since ultimately it is based on "grass roots" participation. Moreover, community organizers increasingly recognize that attempts to foist an organization onto a number of social blocs is apt to be viewed as another example of "bureaucracy" and "outside interference."

The organizational community not only provides an avenue for greater influence to the social bloc, it also encompasses a more cosmopolitan world. In gaining some measure of influence, the social bloc must also come to accept compromises with adjacent neighborhoods. Gains have to be accompanied by some losses. The organizational community, then, provides an instructive or educational setting for the practical politics of urban life.

The organizational community tends to stabilize around the "district" level—the front-line service delivery areas of the schools, police, sanitation, and the like (Jacobs, 1961). Concern about the inflexibility of public agencies persists at this level especially when they are seen as involving the intrusion of wider forms of government and private organization into the front-line delivery agencies. The schools have been a particularly acute source of organizational attention as busing, the selection of teachers, redistricting, and curriculum choices have been bureaucratically or coercively managed by boards of education, teachers' unions, federal agencies, and especially the courts. The school is probably the most sacred repository of collective community investment. It is usually the largest single consumer of their property-tax dollar, it calls for investments that can be profited from only after a full generation, and the gains experienced are not specific to those who invest. The local school especially calls for "sacrifice," and we should not be surprised that local residents feel a particularly strong moral claim upon its management.

In general, the organizational community becomes increasingly preoccupied with the declining independence of front-line service delivery agencies; the centralization of police forces, the sudden appearance of HUD as a "local home owner," or the alteration of bus stops by regional transportation authorities. A bewildering array of local services change, get reduced, or suddenly appear without forewarning. Therefore, the organizational community has been a particular focus for attempts at redress of the quantity and quality of local services and has been drawn increasingly into activist-protest politics. For many older community organizations this has meant reducing their ties to the "regular political process" of pressing their grievances up through the chain of precinct captain, councilman, and political leader. It has meant operating in a wider political arena, using the mass media to dramatize grievances and searching for allies in negotiations with distant and highly pyramided organizations. Thus, the organizational community itself has frequently taken on a confederational form in which different local organizations have leagued together, often temporarily, for limited objectives.

Within the last few years these organizational communities have been brought together in a number of metropolitan areas so that they constitute a third level of community organization. We have labeled this level as the *aggregated metropolitan community* because it represents aspirations as well as realities to organize on a wider and more realistic territorial basis. In the late years of the 1960 decade and thereafter, purely private community action groups arose in the wake of the "War on Poverty"—often making use of the symbolism of the Alinsky type but with a broader, geographical base. They were to be developed throughout the country, some with a concern for multiple issues, others more single-issue-oriented. These metropolitan confederations seem to wax and wane in the inclusiveness of their membership, but they seem to persist despite their fluctuating membership. Usually they have a small staff, regularized funding sources, some type of news coverage and dissemination, and a capacity to monitor local, state, and federal actions. They provide, so to speak, the organizational framework within which more local organizational communities can fit themselves on occasion in the search for allies on specific issues. Often their vitality is linked to specific metropolitan-wide issues. Apparently, many of them have achieved a measure of stability and constitute essential elements of the aggregated metropolitan community.

Such organizations have especially brought into relief the unevenness in the distribution of services and benefits or the differential impact of public decisions on separate communities. Thus, one of their tendencies has been to focus on problems such as redlining, the comparative benefits (or costs) of public investments, and differentials in service delivery. They also provided a vehicle through which a large number of local communities could mount efforts to review investments such as expressways and building programs which impact on more than one organizational community.

These forms of community organizations are similar to the old political machine on the one hand and parallel to the emerging structure of metropolitan decision making on the other. Like the old-line precinct, the social bloc is essentially a network of informal relations in which interpersonal loyalties are the basis for mutual trust and a confidence in the "grass roots opinion" imputed to its members. The organizational community, like the ward organization, gains validity and strength because it is constituted from such "grass roots" groups. And, as in the case of the political party, the aggregated metropolitan community seeks to mobilize or balance common or competing claims. At each level, of course, the issues that attract attention and the capacity for mobilizing local opinion shift. Thus, these forms of community organization reflect the admixture of localistic sentiment and the purposeful effort which are encompassed by concepts such as the "community of limited liability" (Janowitz, 1967). In essence, these levels of community organization emerge in response to the problematic tasks of linking residential localities to the structure of national government. The social bloc is essentially concerned with the informal regulation of its own members and the ability to continue without outside interference; the organizational community with the front-line delivery of services and the dilemmas of the growing scale of urban organization which reduce its autonomy; and the aggregated metropolitan community with the unevenness in the distribution of public benefits as well as the broad impact of public decisions on the organizational communities.

Table 1 attempts to make more explicit this hierarchy of community organization and the emerging specialization among levels. Obviously we are describing a process of institution building that is more nearly in the stage of "becoming" rather than an organizational achievement. It is a process where the outcome is not predetermined. However, we are attempting to provide a conceptual framework which suggests that the discontinuities and trends of local community organization fit less in the tradition of the "decline of community" than in the tradition of the "social construction of community." The local community has moved toward a greater degree of specialization and developed linkages between each level of specialization. It reaches from the grass roots strength of the social bloc to progressively more formal and more instrumental organizational forms; forms that resemble more closely the "community of limited liability." Its structure tends to mirror, on the one hand, the selective concerns of coresidents at each level and, on the other hand, the various levels of public decision making. The hierarchy has the potential to articulate and aggregate community opinion so as to mount a more effective statement at those points of

| Community Type | Territorial Variants | Focus of Shared Interests | Organizational and Ecological Processes Most Closely Associated with Incentives to Activism |
|---|---|---|---|
| *Social Bloc* | | | |
| Informal, face-to-face relations; natural leaders; diffuse expectations | Face bloc; single high-rise building; housing project; ethnic enclave; historic area | "Big government" or "big business"; inflexibility of bureaucracy; intrusion of government into housing choices, property taxes, land conversion. | Separation of place of work and place of residence; increasingly distinct residential areas and concern for "quality of life." |
| *Organizational Community* | | | |
| Formal organization with part-or full-time staff; newsletter | School, police, or ward districts | Delivery of services by front-line agencies; schools, police, streets, parks | Growing scale of metropolitan organizations and declining autonomy of local front-line agencies |
| *Aggregated Metropolitan Community* | | | |
| Formal organization w/professional staff; newsletter; capacity to monitor local, state, and national actions | Confederation of widely distributed organizational communities; shifting membership; aspiration to represent entire metropolitan area | Unevenness in distribution of costs and benefits of broad private and public projects and policies; highways, water supply, transportation | Political and administrative fragmentation and declining capacity of political parties |
| *National Neighborhood Lobbies* | | | |
| National staff; conventions; member confederations; news releases | Effort to recruit widely; membership drives coincide with periodic efforts to influence current legislation, budgets | Formation of Federal Urban Policy, especially a neighborhood policy; federal funding for neighborhood rehabilitation; services | Increasing presence of federal government and financing in regulating government, supporting local services, and imposing standards |

leverage where community leaders must seek influence in the metropolitan community.

Table 1 includes, as well, *national neighborhood lobbies*, which seek influence at the federal level itself. This seems to be increasingly apparent to community leaders themselves, and since 1975 a number of national-level organizations have emerged to lobby for neighborhood groups, the best known being the National Association of Neighborhoods, National People's Action, and National Neighbors. Perhaps the most pointed demonstration of this general approach, however, was provided by a community organizer who asserted that "You simply have to try at each level. And you need an organization for each level."

In almost every large metropolitan area in the United States specific examples of this hierarchy of community organization have come into existence. The scope of these organizations and the linkage among them, of course, are quite ragged, incomplete, and problematic. As of the end of the 1970s, no achievements of great consequence can be singled out, and in any event sociologists may be "wrong" in what they would consider to be accomplishments. These forms of community organization have emerged in part because of the incapacities of partisan politics to provide political aspirants and leaders with a clearer definition of the content of public opinion and its potentials for a working compromise. Political party organization, especially its local forms, seems to remain steadfastly attached to workplace organizations despite a decline in their membership and voting loyalties. Increasingly political aspirants turn to more ephemeral and unstable populist manifestations for a "reading" of popular opinion. By contrast, these levels of community organization represent, in our view, an effort to aggregate public opinion and balance contesting claims within this renewed search for political mandates. This tier of community organizations has not solidified beyond its skeletal structure, and this will be described by some as one in which "big" community organizations are replacing small ones. We doubt this interpretation and suggest instead that it is a systematic effort to construct a more coherent relationship between the local community and the changing structure of the wider society. If it succeeds it will hardly replace partisan party politics, but augment and modify it.

## Social Science Concepts of Community: Traditional and Emerging

If one takes the perspective that the local community is a competitor with the more formal and instrumental bureaucracies of the wider society, these variations in form as well as the short life span of many community organizations may be taken as signs of centrifugal disintegration, dissensus, and the continued "decline of community." This prognosis has been especially appealing since the War on Poverty and the abortive efforts of Community Action Program (CAP). The War on Poverty had such ambitious goals (the total eradication of poverty, delinquency, urban decay, racial antagonisms, etc.) that its defeat in these terms was a foregone conclusion. Goals of this order made Moynihan's subsequent dismissal of community organization appear as a reasoned assessment. By juxtaposing local community organization against local political organization, the two were pitted in what appeared a zero-sum contest in which one would survive and the other decline. Short-run, dramatic achievements were expected in the form of reduced poverty, delinquency, or health problems, and these short-run goals continue to be institutionalized in evaluation research (Rossi, 1978) and the federal grants programs. Consensus was apparently expected at the onset rather than seen as an organized debate both to reveal and reconcile conflicting interests. If one evaluates any other American institution—the Congress, the Executive, local government, or private business—by any similar standard, they also "fail." Yet we would not ordinarily conclude that they are for that reason "unimportant."

In realistic terms, then, what can be the objectives of the local community and within what conceptual framework can it be evaluated or its future forecast?[4] The diffuse and voluntary forms of community organization cannot be studied and assessed in terms of models borrowed from formal organization theory. Some aspects and levels of community organization may fit part of this model, while other levels sharply deviate from it. In our view, then, local community organization is a much more complex—and not always successful—effort to specialize different levels of the local community so as to preserve its informal and voluntary charcter at the lower levels while becoming progressively instrumental and formal at the higher levels. Thus, in this sequence of forms, community organization can preserve the unitary interests of the most localized residential groups while also engaging them in the more adversarial pattern of partisan politics. The potential of communi-

[4]Evaluation research of community organizations seems especially off the mark because it takes as its starting point a definition of the local community as both an all-purpose voluntary organization (an antidote against everything from delinquency to divorce) and one with a highly specific set of agreed-upon instrumentalities. One theme of this research has been to look for changes in various indices of pathology after very short periods of "community organizing." As Henry McKay (1967) has argued, the therapeutic or self-healing capacities of local communities operate over the very long term, probably a generation or more. In addition, these capacities are probably most closely connected with the strength of the social bloc than the more contrived levels of community.

Another line of inquiry in evaluation research has been to focus on the "representativeness" of community organization and its capacity to include previously excluded groups from the local political process. This is probably a more realistic approach to the evaluation of organizational communities, but to be effective, evaluation research needs to be extended to include investigations on the capacity of these more representative organizations to reconcile competing interests and link themselves to broader forms of metropolitan, state, and national political organization.

ty organization is to articulate the interests of differing-ordered social segments and differing streams of public opinion with the partisan political structure of the wider metropolis. In this capacity it is most comparable to the old-line political machine. At its lowest levels (precinct or social bloc) it demands favors and various means of circumventing bureaucratic rigidities, both of which probably reduce hostility to the political system by humanizing some of the contacts between citizen and government. At the next level (ward or organizational community), however, its members are willing to trade their voices or votes to influence front-line service delivery agencies. And beyond that level (political party or aggregated metropolitan community) at least some members are willing to engage in the trade-offs and pursuit of common interests that embrace large regions of the metropolis, and, finally, to press their (political coalition or lobby) voices in the halls of Congress or the White House.

The general task, then, is not a specific objective, for example, to reduce delinquency or increase reading scores—although those goals are laudatory—but is one of mounting public opinion so that the local citizenry achieves a more effective interface with the institutions which are charged with dealing with delinquency and basic literacy. In this respect we believe that the importance of the local community in its variant forms has increased as the capacity of local political parties has declined. In effect, in the past the political parties in metropolitan areas were community organizations. Over time they have, to a large extent, lost their base in the local community with the growing scale of organization, the fragmentation of the metropolitan area, and the separation of place of residence and place of work. As the local political parties have remained attached primarily to workplace organizations, the local community has been faced with the prospect of creating its own parallel organization. This organization is far from complete, but nonetheless the demands of community groups are being pressed with increasing vigor. Indeed, the mainline political parties have become so disarticulated that on many issues concerning the quality of life, citizens' groups are essential in order to overcome legislative deadlocks and inaction.

Broadly speaking, then, community organizations strive to articulate public opinion. Their goals are to (1) mobilize opinion within social blocs, small and intimate enough to trust one another and to be frank with one another; (2) make compromises with other social blocs in order to advance their interests; (3) balance their disagreements and aspirations through compromises and trade-offs with other communities, and (4) seek to shape policies at the highest levels of the nation-state. While community groups perform incidental services, mainly information exchange, they do not do psychiatry, law enforcement, or divorce law. They may be effective in trying to get other people—specialists—to do these services.

If the programs community groups activate fail, it does not necessarily mean that community organization is a failure. At times, the demands we make upon community organization or the services they are encouraged to seek have no precise or clearly operational remedial technology. But there is a real advantage in confronting the shortcomings of social technology. By having a voice in public decisions, at least some community members undergo an educational experience in which they come to recognize the shortcomings of the contemporary professional world. While not all social problems are intractable, numerous are—or at least they are not tractable to ready legislation, professional treatment, or ideological conversion. Therefore, community organizations progressively educate people to the view that many problems are their own. Reconciliation to the possible does represent an advance over professionally inspired utopianism.

In this respect, community organizaton may help eliminate exaggerated expectations and reconcile community members to limited practices, as well as to effective traditional ones. There are, of course, specific goals that can be achieved through public policy and community organization. Learning what they are is one of the signal aims of community organization. Indeed the research findings of sociologists here are probably persuasive only if they can be incorporated in the experiential base of community groups. Being willing to wait—to continue to discuss events and make known one's losses or gains—depends upon a public that has enough involvement in public policy so that the debate is continued rather than foreshortened by bureaucratic fiat or another round of presumed innovations. In the absence of ready and effective solutions, patient debate is a virtue. It is a virtue not only because it continues exploration rather than foreclosing it by coercion, but because it permits differential levels of discontent to surface along with an assessment of the relative needs for remediation. To the extent that community groups halt the advance to "final solutions"—utopian or coercive—they make incremental solutions more feasible. If the goal of keeping debate effective was not a federal assignment to community groups during the War on Poverty, it is clearly vital to their contemporary organizational forms.

## Conclusion

In describing modern urban society, Louis Wirth (1938) was in error in forecasting that the size, heterogeneity, and impersonality would gradually eliminate all forms of territorially based community. Yet he did foreshadow the systemic problems to which community organization is a response. At the time Wirth wrote, the sheer size and anonymity of the city, its ethnic heterogeneity, and its reliance on formal organizations seemed likely to make it a thoroughly impersonal and disorderly place to live. However, these very features of the city seem to have provided the initiative for a variety of new social forms: the residential enclave, ethnic associations, the parish house, the settlement movement, local political organizations, and so on. Indeed, one might almost reverse Wirth's formulation to say that those elements which he saw as barriers to the persistence of the local community were in fact the key conditions which led to its proliferation and transformation. They are not rural communities transported to an urban setting, but significant ways of linking urban residential groups to the wider, impersonal organizations that Wirth thought would replace the territorial community.

W. I. Thomas, Park, and Burgess continually searched for a formula which would reconcile their observation of community life in the city with the obvious large-scale trends in the metropolis and the nation-state. The local community was not just a retreat from the wider society, but a territorial unit which could effectively link itself to the wider society because it possessed some degree of autonomy and internal order. Burgess was especially mindful of this and in presenting his "Community Areas of Chicago" as he sought (rather unsuccessfully) to have the boundaries of major service agencies coincide with them on the argument that residents might better exert influence over these services. As his papers make clear, Burgess saw his community areas as a growing strategy of citizen influence rather than just a documentation of their existence.

Our intent in this chapter has been to explore within the contemporary urban setting the alternative formulation to "the decline of the community" that Thomas and Burgess sought to make explicit. Our approach draws on Julian Steward's more cumulative theory of social change and particularly his notion of new levels of sociocultural integration (1955). The distinctive features of the contemporary metropolis are not encompassed by the dimensions of size, its heterogeneity, and its impersonality; more central are the growing scale of organization, its fragmentation, and the increasing separation of place of work and place of residence. They represent the systemic problems to which community organization seeks a solution just as size, heterogeneity, and impersonality represented the systemic problems of urban life a half-century ago. The emerging result is not a "mosaic of little worlds" but an increasingly specialized hierarchy of territorial organizations linked to one another and linked to the wider society. At the present time these levels of community are still in an "experimental stage" and open to alternative interpretations and different efforts at "institution building." A determinate sequence of evolutionary steps is not implied. Nonetheless, in the context of the 1970s, as other forms of popular representation have been seriously weakened, these experimental efforts at institution building have an enlarged significance.

# 12

# Structural Differentiation and the Family: A Quiet Revolution

*Judith Blake*

MANY OF OUR VENERATED sociological notions about the modern American family are undergoing rapid revision. The ideal type of the "isolated," structurally differentiated nuclear unit—a neat product of the industrial process—has lost credibility (Parsons, 1942, 1943, 1955, 1965, 1971; Smelser, 1968*a*, 1968*b*). This family's social, as distinct from structural, isolation from the rest of kin has been shown, perhaps not surprisingly, to be less than was initially depicted.[1]

Even more serious, historical sociology and demography, blossoming particularly during the past fifteen years, have suggested that many characteristics of the "modern" Western family evolved prior to industrialization, rather than as a concomitant of it.[2] Late marriage, relatively low average fertility, independence of a vast lineage or clan, nuclear residence rules,

[1]Although Parsons and his followers emphasized the structural isolation of the nuclear family from the rest of kin—particularly a neolocal residence rule, a bilateral descent rule, and the separation of the family from work—Parsonians also elaborated on the social isolation from kin as well. The latter has been extensively studied since the 1950s and it seems fair to say that the social isolation appears rather considerably less than the Parsonians believed to be the case (see Litwak, 1965, and (in the same volume) Sussman, 1965; see also Sussman, 1959; Klatsky, 1972; Rosenberg and Anspach, 1973). For a discussion of the literature on child care by relatives among working-class families, see Woolsey, 1977.

[2]The rise of historical sociology and demography has carried with it an inevitable increase in controversy over specifics. For example, Laslett's work on preindustrial households (which, unfortunately, did not clearly distinguish between residence rules and descent groups) has given rise to a considerable "backlash" among historians of the European family (Laslett, 1970, 1972, 1977; Wrigley, 1977). Many feel that the use of census data is too simplistic, that European kinship structure was more complex and varied than was the case in England, and that there were important stratificational differences, as well as differences according to land tenure (see Berkner, 1972, 1975; Goody, 1972; Heers, 1968, 1974; and Goubert, 1977).

structured opportunities for social and geographical mobility—the list lengthens almost annually—set preindustrial Western peoples quite apart from most of the major underdeveloped countries of today. Our preindustrial past, although a "world we have lost," is closer to us in form than had previously been suspected. In fact, the preindustrial Western family may have been an important condition of industrialization rather than vice versa.

We are thus faced with a familiar problem in the study of social change. Research efforts to epitomize a "beginning" and a "terminal" point between which the changes have occurred generate almost instantaneous feedback among scholars, since the specification of such heuristically "frozen" points inevitably raises questions of validity. Consequently, we are seeing an upsurge of research activity about both the nature of the beginning point and of the present state of affairs.[3]

With respect to the latter, most of the controversy in sociology concerning the "structurally differentiated" and specialized nuclear family of modern American society has centered on whether there has, in fact, been as much isolation from kin as the Parsonians supposed.[4] For present purposes, I shall assume that this issue has successfully been laid to rest by Litwak, Sussman, Klatsky, and others.

Here I want to turn to another facet of the problem. This is the diminishing validity, as applied to the nuclear family of the 1970s, of the notion of structural differentiation.

As is well known, according to the Parsonians, the modern nuclear family has undergone progressive specialization of functions. Instead of being a primary economic and educational unit, it has relinquished these tasks to other agencies and "freed" itself to specialize in reproduction, socialization, emotional support (a private "haven" for the man who must "do bat-

---

The fact is, however, that the peculiarities of Western European kinship extend further than mere size of household or residence rules. Although there may have been exceptions among ruling families and the like, it does appear that descent was reckoned bilaterally, that marriage was (by world standards) late, that de facto neolocal residence occurred over most of a married couple's life (even if the stem family was ideal), that Western European society had unique channels for social mobility and major nonkinship institutions such as feudalism and guilds, as well as being dominated by an institution—the Catholic church—that, as world religions go, had a most unusual lack of articulation with kinship. For this kind of information we do not depend entirely, or even primarily, on censuses. I believe it is the entire complex of characteristics, rather than any one, which is so significant. For a variety of data on characteristics other than household size per se, see Hajnal (1965) and, in the same volume, articles by Eversley, Peller, and Helleiner. (See also, Wrigley, 1969; Coale, 1973; Demeny, 1968; van de Walle, 1968; Live-Bacci, 1968; Davis and Blake, 1956; and Blake, 1965.)

[3]For a discussion of the selection of beginning and ending points in the study of social change, see Smelser (1968*c*:192–280, especially 202–5).

[4]See references in footnote 1 above. An additional dialogue of great interest concerns the general relationship of family form (in particular, type of descent) and societal complexity. Goode (1963) has assumed something of a linear relationship between the isolated nuclear family (isolated in the sense of descent and residence rules) and modernization. For an alternative, and comparative, perspective, see Nimkoff and Middleton (1960) and Winch and Blumberg (1968).

tle'' in the outside world), and status ascription for women and children.[5] Moreover, the nuclear family is regarded, by the Parsonians, as increasingly the only source for such functions, and as greatly set apart from the economic and other nonfamilial spheres of American society. Indeed, only one family member is believed to make a significant connection with this outside world—the male breadwinner. This structural differentiation of the nuclear family has not been seriously challenged, and it is this task that will be undertaken here.

I shall argue that we are witnessing a significant decline in the specialization of the ''typical'' nuclear family on its residual, structurally differentiated tasks of reproduction, socialization, psychological support, and status ascription by the breadwinner. I believe that many seemingly disparate indicators of familial changes can profitably be subsumed under the following rubric: a major decrease in the functional specialization of the nuclear family. Alternative mechanisms for fulfilling the functions are becoming salient, but even more significant is the fact that the family as we know it is becoming less bounded and, additionally, more articulated with the rest of the society.

As for the lack of bounding, it is less and less clear that marriage defines whether an adult is inside or outside the boundaries. Nor is it obvious anymore that every child (in order not to be an outcast) must have a sociological father—that is, be legitimate. Moreover, although there is still an inevitable distinction between parenthood and nonparenthood, the social significance of this difference has been diminishing over the life cycle because of the marked decline in family size. Given close spacing and small families, married couples who have had children nonetheless spend a high proportion of their lives without offspring domiciled at home. As for actual articulation of family members with the nonfamilial sectors of the society, it is currently no longer self-evident that one person alone forges the link with the occupational structure, or that the status of the family rests uniquely with that individual. Finally, although at one time it may have been true that the modern middle-class family was emotionally ''privatized''—a refuge from economic engagement and a sheltered cocoon for child rearing and socialization, this interpretation seems questionable today.

Why are these changes occurring and why do they appear to signal a genuine familial transformation, rather than an erratic or temporary stream of events? To begin with, the structurally differentiated family has generated serious internal sources of strain. This was true even when it was functioning as it was supposed to function—perhaps in the 1950s, perhaps only in the minds of its delineators. Parsons himself provided some of the most devastating descriptions of role stress, although he seemed to take them for granted and did not appear to perceive in them the seeds of change.[6] A number of other sociologists viewed them in strongly ideological or revolu-

[5]See references to Parsons and Smelser.

[6]See selections from Parsons.

tionary terms, however (see B. Moore, 1958:160–77; Lasch, 1965, especially pp. 38–68). These sources of strain included the fact that the housewife-mother role was really only a "pseudo-occupation" and that it was cut off from externally validated achievement in a society emphasizing this goal. Also involved were serious problems of youthful socialization and career choice, protraction of the child status until well into chronological adulthood, and severe status changes upon retirement.

Furthermore, the rest of the society could not function adequately under the schedule of assumptions implicit in extreme familial differentiation. For example, although the labor-force concepts of "secondary" or "marginal" workers assumed that the "real" workers were the male breadwinners, the fact is that the economy could not operate without its so-called marginal workers—notably women. Modern industrial societies that have had a less responsive female labor force—for example, Switzerland—have had to import a relatively huge foreign supply of labor to take up the slack. Efforts by European countries to mythologize themselves into believing that these imports were temporary have backfired badly.[7] In effect, the economic withdrawal of women in industrial societies has not proven to be a viable structural pattern.

Other, more ominous, indications of external problems relate to the difficulty of educating young people, solely through the school system, for adult roles (see Coleman, 1972, 1974), together with the unwillingness of high proportions of youngsters to endure the deferred gratification involved in long years of schooling and childlike social status.

Complementing these internal and external sources of tension has been an absence of mechanisms for integrating the differentiated family with the rest of the society. To a great extent, the segregated role structure, described by Parsons, assumed that familial specialization was so "functionally suited" to modern life that the strains outlined above were really idiosyncratic personality malfunctions, or unusual perturbations of the economy. Only a "neurotic" woman would be troubled by a "pseudo-occupation," and only a war economy (or some similar crisis) would require heavy doses of extra workers. It has become increasingly clear that extreme familial role segregation can be regarded as suited to a society like ours only if we overlook entirely the extraordinary dysfunctions of this arrangement.

Finally, intrinsic to the modern American family, like so many family systems elsewhere in time and space, has been an absence of "fall-back

[7]The saga of the "temporary" workers in many European countries during the post-World War II period has occasioned a literature unto itself. In the case of each country, the initial wave of migration was explicitly regarded as temporary—as alleviating a momentary problem. From that point on, each country of heavy immigration experienced a reconfiguration of the status of the migrants, to the extent that Turks, Yugoslavs, North Africans, and so on are now permanent fixtures in many European countries. Although the immigration pattern has not, to my knowledge, been related to the relative inflexibility of the supply of female labor offered, the connection is an important one. For an introduction to this problem, see, for example, Böhning, 1972, and, K. Mayer, 1972. For comparative rates of growth of the female labor force in developed countries, see Blake, 1974.

positions'' for individuals who were not taken care of within the basic set of assumptions. Thus, a cadre of dissatisfied customers was generated—individuals who welcomed a change in familial ground rules.

Given the strains, it is hardly surprising that the need for change would be widely recognized. A number of conditions have helped it actually to transpire. For one, many of the people involved in the major sources of stress have been high on the scale of awareness and personal efficacy. Growing numbers of women and young people have been comparatively well educated and are very knowledgeable about what goes on within the family. After all, they have had the system under observation. This fact, together with the ''demystifying'' effects of the social sciences and the media (taken jointly and separately), have demolished many of the supporting mythologies of the differentiated family. And the inability of the society at large to manage with so much familial specialization has generated an important opportunity structure for nonbelievers in the various myths—whether these be that wifely dependency is advantageous economically for most women, or that a normal teenager is like a character out of the Andy Hardy family.

So, I would argue, we have had a classic set of bases for change. The insiders experience pain, and the people who are left out suffer, too; the society is less well served by familial differentiation than has been alleged; for a variety of reasons, awareness increases; and alternatives emerge that are rapidly being legitimated. These developments are, moreover, occurring without a political revolution, and in a context allowing for impressive amounts of incremental trial and error at the popular level.[8] Such a situation would seem to provide the basis for far more lasting change than one resulting from a major political revolution, in which edicts regarding the family are abruptly handed down from on high.

## Indications of the Decline in Structural Differentiation

Let us now examine some indications of the decline in structural differentiation. I shall consider these in terms of a set of diminishing distinctions between marriage and nonmarriage; having children and remaining childless; legitimate and illegitimate childbearing; being a wife/mother and participating in the labor force; and, finally, between family ''privacy'' and the external society.

[8]This paper does not discuss the revival of the commune tradition in American society, because a semicontractual imitation of a residentially extended family seems to be the least auspicious of recent popular efforts to modify the structurally differentiated unit. Problems of solidarity, control, and succession in communes have been ably discussed by a number of modern sociologists (see, for example, Kanter, 1972; Zablocki, 1971).

## THE BLURRING DISTINCTION BETWEEN MARRIAGE AND NONMARRIAGE

Two salient features of American mating behavior in recent years represent, I believe, a major blurring of the distinction between marriage and nonmarriage. These are the increase in open, informal domiciliary relationships and the rise in divorce.

### THE RISE IN INFORMAL AND OPEN DOMICILIARY RELATIONSHIPS

Since 1960, the number of unmarried couples residing together in the same quarters has more than doubled—rising from 439,000 in 1960 to 957,000 in 1977.[9] Most of this change has taken place since 1970. According to Glick and Norton, by March 1977 some two million persons were involved in such domiciliary arrangements. The largest rise has been among individuals in two-person households. The change is, moreover, apparently even greater than the gross statistics suggest because there has been an apparent decrease since 1960 in the proportion of these domiciles that constituted a landlord-tenant arrangement. According to Glick and Norton, detailed analysis of the ages of the participants over time indicates that more unmarried, cohabiting couples now consist of a young man and woman living together, whereas, in 1960, unmarried couples were composed of higher proportions of older women with young male tenants.

Although increasing, are such arrangements of any proportionate significance in American society? Considering unmarried adults of all ages, some 3.6 percent were in such households. But, taking couple-households where the husband or man was under age twenty-five, 7.4 percent were nonmarital rather than marital. We are still some distance from Sweden, where some 12 percent of all couples live together informally (only 2 percent of all couples are thus situated here), but the younger generation of Americans is approaching the Swedish level.[10]

About 25 percent of unmarried couples under age twenty-five residing together appear to be still students, and unmarried couples generally have a higher probability of being poor. Yet, most informally cohabiting couples are above the poverty line (65 percent of the women and 79 percent of the men in 1977), and a healthy minority (18 percent of the women and 34 percent of men) had annual incomes in 1977 at least three times the poverty level, or about $15,000 on the average.

These arrangements indicate a rise in the number of couples who have elected to be married in every way but formally. Moreover, as most of us

[9]The data included in this section are based on the research of Paul Glick and Arthur Norton (1977 in particular, and especially pp. 32–36).

[10]For a comparative Swedish perspective, see Trost, 1976.

know from personal experience, such configurations do not set the participants apart from normal social intercourse, even if marriage is still generally "preferred." Thus, unmarried couples who wish to reside together and thereby have the convenience, companionship, and many of the economic advantages of being married (but fewer of the disadvantages) are able to do so today with minimal penalties.[11]

Whether such arrangements are of equal respective benefit to the men and women involved depends on an assessment of the relative opportunity costs of marriage and nonmarriage, as well as the freedom each sex has to reshuffle the marital decision as time goes by. The traditional view has been that women, being dependent on marriage economically as well as being the passive recipients of a "proposal," should strike a good match while their physical attractions are greatest—that is, while young (see Davis, 1976, 1977). These ground rules have undergone some revision. The opportunity costs for women in marrying have risen substantially as job opportunities have improved.[12] This is particularly true since the economic security of marriage has greatly diminished. As will be discussed, marriages are deeply threatened with impermanence because of divorce, and it is becoming increasingly evident that a divorced woman is typically left without much support (Weitzman, 1972). Hence, although there has not been a revolution in women's job chances, it is nonetheless true that fidelity to the labor market may pay off better for a young woman than fidelity to a husband.[13] This is particularly true since the law still holds to some genuinely archaic notions

[11] Speaking of the California Supreme Court's landmark decision in *Marvin* v. *Marvin*, Kay and Amyx (1977) say that, "the court fashioned a remedy appropriate for use in any state, regardless of the underlying form of its marital property law. The court has thus taken the lead in recognizing the factual existence of a variety of familial relationships—ranging from marriage through nonmarital cohabitation—affording to each its characteristic set of legal incidents. California's citizens are therefore offered a wide choice among legally sanctioned alternatives within which they may work out their own private arrangements." (In this connection, seel also *Harvard Law Review*, 1977).

[12] William Butz has postulated that the correlation of prosperity with women's job opportunities in the United States has led to an economically countercyclical trend in fertility— an association of cyclical prosperity with declines in the birth rate. For a discussion of new trends in women's opportunity-costs in marriage and childbearing, see Butz and Ward, 1977. For additional discussion, see Blake, 1974.

[13] Kay and Amyx (1977:974–75) say, "The concept that traditional marriage is a status that protects women has been vigorously attacked for some time. As early as 1855 the well-known legal disabilities imposed on married women by the common law which Blackstone had asserted were designed for the wife's protection and benefit were specifically rejected by Lucy Stone and her husband, Henry Blackwell, in their *Marriage Protest*, because such laws 'confer upon the husband an injurious and unnatural superiority, investing him with legal powers which no honorable man would exercise, and which no man should possess.' Some feminists have concluded that legal marriage is inherently oppressive for women and have dedicated themselves to its abolition; others have turned their efforts toward reform laws governing marriage and divorce in an effort to make the institution more nearly analogous to a partnership. Still others have explored contracts that alter the obligations of traditional marriage. Certainly Midge Decter's assertions made in 1972 that 'every woman wants to marry' and that 'marriage is something asked by women and agreed to by men' have been belied by the facts."

of the trade-offs within marriage—the man is the "provider" and the woman exchanges services for support (Weitzman, 1972). Most states regard property as the husband's, unless otherwise specified, and the husband's earnings are regarded as his as well.[14] Since virtually no provision exists for recognizing the market value of the housewife's time, a woman who devotes herself to home and family may, for her efforts, discover herself to be severely undervalued should the marriage dissolve (Krauskopf, 1977). Moreover, public and private social security and pension plans by and large sorely discriminate against a divorced wife, unless the marriage has been of very long duration.

It is thus true that many women may enter nonmarital relatonships today on a basis of greater relative equality than in the past. And it is not necessarily true that their attractiveness is as evanescent as has been claimed. Women's premature loss of attractiveness (compared with men) is itself highly correlated with marriage and childbearing. Insofar as exercise, diet, personal attention, and fashion all take time and effort, many women's preoccupation with keeping up houses, husbands, and children, instead of themselves, itself contributes to a self-fulfilling prophecy regarding diminishing good looks.

### THE RISE IN DIVORCE

Since the late 1950s the divorce rate has climbed precipitously. Although it seems currently to have leveled out, it has done so at a point unprecedented in our statistical history—five divorces annually per 1,000 population. To be sure, during some of the period between 1955 and the present, the rise in divorce was due to the growth of the married population and to changes in the age distribution of married persons. However, in recent years almost all of the rise has been nondemographic in cause.[15] Married persons are just divorcing at higher rates. As a consequence, Glick and Norton (1977:36–37) have estimated that approximately 40 percent of all marriages

[14] Kay and Amyx say, "Within the last 5 years the [California] Legislature has repealed former Civil Code section 5101, which, since the days of the Field Code, had declared the husband to be the 'head of the family,' has equalized family support obligations, has extended to wives a power equal to that formerly held exclusively by husbands to manage and control the community property during their joint lifetimes and after the death of one spouse, and has mandated the extension of credit to married women on the same terms it is granted to married men. As Professor Prager has persuasively shown, California marital property law for the first time in its history now recognizes the spouses as true partners. Similarly, the California Attorney General has acknowledged the right of a woman to retain her birth name after marriage, and the case law has permitted her to resume her former name after divorce regardless of whether she has custody of minor children." (See Kay and Amyx, 1977:952–53.) Glendon (1975) discusses very recent changes in family law in European countries and the United States—changes involving "our increasing recognition of the individual liberty of the spouses."

[15] Plateris (1978) has estimated that the population component of the rise in divorce declined from 47 percent during 1955–1963 to 12 percent during 1963–1975.

of young adults will, at current rates, end in divorce. Such rates mean that substantial numbers of persons experience a divorce in any given year. During 1975, divorces exceeded one million for the first time in our history, and provisional figures for 1977 found us with 1.097 million divorces for that year.

Obviously, this large number of divorces annually does not occur with equal probability among all age groups. Divorce rates by age of husband at decree show that the highest probabilities of divorce occur between the ages of 20 and 34. At ages 20–24, the rate in 1970 was 33.6 per 1,000 married in each age group, at age 25–29 it was 30.0, and at 30–34 it was 22.3. Such rates contrast with 14.2 for married persons of all ages (Plateris, 1978:37). If we had more recent data by age, we know that the rates would be much higher.

The statistical picture thus suggests that the line between marriage and nonmarriage is blurring even among married couples. With almost 1.10 million divorce decrees being granted annually, millions of married couples must be on the road to dissolution at any given time. Moreover, such rates of dissolution imply that the population is building up large numbers of people who have been divorced. Census data for the mid-1970s indicate that among women (divorced at ages 14–75), 9.068 million with a first marriage experienced a divorce. Assuming comparable figures for men, this means that some 18 million Americans alive in 1975 had had a first marriage dissolved by divorce. To be sure, most divorced people remarry (for example, among childless women under age 30 at divorce, some 80 percent remarry), but this in itself makes the distinction between marriage and divorce even less clear.

## A BLURRING BETWEEN FAMILIAL AND OCCUPATIONAL ROLES

A major component of the structural differentiation of the modern nuclear family has been its withdrawal from the world of work. Yet, as we approach 1980, this characterization of the American family has become quaint. It appears that this aspect of the structural differentiation, so vaunted in the sociology of the 1950s and early 1960s, has been obscured almost totally. No longer is there a single breadwinner during most of the family cycle; no longer can one conceive of the status of the family as depending almost entirely on his efforts; in fact, no longer is he always the highest earner, nor does he invariably have the higher-status occupation. The world of work and the family have been reunited in the persons of both husband and wife, father and mother. Finally, as the husband and wife age, the "breadwinner" for them both is typically located in another generation and outside of any direct family connection. The backbone of family sustenance becomes an intergenerational transfer payment from the men and women in the society who are currently working. Let us look at the evidence.

### MARRIED WOMEN AND MOTHERS IN THE LABOR FORCE

Between 1960 and 1975 there was an increase of 28 percent in the labor force participation of married women, husband present. By the mid-1970s almost one-half (44 percent) of all women in this marital status category were market participants. Among young childless women (under age 35), husband present, 77 percent were in the labor force in 1975, a rise of 24 percent from 1960 among even this group of women who were traditionally prone to work. However, the really startling news, of course, has been the 64 percent rise, since 1960, in work participation by mothers, husband present, with children under age three (from 23 to 37 percentage points), and the increase of 43 percent among mothers of three- to five-year-olds (from 29 to 42 percentage points—see Glick and Norton, 1977:11). Thus, the traditional association between legitimate childbearing for women and withdrawal from market work has changed quite drastically over the past fifteen years. This change has occurred, moreover, without any formal policy designed to aid working women with child care, or to provide other ancillary services to them (see Rivlin, 1972; Rothman, 1973; Woolsey, 1977; also, U.S. Bureau of the Census, 1976). We must conclude that women with young children are highly motivated to enter the labor force.

### HUSBAND AND FATHER—THE "STATUS GIVER"

Concomitant with the rise in working pairs among intact married couples is a change in the notion that the husband/father is the status giver for the family. Among married couples in 1975 where both husband and wife were earners, a third of the wives made approximately as much as, or more than, the husband, and 62 percent were in an occupation in the same "major" level, ranked in terms of the Census Bureau's socioëconomic status scores (Glick and Norton, 1977:11).

This pattern of relative income equality between working mates is, of course, far more pronounced among couples where the husband's earnings are under the median for husbands with working wives, than where his earnings are higher. For example, among working couples where the husband earns less than $10,000 a year—41 percent of all working couples—the wife's earnings were approximately equal to his or more in 49 percent of the cases.[16] But among husband's with earnings of $15,000 and over—28 percent of all working couples—only 18 percent of the wives were in roughly

[16] See Glick and Norton (1977:11); the actual median earnings in 1975 for husbands in families where both spouses were earners, was $11,370.

the same bracket or higher. It is nonetheless true that, for a significant proportion of working couples, the wife, through market work, is not only making an important *marginal* contribution to the family's economic status, she is making an *absolute* one equal to or greater than her husband.

Quite clearly, as Oppenheimer has suggested, a major erosion has occurred in the notion of the husband/father as chief status giver or principal earner. "Structural differentiation" theorists were interested in developing a "functional imperative theory." But, as Oppenheimer (1974) says,

> By definition, such theories are statements of the necessity of the status quo—unfortunately, in this case, the status quo of some 35 years ago, not of today. The only change such a theory tends to permit is that from social order to social disorder. As such, theories of this nature are not particularly useful tools in the analysis of the types of change which do not involve the disintegration of the social system.

## Family Status of Highly Educated and High-Status Women

We have seen that women who have attained conventional wifely status are increasingly articulating with the world of work and helping to define the social position of their families. In considering the erosion of familial specialization, it is also important to focus on the familial participation of highly educated women and female occupational stars. Are such women as likely as in the past to remain unmarried, or are they more apt to combine high-level educational and/or occupational status with marriage? In effect, does a feminine "success" role in the nonfamilial world still greatly reduce the probability of being married?

As for educational level, between 1960 and 1975, women with graduate training have scored the largest gains of any educational group (male or female) in the proportion married once with spouse present by middle age (or near it). During the fifteen-year period, these women had a 136 percent gain in this category (Glick and Norton, 1977:10). Even by 1975, however, it was still true that highly educated women (by late adult or middle age) were married to their first spouse in smaller proportions (63 percent) than women of any other educational category except those with 0–11 years of schooling. In addition, they were 19 percentage points lower than men of comparable schooling—a gain, however, over the 25 percentage point differential of 1960.

These results reflect not simply greater marital stability on the part of high-status women, but a higher probability of marrying at all than was the case as recently as twenty years ago. Taking major occupational groupings of employed persons, comparison over the past decade alone indicates that women in the two highest occupational categories—professional and managerial—were more likely in 1976 to be married with a husband present than approximately two decades earlier (1958). For example, proportions in this marital status among professional women increased from 52 to 62 percent, and among managers from 59 to 64 percent. Among the remaining occupational categories combined, the proportions married (husband present) rose from 53.1 to 55.5 percent.[17]

These data suggest important changes in the structural differentiation of the nuclear family and, as well, a major motivational reconfiguration for modern women. A salient goal of women's movements the world over—the freedom of women to combine familial and major occupational roles (just as men do)—is closer to achievement than has ever been the case before (B. Friedan, 1963:381–82; Rossi, 1964; Epstein, 1970:99–100).

### INTERGENERATIONAL TRANSFER PAYMENTS AS "THE BREADWINNER"

As we have seen, married men in intact households are less and less likely to be the sole breadwinners. Moreover, people generally are, as they age, becoming more dependent upon younger workers of both sexes to make transfer payments to them (Kreps, 1965:268). Since the century began, there has been a drastic decline in the labor force participation of older men. Among men aged 65 and over, the rate of labor force participation has fallen from 68.3 percent in 1900 to 20.1 percent in 1977. Since 1960 alone, the rate dropped from 33.1 percent. Even among men aged 55–64 years of age, labor force participation has fallen. Between 1960 and 1977, market attachment among these men declined from 86.8 to 74.0. Most of this change has occurred during the 1970s (U.S. Bureau of the Census, 1977*b*).

As Kreps has emphasized, sources of income of the aged in recent years have reflected the changing work-retirement pattern of older men. The proportion of income from current earnings among older persons declined substantially during the 1950s at the same time that the proportion derived from social insurance benefits increased. Kreps (1965:271) says,

> Of the 1960 aggregate income of persons aged 65 and over, income from earnings totalled between ten and eleven billion dollars, and approximately the same amount went to recipients of old-age, survivors, and disability insurance and to retired government and railroad employees. This one-to-one ratio of earnings to benefit payments contrasts sharply with the composition of the income of the aged a decade earlier, when aggregate earnings of seven to eight billion dollars amounted to several times as much as benefit payments.

By 1967, among all aged units (married and unmarried), earnings represented only 30 percent of income. Of the remainder, 37 percent was from retirement benefits (mostly OASDHI), and 6 percent was from veterans'

[17] Figures derived from *Handbook of Labor Statistics 1977*, tables 18 and 28, and *Handbook of Labor Statistics 1975*, tables 19 and 29 (see U.S. Department of Labor, 1977*a*, 1975*c*).

benfits and public assistance. Income from assets comprised 25 percent of total income.[18]

It is thus true that although direct intrafamilial and in-kind transfers to the older population may have declined, there has been an enormous increase in intergenerational transfers of income—from the working population to the aging. Aging persons are no longer primarily dependent on the direct efforts of the male breadwinner, nor are they economically isolated from the rest of the society.

## THE INCREASING AMBIGUITY OF MARRIAGE AS THE LICENSING OF PARENTHOOD

Two additional trends in American society have served to obscure the structurally differentiated status of the family. Both relate to the notion of marriage as, in Malinowski's (1930) words, the "licensing of parenthood." On the one hand, over the past thirty years there has been a burgeoning of illegitimate births. And correlative with the surge in births without marriage is the voluntary expansion in marriages without births.

### THE RISE IN ILLEGITIMACY AND MALINOWSKI'S "PRINCIPLE"

Since 1940, when national estimates became available, illegitimacy rates have risen from 7.1 per 1,000 unmarried women aged 15-44 to 24.7 in 1976.[19] The increase has been remarkably steady. Moreover, although nonwhite illegitimacy accounts for a disproportionate share of total illegitimacy, it is the rate for whites that has risen over time. This rate has increased from 3.6 per 1,000 unmarried women in 1940 to 12.7 in 1976. Although it has been declining slightly among white women over age 20, it has inflated inexorably among teenagers—from 3.3 per 1,000 unmarried white women aged 15–19 in 1940 to 12.4 in 1976.[20] Partly as a result of this advance in the illegitimacy rate, the proportion of all births that were illegitimate swelled between 1940 and 1976, from 3.8 to 14.8 percent.[21] The

[18] See Bixby, 1970, especially p. 14, giving estimates by source, using a variety of data in addition to the Current Population Survey.

[19] For data for 1940, see U.S. Department of Health, Education and Welfare, National Center for Health Statistics 1972, tables 1–30, pp. 1–30; data for 1976 from HEW National Center for Health Statistics, 1978, table 12, p. 17.

[20] The magnitude of the change in illegitimacy rates in the United States among teenagers, and between blacks and whites, is open to considerable question. On the other hand, it appears that illegitimacy in the 1950s may have been underestimated and that reporting may have been better in recent years. On the other hand, the recent official statistics cited above from the National Center for Health Statistics appear to underestimate illegitimate childbearing because they do not include data for twelve major states having high rates of illegitimacy. At the present time, we do not have corrected illegitimacy rates dating from the 1940s. For a discussion of some of the methodological problems involved, see Berkov and Sklar, 1975, and also O'Connell, 1978.

[21] For source data on illegitimacy ratios for 1940 and 1976, see footnote 19 above.

expanding illegitimacy ratio (the illegitimate proportion of all births) results as well from the decline in average family size and the effect of this trend on annual legitimate fertility.

The so-called principle of legitimacy—as enunciated by Malinowski—was a statement about institutional norms. It referred to an astonishingly widespread—if not absolutely universal—rule that for a child to have a socially legitimated status in a society, it must be acknowledged by a sociological father—"the male link between the child and the rest of the community" (Malinowski, 1930). Obviously, however, the "principle" is not fixed in time and space like a fly in amber—it is based on certain prior assumptions. Among these are the following: that a "father" is *the* person who links the child with the community and accords status; and that, in general, the society strongly supports status ascription on the basis of familial origin.[22] As Malinowski knew, the "principle" is a theory not just about the family, but about society.

In most societies where legitimacy is not the statistical norm, such as the Caribbean and parts of Latin America, the principle really still holds in spite of the frequency of illegitimacy. This is because in these societies, men are the status givers and the societies are highly ascriptive (Blake, 1961). On the other hand, as Goode and others have pointed out, the "principle" obviously carries less weight, on a day-to-day basis, in a society where most births are illegitimate than in one where such deviation from the norm is unusual. Illegitimate children are nonetheless punished for not having a father because the role of women is not such as to compensate for this lack.[23]

In the United States, I believe that we must not regard the rise in illegitimacy as primarily indicating a breakdown of "control" over sexual relations and reproduction, while reproductive and familial norms remain unchanged. Rather, this rise is a natural result of the fact that we are subscribing less and less to the assumptions upon which the so-called principle is based. Consequently, the sanctions for premarital childbearing are less awesome. The trend in illegitimacy is, therefore, no longer so much an indicator of deviance as of the abrogation of many prior norms supporting the principle of legitimacy.[24] Obviously, in almost every conceivable

[22] For an analysis of the status-ascriptive assumptions involved in the "principle," see Goode, 1960, Coser and Coser, 1973.

[23] It may be true that, given economic and social conditions in such societies, a father would not add much economically and, hence, in such conditions it is hardly worth bothering to legitimize offspring. However, I believe that this interpretation is overdrawn because all such calculations are made at the margin and in context. In *that* context, the man can make a contribution, and this would be particularly true were his involvement with only one set of children. Societies experiencing far more intense poverty than in the Caribbean and Latin America will nonetheless adhere in practice to the principle of legitimacy.

[24] In a number of Euorpean countries, and to a great extent in the United States, illegitimacy has become virtually irrelevant legally (see Fritz, 1977). Coser and Coser's (1973) analysis concentrates on the case of genuine, acknowledged social revolutions in which the "principle" was abolished for the explicit purpose of abolishing the status-conferring role of the

respect, illegitimate children still fare less well, on the average, than legitimate ones (Berkov and Sklar, 1972). Indeed, even if, for example, the large wage gap between men and women lessened, welfare payments to single mothers increased, and child-care arrangements expanded and improved, parity might never be achieved. That it should be both considered and attempted, however, is momentous.[25]

The rising refusal to allow a child's fate to be hitched to whether its father serves as a status giver correlates with a legally enforced norm that life chances should be decreasingly family-dependent. Such legal enforcements, as, for example, in Supreme Court decisions regarding school integration, may not accord proportionate advantage to the disadvantaged. These decisions do, however, keep the advantaged on the run and have the effect of damping the de facto enjoyment of superior social and economic status, and lessening the subjective sense of advantage due to birth.[26] In this sense, the more redistributive the society becomes, the less "status" either parent has to confer on children and the more blurred are the distinctions between legitimate and illegitimate offspring.

In effect, for the principle of legitimacy to operate in a true Malinowskian sense presupposes a society very different from the one we now live in or toward which we appear to be headed. In particular, it is a society in which the accident of familial origin means far more for life chances than is

---

family and thereby creating greater equality of life chances. The redistributive trends in many advanced industrial societies, including our own, also bear watching, however, since numerous public policies are *implicitly* vitiating the assumptions of the principle of legitimacy, and doing so in ways that may have more staying power than has been the case with the social revolutions studied by the Cosers. In particular, the role of women in such advanced societies today is potentially somewhat different from their roles after the French, Russian, Chinese, or Cuban revolutions. There is, of course, nothing less ascriptive about inheriting status from one's mother than from one's father, and many women are, indeed, in the labor force in order to give their children "advantages," even when there is a father present.

[25] The provisions of AFDC as they apply to men and women, respectively, assume that traditional sex roles are the desideratum, i.e., that the woman stays home with the children and the man finds a job (see Kinsley, 1977). However, given the difficulty that mothers of illegitimate children have in locating fathers and fixing responsibility, the AFDC program increasingly *functions* as a proxy second parent and cannot help but make a sociological father seem less crucial to many women. Indeed, there is a genuine trade-off for some women between having full control of less money from AFDC, as against being "supported" by a man who may himself spend most of the money he earns, and against whose physical violence the woman may actually require protection (see Straus, 1977; also, Steinmetz and Straus, 1974: passim). Taking such problems into account in assessing AFDC, we are faced, as a society, with the question of whether we wish to support family relationships or the almost unfettered dominance of a male-headed family. The two are not necessarily synonymous. The fact that this dominance is often buffered in middle- and upper-class families does not make it any less real for those women and children at poverty and working-class levels, among whom even the police and the courts tend to regard a husband's physical violence against his wife as permissible (see Straus, 1977).

[26] Indicators of economic redistribution inevitably fail to take account of the redistributive effect of changing access to public resources. Cheap means of transportation, such as the automobile and the airplane, have opened up access to recreational areas previously reserved, on a de facto basis, almost exclusively for the well-to-do. Some of the same forces have made suburban living far less safe from both crime and accident than in the past.

the case today, and in which social status depends on paternal "placement" almost exclusively.[27] As a consequence of our current situation, the designations "legitimate" and "illegitimate" have dwindled in meaning and are even becoming increasingly difficult to discover.[28] If being illegitimate is a "private" matter, supported by an individual's "right to privacy," the "principle" must have suffered a telling blow!

### THE DECLINE IN MARITAL FERTILITY AND RISING PROPORTIONS OF CHILDLESS COUPLES

If premarital childbearing is mounting, reproduction within marriage is lessening. Not only has voluntary family size been reduced substantially since the height of the baby boom, but a growing number of young people are deciding to remain childless.[29] Under current conditions, young (18–24-year-old) American women expect to complete their fertility with an average number of two births. Among these same young women, 11 percent expect to be childless, and 12 percent expect to have one child (U.S. Bureau of the Census, 1977*a*). Such expectations, combined with actual behavior that (to date) appears to be highly congruent, mean that most people will spend all but a fraction of their conjugal lives without young children at home, and that a rising proportion of couples will never expand beyond the dyad.

Not surprisingly, growing numbers of young people believe that marriage is something quite different from, or more than, the "licensing of parenthood." Although a recent national survey of attitudes toward childlessness revealed that nonparenthood lacks a "glamour" image, a scale of attitudes toward childlessness demonstrated a marked division by sex in respondents' views on children as a social investment (Blake, 1979). Men were more likely to regard childlessness as disadvantageous than women. Moreover, a multiple classification analysis showed that this difference was greater, rather than less, when a range of social and demographic background variables were controlled. Men were particularly likely to think that childlessness makes a marriage more prone to divorce. It is thus possible

[27] For a summary of trends in social mobility in the United States and in European and Soviet states, see Lipset, 1972. Lipset pays particular attention to the role of the family in perpetuating inequality through the transmission of cultural differences. See also Bell, 1972, for a discussion of some of the combined implications of the Coleman Reports, Jencks, and Rawls.

[28] In addition to the fact that most of the assumptions on which the "principle" is based are receiving diminished support, there is also strong societal backing for not directly stigmatizing the illegitimate child. Increasingly, states are becoming reluctant to include legitimacy status on birth certificates and, when it is included, efforts are made to ensure confidentiality (see Clague and Ventura, 1968; also Berkov and Sklar, 1975).

[29] During the period since 1973, the total fertility rate in the United States has averaged about 1.8 births per woman in the reproductive ages. This means that, under current age-specific birth rates, women will bear fewer than two children per woman, on the average, by the end of their reproductive years. Actual completed cohort fertility for today's young women may, of course, be higher (or lower), since annual rates may change during the next ten or fifteen years.

that the "principle of least interest" in family life, in which it is assumed that women have the largest stake in home and family, may be undergoing some reversal. Elsewhere I have suggested that a change in women's "market" situation regarding marriage and childbearing—namely, a scarcity of women available for conventional wife and mother roles—could greatly alter the terms on which such arrangement were entered (see Blake, 1974, especially p. 147).

We are thus witnessing a de facto redefinition of the social, as well as the legal, institution of marriage. Most people are, of course, almost completely unaware of the traditional legal provisions of the marriage contract. As Weitzman (1972) says,

> The marriage contract is unlike most contracts: its provisions are unwritten, its penalties unspecified, and the terms of the contract are typically unknown to the "contracting" parties. Prospective spouses are neither informed of the terms of the contract nor are they allowed any options about these terms. In fact, one wonders how many men and women would agree to the marriage contract if they were the given the opportunity to read it and to consider the rights and obligations to which they were committing themselves.

The legal realities of marriage typically only impinge on couples' definitions of their marital behavior when there is conflict. Until then, they may behave as if it were irrelevant that the husband is legally the head of the family, that he is responsible for support, that the wife is responsible for domestic and child-care services, or that marriage legally presupposes reproduction.[30] The surge of divorces is, however, making explicit the sharp divergence between current marital behavior and the state's presumed interest in preserving the traditional family. Increasingly, it is becoming evident that the anachronisms embedded in family law and the law of marriage will have to succumb to the realities of family life today (Weitzman, 1972). It would thus be foolhardy to look to family and marriage law as providing the bedrock of support for the family as it "really" is, or as indicating what familial and marital norms actually are. This area of the law is so at odds with major trends in modern family life that it must be considered a candidate for revision, rather than a guardian of stability.

## THE DEMISE OF "PRIVATIZATION"

The physically private nuclear family in its separate household has been part of the Parsonian characterization of familial specialization. Similarly, historians of the family, coming from another tradition, have argued with

[30] For recent changes in family law, both here and in Europe, see Kay and Amyx, 1977, and Glendon, 1975. See also the article by Fritz (1977) on the legal status of illegitimate children.

some force that the preindustrial, or premodern, family was far more community-oriented than the nuclear unit of modern times (Ariès, 1962; also Shorter, 1975).[31] Certainly the physical privacy of the couple and their children, so typical of the modern family in its separate quarters, did not exist in past times. Moreover, a fairly extensive historical record has been accumulated of rough and insensitive personal relationships among nuclear family members, and of singular disregard for the health and welfare of children (Ariès, 1962; Shorter, 1975). The preindustrial family was not, apparently, a tenderly guarded haven for any of its members. Interests, activities, "life," were in the community, not in the family. From this contrast with the past, some historians, like the Parsonians, have created the edifice of the "privatized" family of modern times—a family turned in on itself in the interest of performing its highly specialized functions.

Although it would be hard to argue that adults (or even children) today spend their leisure time in the community in the same way that characterized the denizens of the Middle Ages about whom Aries has written, it seems inaccurate to speak of the family of the past fifteen to twenty years as "privatized." Rather, through the mass media, the outside world has entered the home in force. Not only do the invidious comparisons of the status system impinge incessantly, but the existence of a "youth market" has generated a socializing force directed explicitly at the young (Bernard, 1961). Moreover, in recent years, radio in particular has functioned as a source of information for adolescents concerning topics such as birth control and abortion clinics, where teenagers may be assured of privacy *from* their parents.

In contrast with the 1940s and 1950s, suburban living is no longer isolated and protected from urban ways. As the city has expanded toward the suburban lands that, years ago, seemed so "countrified," and as children find themselves traveling long distances to school, the splendid isolation of midcentury has disappeared. Thus, suburban parents have today far less control over youthful environments than was the case twenty-five years ago (Friedenberg, 1959; Bensman, 1973). As a consequence, in addition to sharing its socializing function with the legally legitimate sponsors of radio and television, the family is increasingly being touched by the underworld's insistence on its quota of the youth market as well. As children mature and move into schools, playgrounds, and streets, they soon learn that they have the opportunity to "deal." This opening does not presuppose the stigma of membership in a gang of hoodlums. The chance to peddle drugs is readily afforded by the adult underworld and by the availability of customers among the peer group. In effect, the protected and sheltered child who is a product of the privatized family is, in these days, something of a myth. The off-limits cultures that impinge on middle- and upper-class children today

[31] Questions concerning the privatization argument have been raised by Lasch (1975*a*, 1975*b*) in "The Emotions of Family Life," and "What the Doctor Ordered." See also Moore, 1958.

are, by and large, not merely the covert cultures of their parents. For many parents, much of the environment of youth is genuinely foreign territory.

## Fall-back Positions, Safety Valves, and the Modern Family

We have considered familial change in relation to societal needs and functions. What about the fate of individuals in this period of domestic transformation? Here we may note that, on a per capita basis, the family has not been a wholly benign institution (see Ariès, 1962; Shorter, 1975; also Blake, 1975; Goode, 1963). Not only has it involved much strong-arming, induced dependency and status ascription, but even in the most traditional societies not everyone has been included in the tidy web of rights and obligations that it represented. Individual deviance aside, large proportions of people, in the past, have been involuntarily left out of the "typical" pattern (Levy, 1949; Homans, 1941; Uhlenberg, 1974). Not all men could marry, if some had plural wives. Indeed, if many were landless they may have been unable to marry because of this as well. Not all women have been able to bear children, nor will all have had husbands who lived out the normal life expectancy. And so it has gone.

What has happened to these people? Did they spend their lives on the outside looking in? At times, they have provided revolutionary cadres, as Levy (1949) suggested for China. At times, they have helped conquer and colonize foreign lands, or they have risen within celibate organizations such as the Catholic church, or peopled the bohemian world of the arts and other pleasures. Since, on the average, they have been nobodies rather than somebodies, we do not know a great deal about them. No history has been written from the standpoint of familial leftovers.

One thing is clear, however. Societies, generally, have been most grudging in providing fall-back positions and safety valves for familial malfunctions or failures.[32] Until very recently, ours has been no exception.[33] Why

[32] Insofar as compensatory mechanisms have existed, their low or despised status has served to emphasize the exclusive legitimacy of the family as a sexual, reproductive, status-ascribing institution (see Davis, 1937).

[33] Of nineteenth-century America, Smuts (1959:51–52) has said, "Aid was available only as charity, which was reserved for paupers, and was still influenced by the philosophy that the way to control pauperism was to keep its victims as miserable as possible. The only help a widowed mother was likely to get from public or private charity was an offer to place her children in an orphanage. The states did not begin to provide public assistance to widowed or abandoned mothers of young children until the decade before World War I." The double standard of dependency suffered by women and children is well illustrated by the following quotation, also from Smuts (1959:53): "Even if a widow was in easier circumstances, her position in the community was awkward. In recalling the death of her father from a chronic ailment which the doctors could neither diagnose nor treat, Mary Austin wrote with bitter sympathy of her mother's humiliation: 'At that time . . . the status of Wife and Mother,

have backups been proffered so stingily? The stock answer has been simple: because of the feedback effect. People would not behave in accordance with familial norms unless societies "kept up the pressure." To provide alternatives, to work out fall-back positions, to mop up tenderly after role failures, would constitute sending the wrong messages. People would be led to think that some other entity was prepared to shoulder the responsibilities *belonging* to the family. The incentive system would break down. Hence, individual suffering has been accepted in the interest of maintaining the functionally specialized system. Orphans and bastards have gone to almshouses and died, widows lived at starvation wages, premaritally pregnant women been ostracized so that they often committed suicide, spinsters functioned as servants, and noninheriting men left as rootless, itinerant laborers.

The streamlining of the modern family is allowing for fall-back positions and safety valves. As a consequence, people are in a far more discretionary and flexible position regarding family statuses, and are far less penalized for not being squarely a part of traditional family life. Alternatives are available, and, as I have tried to illustrate, the conventional family is markedly less conventional. For individuals, this means that the trade-off for losing the idealized and romanticized solidarity of the traditional family is not only a more adaptable set of familial statuses, but a more satisfying set of nonfamilial ones. One can deny the importance of this to individuals only by overlooking centuries of negative instances—of people pressed into marriage and parenthood whose talents and spirits were mutilated by domesticity; or of those who, in spite of personal desire to participate, were not absorbed into the mainstream of familial life and left, without options, to languish and suffer in the shadows.

## Conclusion

I have suggested that we are witnessing a large-scale redefinition of the normative assumptions of the American family. This respecification is occurring with respect to almost every institutional feature that has characterized the modern, structurally differentiated familial unit. Since this change is taking place informally, there is no concrete manifesto or policy which blueprints the alterations that are transpiring. Only when one assembles some of the pieces, as I have attempted to do here, can one begin to sense the magni-

---

always spoken of in capitals, was sentimentally precious. . . . No matter how poorly, through incompetence, neglect, or misfortune, her husband "protected" her, she was allowed the airs and graces of a woman apart. . . . Then the blow fell and the treasured Wife became the poor Widow, the object of family bounty, not infrequently grudged, the grateful recipient of leftovers, the half- menial helper in the households of women whose husbands had simply not died. The more precious and delicate her wifehood had been, the less chance there was of her being equipped for earning a livelihood.' "

tude of the modifications that are under way. It is their combination and interaction that is so noteworthy, for in no particular instance do they dazzle the eye. For example, if one focuses on the labor force participation of women, their occupational statuses, or their wage rates, they have a long way to go before achieving parity with men (Blake, 1974; Kreps, 1971; Fuchs, 1974, 1971; Cohen, 1971, 1973). If one glances at American fertility, it is far from approaching zero (as some analysts have suggested), nor are we at the fabled ZPG.[34] If one turns to illegitimacy, many countries are higher; as is the case for nonmarital, domiciliary unions. And so with the other changes I have discussed. I am arguing here that it is the cumulative redefinition of the entire structure that is significant.

What does this mean for the future of the family? Far from a disastrous breakdown at whose door every social ill may be laid, I would argue that we seem to be experiencing a readjustment of the normative assumptions of this group to the actual demands and needs of a modern society. The unit described by the Parsonians, although allegedly so functionally suited to industrial society, was far from modern. Its legal bases alone had not changed greatly during hundreds of years (Weitzman, 1972; Kanowitz, 1969: passim; Krauskopf, 1977). Moreover, these legal presuppositions were a fairly accurate description of the social role definitions of the participating parties. The behavior these definitions were generating was positively dysfunctional demographically (witness the "baby boom"), and largely unsuited to the other trends and goals of the society—rising educational levels for women, labor force requirements, diminishing emphasis on status ascription, an obvious need to find ways of educating and socializing many young people other than by the school system. The list could be lengthened substantially. We are beginning to watch the family become more flexible, externally connected, and appropriate to modern living than has previously been the case.

Part of this streamlining inheres in the tolerance of alternative and varied mechanisms for meeting needs formerly so rigidly assigned to the family. This means that the unique delegation to the family of certain kinds of functions is lessening. Even more telling, we are beginning to see a diminution of many of the dependencies that were *induced* by familial role definitions. A large share of the problems the family has allegedly "functioned" to solve were actually *created* by familial role definitions which *demanded dependency as a condition of the familial status.* The nuclear family has been locked into a vicious circle of trade-offs—authority of the male breadwinner in exchange for dependent service by the wife and, to cap it all, legislated leisure for children and adolescents. During the period of industrialization, economic dependency for women and children became socially, and, in many cases, legally mandated (see Myrdal and Klein, 1956:

[34] Butz and Ward (1977) and Moore (1958) believe that the opportunity costs of childbearing for women are becoming so great that fertility will tend to approach zero very shortly. For a discussion of this point, see Blake, "Is Zero Preferred?" (1979).

chap. 1; Chafe, 1972:60–65; Rossi, 1964; Kanowitz, 1969; Epstein, 1970: Gates, 1976; Ariès, 1962; Plumb, 1972; Coleman, 1974). Then, having created such enormous burdens of dependency, all nominally devolving on one social role, the society was confronted with trying to enforce "controls" to compel husbands and fathers to meet their obligations. This effort has been far less successful in actuality than the institutional role definitions might lead one to believe (Griffiths, 1976; Weitzman, 1972; Gates, 1977). In fact, the welfare side effect of familially induced dependency has proven to be so intractable that some economic analysts have suggested that the society should just redefine public dependency as "honorable" and quietly foot the bill.[35] Rarely is it recognized that much, if not most, dependency is induced as a condition of familial role definitions. In fact, welfare has served to bolster dependent familial role definitions.[36]

In sum, from a societal point of view, the family can afford to be more streamlined because many of the societal functions to which it is geared, such as reproduction, are, today, minimally required. Others of its functions, such as assigning responsibility for the dependent persons, like wives and children, remaining in the wake of curtailed fertility, are being reduced by a lessening of mandated dependencies, particularly among women. In spite of policies and laws that, at every turn, have attempted to keep women in the home, they have broken out and attained a significant measure of economic and social independence. Concerning young people, the problem of prolonged dependency is still critical. However, a first step toward change would appear to be the greater legal emancipation of the young which is taking place, plus a recognition that a protracted period of formal schooling is not necessarily universally appropriate as a learning situation.[37]

[35] Steiner (1971) views the welfare problem from the point of view of an economist and comes to the conclusion that economic disincentives to welfare are, for most welfare cases, too weak to be operative. His advice is, essentially, to recognize that large welfare burdens are here to stay and to bear them graciously, rather than doling out insufficient amounts in a grudging fashion. This economic viewpoint accepts the *social* definition of feminine and juvenile dependency as given. It is not regarded as the economist's job to question familial role definitions. These fall in the arena of "tastes," which are both too sacred and too nonrational to be of concern to the science of economics. Fortunately, sociology has a more catholic perspective.

[36] Steiner (1971: chap. 2) emphasizes the *mère-au-foyer* bias of AFDC; see also Kinsley (1977). Recent public controversy about federal and state support for abortions illustrates how readily familial role definitions generate dependency. Backers of state-funded abortions contend that abortion is a bargain in the long run since it saves huge outlays downstream for AFDC, education, etc. Opponents argue (over and above religious and moral issues) that state-funded pregnancy terminations induce more contraceptive carelessness and constitute just one more example of taxing the public for private mistakes. Actually, of course, there is today an enormous shortage of babies for adoption, so that a decline in state-funded abortion would not necessarily affect the public fisc at a later date. However, our maternal role expectations have been translated into welfare policies that short-circuit this fortuitous outcome. Unmarried mothers are now being strongly encouraged to *keep* their babies, thereby creating a dependency problem that might readily have been averted.

[37] For a discussion of the legal status of children vis-à-vis parents, see Kay, 1969; Cohen, Robson, and Bates, 1958; Katz et al., 1973; also Coleman, 1972:72–75, 82.

The role segregation of older people is also in the process of change attendant upon legal proscriptions of mandatory retirement. Moreover, although, technically speaking, increased reliance on Social Security constitutes a rise in dependency, from a social and equity point of view, Social Security is a form of insurance, since its recipients have paid into the system for the benefit of a prior generation.

As for individuals, their interests are being increasingly safeguarded in the event that crucial family statuses are either unavailable or undesired. The diminution of familial segregation and differentiation, although perhaps according the family less saliency and importance than at times in the past, is also opening up more opportunities for individuals to realize diverse talents and goals outside of a family context. In evaluating the importance of this change, it is probably well to remember that the "family"—fixated in our minds as of some particular time—is not possessed of an immutable validity from which deviations are either suspect or tragic. As far as we know, there has always been a tension between individual interests and familial demands. There still is. Today, however, there are many more ways of resolving this conflict than have ever existed before.

13

# Job Assignment in Modern Societies: A Re-examination of the Ascription-Achievement Hypothesis

*Harold L. Wilensky and Anne T. Lawrence*

RECENTLY, U.S. SUPREME COURT JUSTICES have grappled ambiguously with affirmative action cases involving access to education and jobs by age, sex, descent, seniority, and ability. They have thereby once again revived for popular discussion classic debates in sociology. It is a good time to reassess the state of theory and research on the impact of industrialization on criteria for role assignment in modern economies.

We begin with an apparent paradox. In their search for the shape of modern society, many scholars have arrived at the basic generalization that modern society tends toward the structural and cultural integration of minority groups. There is considerable consensus that industrialization and urbanization together foster increased equality of opportunity, if not absolute equality between races, religious-ethnic or ethnic-linguistic groups, young and old, men and women. The drift toward equal opportunity is said to reflect a general shift from ascription to achievement in role assignment. Yet there is also considerable consensus that even in the richest countries many, perhaps most, jobs are assigned on the basis of a combination of sex, age, and descent (race, religion, ethnicity); that powerful barriers to social mo-

☐ This chapter is based on research made possible by the support of the National Science Foundation (Grant SOC77-13265), the German Marshall Fund, the Institute of Industrial Relations, and the Institute of International Studies of the University of California, Berkeley. We are grateful to Martin A. Trow, Susan Abbott, and Natalie Rogoff Ramsøy for critical readings, and to Susan Reed Hahn, Jeffrey Haydu, and Theodore Crone for research assistance.

bility for able young people from lower-class families are still more powerful for deprived minorities; and that political criteria for important posts remain important.

In this chapter we argue that the paradox is merely apparent. Obviously, a long-run shift toward greater emphasis on achievement and a cross-sectional picture of discrimination by age, sex, and so on are consistent. But beyond the distinction between the long-run and the short, there are three ways to resolve the paradox. First, ascription and achievement are not mutually exclusive categories; ascriptive criteria are sometimes relevant to performance. Second, because of past discrimination, disadvantaged groups bring distinct configurations of abilities and handicaps to the labor market. Thus, even with no bias at the point of hire, the complete occupational integration of minority and other communal groups will still elude us. Third, managers who rely on established ascriptive networks for job assignment have powerful economic incentives for maintaining the status quo. They abandon older ascriptive criteria only in the presence of (1) severe labor shortages, (2) political pressures from above by government, or (3) political pressures from below by social movements and organized workers. Under these conditions, managers move toward new combinations of ascription and achievement.

Because education is central in job assignment in modern society, we will address the debate about whether education is in fact a measure of achievement or merely "a symbol of status" mainly irrelevant to "technical function"; we shall argue that these terms are misleading and, instead, assess evidence on the relevance of education to job performance, career development, and economic growth.

An exploration of the deviant case of South Africa, where heavy reliance on race in job assignment has not prevented rapid and sustained economic growth, will help us understand the political economy of job assignment. We close with an interpretive summary which reviews the state of theory and research on the ascription-achievement hypothesis. Our ultimate aim is to connect our analysis of trends in job assignment to the larger question of the integration of minority groups. By specifying the conditions under which occupational integration weakens or strengthens ties of ethnicity, language, religion, and race, we can better understand the fate of local communal groups in modern society.

## The Ascription-Achievement Hypothesis

The proposition that modern society tends toward equality of opportunity derives from the so-called functional theory of stratification (Davis, 1942; Davis and Moore, 1945; Levy, 1949). The opposing emphasis on discrimination derives from its critics (Tumin, 1953; Lopreato and Lewis, 1963; Stinchcombe, 1963; Goode, 1967; Broom and Cushing, 1977). Our purpose is not to revive that debate, which concerns the relationship between rewards and the functional importance of positions, between rewards and qualifications, and between qualifications and performance in all social systems; but instead to reexamine a subclass of propositions derived from it, which concern the shifting criteria for allocation of work roles in modern societies. We do not deal with differential rewards other than access to jobs. (For a discussion of earnings, income, and wealth differentials, see Wilensky, 1978.)

The idea that industrialization (the extensive and increasing use of high-energy technology and inanimate sources of power) and its structural correlates induce a shift from ascription to achievement is recurrent. For at least fifty years major students of modern society have presented one or another form of this argument (e.g., Sorokin, 1927; Linton, 1936; Schumpeter, 1942, 1951; Levy, 1949; Parsons, 1951; Parsons, Bales, and Shils, 1953).

Some definitions of "ascription" emphasize social attributes of the person which are clearly known at birth (Linton, 1936:115) such as sex, race, ethnic-religious or ethnic-linguistic origins, and social class origins. Everything else (ability, effort, education) is a residual category labeled "achievement." Other definitions characterize achievement more narrowly as "an actual or expected specific performance" (Parsons, 1951:94); everything else such as biological attributes or personality—the person's "attributes or qualities, independently of specific expected performances" (ibid., p. 88)—is a residual category labeled "ascription." In the latter view, ascription covers all that is thought to be irrelevant to performance even if it is not inherited—seniority, age, political or religious preference, physical appearance, and dress.

Popular discussion of these matters combines both views. No neat separation of qualities present at birth and other qualities appears as Supreme Court justices and civics textbooks endorse equality of opportunity "regardless of race, creed, color, or previous condition of servitude." In this paper, we follow popular concerns and ask whether there is a shift from criteria of job assignment irrelevant to role performance (ascription) toward criteria relevant to role performance (achievement).

Giving the ascription-achievement hypothesis a sympathetic reading and drawing mainly upon Linton (1936), Parsons (1949:189 ff.), Moore (1951), Levy (1949, 1952), and Wilensky and Lebeaux (1958:63–65), we can briefly summarize the argument:

1. Work in the primitive tribe or peasant village is traditional; the division of labor is simple. This means several things. Work does not change much from generation to generation; the son can do what his father did, the daughter what her mother did. There are only a few special roles to

fill; practically anyone can learn any of the few specialized roles available. Work can be assigned on the basis of traditional criteria, criteria often irrelevant to the performance of the role—age, sex, and perhaps, as in the Indian caste system, family origin. The elders of the tribe or village may occasionally look for promising young people and, in some societies, as among the Manus and the Chukchi, "adopt" them and sponsor their progress. But generally, even in these cases, little competition need accompany the "placement" of the individual in the economic order.

2. Contrast the industrial society. Work changes with changing technical and social organization and the pace of change accelerates; the division of labor is complex; and work is assigned more often on the basis of ability. Large portions of the population cannot do what their parents did, cannot inherit occupations because the occupations change too rapidly. Further, there are not enough age and sex differences to represent the vast number of specialized roles that need to be filled. For example, we cannot expect all American males to learn to be carpenters, barbers, doctors, lawyers, research chemists, labor leaders, corporation executives, and so on. Some of these roles are so complex that they cannot be left to the accidents of inheritance. Despite the great plasticity of human nature, some individuals are born without the capacity to fill some roles; and modern society cannot afford too many idiots in high places. In fact, industrialization, by creating complex and important occupational roles, accents the importance of even *small* differences in ability. For these small differences may mean enormous differences in output. Compare, for example, the different amounts that can be accomplished by two machine-shovel operators of different degrees of skill and reliability.

   In short, the number, complexity, importance, and frequency of change of occupational roles in industrial society have meant a shift in the basis of role assignment. "Who you are" becomes less important; "what you can do or learn to do" becomes more important.

3. That work roles in modern society tend to be achieved, assigned on the basis of ability, intensifies competition for these roles. If few are excluded from consideration, then the number of potential competitors is vastly increased. This is why there is less chance for the development of a hereditary elite. This is, moreover, why modern industry everywhere is such a sifter, sorter, and above all a *mixer* of diverse racial, ethnic, and religious groups (Hughes, 1946). It is a major reason, too, for the increased proportion of women who work outside the home. Everywhere industrialization, by challenging traditional criteria of work assignment, by accenting ability instead of sex, invites women to participate as occupational equals.

4. If industrialization means increased competition for work roles and increased mobility opportunity, it also fosters a mobility ideology appropriate to the changing structure. Industrialization has everywhere been accompanied by agitation for equality of economic opportunity—movements for improving the life chances of women, minority groups, and lower classes. Thus, a system accent on achievement or "economic indi-

vidualism'' marks modern societies, whatever their political and cultural differences, and despite counteracting ideologies of ''economic collectivism.''

None of these writers ignore discrimination; they merely assert that placement criteria relevant to role performance are becoming more prominent, ascriptive criteria less important.

## The Persistence of Ascriptive Criteria

To gauge the extent and rate of change of discrimination against women, ethnic and racial minorities, the aged, and those from lower-class backgrounds is complicated. It requires not only measures of the occupational distribution of various groups but also a control for relevant measures of ability—such as educational attainment, physical capability, and job-acquired skills and experience. From a review of the evidence for the United States in the last half-century or so and of more scarce cross-national data, we have the impression that the extent and rapidity of occupational integration—the shift toward achievement—has been greatest for white ethnics and broad religious groups followed by blacks and women. The relative position of young people from lower-class backgrounds has improved only slightly, if at all; and the situation of the aged has actually deteriorated.

### ETHNICITY AND RELIGION

Structural assimilation has proceeded more rapidly for some ethnic groups than for others, but by the second generation most white ethnics have achieved an occupational profile which closely matches that of the native white population. In his study *Immigrants and Their Children*, Hutchinson (1956) found marked specialization among first-generation ethnics.[1] Between 1910 and 1950, however, the advance of foreign-born Americans from unskilled manual to nonmanual employment—especially in professional, technical, managerial, clerical, and sales jobs—was more rapid than that of the native white labor force as a whole. Second-generation immi-

[1] Studies of occupational integration which rely on census data are subject to three limitations. First, the occupational data on which they are based, even when adjusted, are not strictly comparable over time, making between-period comparisons difficult. Second, most indices of segregation developed on the basis of census data underestimate its degree, since even the most detailed census categories are broader than those into which ascriptive groups are segregated (cf. Oppenheimer, 1970:69, 86–88). Most important, to compare the decennial census distributions is not to compare parents and their children. The crucial intergenerational comparisons require either cross-sectional surveys of individual family histories or longitudinal studies.

grants—the children of foreign-born or mixed parentage—had almost no marked occupational specializations; their occupational profile was very close to that of native whites (1956:273–78). Using more direct measures than Hutchinson's decennial census comparisons, Duncan and Duncan (1968) found similar evidence of occupational integration, melting-pot style, among ethnic minorities. National origin had much greater influence on the occupational fate of fathers than of sons in the Duncans' 1962 national survey data. When matched for education and social origin, respondents of different nationalities differed little in their occupational achievement, with the exception of the "overachievement" of Russians (mainly Jews) and WASPs, and the "underachievement" of persons of Hispanic, Italian, Canadian, and Polish descent. Greeley's (1974) analysis of more recent survey data for the 1960s demonstrates a continuation of the pattern documented by earlier researchers, with Irish and German Catholics registering the largest gains. Thus, although the rate of absorption has varied, and is not simply a function of the time of arrival as ideas of ethnic succession suggest (cf. Wilensky and Ladinsky, 1967:560), the occupational integration of most of America's ethnic-religious groups has been fairly complete.

## RACE

The pattern of structural assimilation over several generations experienced by many white ethnics has not been replicated for black Americans. Analysis of the jobs of blacks over the last four decades reveals a pattern of slow occupational integration which is either speeded up or slowed down by the business cycle and by shifts in the political climate which favor or block antidiscrimination measures (Price, 1969:131; Humphrey, 1977:13). An analysis of census data by Price (1969) shows that blacks made significant occupational gains in the 1940s, largely because of labor shortages and economic growth associated with World War II (p. 131). Using an index of occupational change which compares shifts in the occupational distribution of blacks and whites between time periods, Price found that between 1940 and 1950 black men registered particular gains in clerical work, with black women gaining most in the clerical, sales, craft, and laborer categories (p. 116). In general, gains were greater for women than for men and were greater in the West than in other regions (pp. 115–30). The dozen years from 1949 to 1961, however, encompassed four recessions and a related slowdown in the gains of the war years—in some categories an actual reversal. Although blacks continued to gain in the clerical and craft sectors, in defense industry, and in the West, their representation among managers and officials (except farm) declined and in most other sectors remained stagnant (chap. 5, passim). Then, during the 1960s, the occupational position of blacks relative to whites advanced again, with the proportion of black workers represented in professional, technical, and managerial positions increasing from 9.4 percent to 12.6 percent compared with a shift from 24.7 percent to 26.0 percent for whites (Wilson 1978:131).[2]

It is possible that the occupational advance of blacks has recently been slowed by the recession of 1974–75 and a political climate less favorable to affirmative action. Wilson (1978) shows that although blacks continued to gain during the early seventies, the rate of occupational upgrading in 1970–74 was slower than that of the 1960s (p. 130). Moreover, the movement of blacks out of the least desirable jobs (service workers and laborers) is proceeding more slowly than their advance into the most favored jobs, contributing to "a deepening economic schism in the black community" (p. 134).

Recent data on occupational attainment by education suggest that discrimination against blacks is more pronounced for those with less education. Black men appear even to have achieved parity at the upper educational levels: 58 percent of black men with a college education are employed in professional and technical occupations, compared with 54 percent of college-educated white men. For blacks with a high school education, however, the situation is reversed: 30 percent of black men with only a high school education are service workers or laborers, compared with 14 percent of white men (U.S. Department of Labor, 1975*a*, 1975*b*). Similarly, if we consider age and job experience, by 1972 the occupational status of black males who had recently entered the labor force approached that of equally experienced whites (Hall and Kasten, 1973:790). The position of older, less educated blacks had not improved comparably (Freeman, 1973:118).

In sum, despite long-term gains for blacks and a marked improvement for employed, young, educated blacks in particular and for the black middle class in general, there remains a significant gap between the occupational distribution of whites and that of blacks in the American economy, accounted for only partly by amount of formal schooling.

## SEX

Industrialization has everywhere been accompanied by a swift increase in female labor force participation, a slower decline in sexual segregation in occupations, and a still slower increase in the relative and absolute occupational status of women. In the United States, the labor force participation rate for women has climbed steadily from 20 percent in 1900 to almost 50 percent at latest count (U.S. Department of Labor 1977*b*:24; Oppenheimer,

[2]These figures are actually for "whites" and "blacks and other races." However, the latter category is approximately 90 percent black. Within the "black and other races" category, blacks clearly bear the brunt of occupational disadvantage. Duncan and Duncan (1968) report, for instance, that adjusting for social origin and educational attainment, Hispanic-Americans fall one point below the mean socioeconomic status score for nonblack, nonfarm, native males; blacks fall twelve points below the mean (p. 364).

1970: 3). During the same period, the occupational integration of women also advanced, but less rapidly. For instance, Oppenheimer (1970) found that sexual segregation in the United States (measured by the ratio of the number of women found in predominantly female occupations to that expected by chance) declined from 3.5 in 1900 to 2.1 in 1960 (p. 69). Using different indices, Gross (1968) and G. Williams (1975) also show a drop in differentiation during this period. Cross-national data by industry are consistent. In a rare, detailed study of trends in sex segregation by industry covering ten European nations and the United States, Cooney (1978) found that from the early 1900s until about the 1960s sex segregation within broad industrial sectors declined in all countries examined, although rates of change varied by period and country.

Whatever the pace of change and by any measure, the absolute amount of occupational differentiation in the United States remains high. In 1969, half of all male workers were concentrated in only 63 occupations, while half of all women workers were concentrated in only 17 occupations. And one-fourth of all women at work were concentrated in just five jobs: secretary, household worker, bookkeeper, elementary school teacher, and waitress. (Hedges, 1970: 19.)

Sexual segregation does not necessarily measure discrimination. Indeed, Cooney shows that in all eleven countries she studied, sex desegregation proceeded faster than the pace of improvement in the absolute and relative work status of women (Cooney, 1978:70–71). To measure discrimination more directly we must take account of at least some indicator of relevant abilities.[3] Holding education constant, we find that college-educated women are more likely than similarly educated men to be found in professional and technical jobs: 69.4 percent of women, compared with 54.1 percent of men, were in this favored category in 1975. However, college-educated women are less than a third as likely as men to become managers or proprietors (7.1 percent to the men's 24.1 percent). High school–educated women are concentrated in clerical jobs; high school–educated men in the "craftsmen and foremen" category (U.S. Department of Labor, 1975*a*, 1975*b*).

Of course, once again broad census categories obscure considerable variation within categories. For instance, Epstein (1970) shows that within the professional and technical category, women are concentrated in those sections of the professions with the least pay, prestige, and opportunity for advancement. The 1970s, however, saw an accelerated shift toward equality. In five years, from 1969–70 to 1975–76, women tripled their enrollment in medical schools—up from 9 percent of the total enrollment to 20.5 percent (Walsh, 1977). Similarly, from 1971 to 1977 women moved from one in ten to more than one in four of total law school enrollment (American Bar Association, 1977). In both of these male domains, women have now pene-

[3]The question of preferences and motives is discussed below. The rest of this paragraph refers to whites only. Black women with little education are still disproportionately clustered in private household and service jobs; they are a special case.

trated even the most powerful and lucrative specialties (Epstein, forthcoming).

While industrialization has clearly improved job opportunities for women and the occupational integration of highly educated women has recently accelerated, women in the most modern countries still remain concentrated in nurturant, expressive, and subordinate roles (cf. Wilensky, 1968).

## SOCIAL CLASS

The most dubious data we must cope with concern changes in the intergenerational transmission of occupational status in the United States; cross-national comparison is even more shaky (cf. Wilensky, 1966). Nevertheless, based on recent mobility studies in the United States, we can venture some guesses about shifts in the links between social class origins and the occupational fate of sons. Blau and Duncan (1967) and Duncan, Featherman, and Duncan (1972) have demonstrated that social class origins (as measured by father's occupation and father's education) greatly affect the success of nonfarm white males in the United States. However, most of the effect of a man's origins is mediated through his educational attainment and early job experience—an effect that diminishes over the course of the life cycle. Together, social origin, education, and first job account for about half the variance in achievement. The strength of this link between class origins and occupational fate has remained remarkably stable over time. In an analysis of changes in intergenerational mobility rates within and between cohorts of 1952, 1962, and 1972, Hauser et al. (1975*a*, 1975*b*) found a slight weakening of the relationship between the occupational achievement of fathers and sons and a slight rise in the total level of mobility. However, these shifts were quite modest and could be accounted for almost entirely by shifts in the occupational structure. Holding the job structure constant, Hauser et al. found "remarkable homogeneity in the patterns of association between father's occupation and son's first occupation" from 1952 to 1962 (1975*a*: 288; cf. Rogoff, 1953). In short, through its heavy influence on education, social class remains an important and relatively constant determinant of occupational achievement in the United States. What meager cross-national data we have are consistent (cf. Svalastoga, 1965, and the citations therein).

## AGE

Disadvantaged as they are in the labor market, minorities and women have generally enjoyed some labor market gains with continued industrialization. Not so for the aged, many of whom are chronically unemployed or underemployed in modern economies. Older people who are employed evidence an occupational profile similar to that of other adults; they tend to be slightly overrepresented in managerial posts and in the farm sector and underrepresented in professional and technical jobs and in clerical work (Riley and Foner, 1968: 50, U.S. Bureau of the Census, 1977*c*: 406). However, employed or not, their skills are plainly underutilized. Although older workers are less likely to be laid off than their younger workmates, they are more likely to experience difficulty being rehired. Recent cross-national evidence shows that the duration of unemployment rises steadily with age in the United States, Canada, Belgium, and the Netherlands (Riley and Foner, 1968:47). Job opportunities decline markedly with advancing years after the age of forty-five (Wirtz, 1965:4). For instance, a survey of employers conducted by the Bureau of Employment Security in 1965 found that only 9 percent of the previous year's new hires were over forty-five. Yet the percentage of unemployed workers in the older age group was more than three times as large.[4]

Most important, there is no doubt that for many decades increasing numbers of talented older people have been forced to retire before they choose to. Since 1890, in almost all industrial countries there has been a steady decrease in the labor force participation rates of older men. The main causes: the rise of compulsory retirement rules in legislation and in collective bargaining contracts and the growing occupational obsolescence of the aged. (Long, 1958; Riley and Foner, 1968; Fisher, 1978). At the same time, increased longevity and improved health have prolonged the years of productive life. The inevitable result of the intersection of these trends is a growing number of able older workers who are excluded from the labor market completely or are chronically unemployed or underemployed. Thus, discrimination against older workers accelerated as rich countries got richer. Whether recent political pressure applied by the aged and their allies will reverse this trend is uncertain.

## Resolving the Apparent Paradox

Aside from the obvious compatibility of contemporary cross-sectional data showing substantial discrimination against the abler aged, women, minorities, and lower-class young people on the one hand, and a long-run tenden-

[4]Although the Bureau of Employment Security survey did not directly collect data on the abilities of older workers, employer responses indicated widespread discrimination on the basis of age. Of the employers surveyed, only one in six had in force a policy of hiring without regard to age. On the other hand, one in four had established age limits above which they would not hire, and another quarter replied that although no formal restrictions were in effect they preferred not to hire older workers. The most prevalent reason for restricting the employment of older persons, cited by 34 percent of the employers, was physical incapacity. Less than a third of those citing this reason, however, reported any objective basis for their assessment that older workers were less capable of performing the job (Wirtz, 1965: 5–10).

cy toward use of criteria relevant to role performance on the other, there are several ways to resolve the apparent paradox.

## AMBIGUITY ABOUT THE RELEVANCE OF "ASCRIPTION" AND "ACHIEVEMENT"

At the point of hire or promotion, the opposite of performance-oriented criteria is not necessarily ascriptive. That *age* and its close correlate, *seniority*, are relevant to job performance is obvious for many complex jobs in which accumulated work experience both in similar lines of work and similar work places is indispensable. As labor unions have argued for decades, seniority is an important measure of ability, perhaps the best measure of ability for most jobs in modern economies. Think of a stillman in an oil refinery—an operator who has heavy responsibility for expensive processes and equipment. If he goes to sleep on the job he can ruin machinery and material, as can many semiskilled machine operators. A long-service stillman who has never made a drastic error (like blowing up the plant) has demonstrated his reliability, which for many jobs *is* ability.

We can easily recognize the relevance of experience for top positions such as political leader, judge, executive, and military officer. To note incompetence, even senility, among some of these powerful people is not to deny that an equal incompetence is more prevalent at the other end of the scale among the young and very inexperienced.[5] In short, age or seniority is often the best single test of steady performance.[6]

The question of age is like the question of *"politicking"* and *"pull,"* which, if not "ascriptive" in the sense of inherited, are popularly viewed as irrelevant to performance. Yet, upon close inspection, their relevance is clear. Political loyalty is a measure of ability in all organizations and all na-

[5] In the minds of recruiters, age and seniority are often merged with marital status. That such measures of ability are not remnants of the past is suggested by an interview with an executive of the most modern assembly plant in Sweden—a kind of workers' paradise set up to deal with the new demands of the new worker. Each team of twenty five workers has very little supervision, some control over work pace, some variety in work, quiet, pleasantly lighted work space, with music the group chooses, topped off by a coffee bar and sauna of its own. The manager, explaining why all this has not sharply cut down absenteeism and turnover, said, "Age is a problem. The best workers are twenty five to forty years old. The young worker—girls or boys just out of school, sixteen or seventeen—single, without family responsibilities—they are absent five to ten times more than the rest. These are short absences. And they quit in a few weeks or few months. The older worker is absent much less often but that may be a long absence because he is really sick. He could have been doing heavy work most of his life and have a sore back. The most desirable is in between. But it's getting harder to recruit them. The recession has not helped. The twenty-five-to forty-year-olds—the most reliable ones—are afraid to leave their jobs. They have family responsibilities" (H.L.W. interview, 1978). Vanguard technology in a mecca of participatory democracy, but the recruitment criteria and problems remain the same.

[6] For an analysis of the interplay of age and eminence (measured either by productivity or honors) in the achievement of a full professorship see Lazarsfeld and Theilens (1958: 402–7). For a satirical treatment of the illusion that a promotion system based solely on precisely measured merit—ignoring years of experience—is possible in academic life, see Stigler (1947).

tions—ability to further the goals of the system through political connections and demonstrated loyalty. A growing number of mediating roles require knowledge of who can make what decisions or has what information and how to reach him; "contacts" which are so well developed that they become nontransferable; skills in exploiting such contacts. The military officer in defense procurement becomes the corporation vice-president in charge of sales; the regulatory-agent staff person goes over to the regulated industry; the NLRB Regional Director becomes the union lawyer. The "training" or "preparation" of these contact men is heterogeneous: law, politics, journalism, business, and religion (Wilensky, 1967: 10–13; cf. Perrow, 1972: 12 ff.). Achievement? Or ascription? Universalism or particularism? Whatever the label, this sort of political loyalty, these skills and connections—which almost always require many years of cultivation and hence combine politics and age—are directly relevant to role performance. Such political criteria count in sensitive, authoritative posts everywhere. But they probably weigh most heavily in totalitarian and authoritarian regimes.

So far we have discussed such elusive "skills" as reliability, wisdom, and loyalty where role demands are fairly clear and where ascriptive criteria are relevant to performance and hence are also achievement criteria. Now consider the case where the demands of work roles are vague or rapidly changing—perhaps the typical job in a modern economy. In these roles, it is logically impossible to specify precisely the skills required or devise measures of those skills. Neither the hiring agent nor the applicant can know what criteria *are* relevant. Naturally where such vacuums exist management stereotypes of the right type of personality, which will often involve a combination of sex, age, marital status, descent, interaction style, style of speech and dress and the like will have freer play.[7]

Thus, in some cases—age, politics, pull—ascription is directly relevant to job performance; "who you are" shapes "what you can do." In other more numerous cases—where the demands of work roles are vague or rapidly changing—ascriptive and achievement criteria are inextricably meshed.

## AMBIGUITY BECAUSE ABILITIES INTERACT WITH MOTIVATION, INFORMATION, AND OPPORTUNITY

Even if we could neatly distinguish ascribed from achieved characteristics by specifying the demands of work roles, listing the abilities required, and devising appropriate measures, we would still encounter a major obstacle in research on the place of abilities in job assignment or in public

[7] Where the demands of work roles are unclear or rapidly changing, the ritual of objective testing or the ritual invocation of the company type of person are prominent techniques of job assignment. In these situations of great uncertainty, tests, objective merit-rating systems, or personality stereotypes applied in employment interviews all serve the same function for management—increase the speed of decision and lighten its moral burden. Such devices are also used as evidence of fairness and legitimacy in a selection process.

policies designed to expand equality of opportunity: In both individual lives and organizational systems most abilities themselves depend upon opportunity, motivation, and information, especially during pre-adult socialization. It is the interaction of these four forces that determines the occupational fate of persons and the shape of systems of job assignment.

The judgments made in the family and school concerning capacities and abilities affect the child's motives and aspirations. These in turn will affect performance—abilities developed in school and displayed on jobs. Although the point can be exaggerated, if you tell someone every day in every way that he is no good, he will likely fulfill your expectations; if in contrast you affirm the better self, he might come alive; he might become trainable. In other words, Shaw's Pygmalion is everywhere—in the living room, classroom, street corner, and work place.

Both motivation and trained abilities will influence the information the child acquires about jobs and careers, as well as the occupational role models to which he or she attends. For instance, if both parents and all siblings are in unskilled or semiskilled jobs, if the school is of low quality—its teachers distracted, overworked, preoccupied with keeping order—the typical child will not acquire the motivation to develop his abilities, seek information about desirable occupations, or identify with real-life high-status role models; he is therefore unlikely to travel the road to higher education. (Although research on this matter is limited, fantasy aspirations derived from the mass media are unlikely to inspire effective action.) In other words, the structure of opportunity in family, school, and labor market shapes abilities and motivation and channels occupational information.

Thus, by the time they have been in the labor market for two or three years, various groups—majorities and minorities, men and women—differ systematically; employers react accordingly. Sex, for example, is by definition purely ascriptive but, again, on average and at the point of hire or promotion, it is relevant to performance in some roles. That nursery school teachers are typically women is partly a product of discrimination; but it is also a product of self-selection and recruitment of persons whose skills in nurturing small children are highly developed. Until the agencies of socialization make men equal to women in those skills, the rational recruiter will play the probabilities. Similarly, social origin, to the extent that it is associated with a handicapping configuration of traits at the point of hiring—weak motivation, meager information, low IQ, limited literacy—becomes relevant. Of course, the recruiter who stereotypes an entire minority group as sharing such characteristics and fails to assess individual members is discriminating.

In sum, with no discrimination at all at the point of hire or promotion, the promised land of proportional representation in desirable jobs by sex, age, social class, and descent would still elude us. "Job qualifications" are the end product of all these interacting forces, especially powerful during pre-adult socialization. The discrimination and the differential socialization that do not occur at the point of hiring occurred earlier (that part of the case for affirmative action that does not claim equal qualifications).

## Recruitment Systems

If part of the explanation of the persistence of ascription is ambiguity in the distinction between ascription and achievement and the heavy dependence of job-relevant abilities on motivation, information, and opportunities (characteristic of diverse families, schools, and early work situations), the rest of the explanation is the nature of recruitment systems. From the viewpoint of the recruiter, as Mayhew suggests (1968:110), the main source of the staying power of ascription in job assignment can be summed up in three words: It is cheap. Personnel decisions in complex systems are like any other decision: Managers do not maximize or optimize; they rest easy with the minimally satisfactory alternative.[8] Thus, managers who must recruit and maintain a labor supply almost never set up an elaborate structure for recruitment, training, and evaluation; they seldom mount an intensive search for the *best*-qualified persons, because the potential gain from such action is not justified by the costs in time and money. Given all the ambiguities of defining the requirements of hundreds or thousands of work roles, given the further ambiguities of performance criteria even where job demands are clear, it is too costly to launch the grand-scale program for comparing all or most potential applicants for all or most vacancies. The problem is instead to fill positions with adequately qualified applicants at a minimum cost to the organization. In other words, in the absence of unusual shortages or other strong pressures, managers fill vacancies in the easiest way. In the United States, which lacks an active labor market policy, that easy way is to rely overwhelmingly on word of mouth—the natural cheapest route to a reliable labor supply. Information passes through informal networks of kin, friends, and co-workers which, of course, are based on ethnic, religious, and racial groups and social strata. This observation is confirmed in several studies of hiring transactions.[9]

[8]March and Simon (1959: 140–41) note that "finding the optimal alternative is a radically different problem from finding a satisfactory alternative. An alternative is *optimal* if: (1) there exists a set of criteria that permits all alternatives to be compared, and (2) the alternative in question is preferred, by these criteria, to all other alternatives. An alternative is *satisfactory* if: (1) there exists a set of criteria that describes minimally satisfactory alternatives, and (2) the alternative in question meets or exceeds all these criteria." To optimize is to search a haystack for the sharpest needle in it; to *satisfice* is to find a needle sharp enough to sew with (p. 141). We leave aside the question of whether the satisficing manager is, in fact, maximizing enterprise welfare in the long run; clearly, at the point of decision he is not optimizing.

[9]In 1960 the State Employment Services accounted for only an estimated 16 percent of all new employment, and that was concentrated among unskilled, often temporary workers. These agencies accounted for about three times as many new hires among unskilled workers as

Only when they confront severe cost pressures do managers create and maintain expensive new structures and strategies for recruitment, training, and evaluation. Four major external forces, one economic and the rest political, can shake them up: shortages of labor (chronic in some demanding occupations, variable in economies, industries, areas); government coercion (as in antidiscrimination or affirmative action programs); active labor market policies (as in Sweden and West Germany); and social movements for equality.

## LABOR SHORTAGES: FROM ASCRIPTION TO ACHIEVEMENT

Confronted with a severe shortage of applicants, managers do search more widely and offer special inducements (pay and privilege) instead of relying on normal attrition and the principle of "Available Jones." Only then do they invest in a formal training apparatus to improve the qualifications of insufficiently qualified applicants rather than letting them learn casually on the job. And only when the labor shortage is both unusually severe and chronic do they move to the last resort—restructure the jobs to fit the available applicants (cf. Moore, 1962:40). Thus, there is nothing like a brisk labor market to make an elementary school dropout look useful, an old man look strong, an unskilled woman skilled, a black acceptable, an "unemployable" a good bet for the next opening (Wilensky, 1965:*xxxiii*). The other case where costly search and evaluation are common is the unusually complex and demanding positions at the top where a shortage of talent tends to be chronic; but such positions are a tiny fraction of the labor force.

The prevalence of labor shortages is linked to economic fluctuations by area, occupation, industry, and nation—to the business cycle in general and to the market position of highly educated or highly trained people in particular. It is likely that rate of growth of an upper stratum affects the degree to which new entrants will be admitted on the basis of achievement or trainability. On the upswing, there is less resistance to new entrants from below; on the downswing, ascriptive criteria will once again be combined

---

they did among skilled workers or professional and managerial personnel (for whom the agencies placed only about one in ten (Lester, 1966: 72–73, 31). The distribution of hiring transactions according to the two most frequent channels workers used were recruitment by relatives, friends, other employees of the firm (23 percent), and direct application to the employer (36 percent), most of which were probably triggered by networks of kin and friend (since newspaper ads accounted for only 11 percent). In other words, the principle of "Available Jones" is applied in the majority of hiring transactions. Similar results appear in a study of job-seeking behavior of unemployed workers in Erie, Pennsylvania, in 1963–64 (Sheppard and Belitsky, 1966). Despite many years of effort to strengthen such labor market services, the situation in the U.S. remains much the same today (U.S. Deparment of Labor, 1975*a*, 1975*b*: 7, table 3). For microsociological analysis of how job openings become known by word of mouth from current employees via networks of ethnic group, political affiliation, and social club, see Dalton, 1959.

with criteria more obviously relevant to role performance. The formula is: In good times the employee outside the usual acriptive network gets the glad hand; in bad times he gets the brush-off.

## POLITICAL PRESSURES: FROM ASCRIPTION TO ASCRIPTION?

Beyond the economic shock of urgent shortages of labor, there are three political shocks that either increase employer costs of using established ascriptive networks of labor supply or reduce the costs of alternative channels sufficiently to change job assignment strategies. First is government coercion via fair employment practices commissions such as those of the 1940s and 1950s or affirmative action programs such as those of the 1960s and 1970s. As we have shown, the occupational integration of blacks—their penetration of middle and upper-middle professional and technical jobs—proceeded faster in the prosperous periods of World War II and 1960–73 than in the slumps of the 1950s or midseventies. But there was more than the business cycle at work. The armed forces during and after World War II led in occupational integration (Moskos, 1966). And most of the civilian gains since World War II have been in occupations in which a large portion of the nonwhites are hired by government (Wilensky, 1965:*xxxvi–xxxvii*). All of this suggests that vigorous antidiscrimination policies can make it too expensive for employers to stick to the older ascriptive networks.

A second political force that inspires employers to rely a bit less on the cheap ascriptive networks is heavy government subsidy of an active labor market policy designed to reach the hard-to-employ and to place everyone. Sweden, West Germany, and several Western European welfare-state leaders, in contrast to the United States, have developed strong labor market boards and labor exchanges coupled with a great range of policies to match people and jobs. As early as 1960 the fraction of hiring transactions accounted for by the labor exchanges was about one-third in Sweden and about two-fifths in Germany, compared to our 16 percent (Lester, 1966:73). European strategies to deal with the hard-to-employ include the following: tight links between employment officers and social welfare and medical personnel and between rehabilitative units and work training centers; quotas and reservations geared to rehabilitation and training; wage subsidies and tax incentives to employers; requirements that employers who lay off workers find them suitable alternative jobs; work sharing; reconversion allowances; lowered Social Security contributions for employers willing to hire designated groups; mobility allowances; and the usual unemployment insurance, lump sums, and, increasingly, preretirement pensions to ease the shift to part-time work for the older worker. Confidential notice to government of impending layoffs is common (Reubens, 1970). Recently Sweden has experimented with compulsory vacancy notification in order to strengthen its already strong employment offices (Swedish Labour Market Board, 1978). By the standards of other industrial countries, the process of linking people to jobs in the United States is casual. In contrast to Sweden, West Germany, and other European countries, we have a weak, understaffed employment service whose operations are only loosely related to school counseling, testing, tracking, and guidance. And our high school counselors are only slightly attuned to occupational information; they are primarily talent scouts for the colleges, especially local and state colleges (Wilensky, 1967; cf. Cicourel and Kituse, 1963).

We should be clear that what employers are doing in response to active labor market policies and government pressure for occupational integration is substituting one rational ascriptive criterion for another. When American Telephone and Telegraph, using customary low-cost combinations of established informal networks and achievement criteria, is faced with unmistakable costs of government action and court orders, it widens its recruitment networks and elaborates its affirmative action machinery to place women and minorities in crafts and management positions and men in clerical and operator positions. (For background on the case, see *New York Times*, Jan. 19, 1973, p. 1; *Wall Street Journal*, Jan. 19, 1973, p. 3.) The ascriptive criteria that favored sufficiently qualified white men are expanded to include numerical "targets" for sufficiently qualified women and members of racial minorities. Similarly, like affirmative action in the United States, an active labor market policy may cut through established local ascriptive criteria, but this does not imply the substitution of the more obvious achievement criteria. European labor market policies aim to keep the vulnerable populations—usually concentrated among the aged, the young, the disabled, women, and minorities—from joining the ranks of the chronically unemployed. Such programs necessarily rely on informal networks in which disadvantaged groups are embedded.

Government coercion and active labor market policies interact with a third political pressure for change in employers' job placement strategies: social movements for equality, which are a product of industrialization everywhere. We must consider the push from below as it affects employer costs calculations.

Social movements—whether based on minority group interests or class—aim to introduce their own ascriptive criteria within a category of sufficiently qualified, just as employers in the absence of pressures for change had previously used ascriptive criteria for their own convenience. Before the rise of French nationalism in Canada, Anglophone employers typically preferred English-speaking Protestants to Francophones for supervisory and managerial positions (Hughes, 1943). After four decades of agitation for Francophone equality and the recent rise of a separatist government in Quebec, the tables have been turned: Anglophones in Quebec must now speak French in work place and community; in Ottawa French fluency gets you points for promotion. In a systematic study of men aged twenty-five to forty-five at midcareer in five agencies of the Canadian federal administration, Beattie (1974) demonstrated the effect of this social movement on career development among Francophones. Although by 1965 older unilingual Francophones were still suffering disadvantages in both salary and career mobility in "English" organizations, young minority men were doing as well or better than their majority counterparts (holding constant level and type of education, linguistic skill, age, and seniority).[10] In private and public sectors alike the effects of political pressure on managers' cost calculations are plain.

A related aspect of the managers' calculations goes beyond the cost of recruitment, training, and job evaluation. Where unions, workers' councils, or informal work groups press for seniority or other preferences in hiring and promotion, the manager who ignores their demands can provoke labor disputes, decrease morale, increase absenteeism and turnover, and lower product quality. At various times and places managers have confronted a wide variety of demands to modify placement practices. Consider this list for preferential treatment:

- superseniority for labor leaders and activists or war veterans
- preference for relatives (craftsmen in the U.S.A.)
- credit for peasant and worker parentage (university and hence job entry in modernizing Poland)
- ethnic-linguistic background (Belgium, Canada) or race (U.S.A.)
- confessional-political affiliation (Holland)
- physical handicaps or sex (many countries).
- region (In Italian politics and the bureaucracy, the preference for Sicilians has provoked the label "the southernization of Italy.")

Groups threatened by such movements are not without resources and motives to fight back. White ethnic backlash in the United States, tax-welfare backlash in Denmark, Switzerland, the U.S.A., and Britain are signs of resistance to the push for equality (see Wilensky, 1976).

Most employers must make judgments, however imperfectly, about these costs. Since there is no predetermination of the outcome of struggles among minority groups and between minorities and majorities, the particular combination of ascription and achievement employers adopt will vary by country and region, and over time. Further, in some situations, employers see a cost advantage in playing one minority group against another. The

[10] As a group, the older Francophones were handicapped by a higher and selective fallout rate (more ambitious Francophone civil servants left Ottawa for the action in Quebec in the 1960s) and by discrimination both on the job and in education before entry. The attraction of energetic, talented members of minority groups to social and political action (by criteria directly relevant to performance) is seldom considered in analyses of "discrimination" against those left behind in the sectors under study.

point for us is that in no sense can we see the effort to substitute one ascriptive criterion for another—within the broad category of "adequately qualified"—as premodern. In fact, it is the universal correlates of industrialization—modern communication and transportation networks, mass education, urbanization, high rates of residential and occupational mobility—that have given force to the push for equality. The result is new self-consciousness, new aspirations, and new political and economic resources for minority groups (cf. Williams, 1977: 155–56).

In Norway, Sweden, and other countries with long periods of social democratic rule, the push for equality no longer comes mainly from below; those "below," now in control of the government, go to great lengths to assure full employment of minorities and majorities alike. Norway, for instance, has written into its constitution the right to work, with the proviso that anyone "fit" to work may exercise that right. In such circumstances, the employer's cost calculations become even more complex because a large medical-psychiatric-administrative apparatus must certify everyone's "fitness" for the job entitlement.

Where does this leave the counteracting meritocratic thrust of modern society? Very much alive. Although equality of opportunity (a heavy accent on achievement criteria for job entry and placement) is at war with absolute equality or equality of results (a heavy accent on ascription), both principles have powerful roots in the structure of modern society (Wilensky, 1975:28–39). The modern complex work place mirrors this larger conflict. We can best see the workings of these conflicting principles of organization by examining the role of education and training in job assignment.

## Education: "Status Group Conflict" or "Technical Function"?

In the analysis of modern stratification systems and criteria of job placement, no issue has created more confusion than the ambiguous role of education and training. From theorists of the managerial revolution (e.g., Veblen, 1921; Burnham, 1941; Galbraith, 1968; Bell, 1973) to status attainment researchers (e.g., Blau and Duncan, 1967; Duncan, Featherman, and Duncan, 1972; Sewell and Hauser, 1974), scholars have argued or demonstrated the relevance of education and training to occupational achievement. Many of these writers have assumed that education enhances job performance or develops job skills or both. This assumption has provoked a counterattack in which education is seen as a symbol of status substantially irrelevant to technical function, and vocational education as the "Great Training Robbery" (Berg, 1970). America has become the "Credential Society"

(Miller, 1967:2) in which degrees and certificates function to protect the status and power of privileged groups and strata.[11] Collins's (1971) more careful analysis emphasizes that increased schooling as an employment requirement reflects an effort of competing status groups to monopolize or dominate desirable jobs by imposing their cultural standards on the selection process. Some authors of this persuasion also imply that employers are giving decreasing weight to criteria relevant to role performance and therefore the long-run period trend toward achievement is a conservative mirage.

Whether they accent status protection and power or technical function, all these writers underplay or miss entirely at least five major findings about modern education and occupations—findings which, if they are not firmly embedded in the literature on the sociology of economic life, should be. The findings are as follows: (1) Employers increasingly recruit not only for entry jobs but for future jobs, job patterns, and careers. (2) When employers talk about "skill" they mean many things beyond technical function, all relevant to job performance. Although education often cannot produce "technical" skills, it does have an enduring effect on the capacity to learn new jobs quickly. (3) "Vocational education" is an illusion unless it builds on basic literacy, discipline, and flexibility of mind. (4) Modern mass education systems are so diversified that quality variations within the same level of education are more important for occupational fate and job performance than the sheer levels of education commonly analyzed. (5) Test bias, which has received so much attention in debates about equality of opportunity, is a tiny part of the complex of interacting determinants of job placement. A word about each of these propositions follows.

## ENTRY JOB VERSUS JOB PROGRESSION

Modern employers increasingly try to select not for entry jobs but for several jobs, job sequences, and progression lines. (cf. Wilensky, 1960: 552–57, 1964*b*,1967). The more employees organize to protect their job security, to assert property rights to the job, the more employers screen for long tenure. This is especially true where there are long promotion lines and where the more desirable jobs are demanding. For instance, managers of oil refineries of the 1930s, in the vanguard of automation, knew that they did not need a high school graduate for the dirty job of cleaning out the pipe stills. But they also knew that the "overeducated" high school graduate would very likely end up in a skilled job requiring much more responsibility

[11] Max Weber embraced both arguments. Compare his early version of the managerial revolution (Wilensky, 1956: 15ff.; Bendix, 1960: 451ff.) and his caustic reflections on the spread of educational requirements for favored civil service positions (Weber, 1968: 1000).

for expensive equipment. With more modernization of industry, higher educational requirements for entry jobs spread rapidly and for the same reason—employers prefer to cover their bets with educational criteria they believe relevant to the learning of later jobs.

Thus, the frequent observation that educatonal credentials are often irrelevant to job performance and that increasing numbers of workers are "overqualified" for their current jobs ignores the central fact of job progression. Hanging on to the educatonal requirement makes sense even in "technical" terms if employers think they are hiring workers on job ladders.

The combination of an increased supply of college graduates, government pressure on behalf of the disadvantaged, and social movements based on race, ethnicity, and sex will accelerate the long-term trend toward raising the educational requirements for employment. Employers who must act affirmatively for minorities and at the same time respond to union demands for further job protection will spend more time and money in their initial screening of applicants. If the opening scene of the play is going to determine the course of a lifetime drama, all the actors will give it their keenest attention.

In the more advanced welfare states of Western Europe, job protection is becoming a religion. Strong labor movements and social democratic governments have made it quite difficult for employers to fire anyone. They have also made it costly for employers who fail to take manpower planning seriously.[12] By comparison, American employers are sloppy in planning and hard as nails in firing and layoffs.

It can be argued that hiring rules that set goals and targets for minorities and women will force employers to lower educational requirements. Two tendencies make that unlikely. The demand for minority educational opportunity is being met somewhat faster than the demand for job opportunity—a trend that was apparent before affirmative action programs (Wilensky, 1966: 133; Schiller, 1971; Freeman, 1973:70). Second, employers confronted with demands to prove that they are not discriminating cling more tenaciously to certificates and degrees as third-party validation of ability. Even if the thrust for equality compels a lowering of the line defining "sufficiently qualified" the forces motivating employers to screen in the most qualified minority applicants will not lessen.

[12] Consultations or negotiations with unions or worker representatives on the need for and extent of layoffs is required by law or collective bargaining agreement in Sweden, Norway, Finland, Italy, and France. In France and the Netherlands, prior authorization by a public agency is required before any work force reduction may take place. In West Germany and Austria, an employer must consult a works council before dismissing anyone for cause; the Netherlands requires prior authorization of an employment office. To protect older workers in several sectors of West German industry there is outright prohibition of dismissal of workers between a given age and the age of retirement with pension (Yemin, 1976; International Labour Office, 1974*b*; Delamotte, 1972).

## DOES EDUCATION PREPARE FOR WORK?

Leaving aside the central fact that entry jobs requiring little skill are linked to future jobs requiring more skill, what do employers think they are doing when they require college graduates for "skilled" jobs which we all know can be done by three-quarters of the population? What they are doing is assuming that the vast majority of jobs can be learned only on the job—a bit of sociological wisdom that most managers have always known and that has recently been picked up by a few unconventional economists, too (Thurow, 1975, cf. Berg, Freedman, and Freeman, 1978). So the question is "Who can learn quickly what must be learned?"

Insofar as sociologists of work have contributed to an answer regarding "what," there seem to be two broad categories of demands modern work places impose on their employees. First, they must learn a set of tasks and the social relations that flow from the tasks—the core of work roles. Few of the tasks can be learned in school and then only by close simulation of the real thing or by supervised practice—as in some skilled trades (tool and die making), office jobs (typing), and some technical jobs (X-ray technicians), or in sports (jobs with the most easily measured performance), music, or the most abstract aspects of science and mathematics. In fact, where schools attempt to transform themselves into vocational training institutes, their graduates, upon entering the work place, typically must unlearn much of what they have painstakingly mastered—a process Everett Hughes labels "reality shock." This is the sense in which Berg's phrase the "Great Training Robbery" captures half the truth. The other half is that although most jobs are not learned in school and although we need shorter periods of special training for semiprofessional, semitechnical people, all job training must build on a good general education—a point to which we will return.

Regarding the other component of the work role—social relations that flow from the tasks—schools do provide some guide to work, however indirect. The school as a factory, a bureaucracy, a colleague group has some resemblance to modern work places. But when we glance at the internal dynamics and functions of work groups, when we consider the subtle rules by which newcomers are inducted into work groups and learn patterns of cooperation and competition, authority and subordination, success and failure, conformity and deviance—richly described by sociologists of work—we can understand why newcomers need old-timers to become adequately oriented to both tasks and social relations on the job. (Another reason employers are willing to count seniority as a measure of ability is that it gives the old-timers enough security to share their know-how with the newcomers who would otherwise be seen as a threat to jobs and wage standards and therefore be kept in the dark.)

Going beyond the immediate work milieu, the second challenge many employees must eventually master is learning the social and political map of the work place and its environment. Again the school can be of only limited relevance. The new employee cannot know the organizaional character of the enterprise or any unit within it; the school cannot provide a grasp of the distinctive outlook and habits of its members and leaders, of the organization's central mission and subordinate goals (cf. Selznick, 1957). Those, too, must be learned on the job.

If tasks and social relations constituting work roles and the social and political topography of the work place and its environment are what effective employees must know, and if most of this must be learned on the job, why should employers prefer college graduates to highschool graduates and highschool graduates to the rest? The "status-power protection" argument holds that managerial elites favor high-level degrees for top positions because they want carbon copies of themselves while they favor formal (if lesser) credentials for lower-level employees because education level signifies degree of indoctrination in elite values. In recruiting both members of the elite and the "aborigines," employers seek recognition of their own cultural superiority (cf. Collins, 1971:1010).

The argument underestimates the casual effectiveness of the self-selection process (by which Available Jones shows up at the place he thinks he fits) combined with informal recruitment tapping a great variety of subcultures. Most important, the argument underestimates the power of the organization's own resources for socializing new members at every level—training, indoctrination, salaries and careers, transfers and rotation; location (top floors for top dogs, etc.), the control of informal groups, at the extreme, complete segregation from all counterinfluences (the priesthood, the military officer corps). With all that, who needs degrees?

Whatever the weight of their desire to recruit employees who share their own values, employers who use educational credentials to define eligible pools of workers are acting on a more reliable assumption: Schools and colleges on average recruit and pass on people who can quickly learn new work roles, thereby lowering training costs; more than serving as a mere conduit, educational institutions on average also sharpen the job-relevant cognitive and social skills of their students. What employers think they are getting and what schooling in fact produces are not far apart.

When employers speak of "skills" they mean not only manual dexterity, accuracy in task performance, and a variety of mental abilities (verbal, quantitative, other) but also a willingness and ability to take responsibility (for equipment, tools, files, records, money), "good work habits" (punctuality, reliability, a willingness to comply with orders), and social skills that minimize costly strains and permit work to go on. Occasionally they mean "creativity" and "initiative"—somewhat vaguer labels for qualities they are sure exist.

Whatever else the endurance contests we call education do for the graduates, they surely do something to develop their responsibility, work habits, and social skills; schooling at times may even foster creativity and nourish entrepreneurial talent.

From two types of study we can infer that schools typically enhance the motivation and capacity to learn: intensive studies of distinctive colleges (Newcomb et al., 1967; Feldman and Newcomb, 1969; Clark, 1970; Grant and Riesman, 1978; Trow, 1974*a*; and Clark et al. 1972) and a massive inventory of data on the effects of education at every level among cross-sections of the United States population. In a careful secondary analysis of fifty-four national sample surveys done between 1949 and 1971, Hyman, Wright, and Reed (1975) found that education produced "large, pervasive, and enduring differences in knowledge" of a wide range of topics (p. 60).[13] More important for our argument, much of the knowledge which the more highly educated displayed could only have been learned after the completion of formal education. Education thus inculcates not only factual information, but also the "motivation, outlook, and skills that will give [a person] the power to continue to learn, to seek, and to be receptive to new information and culture" (p. 80).

Our theme that education is relevant to work performance and probably has an enduring effect on the motive and ability to learn new roles must be accompanied by several caveats concerning the possible effects of a surplus of college graduates; a related impulse of governments to make education more narrowly vocational; the importance of quality variations as education becomes more universal; and, finally, the place of ability and aptitude testing in occupational fate.

## "OVEREDUCATION" AND THE NEW VOCATIONALISM

In the competition for preferred jobs over the work life—jobs with relative security or freedom or status—it is unlikely that the advantage of a solid base for lifetime learning will lessen much if any. Even if income from human capital investment continues to slide, from the individual's point of view education will continue to pay off for job placement. In fact, given the central relevance of education in recruitment, the advantage of college and

[13] Hyman and his collaborators selected survey questions which revealed a knowledge of public affairs, notable persons, popular culture, the tools and duties of various occupations, and general academic knowledge of history, geography, the sciences, and the humanities (pp. 15–21). In various surveys, for example, respondents were asked to identify Sigmund Freud or George Meany, to name the planet closest to the sun, or to locate the Parthenon (appendix D). Differences by education in information about such matters persist even when the independent effects of age, sex, religion, ethnicity, and class and residential origin were controlled; such educational differences characterized individuals who represented "several generations and several historical periods in the functioning of the schools"( pp. 58–59; chap. 3 passim).

high school graduates over the rest should widen, thereby adding to the diminished hope of the underclass, as the least successful college graduates compete for jobs held by high school graduates and the least successful high school graduates take over the best jobs of the remaining elementary school graduates.

However, education can become somewhat less relevant to job performance and occupational fate if current trends are carried far. In their zeal to save public funds and reduce the "underutilized," "overeducated" population, many politicians and some educational planners in the United States are trying to phase out liberal arts colleges and general high school education in favor of shorter, more vocational curricula; their European counterparts, never having developed the concept of a liberal education, are continuing to search for more practical work-oriented curricula. Leaving aside the values of education beyond the vocational, it is grossly misleading to think of vocational education apart from basic literacy of a high order, disciplined work habits, and flexibility of mind. Narrowly vocational education is the enemy of both literacy and flexibility, crucial qualities for finding one's way about a modern labor market. Such fragmentation of curricula will assure the repeated obsolescence of skills, which, to be useful over the work life, must reflect a common core permitting quick retraining and refreshing. It is not the overeducated person but the overspecialized person who is a positive danger to himself and to a democratic society.

Industry, like government, helps to create these educational fashions. Consider the current enthusiasm for the certified master of business administration (M.B.A.). Although the M.B.A. boom in part fits our theme of the "technical" functions of education, it also is a symbol of the overprofessionalization and narrow vocationalism now developing in response to the fiscal crisis of universities. On the one hand, the standard courses in accounting, finance, and quantitative methods certify that the M.B.A. can read a balance sheet and quickly learn some other relevant things. People strongly motivated for business careers are attracted to this degree; recruitment costs for the firm are low. Universities under fiscal pressure respond by reallocating resources to the hot topics where the job market of the moment seems active, thereby increasing the supply of this easily sold package and reinforcing management predilections. On the other hand, some managers who are impressed by the technical virtuosity and personal cool of M.B.A.'s at the same time complain of lack of breadth and weak communication skills. It has yet to be proved that a four-year liberal arts major trained on the job would perform worse or cost more than the MBA. And beyond technical function, the M.B.A. symbolizes legitimacy. As Arnold R. Weber says, "The MBA degree attests to the professionalism of management and strengthens the argument that corporate leaders exercise power by virtue of competence and not usurpation. Historically, a mastery of cost accounting has provided a more credible basis for managerial legitimacy than

Social Darwinism" (*Wall Street Journal*, May 15, 1978). In short, a handy blend of technical function and status affirmation.

If these recent trends accelerate and persist, the liberal arts degree will become more a status symbol and less a ticket of admission. Highly "professional" and "technical" credentials will become more important as an entry requirement but less of a base for lifetime learning. The question for research remains "Among various kinds of professional-technical curricula, which are too narrowly vocational (a poor base for lifetime learning) and which facilitate the easy redevelopment and transferability of skills?"

## THE INCREASING IMPORTANCE OF QUALITY VARIATIONS

As the brisk demand for Harvard-Stanford-Chicago M.B.A.'s illustrates, level of education, type of education, and particular schools all count in job assignment. As rich countries become richer and mass education spreads, however, quality variations within the same level of education will become increasingly important. For mass education necessitates a riotous diversity of schools, colleges, and universities to meet the great variety of demands on the system and people to be accommodated (cf. Jencks and Riesman, 1968; Trow, 1972, 1974b; Riesman, Gusfield, and Gamson, 1971; Wilensky, 1975: 3–7). That about a third of the age grade eighteen to twenty-one in the United States are in college (U.S. Bureau of the Census, 1977*a*: 7; 1977*b*: 8) reinforces a long-established diversification.

The specialization and institutional stratification of modern educational systems means that the higher quality, resource-rich schools and colleges graduate people whose abilities, motivation, and information give them a competitive advantage in the job scramble over people with identical formal levels of education. Yet few systematic studies of the links between education and occupational fate—or of any other outcome of education— have taken account of these crucial quality variations.[14]

## A FOOTNOTE ON ABILITY TESTING

Insofar as aptitude and achievement tests become a gate through which one passes to desired colleges and professional schools, they are, of course, crucial for occupational fate. But no amount of complaint about test bias will change the overwhelming evidence that, in itself, debiasing tests

[14] For a demonstration of the utility of measures of quality variations, see Wilensky, 1964*a*: 187–89, and Ladinsky, 1967: 222–32. For evidence of the links between types of educational institutions and broad types of occupational positions attained by graduates, see Crozier, 1964, and Ben-David and Zloczower, 1962. For differences between graduates of contrasting types of British universities, see Halsey and Trow, 1971.

changes nothing. Thirty years of effort to remove cultural bias from such tests have had no effect in reducing the differences in average scores between advantaged and disadvantaged groups (Haggard, 1954; Green, 1978; Flaugher, 1978; Schmidt and Hunter, 1974; Stanley, 1971). For social research and social action alike, "test bias" is a dead end. Unfortunately, that has not stopped sociologists and the Supreme Court from riveting public attention on the nonissue of test bias in entry jobs, thereby diverting energies from research and action on more important problems: the interplay of opportunity, motivation, and information as determinants of both test performance and occupational fate over a forty-six-year work life.

There is a more fruitful way to frame the debate about the uses of tests in hiring and promotion. We should focus on two questions: What measured abilities and what additional qualities—of common sense, judgment, motivation, leadership—are relevant in what organizational contexts and job patterns? What combination of ascription and achievement can be defended by what set of values and political purposes?

## NEEDED RESEARCH ON EDUCATION

Systematic tests of the ascription-achievement hypothesis and of the argument about education as "technical function" versus "status group conflict" are rare. What is required is cross-sectional studies of job assignment by type of organization, historical studies of changing criteria of job placement in one country, and, most difficult of all, comparative historical studies of systems of job allocation. The few we have found show an intricate admixture of ascription and achievement in hiring and promotion. They are consistent with our argument that education both fosters economic growth and provides a base for lifetime learning and mobility, especially for the least privileged populations. These studies are consistent, too, with the idea that industrialization has thus far meant a slow shift from ascription to achievement. A summary and evaluation of the best of them will indicate the research possibilities. We can then turn to what appears to be a spectacular deviant case, the economic growth of South Africa despite its overwhelming reliance on ascription in job assignment.

### MANAGERS IN ACTION

The most suggestive study of employers weighing various criteria in job assignment is by Collins (1971). Using the University of California Berkeley Institute of Industrial Relations survey of entry requirements in 309 organizations with 100 or more employees in the San Francisco, Oakland, and San Jose metropolitan area (Gordon and Thal-Larsen, 1969), Collins tried to test functional and conflict theories of educational stratification by exploring the meaning of education as a criterion of recruitment. He measured a normative control emphasis versus a technical function emphasis. Among his findings: Educational requirements are highest in organizations with the strongest emphasis on normative control ("public trust" organizations in the fields of finance, professional services, and other public services and any other organizations where recruiters emphasize a record of job loyalty and the absence of a police record). That relationship holds for entry to managerial and white-collar jobs generally but does not affect blue-collar education requirements. He also found, however, that an organization's technological modernity (measured by the number of technical and organizational changes in the previous six years) independently affected educational requirements at the same managerial and white-collar levels (Collins, 1971: 1013–14). In other words, criteria relevant to organizational commitment and reliability were meshed with criteria relevant to technical performance—a good demonstration of our picture of what employers look for in hiring and promotion. (For those who believe that educational requirements for blue-collar workers are a means of keeping the working class under managerial control, these findings provide no support.)

Comparative analysis of various types of organizations in action on job assignment is needed to sort out the processes by which various mixes of achievement and ascription are developed.

### Historical Studies

In addition to cross-sectional studies of job assignment by type of organization, historical studies of changing criteria of placement can help test the ascription-achievement hypothesis. The conflict theory is based partly on historical grounds. For instance, many students who believe that education is basically irrelevant to work performance and economic growth note that mass education in the United States and England preceded the big push for industrialization and therefore educational expansion cannot be explained by the technical demands of modern organizations and occupations. The argument is not entirely persuasive. A mass demand for citizenship rights, expressed in political action to expand education, may come first and economic growth later but as modernizing countries get richer, the interaction between the two is subtle and complex. Further, at higher levels of development "political demands" (for medical care, pensions, higher education, and other entitlements) are themselves generated by economic growth; logically, they are intervening variables (Wilensky and Lebeaux, 1958; Wilensky, 1975; Cutright, 1965) and do not show the irrelevance of demands of modern work roles and work places.

The possibility of systematic analysis of the role of education through one-country historical studies is illustrated by Donovan (1977). She explores the specific question "Is secondary school enrollment in the United States a response to expanding labor market opportunity or is it an attempt by higher-status groups to maintain their privileges?'' and specifies the populations and times for which education did or did not function as a means of mobility. She regressed the proportion of fourteen- to seventeen-year-olds enrolled in all types of secondary education from 1870 to 1910 on the proportion of the economically active labor force in nonmanual jobs, taking account of variations by region, differential migration of educated labor, white and nonwhite. Her main conclusion: Established elites (native-born whites) could rely on ascription for access to white-collar jobs, but less favored groups—the foreign-born and blacks—got access to such positions only by achievement through secondary schools. A century later, as we have seen, the same educational road is travelled by blacks: Where it once took a highschool diploma, it now takes a college degree for such minorities to secure entry to upper-level occupations.[15]

In one-country historical studies, part of the missing evidence should be answers to these questions: At various levels of education, do compulsory school laws and increases in actual attendance lag or lead various levels and rates of economic growth? What occupational profiles characterize these levels and rates? And, finally, for which populations does ascription outweigh achievement?

## EDUCATION AND ECOMOMIC GROWTH

In further specifying the idea that modern society tends toward placement by relevant performance criteria and that education becomes increasingly relevant with industrialization, especially for excluded groups pressing for equality, we need to compare societies at various levels of development and explore the interplay of education and economic action.

If students who reject the technical function argument want to find places where education is purely an index of status, they should look not to modern countries but to a range of least developed countries where formal education is the primary criterion of merit, is tightly connected to elite socioeconomic status and high caste, and is totally irrelevant either to economic action or to the expansion of bureaucratic discipline and a power base necessary for economic development. In many poor countries, educated strata learn a distaste for manual labor and practical action in upper-income, high-caste families—later reinforced by education; they then staff a bloated bureaucracy which generates numerous development plans. Absent are the middle-level technicians and managers in agriculture, veterinary medicine, engineering, health, commerce, and public administration needed

[15] Similarly, an analysis of the introduction of educational standards and examinations in the civil services of Prussia and England suggests that education served different functions for populations differently situated: To Prussian middle-class careerists at the beginning of the 19th century it meant gaining administrative power; to Victorian gentlemen, it meant holding onto power (Mueller, 1974).

to put such plans into effect. Present in abundance are college graduates from the arts, humanities, law, and social sciences (cf. Shils, 1960*b*; Boggs, 1978). For education to foster economic growth it must be broadly based and diversified. Homegrown or imported, the products of schooling must connect with the political and practical tasks of modernization.

That an appropriate educational mix facilitates economic growth is shown by both time-series and cross-sectional analyses of the links between educational expansion and increases in real income per capita. Whether one uses the data of Kuznets, Clark, Maddison, or the United Nations, the comparative evidence suggests that after universal primary education is substantially attained, a swift rate of growth of secondary enrollment results in a high rate of economic growth per capita, and that a subsequent step-up in university enrollment rates contributes to further economic growth. (For a review of this literature and results of graphs of educational and economic growth for thirty-seven countries from about 1900 to 1962, see Peaslee, 1969; cf. Carnoy, 1970.)

The issue of the relative effects of education and other institutions remains unsettled. Two recent studies of countries at low to medium levels of development illustrate fruitful avenues for research. Inkeles and Smith (1974), analyzing interviews with almost 6,000 men in six countries, establish that modernizing institutions produce modern persons. In descending order of strength as producers of people with orientations appropriate for economic growth and effective government, they find, are the school, the mass media, and the factory. No evidence is presented, however, that modern individuals in fact produce economic growth. The second study focuses on actual growth in forty-nine poor countries; it abundantly confirms the central role of the school, contradicts the importance of the media, and adds a demonstration of the effect of political context. Controlling for the economic constraints imposed by initial poverty and world system position (trade dependence), Delacroix and Ragin (1978) find that the school (secondary school enrollment as a proportion of secondary school–age population circa 1953 and in 1965) furthers economic development, while exposure to the cinema, interpreted as exposure to Western values, hinders it. Mobilizing regimes (''hard'') such as Cuba and Mexico enhance the positive school effect; nonmobilizing regimes (''soft'') such as Guatemala and Nigeria enhance the adverse effect of the cinema.

In sum, by riveting attention on entry jobs instead of job patterns, by accenting the oversupply of college graduates, by noting the age-old tendency of privileged groups to protect their privileges and economic groups to seek a monopoly, by failing to make the necessary comparisons, historical and contemporary, and by diverting attention to sideshows such as the test bias controversy, sociologists have obscured the real relevance of education to job performance, career development, and economic growth. More balance in this debate should be restored.

## South Africa: A Deviant Case?

Among industrial societies, what appears to be the most glaring deviation from the hypothesized shift from ascription to achievement as the basis of role allocation in modern economies is the Republic of South Africa. Between 1946 and 1966, the rate of economic growth exceeded 8 percent annually, the highest in the world after Japan (Rogers 1976*b*: 23). In per capita gross domestic product, South Africa now ranks somewhat below Portugal—and at a par with Japan ten years ago—in an intermediate position among the world's nation-states.[16] During the postwar period, the South African economy successfully diversified its base from an almost exclusive reliance on commercial agriculture and gold and diamond mining. By 1963, secondary manufacturing industry had overtaken the two primary sectors' contribution to the gross domestic product and is today the most dynamic sector in South Africa's economy (Gervasi, 1970). In recent years, growth has been particularly rapid in the automobile, metals and engineering, and chemical industries, all of which use technologically advanced production techniques. Although industrial expansion varies by area and the economy still depends heavily on extractive industry, most economic historians agree that South Africa has largely completed the transition to a modern industrial economy (Houghton, 1967: 40, 1971: 32–48; Trapido, 1971: 313).

Despite its rapid industrialization, South Africa continues to maintain rigid restrictions on both the geographical and occupational mobility of nonwhites in the labor market.[17] Under the policy of apartheid, or "separate development," all Africans are required to become citizens of

[16] In 1975, per capita gross domestic product in South Africa was $1,330 compared with Portugal's $1,517 in 1974. Japan's per capita GDP in 1965 (in 1975 dollars) was $1,546 (United Nations, 1977: 634–36, 686–88). However, for South Africa, per capita gross domestic product may be an inadequate indicator of industrialization. As the South African Department of Information notes, "the dualistic nature of the economy needs emphasis. It comprises a highly sophisticated Western type industrial sector, together with a fairly large subsistence sector." In 1973, 32 percent of all economically active Africans were engaged at least part time in subsistence agriculture, which is not computed in the national product (Republic of South Africa, 1976*b*: 115). Thus, the gross domestic product per capita underestimates the degree of industrial development in the most advanced sectors of the South African economy.

[17] The South African population is officially divided into four racial groups: White, Coloured (a term referring to persons of mixed racial ancestry), Asian, and African. According to the South African government's population estimates for 1977, these racial groups are distributed as follows: White, 4.32 million (17.6 percent), Coloured, 2.39 million (9.7 percent), Asian, 0.77 million (3.1 percent), and African, 16.95 million (69.1 percent). These figures exclude the estimated population of the Transkei. Following customary usage, we will use the term "nonwhite" to refer to Coloured persons, Asians, and Africans (Republic of South Africa, 1978: 1.1).

one of ten "bantustans," rural reserves set aside for African residence. Comprising only 13 percent of the country's land area, the bantustans include few cities, ports, mineral resources, or major industries, and their land is overcrowded, and typically badly eroded (Carter, Karis, and Stultz, 1967; Horrell, 1973; Rogers, 1976a). However, the South African economy continues to rely heavily on African workers, who currently constitute 70.4 percent of the labor force (Republic of South Africa, 1978: 2.1). The result of government policy has been the institutionalization of a migrant labor system, in which Africans enter the "white" areas as temporary migrant laborers who oscillate annually between jobs in the cities and their families in the rural homelands. In 1970 43 percent of all economically active African men in South Africa were migrants, and this proportion, contrary to the general pattern in industrializing countries, has been increasing (F. Wilson, 1975: 178; Rogers, 1976*b*: 49; Nattrass, 1976: 69, 78). The geographical separation of the races is maintained by an elaborate "influx control" system which regulates the movement of Africans in the "white" areas. Thus, apartheid has institutionalized a massive disjunction between the geographical location of job opportunities and the location of the African population.

The migrant labor system is complemented by an industrial "color bar" which substantially blocks the upward mobility of African workers into skilled occupations. Until 1978, the South African government had legal authority to reserve jobs on a racial basis and to set quotas on the number of Africans who could be employed in particular industries. Although in recent years the government seldom used that authority, the threat of government intervention, coupled with pressure from powerful white trade unions which have virtually monopolized access to skilled positions, has constrained the upward mobility of nonwhite workers. The power of the color bar is reflected in the occupational distribution of racial groups. According to the 1970 census, a mere 4.7 percent of economically active Africans are employed in white-collar occupations (professional and technical, managerial, clerical, and sales). Most of these are employed as ministers, teachers, health workers, and salesclerks in segregated establishments. By contrast, 57.8 percent of whites are working in white-collar jobs (Republic of South Africa, 1976*a*: 1-15).

Through the mechanisms of influx control and the color bar, the South African labor market has become effectively bifurcated into two relatively noncompeting segments: one nonwhite, unskilled, and migrant, the other white, skilled, and settled.

There is considerable debate in the literature about whether or not apartheid is, in Heribert Adam's phrase, an "outdated relic" which will inevitably give way to more rational forms of social organization as industrialization proceeds (1971*a*: 16). Many scholars argue that South Africa's ascriptive system of racial segregation is incompatible with a complex industrial economy and has survived only because of the increasing use of coercion. Because of its dysfunctional character, they say, segregation in the labor market will erode as the economy develops (Hutt, 1964; Thompson, 1966; Horwitz, 1967; van den Berghe, 1967; Marquard, 1969). Generally, such scholars maintain that pressures for reform will be initiated either by economic elites associated with the most advanced sectors of industry, particularly English-speaking businessmen and those allied with foreign corporations (Van der Horst, 1965: 135–36), or by the small but growing number of *verlighte* ("enlightened") Afrikaner businessmen, who may be in a better position than the English-speaking group to influence government policy (Adam, 1971*a*: 180–82).[18] In contrast, a second group of scholars has argued that apartheid and industrialization are compatible. Historically, they say, the migrant labor system and the color bar have given the politically dominant white minority a mechanism for holding down the wages of African workers, thereby generating the surplus to sustain both rapid economic growth and a high standard of living for the white population. Thus, further economic development will not be enough to eliminate the political disabilities of nonwhites in the South African labor market (Johnstone, 1970, 1976; Wolpe, 1970; Arrighi and Saul, 1973; Legassick, 1974; F. Wilson, 1975; Rogers, 1976*b*; Litvak, DeGrasse, and McTigue, 1977; Lawrence, 1977; Milkman, 1977).

In our view, the first group of theorists is correct in pointing to the economic strains caused by the rigid racial stratification of South Africa's labor market. Restrictions on the geographical and occupational mobility of African workers have in recent years caused serious dislocations in the South African economy, including shortages of skilled workers, low rates of productivity, and an artificially restricted domestic market. However, these pressures have not been sufficient to undermine apartheid. As the second group of theorists stress, the continuing profitability of cheap African labor, coupled with the political support for apartheid among the dominant white electorate, assures that industrialization alone will not destroy the system. Industrialists and state policy makers have responded to the economic costs of a racially stratified labor market not by eliminating apartheid restrictions altogether, but rather by developing increasingly innovative techniques of racial domination which bring these restrictions into line with the demands of a modern economy.

[18]The South African white population is divided into two language groups: the Afrikaans-speaking Afrikaners (57 percent), descendants of the Dutch immigrants of the seventeenth century, and the English-speaking whites (43 percent), descendants of the British settlers of the eighteenth and nineteenth centuries. Historically the Afrikaners have been less urbanized, poorer, and less well represented in the business, mining, and banking sectors than the English, although the discrepancy between the two groups has lessened considerably in the postwar period.

## THE COSTS OF APARTHEID

Among the most serious economic consequences of apartheid have been growing shortages of both white and African workers. In 1960, skilled jobs accounted for 13.1 percent of total employment. By 1970, this proportion had risen to 16.0 percent and the demand for white-collar workers will continue to grow rapidly with further industrialization (Republic of South Africa, 1978: 2.1; Horrell, 1977: 288–89). Since such jobs are customarily filled by whites, these trends have meant a dramatic increase in the demand for white workers. The natural increase of the white population, however, has not been sufficient to meet this demand. During the early 1970s, vacancies in all "white" jobs varied between 40,000 and 50,000 annually, with particularly severe shortages registered among artisans and professionals (Feit and Stokes, 1976: 490). Such shortages give white workers improved bargaining power and drive up wages, exacerbating South Africa's already severe double-digit inflation.[19]

Paradoxically, despite the great abundance of nonwhite labor in South Africa, the barriers to the free mobility of Africans in the labor market have caused short-term shortages of African workers as well. Because Africans seeking employment outside the bantustans must obtain the approval of the tribal labor bureau before entering a "white" area, they are not able to respond to changing employer demand for labor as quickly as would be the case in a free labor market. Employers have found it difficult to obtain adequate supplies of unskilled African workers, particularly if their labor needs change rapidly and unexpectedly (Steenkamp, 1973: 448–49).

Racial restrictions in the labor market also mean lower labor productivity, on both sides of the racial divide. From a standard baseline of 100 in 1953, worker productivity in South Africa rose to only 128 by 1968, as compared with 168 in the United States, 194 in West Germany, and 398 in Japan (Horner, 1972: 12). Both whites and nonwhites play their part. Although the productivity of skilled white workers did advance during the postwar boom (Houghton, 1967: 213), the rate was slow: They were in such scarce supply that they had little incentive to improve efficiency (Doxey, 1961: 184; van den Berghe, 1967: 199). On their side, the productivity of African workers is currently only one-quarter that of whites and is growing sluggishly at a rate of 1.4 percent a year (Horner, 1972: 12; Kessel, 1972: 364). The wages paid Africans are generally inadequate to maintain a decent standard of living; black workers often come to the job malnourished and suffering

[19] In 1974–75, the South African inflation rate was close to 14 percent—no more than that of many other countries, but high enough to alarm South African policy makers (United Nations, 1977: 534–36).

from a variety of poverty-related diseases (van den Berghe, 1967: 185).[20] Restricted opportunity for upward mobility seriously diminishes incentives for improved performance. More significantly, the migrant labor system discourages employers from providing training, since turnover is so high. The combination of an abundant cheap labor supply (much of it reflecting "overmanning") and swiftly growing capital investments partly explains why South Africa can have both persistently low labor productivity and a rapid growth in GNP.

The low wages of African workers have resulted in an artificially restricted domestic market. In 1973, the per capita annual income among whites in South Africa was approximately $2,539, approaching that of the United Kingdom ($3,145 in 1973) (United Nations, 1977: 686–88; Horrell, 1976: 163). The consumption by whites of all manner of consumption goods, from automobiles to swimming pools, is extremely high. Yet whites constitute only 18 percent of the potential internal market for consumer goods, and there is evidence that the affluent but numerically small white market has become saturated (*Business Week*, 1977: 68). Africans, by contrast, spend about 70 percent of their incomes on food alone; the consumption of other items is correspondingly restricted. Thus, South African producers have found it difficult to expand the local market to keep pace with expanding production.

Finally, the cost of the repressive apparatus necessary to enforce apartheid is large. As the subsistence sector in the bantustans declines with soil exhaustion and overpopulation, growing numbers of Africans seek to leave the reserves for the cities, in direct conflict with the South African government's policy of geographical separation of the races. After a long lull, since 1976 South Africa has been shaken by increasing political unrest, as students and relatively urbanized workers in Soweto and elsewhere have challenged legalized discrimination in education, housing, and job opportunities (Callinicos and Rogers, 1977: 157–73). Under these conditions, the government has escalated coercion to enforce influx control and other apartheid legislation. Since the passage of influx control legislation, there has been a steady increase in the proportion of Africans prosecuted for pass law offenses (Wilson, 1975: 181). South Africa's prison population now averages 100,000 daily, proportionately the highest of any Western country (Burns, 1978). If internal tensions continue to mount, the costs of enforcing the laws which regulate the occupational and geographical mobility of Africans will grow still further.

[20] In 1976, the average wage for an African worker in Johannesburg (where wages are above the national norm) was $60 a month (Horrell, 1977: 275–76); the average monthly wage for whites was $562 (Republic of South Africa, 1978: 2.3). Although African wages have risen, the absolute gap between the incomes of African and white households is growing (Horrell, 1977: 276).

## THE "BENEFITS" OF APARTHEID

Despite the clear economic costs of apartheid and recent demands for liberalization, the ruling National party, in power continuously for thirty years, has stuck to its racial policies. Historically, the party has drawn its support primarily from white workers of both languages and Afrikaner farmers, small-businessmen and professionals, all of whom benefit from white supremacy. During their tenure in office, the Nationalists have aggressively pursued a policy of secondary industrialization under state auspices while adhering to their ideological commitment to strict racial separation in all spheres (Milkman, 1977: 61–78). These policies have benefited not only the Nationalists' traditional supporters, who are protected from nonwhite competition, but all whites, who have enjoyed a rising standard of living. Since 1948, the National party has gradually increased its support among the white electorate from the bare majority which brought the party to power to the overwhelming 70 percent of the popular vote it received in the 1977 general election (*New York Times*, Dec. 1, 1977).

In contrast to white workers and small-businessmen, leading industrialists do not need government intervention to protect them from competition from nonwhites; they have a different incentive to support Nationalist policies: apartheid has delivered a cheap labor force with few political rights and little bargaining power. The geographical separation of the races helps keep labor costs low, since the separation of the migrant worker from members of his family, who remain dependent on the subsistence economy in the bantustan, allows the employer to pay a wage and fringe benefits sufficient only to support a single individual. Industry is thereby able to transfer to the reserve economy such social overhead costs as unemployment compensation, family education, medical care, and support of the aged (cf. Burawoy, 1976; Moore, 1951). The savings to the employer in wages and benefits and to the government in welfare costs must be considerable. In addition, as noncitizens in the areas of South Africa reserved for whites, Africans are denied the right to vote, to organize political parties, or to dissent (Friedman, 1974: 17–23). Their papers can be revoked and they can be deported to the bantustans at any time, a powerful lever of social control since prospects for employment in the reserves are bleak. Without political rights in the "white" areas, Africans are severely hampered in their efforts to organize. Although African labor unions are not prohibited by law, their activities are tightly circumscribed.

Apartheid policies also weaken the position of African workers indirectly. First, the migrant labor system has helped prevent the formation of a unified urban working class which could act on its own behalf to gain improvement in wages, working conditions, and political rights. African migrants do not develop the skills that have given white workers improved bargaining power in urban industry. Second, the continual turnover of migrants, who often return to another employer after their furlough in the reserves, creates formidable obstacles to developing the leadership and common organizational experience necessary for an effective union, quite apart from the legal obstacles to organization.[21]

## CHANGING PATTERNS OF RACIAL DOMINATION

In view of the clear advantages of racial repression, most industrialists and state policymakers have sought to circumvent or counteract those aspects of apartheid that impede the efficient functioning of business operations without fundamentally challenging white supremacy itself. They have pursued two main strategies: recourse to markets for capital, goods, and labor outside South Africa, and the internal reorganization of labor recruitment and jobs to make more efficient use of existing resources.

The government and employers have looked beyond South Africa's borders for capital and technology necessary for industrial development and for markets for South African goods they are unable to sell to their own impoverished population. In the postwar period South Africa has relied heavily on foreign capital, through direct investments and bank loans, to offset some of the costs of its racially skewed economy. By 1976, approximately $10.4 billion had been invested directly in the South African economy by foreign firms (U.S. Senate, 1978: 8). These firms have helped provide the technological and managerial expertise and the capital to facilitate South Africa's rapid economic growth in the postwar period. The surplus thus generated has helped pay the costs of apartheid and, at the same time, raise the living standard of the white population, thereby consolidating political support for National party policies. Regarding external markets, although South Africa ranks only twenty-third in total economic output internationally, it is fifteenth in the volume of foreign trade (Rogers, 1976*b*: 99; Litvak, DeGrasse, and McTigue, 1977: 31). Thus, in several ways South Africa has been able to "externalize" the cost of its racial policies.

In solving the labor shortages induced by apartheid, South Africa has sought both external and internal solutions. The government has augmented existing supplies of white labor through immigration. The regime

[21] The political repression of African workers and the difficulties of organizing migrant labor are reflected in the weakness of the African labor movement. In 1975, only 59,440 Africans, approximately one percent of those in the labor force, had joined one of the twenty four known underground African unions (International Labour Office, 1976: 3). In 1977, there were only ninety work stoppages in South Africa (Republic of South Africa, 1978: 2.31). Many leading industrialists are ambivalent toward apartheid. A survey of businessmen's attitudes concludes that their recognition of the losses from restrictions on their use of African labor is outweighed by their appreciation of internal stability and access to cheap labor which together guarantee a high return from investment (Adam, 1971*b*: 89).

maintains an extensive network in all major western European countries to attract skilled workers affected by technological unemployment in their native countries, and private firms also initiate their own recruitment efforts abroad (African National Congress, 1971: 52; *Africa Today*, 1970: 35–36). The result: throughout the 1960s and 1970s, the inflow of white immigrants averaged around 30,000 annually, overwhelmingly persons whose occupational training fits current job vacancies (State of South Africa, 1978: 52; International Labour Office, 1974*a*: 35–36).

Internally, labor recruitment has been reorganized to make the most efficient use of existing labor supplies, both white and nonwhite, within the framework of apartheid restrictions. As the demand for skilled workers increased, employers attempted to increase the labor force participation rates of whites. Some companies have recruited women for jobs previously defined by custom as men's work and have encouraged retired whites to return to work, while the government has proposed to incorporate sections of the military into the labor force (cf. *Africa Today*, 1970: 11, 26; Houghton, 1967: 213).

In their use of Africans, employers generally adjust to the migratory pattern by assigning the minority of African workers who are relatively settled in the urban areas to upgraded jobs, while relegating oscillating migrants to the least skilled, least desirable jobs (Wilson, 1975: 182–83). However, they have recently developed new kinds of labor controls to upgrade African workers without threatening the migratory labor pattern. A prime example is the "call-in card." In the past, employers found that the high turnover rates associated with the migratory pattern made it difficult to train workers for semiskilled work. In 1973 the influx control bureaucracy was centralized and the "pass book" system computerized, thereby enabling employers to use a "call-in card" to recall former workers after their furlough in the reserves. In 1975, 225,000 migrants were returned to their previous place of employment by this device (Wilson, 1975: 182; Litvak, DeGrasse, and McTigue, 1977: 21). Under discussion is a new regulation which would prohibit a worker from entering the urban area at all until he or she first reapplied for work with the previous employer.

While most employers try to find workers to fit available jobs, some change jobs to fit the available labor supply. At times, jobs are simply reclassified without changing their content. The South African Railway, for instance, recently employed a number of Africans as "shunters" on the trains by relabeling the job "train marshal" (SPRO-CAS, 1973: 23, 69). More frequently, a skilled job previously performed by whites is subdivided so that its component elements may be performed by less skilled African migrants (*Africa Today*, 1970: 35–36; Litvak, DeGrasse, and McTigue, 1977: 21; Myers, 1976: 58).

A final response to labor shortages is to allow the color bar to "float" upward. Many African and Coloured workers now perform skilled work in

South Africa illegally and without corresponding status or reward (Doxey, 1961: 276). In the South African automobile industry, for instance, the ratio of skilled mechanics to automobiles produced is 1:145, as compared with the international ratio of 1:85, reflecting the tendency of smaller workshops to assign nonwhites to skilled work unofficially (SPRO-CAS, 1973: 66). Although job reservation rulings are often circumvented informally, important cases must be negotiated between the company involved and the government. In 1975, over 4,000 exemptions from provisions of the Industrial Conciliation Act were granted individual employers (Horrell, 1977: 285–86).

The recent gains of nonwhite workers in the job market have typically *not* been at the expense of white workers. Statistics on trends in the occupational distribution of workers by race suggest that the upgrading of Africans has been occasioned by the upward movement of whites into more skilled positions in secondary industry or into service or white-collar employment (Steenkamp, 1971: 109). In most cases, the government grants exemptions from job reservation laws only on the condition that there is no white unemployment in the industry and that no nonwhites, as a consequence of the exemption, either supervise or replace whites (Rogers, 1976*b*: 41–2; Horrell, 1976: 170). Often, white workers negotiate salary increases or other benefits in exchange for their support of an upgrading scheme for nonwhites (International Labour Office, 1976: 19). The gradual upgrading of nonwhite workers is thus better interpreted as a shift of the entire color bar upward—a case of uncontested ethnic succession—rather than as a breach of the color bar itself (First, Steele, and Gurney, 1973: 59–80; Johnstone, 1970).

Through all these strategies, official and unofficial, employers seek to resolve the economic dilemmas posed by apartheid. Although systematic data are not available, scattered evidence suggests that pressures on employers to reorganize jobs and recruitment systems and to push up the color bar are most intense in those industries in which changes in skill composition have been most rapid. Government records on employers exempted from job reservation laws—or prosecuted for failure to comply with them—show that evasion and avoidance of apartheid restrictions have been most substantial in the construction industry, motor vehicle driving, motor vehicle assembly, and liquor and catering (International Labour Office, 1974*a*: 12; Horrell, 1977: 286–87). With the possible exception of liquor and catering, these are industries which have been characterized in recent years by rapid shifts in skill composition, increasing shortages of skilled workers, or both (Scheiner, 1977). If this is the case, further technical and organizational change in the South African economy will bring heightened pressures on apartheid restrictions.

In sum, while the South African government and many employers have not wavered in their commitment to white supremacy, they have shown considerable tactical flexibility in shaping these ideological goals to the requirements of a dynamic industrial economy. Forces for a shift to the use of achievement criteria exist in South Africa, as in other modernizing economies. As a result of its racial policies, South Africa has experienced shortages of skilled labor, low rates of productivity, a restricted domestic market, and high costs of law enforcement—all of which could be eased by a breakdown of apartheid policies and the more rapid advancement of nonwhites in the labor market. However, a major shift in policy has so far been thwarted by a politically dominant racial minority which has sought to preserve its privileges even at the cost of some short-term disadvantages for the economy as a whole. To be sure, the costs of South Africa's "modernizing racial domination" have been extremely high. But, to date, the South African experiment has been, in its own terms, a success, and it is unlikely that pressures internal to the system will soon destroy it.

In some ways South Africa is deviant from ethnically pluralist societies, in others it fits general patterns. Our interpretive summary explores its significance for the ascription-achievement hypothesis.

## Summary and Interpretation

Whether we restrict "ascription" to attributes of persons clearly known at birth (sex, race, social origin) or include all placement criteria frequently viewed as irrelevant to job performance (age, seniority, political or religious preference, personality, physical appearance), it is likely that in general and for the past century continuing industrialization in rich countries has fostered a slow decline in ascription in job assignment and an increase in the weight of achievement. "Who you are" has become less important; "what you can do or quickly learn to do" becomes more important. Further, in some occupations certain ascriptive criteria (e.g., age, personality) are, in fact, relevant to performance.

The predominant institutionalization of one alternative of these polar opposites does not exclude its counterpart. To go beyond the very general proposition, we can fruitfully view ascription and achievement, like tradition and modernity or community and society, as conflicting principles of organization built into the structure of modern society (cf. Bendix and Berger, 1959; Moore, 1960; M. G. Smith, 1966; Gusfield, 1967; Mayhew, 1968) and then specify the conditions under which one or another placement criterion is dominant, discover which is ascending or fading in various types of roles, organizations, and societies, and which groups competing for advantage are least and most successful. The persistence of ascription will thereby be rendered less puzzling.

Taking account of level but not quality of formal education, the pace and extent of occupational integration among white ethnics or ethnic-religious groups in the United States appear to be fastest. Minority groups which enter the economic system with child-rearing philosophies and practices favorable to their children's occupational mobility (e.g., independence training), who arrive with resources of urban experience, credit, money, or occupational skill, and whose schools are not segregated and unequal achieve occupational parity quickly. Thus, among immigrant groups in America, Russians, (including Jews), Scandinavians, Austrians, Romanians, and Greeks and most northwestern European Protestants were occupationally advantaged, while Italians, especially those from rural Sicily, Poles, Yugoslavs, French-Canadians, and some of the Irish were disadvantaged. Occupational integration among Spanish-speaking Americans has been slower, and among blacks, much slower. Although racial discrimination has recently declined sharply for young educated blacks and the black middle class, the vast majority of blacks are falling behind in relative occupational status.

The occupational integration of women in all rich countries is perhaps closer to the slow pace of American blacks than to the swift pace of white ethnics. Again, college education speeds up the process, although a substantial majority of women in all rich countries still remain in nurturant, expressive, and subordinate roles.

Still slower is the change in the permeability of social classes; what increases we see in intergenerational occupational mobility in the United States are almost entirely caused by changes in the occupational structure, especially the expansion of middle strata. Short-step intergenerational upward mobility is increasing, downward mobility decreasing. However, social class origin—indicated by either education or occupation of father—is less important as a determinant of occupational fate than education.

The only major form of discrimination that has increased with continued industrialization is discrimination against the aged. Because age and seniority—in other words job experience—are important indicators of ability and reliability, this trend contradicts the ascription-achievement hypothesis. There are minor variations on the theme of accelerated discrimination. For instance, where wisdom and mature judgment are thought to count most, as in established politics or religion or academic history, discrimination against the aged does appear to be least; indeed reverse discrimination is apparent. But there remains massive and increasing discrimination against older workers in semiskilled manual and lower white-collar jobs. This deviation from the general rule, like the South African deviation, underscores our conclusions concerning the politics and economics of job placement.

Examining modern systems of job placement, we have seen that when work roles are more or less clearly defined and criteria of performance can be specified which can be met by a wide range of people, the satisficing manager assigns employees on a cheap ascriptive basis (white male, Italian Catholic, or whatever established network of co-workers, relatives, and friends his employees connect with). When roles are vaguely defined or rapidly changing—perhaps this applies to most jobs in a modern labor force—room for ascription is even wider. Four economic and political forces can shake managers up enough to change their job assignment strategies: shortages of labor (which foster an accent on achievement); government coercion, active labor market policies, and social movements for equality (which break down older ascriptive networks in favor of newer ones).

The deviant case of the aged fits this picture: When labor shortages are severe, they are called into service. But usually government pressure is strongest on behalf of minorities other than the aged; employers prefer young educated men and women and middle-aged women to older men (who are more costly and less pliable); unions fight for the average member who wants the older worker's job; and, finally, the changes in family structure and economic opportunity that accompany industrialization create a strong constituency of middle-aged and young workers who press the state not only to open up opportunities by getting the aged out of the labor force but also to relieve adult workers of the burden of support for their aging parents. Generous pensions and disability benefits are developing to coax the aged worker into retirement. Where the aged become a large fraction of the population and organize, their labor market position improves (as we can see from flexible retirement rules, preretirement pensions, special job protection, and preferential unemployment benefits and tax treatment in Sweden and West Germany). Finally, where some other very large category of workers is selected for subordination, thereby creating labor shortages, the aged may be utilized more fully, as in South Africa.

However imperfectly, managers must make judgments about how these economic and political pressures affect their costs. Because industrialization—through modern communication and transportation networks, mass education and entertainment, high rates of residential and occupational mobility—gives force to the push for equality, managers will often calculate that the shift from one ascriptive network to another, within the broad category of "adequately qualified," is the easy way. Moving from Anglophone to Francophone, from white to black, from male to female, are signs of these shifts from ascription to ascription.

That education has become increasingly prominent in job assignment has been misinterpreted by many sociologists as a major contradiction of the ascription-achievement hypothesis. Education and its associated testing apparatus, they say, is part of the "Great Training Robbery" in the "Credential Society," where hiring and promotion based on formal education function increasingly to protect the status of privileged groups and strata. In an attempt to restore balance in this discussion, we have emphasized five themes:

1. Employers increasingly recruit not only for entry jobs but for future jobs, job patterns, and careers; the push for equality will accelerate that trend.

2. On average, formal education provides a base for lifetime learning and enhances the capacity to learn new jobs quickly. That is one major reason that employers who recruit for job ladders prefer college graduates. To repeat ritualistically the old observation that education functions to inculcate the young with core values of society (Durkheim, 1922), to reiterate the more venerable observation that privileged groups everywhere try to stake out their economic territory by seeking monopoly power (Adam Smith, 1789), is to obscure these other major functions of education.
3. All the talk about "technical function" in "conflict models" of education and job placement is misleading as a guide to work roles and their skill requirements. Effective employees must more or less quickly learn the tasks and social relations constituting work roles and the social and political topography of the work place and its environment; most of this must be learned on the job. Although schooling can provide specific skills for some entry jobs, typically it is relevant because it sharpens the cognitive and social skills which permit the speedy learning of new jobs and job sequences.
4. Modern mass education systems are so diversified that quality variations within the same level of education are more important as a job-relevant base for lifetime learning than the sheer levels of education commonly used in analysis of the relation of education to job placement and performance.
5. Education mediates the relationship of social origin to occupational fate. Insofar as access to education is shaped by aptitude and achievement tests, test bias could be an important barrier to achievement of disadvantaged populations. But repeated attempts to remove cultural bias from such tests have had no effect in reducing the differences in average scores between advantaged and disadvantaged groups. When we consider the interplay of ability, opportunity, motivation, and information as determinants of occupational fate over a forty six-year work life, when we review the behavior of employers in job assignment—and the vast variations in constraints imposed on their recruitment and promotion practices—we can see test bias as a trivial problem.

The few systematic studies of the links between economic growth, education, and changing criteria of job assignment are consistent with the following propositions:

1. Insofar as any poor countries take off and become modern, they must among other things develop primary, then secondary mass education (ultimately a diversified system of higher education)—or else import the products of such systems from abroad. Consistent with the ascription-achievement hypothesis, education is a major force for economic growth, although tough "mobilizing" regimes are able to make most effective use of mass education.

2. Among highly industrialized countries, marginal groups must use education for occupational achievement; established groups can rely mainly on ascription in intricate admixture with achievement.
3. In all modern countries, the push for economic equality is strongly resisted by those who occupy favored positions. The success of resistance seems to be greatest among the young and middle-aged facing older workers; majority people (now including white ethnics) facing racial minorities; and men competing with women. That no dominant group readily yields its occupational privileges is obvious.

The deviant case of South Africa underscores our conclusions regarding the political economy of job placement and at the same time sharply poses classic problems in sociology regarding communal versus class loyalties and the relation of political to economic and educational dominance.

The costs of apartheid and concomitant pressures for its breakdown are far from trivial. Severe labor shortages and problems of productivity have brought the familiar employer response: Use existing labor supplies more effectively (recruit women and retired whites, even move the color bar up in the typical pattern of uncontested ethnic succession); import skilled labor from abroad; reorganize work to permit less skilled workers to do it (job dilution). Moreover, like American employers in wartime, South African managers bend or break wage and labor regulations to get the work done. Like American employers bypassing unions in the building trades, South African employers pay lower rates to willing workers, employing Africans above the quota and illegally assigning Africans to skilled work. Ideological rigidity has not prevented tactical flexibility.

That pressures on the color bar are most intense in those industries with the most rapid technical and organizational change is consistent with Collins's finding that in the San Francisco Bay area achievement criteria in recruitment (e.g., educational requirements) are highest in technologically modern firms. In short, the pressures on South African employers for a shift from ascription to achievement are similar to those in other industrial countries.

The benefits of cheap and tractable labor are not sufficient to explain the stability of apartheid; the similar use of immigrant labor in the history of American industrialization did not prevent their incorporation into society; even the tough policies to control the guest workers in Switzerland and Germany, or American employer reinforcement of race supremacy and segregation in the Deep South, did not block substantial changes in the social, economic, and political rights of these workers.

In contrast, South Africa has not experienced the political pressures that elsewhere move modernizing societies toward increasing equality of opportunity and some equality of results—toward the combinations of ascription and achievement we have described in this chapter. First, the substantial monopoly of the best upper working-class jobs by white unionists and the vigorous yet flexible enforcement of the migrant labor system have so far prevented the emergence of a critical mass of skilled, settled urban workers who could organize a movement for change from below. Second, the African intellectuals and professionals who could lead such a movement, while not absent, are few. If we could compare the number and political careers of black South African intellectuals educated over given time spans at particular foreign and domestic universities with the number and careers of their counterparts in the former colonies of Britain and France, we could test this hypothesis: Left-wing university circles in Oxbridge, London, and Paris nurtured the colonial protest leadership for the overthrow of empire; equivalent inspiration and training have been rare among South African blacks—their university and political opportunities fewer, the content emphasizing amelioration rather than revolution. Ironically, the very absence of a recent history of colonialism may contribute to the weakness of the opposition.

What the South African case suggests is that with industrialization, if political subordination of a large, economically essential racial minority is to persist, the regime must maintain economic, educational, legal and social subordination in equal measure. A speculative comparison with Northern Ireland illustrates the theme. Protestant political subordination of Catholics in Northern Ireland has created much more organized protest than we see in South Africa. Among many reasons for ethnic resurgence in Northern Ireland, one is critical for our argument: a disjuncture between the political sphere and other institutional spheres, especially the interrelated educational and economic sectors. Although Catholics are underrepresented in the middle and upper-middle classes, their political subordination has not been matched by equally extensive educational and economic disadvantages. In fact, largely because of the British connection, Catholics experienced a rapid rise in education, occupational status, income, and social services during the 1950s and 1960s—more rapid than that of the Protestants (Thompson, 1978: 12, 14; R. Rose, 1971: 289). Thus, the resource base for a civil rights movement and for still further occupational and economic equality has been strong. Specifically, organizational skills and literacy and a related rise in aspirations—so limited among nonwhites in South Africa—were highly developed in Northern Ireland at the same time that Protestant political domination continued. The result: highly organized rebellion in one case; less effective, sporadic protest in the other. Similarly, the stability of the racial system of the Deep South until World War II was a product of successful subordination of blacks in every sphere, sustained by a level of coercion similar to that of South Africa.

Our analysis of ascription and achievement is part of a larger theoretical concern with the fate of local communal groups in modern society. Whether as rich countries get richer communal groups based on descent are greatly weakened and class structures replace them or whether they become stronger remains a central issue in sociology. (Park's formulation that after race comes class is today being reexamined as evidence of mounting racial, ethnic, and religious conflict accumulates and a spate of books on white ethnics appears.)

In our view, ties of locality indeed do give way to more powerful forces of residential and occupational mobility, the media of mass entertainment and communication, mass education, and those great mixers of minority and majority groups—union, corporation, and political party.

Nevertheless communities do persist. What can we make of the recurrent rediscovery of ethnic, racial, or religious "neighborhoods" and "subcultures"? (cf. Gans, 1962; Suttles, 1968; Liebow, 1967; Glazer and Moynihan, 1963) We would like to venture a clarifying generalization that locates these subcultures and their structural base. The hypothesis: *Kinship, minority status, and locality are meshed only where economy provides the cement*. When ethnic-religious or racial groups are segregated residentially and at the same time experience economic reinforcement for minority identity and solidarity, then a subculture with political potential flourishes. Neighborhoods composed of craftsmen in the needle trades, truck farmers, and retail merchants, or intellectuals, artists, and entertainers, sometimes have an ethnic-religious or racial recruitment base. Their members derive job information or even entrepreneurial capital from propinquity and friendship. Similarly, marginal groups band together to protect themselves and share their misery as in ghettos, *barrios*, and even skid rows (cf. Wilensky, 1966: 127; Light, 1972). The extreme case of persistent ethnic and tribal ties in the urban ghettos of South Africa is consistent.

What happens when such a neighborhood is bulldozed or its population moves up and out? In some circumstances that is the end. But if the local communal group continues to share a common occupational and economic fate, it can remain viable. It can reconstitute itself in a new locality, as illustrated in the move of Jews in Chicago from Lawndale to the northern suburbs and their reconcentration—a case of group social and residential mobility (Glazer, 1971: 452) common in modern life. Or the locality ties can become regional and national and still remain minority based. Gusfield notes the emergence of new, wider castes among educated occupational and governmental elites in the modernizing sectors of India. Education and occupational mobility combined with modern transportation and communication have "enhanced the cohesion and widened the scope of castes, religious and linguistic groups in India" (1975: 70). Caste struggles, he argues, are not replaced by class struggles. "Caste communities . . . operating through associations or political parties, find national and state politics an effective channel for achieving better allocation of resources, recognition of status through caste candidates and even legitimation through name changes" (p. 73). "Even where old caste lines are breaking down, new communal groups are being formed through sub-caste intermarriages," wider forms of endogamy (pp. 50–51). The analogy with the history of ethnic-based politics and ethnic occupational life in the United States is suggestive.

Just as ascription in job assignment remains strong despite a long-term shift toward achievement, so some communal groups retain their vitality despite a slow drift toward a society that is more corporatist, more centralized, more massified.

# 14

# Societal Growth and the Quality of Life

*Philip E. Converse*

## I

V. O. KEY ONCE REMARKED that studying public opinion was much like trying to come to grips with the Holy Ghost. I fear that the concept of "the quality of life," which surely is every bit as holy these days, is more ghostly still. Indeed, by comparison, the construct of societal growth, for all its ambiguities, is a perfect model of precision of reference. Hence, while it may be tedious to begin a discourse with an extended definitional exercise, I see little relief from such an obligation in this case. We shall not hope to capture the ghost, or get it truly "pinned and wriggling on the wall"; but we can at least sketch out a few of the regions where we can imagine the ghost to be immanent.

For very simple reasons, I shall deal in the plural in localizing the notion of the quality of life. Of course, the phrase is scarcely abstruse, and seems pregnant with meaning for almost any speaker of the language. Nonetheless, the meanings conjured up, and more especially the tests which might be applied to know a better life from a lesser one, can differ distressingly from observer to observer. Although definitions are dealer's choice and I could proceed with any variant of the concept I wished to specify, it is not my purpose here to make any single selection. Instead, I should like to begin by recognizing one or two of the main variants on the construct, noting both where these variants match and where they collide. Where they are actively discrepant, as they sometimes are, I shall often want to keep the differences in view in spinning out my subsequent remarks, even though this may afflict us with the intricacies of a two-track tape.

The most dramatic watershed separating rival conceptions of the quality of life divides subjective conceptions from those which claim to be more objective. For some, the quality of life ultimately resides in the eye of the beholder, and it is the individual's perceptions of the quality of his personal experience that provide the unimpeachable, if idiosyncratic, definitions of the term. For others, the quality of life of either individuals or groups is best assessed by outside observers who, if not omniscient, are at least well informed as to the objective details of the life situations involved.

While the "good life," as defined by the person experiencing it, can indeed be quite idiosyncratic, subjective definitions can nonetheless claim some underlying unity, inasmuch as "quality" is whatever ego says it is. Third-party definitions may be as disparate, but leave us with no obvious way of choosing between judgments. The community that one observer gives high grades as natural and wholesome, another may grade out as squalid and backward, and whom should we believe?

It seems obvious that both types of definitions have their strengths, but also their shortfalls. Few would claim that people invariably know what is good for themselves, and fewer still would claim that people are very good at knowing what is best for others in any general way, although of course such a claim might be sustained with regard to very narrow domains of professional expertise such as medicine or law. Perhaps if we were to string together the judgments of a full catalogue of experts, restricting each to his arena of true competence, we could assemble a mosaic of assessments of the quality of life of a person or group which would be moderately satisfying. However, expert opinion even within a domain of expertise is not infrequently contradictory; and the instances in which putative experts have badly misjudged the sincere tastes and needs of target clients are of course legion. Obviously, we need to remain attuned to both definitions of the quality of life.

There is no need to exaggerate the discrepancies which may arise between assessments of the quality of life in concrete situations according to relatively subjective or objective points of view. Many facets of experience, especially those involving consensual resources, are likely to be rated rather similarly most of the time. However, noteworthy discrepancies are not entirely uncommon. In the small, one may think of such seeming anomalies as the discovery of low or even negative correlations between neighborhood victimization rates and expressions of the fear of crime in a metropolitan area.[1] A finding of this sort is likely to touch off strong feelings of disdain at the silliness of human perceptions, and anything that can be written off as baseless bravado in the inner city, or paranoia in the suburbs, may not seem well suited to make a contribution, however small, to a balance sheet concerning the quality of life. On the other hand, it is a little cavalier to de-

[1] "Prototype State-of-the-Region Report for Los Angeles County," School of Architecture and Urban Planning, University of California, Los Angeles, March, 1973, pp. 272–89.

cide that such fears for safety, seeming poorly grounded, somehow need not be seen as corrosive of a sense of personal well-being.

Writ larger, there are a variety of phenomena that have classically attracted sociological attention which address the fact of broad discrepancies between the quality of life as imputed by the outsider on the basis of "objective" data, and the quality of life as experienced from the inside. The concept of "false consciousness" is one of these. Another is reflected in the cluster of findings which suggest that man's deepest outrage at his condition occurs not when objectifiable social forces about him are in stagnation or even, perhaps, decline if it sets in gradually enough; but rather when positively valued growth is patently not as fast this year as it was last (see Davies, 1962; Gurr, 1970). Similarly, the "revolution of rising expectations" over the face of the earth mounted toward a crescendo in a period when most conventional resource indicators for most world regions were on the upswing. Objectively, the quality of life was improving; but subjectively, for a variety of reasons including a keener awareness of social and economic alternatives, it was appearing to deteriorate.

It does not take long to think of a variety of reasons why subjective feelings of the quality of life can occasionally become quite unhinged from what would seem to be benign or malignant trends in the objective sense. Chief among these, perhaps, is the role played by expectations, which from time to time evolve in directions that are only loosely connected with some of the objectified facets of reality. Research shows that changes in situations, particularly if they are unexpected, produce subjective reactions well beyond what might seem warranted by the absolute change in objective levels. Thus, for example, recent changes in income can predict more accurately current feelings of satisfaction with income than absolute levels of income do (Strumpel, 1974). Meanwhile, change which can be anticipated and settled into slowly, or which seems no more than a just entitlement, may produce very little reaction at all. The perspectives of a worker who finds his income halved at age sixty five are likely to be vastly different from those of a worker who finds his income halved at age forty five.

At a risk of some oversimplification, we might say that relative to apparent objective trends, the mediation of expectations means that subjective experiences of life quality are in the short run hypersensitive to change, but in the longer run remarkably adaptable. A useful paradigm for this aspect of the fit between objective trends and subjective responses may be something as simple as reactions to temperature. In a climate with four distinct seasons, the first chill weather in the fall can be experienced as utterly bleak and penetrating. With the ambience so unpleasant at a temperature of 35 degrees even if one is properly dressed, it seems hard to conceive of surviving temperatures still lower by thirty or forty degrees. Each new drop in temperature, particularly if it occurs abruptly, produces something of the same experienced pain, but is adjusted to in turn. Then on the back side of winter, the first thaw that brings the temperature up to 35 degrees makes a day seem positively warm and balmy, such that it is unbelievable that it is no warmer than the day, a dozen weeks before, which was chilling to the bone.

Although the difference between subjective assessments of life quality and those which might be constructed on the basis of objective indicators is the primary difference of importance to us, other connotational distinctions have some currency. Thus, for example, the referent for the "quality of life" in some minds rigorously excludes money as a resource or, for that matter, anything economic that can be accounted for readily in monetary terms. This construction has an obvious genesis in the discussions of the later 1960s that brought the notion of the quality of life into broad public visibility in the first place. These discussions arose because of a felt disjuncture between a soaring growth of GNP since World War II and dramatic gains in public affluence on one hand, and a rising discontent with a variety of other conditions afflicting the society. It was keenly felt that the national economic accounts gave an exceedingly misleading picture of trends in the actual general weal in American society, and the "quality of life" term was coined to encompass a much broader view of the assessment of national progress than what was felt to be a prevailing "economic philistinism" of official assumptions (U.S. Department of Health, Education, and Welfare, 1969). For some, of course, the quality of life concept merely meant "not only economics, but well beyond it also." For others, however, it seemed designed to remain purified of economic referents.

There is no question but that a national sense of malaise and disenchantment beginning in the 1960s was real and pervaded to the very grass roots of the American citizenry. It registered in a tide of public disorders, as well as in a number of the limited set of public attitudes that were monitored at all continuously through the 1950s, 1960s, and 1970s, including such seemingly direct indicators as reports of personal happiness, as well as public confidence in national institutions or feelings of the utility of political participation. There is also no question but that these retrograde trends in public morale occurred in the face of striking gains in public affluence that continued unabated into the first years of the 1970s. The question is one of how one wishes to interpret these contrapuntal trends, if a definition of the quality of life is at stake.

We would obviously reject one simplistic interpretation which would suggest that such a sequence of events merely shows the irrelevance or epiphenomenal character of subjective views of life quality, relative to the testimony of objective economic indicators. But we would similarly reject the opposite simplistic interpretation that trends in purely economic welfare are at the very least irrelevant for considerations of life quality.

We certainly could not leave questions of financial resources out of assessments of life quality if we proceed with subjective definitions, since people consider such resources of very considerable importance in the gratifications they can draw from life. This is not to say that any majority would subscribe to the proposition that money is the most important thing in life. Indeed, most of the relevant interviewing we have done would suggest that the quality of the network of one's most immediate social relationships is more important in creating a sense of well-being than are financial resources. Nonetheless, such resources remain important in people's assessments of their situations. And the importance attributed is scarcely exhausted by the amassing of durable goods or the other crasser forms of materialism that are decried by those who find economic measures of the good life repugnant. By personal testimony, at least, limitations of financial resources are among the primary barriers for Americans to the kind of self-development represented by more extended education, or the broadening of travel, or any of a large variety of more constructive uses of leisure time. All of these are ends typically applauded by those who are skeptical of economic elements in definitions of life quality.

In short, while we need a view of the quality of life which is not defined by purely economic yardsticks, it would seem manifestly inappropriate to pursue a definition which leaves them out entirely. Clearly we see the quality of life as involving a large range of criteria beyond the economic, without excluding the economic along the way.

## II

If I had been asked to comment on the quality of life in a context of societal shrinkage, I might have been able to venture that such constriction was actively subversive of the quality of life, although even here one would need to say a good deal more as to what the nature of the shrinkage was. And I am quite sure that I would not care to hazard any simple judgment as to the evolution of the quality of life in a context of societal growth.

It is obvious that societal growth is a matter of enormous complexity, marked by an intertwining of an almost infinite number of more specific facets. It would be remarkable if there were not some facets of this growth which can plausibly be seen as promoting a better life. It would be equally remarkable if there were not other facets, perhaps even related to the first, which have noxious consequences. We can make few telling points about societal growth without beginning to specify "growth with respect to *what*?" But if for the moment we take what is probably the most obvious and simple form of societal growth—the sheer expansion of population numbers—it is clear that too much growth too fast can, in the purely Malthusian sense, be calamitous, at least with regard to most conventional views as to what the quality of life is about. Thus even for any specified form of growth, the significance may be quite ambiguous until one also specifies how much of this growth, how fast, and in what relationship to concomitant forms of growth.

In addition to the facets of growth which may reasonably be thought to hinder or promote a better life, it seems worth recognizing that there are many other facets—perhaps a vast majority—which have no particular relevance for anybody's definition of the quality of life, or at least have no net relevance which can be discerned on the basis of the limited information available at this time. One of the delights of the popular media is to descend upon some recent trend, real or imagined, and show why if carried much further it will be the utter salvation or ruination of society. More serious commentary, such as the symposium of papers in *The Annals* (January 1978) discussing the behavior of the trend data laid out in the Office of Management and Budget's (OMB) *Social Indicators, 1976* frequently arrives at the conclusion that while this or that trend is certainly real and even dramatic, its overall significance for the quality of human experience is at best obscure.[2]

Even trends which seem to have some general positive or negative significance may have concomitant or second-order implications of an opposite sign which serve to cloud the issue. The rising divorce rate is a classic instance of a trend first viewed with almost unalloyed alarm as a symptom of vital deterioration. Its connotations still remain on balance negative, but a variety of mitigating appreciations have grown up around the increase of marriage dissolution. The evidence is clear enough that the immediate breakup of a marriage is one of the more traumatic events of relatively common experience, and is so for all parties involved, including certainly children and to some degree close bystanders. On the other hand, some of this evidence comes from the late stages of withering marriages, and it is not clear that an ethos which would enforce the preservation of such marriages at all costs would represent any gain, particularly as there is also evidence that on balance the depth of the trauma is reasonably short-lived once actual termination occurs. The evidence of effects of divorce upon children is often not particularly pleasant, but this evidence is typically short-term as well, and not explicitly offset by parallel evidence as to the deleterious effects on children of severe parental discord and abuse which persists over large spans of childhood when laws and the culture set the divorce threshold very high. And even if a superbly comprehensive study of all of the long-term first- and second-order effects of divorce had been carried out, say, in the 1920s, it is unlikely that the results could safely be generalized to the current period, when association with a divorce, either as a child or as a principal, has become far less of a social curiosity and stigma.

Similarly, but on the positive side, current-day parents whose children have suffered bouts of moderate illness may well reflect with a shudder

[2] "America in the Seventies: Some Social Indicators," *Annals of the American Academy of Political and Social Science*, January 1978.

upon the time, not more than two or three generations ago, when such a sickness entailed probabilities that were far from trivial that the sick child, and perhaps other contaged family members as well, could be swept away at any moment. Certainly the dramatic lightening of this burden of intense alarm through the growth of of medical technologies must stand as an uncontested advance in the quality of life. However, once again the matter is somewhat less than utterly clear-cut. At a more aggregate level, we have the less fortunate consequences of the demographic transition, which can impinge on both parent and child in second-order ways which will rarely if ever be cognitively associated with or weighed against the liberations from alarm. And we have the fact that the same medical technologies, applied in a democratic and humanitarian way, succeed in postponing death more and more years into the deepening twilight of old age, in a fashion which does not in any obvious way add to the quality of person-years lived in the society. Once again, few would question the net positive balances of these advances, even short of further adjustments. Yet the conclusion is not as unequivocal as appears at first glance.

The important point throughout all of this is that there is no simple, one-to-one relationship between societal growth and the quality of life. The engines of growth roll onward, powered by a whole nexus of causal factors, most of which have limited or unknown relationships to the quality of life. To be sure, man attempts to enter his editing hand, biasing the selection of trends in directions which are benign. And in some small measure he may enjoy a limited success, although even at points of apparent success, there are often unforeseen second-order consequences which can undercut much of the apparent gain.

## III

Since we do not escape ambiguity by focusing on more specific facets of societal growth, it may be useful to take a somewhat different tack. I would like to move up a level of abstraction, where the forms of societal growth are concerned. I shall try to isolate a property of societal growth which strikes me as thoroughly generic to the process of social growth across all or most of its specific forms. And, quite naturally, I shall deliberately be abstracting a property which can be conceptually coordinated with the peculiarities of the notion of the quality of life, so that we can scrutinize the potential relationships between the two, complicated though they may be.

When I speak of "peculiarities" of the life-quality concept, what I have in mind is the fact that this concept, unlike some of the others with which we commonly deal, is addressed to the individual-level "bottom line" of social process. Now, where our definitions of life quality are subjective, the individual and his perceptions are obviously the bottom line. But even where definitions are intended to be objective, the ultimate referent remains the individual and his well-being. That is, if we opine that a certain objective trend has positive implications for the quality of life in a population, we are saying that on balance it improves experience for population members whether we care to talk in the language of utility, or satisfaction, or happiness, or fulfillment, or a greater "good" for a greater number.

This scarcely means, of course, that trends in collective properties or in social institutions are ruled out of view in speaking of the quality of life. Indeed, many of the most time-honored hypotheses of the sociologist purport to establish links between collective properties of human groups and the goodness of individual experience. Thus, for example, a group property like communal solidarity is often supposed to have, among its benign effects, the capacity of improving the sense of well-being and the palatability of life among individual members of the community. Thus any number of collective or institutional properties can become implicated in questions of the quality of life, provided only that the significance of the properties in question is drawn, implicitly or explicitly, to individuals' positive and negative experiencing of these properties.

Therefore, the kind of property I would like to abstract from the nexus of specific forms of societal growth can only be conceptually coordinate with the notion of the quality of life if it involves the individual's confrontations with social experience. This is the individual as "user" of experience. And a property which seems to me rather generically associated with virtually all forms of societal growth is a multiplication of options or alternatives available to the individual.

I do not know whether this proposition will seem debatable or self-evident, but let me address my claim that the equation between societal growth and the multiplication of options, if not utterly generic, is at least highly so. And for such explication, it is useful to take at least a partial survey of the more specific forms of change treated in these thematic addresses.

Certainly the multiplication of tool options is the very hallmark of technological advance. It is just about saying the same thing in other words, taken from the point of view of the user. And in this instance, at least, the word "multiplication" can be taken quite literally, since the growth of invention is exponential. From the user's perspective, the increase in tool alternatives may not always be secular over all segments of time. Thus, for example, the development of a viable steam engine undoubtedly rendered obsolete dozens of other cruder mechanisms for generating power, so that momentarily a set of multiple choices is superseded by a single "best" choice. But as adaptations of the basic principle of the steam engine proliferate, a multiplicity of options is soon revived, and these continue to branch exponentially in the familiar way.

If an explosion of options is obvious in the case of technological growth, it is not much less obvious if we traverse to something of an opposite extreme, and consider pure population growth. A social indicator which would be fascinating, although not reconstructible, would be data over long periods of time as to the sheer numbers of other people that a given individual will encounter in a lifetime at varying levels of intimacy, ranging from merely laying eyes on the person to passing words with him, and on to friendship formation of varying kinds. If it is true that one person out of twenty ever born is alive today, then it is easy to see by how much such numbers must have increased in the recent period of population growth. This means in turn a multiplication of alternatives available where partners for various forms of social interaction are concerned. Other major growth trends merely serve to exaggerate the gain in options for social partners, including advances in transportation and communication technology, or the urbanization trends which draw individuals from the countryside into more and more dense agglomerations. Thus where something as simple as the formation of a circle of friends is concerned, the pool of alternatives from which choices can be made must have expanded astonishingly, even taking account of the historical evidence that supposedly isolated and sedentary populations five centuries ago were rather more peripatetic than has usually been assumed.

We could run through much the same litany for that part of human culture which remains after pure technology is set aside. A basic property of culture is, of course, accumulation; and with the written word and capacities to reproduce it, the rate of loss around the edges declines. Accumulation obviously means expanding options. I do not know what the *x* is in the sentence "Half the books which have ever been published have been published within the past *x* years," but I suppose as usual the number would seem ridiculously short. Naturally, a great deal of the accumulation moves mercifully to the rear of the shelf, and the sheer bulk of it consumed by any given type of person may remain relatively constant. The student of the drama may now give shorter shrift to some of the minor Elizabethan playwrights than he might have fifty years ago because he has a vastly greater store of quality work to cover than before. But the important point is that the options are there and constantly expanding. Indeed, for recorded culture, options are expanding at the level of the modality: not only books and journals, but records, tapes, television cassettes, and the like.

Another way of slicing the matter is to consider the major choice points in the life span of the individual, and note the degree to which the options available have increased even in the past generation or two. Choices as to types of education have radically increased, and the presence of genuine options occurs earlier and earlier in the education cycle. In high schools, and now down to middle schools, we have moved from a relatively standard curriculum to a growing proliferation of curricula, and then on the "alternate schools" and now the kind of "magnet school" plan which pushes educational specialization to its extreme, even at relatively early ages. The expansion of alternatives for occupational choice is equally obvious. Immediately in the wake of difficult and portentous decisions as to whether to become a doctor, lawyer or business chief comes a round of further decisions, nearly as portentous, as to what *kind* of doctor, lawyer, or chief to be.

The choice as to whether to have a mate of the opposite sex is at least somewhat more open today than a generation ago. If the decision is to go ahead, the pool of possibilities is greater in principle, at least, although it may not seem that way to those who wait late in the pairing game. The decision whether to have children and, if yes, how many, is likewise a more open choice today for reasons of both biological technology and social norms. We are imminently threatened with the still further option to exercise concerning the sex compositon of the family.

Even retirement from normal occupational roles is beginning to take on such a variety of shapes that a good deal of new tactical thinking is required to steer through the options. Basic choices as to lifemanship and life style have expanded across the life span, very nearly from cradle to grave.

Now it is obvious that over much of the ground I have covered, the increase in options flows in a most direct way—almost tautologically, in fact—from increased specialization and increased societal complexity. It is worth recognizing this, but it should be remembered that the change in vocabulary is quite deliberate. For one thing, we have agreed to look at aspects of societal growth from the point of view of the user of experience, and from such a point of view, one implication of specialization is increased choice. But I should also make clear that while many of our increased options—especially those surrounding education and occupational choice—are direct matters of societal specialization, the term "specialization" scarcely evokes many of the other points at which options are increasing, and hence would be inadequate for our purposes in any event.

Thus, for example, the additional options about family formation would not normally come to mind as products of greater societal specialization. Neither would a variety of other clusters of expanding choices. While we all know that modern democracies are not the first communities to confront the citizen with voting choices, it is very likely that the number of options posed per unit time per capita has advanced considerably in the past one hundred years, and this is another class of options we would be unlikely to enter under the rubric of "specialization." Indeed, there is a clear sense in which the long-term shifts from ascribed to achieved statuses, again seen from the point of view of the user or occupant, entails an increase in options.

Is the universe of options therefore expanding with the same inexorability as the physical universe is said to be? Probably not, if this means that countertrends are impossible to discover. One can think of certain aggregative processes that can be seen as restricting the number of options available to the user. Because of the advance of nation building over larger and larger territorial domains, a stateless person looking for some principality to which to pledge his allegiance would have a more limited set of choices today than he could have counted a hundred years ago. Similar aggregative processes are characterizing the economic order: If I decide that I wish to take a stand against policies of Exxon or IT&T by refusing them my business, I would have a much harder time avoiding them than would have been true for parallel enterprises a hundred years ago.

In the domain of the mass media, the progressive disappearance of multiple local newspapers in American towns and cities, along with the establishment of national wire services and television networks, can easily be construed as reducing the information channels available for selection by the news seeker. This is a much shakier case, since persons in the limited stratum of avid newspaper readers today have no trouble maintaining multiple subscriptions: The two other local newspapers of yesteryear are now replaced by the *New York Times* or the *Washington Post* or the *Wall Street Journal* as well as a host of other more specialized periodicals. And as direct add-ons to the newspaper fare are the further channels represented by the various radio and television network news sources. In other words, by comparison with the news seeker who could have been in every one of the nation's towns at the same time in the 1870s, it may well be that the number of voices purveying news has shrunk, the total number of channels diminished, and the news homogenized. But for a less hypothetical user who could not be everywhere at once, the case for overall shrinkage is far from clear.

In any event, it is not my point to insist that in all domains of experience, choices are everywhere and forever expanding. All I care to establish here is a general tendency for societal growth in forms as diverse as technological advance or the multiplication of population to confront the individual with increasing options from which he must choose in arranging his behavior. And this much seems clear to me, even though occasional countertrends can be documented.

## IV

We have now arrived at our ultimate question. Let us grant that from the point of view of the individual actor, most forms of societal growth entail increases in his options. What difference does this make for the quality of life he experiences?

I took pains originally to distill from the varieties of societal growth an abstract property which shared a conceptual venue with notions of the quality of life, but I did not promise you that the relationship between an expansion of options and the goodness of life would necessarily be either simple or pat. At first blush, most of us would be likely to rush to the judgment that, other things being equal, more options are obviously better than fewer. Indeed, in a moment I shall review a purely rational argument which is probably too precious by half, but which says that such a judgment *has* to be true. But without any extended argument at all, increased options seem to mean increased freedom and increased control over one's destiny, and surely these are desiderate.

Options seem to be a very generic form of resource—more generic, say, than wealth. Of course, one of the many things that distinguish the rich from the poor is that the rich have vastly more options. Yet there are many forms of options that money cannot buy. In fact, one of the things that we find felicitous about dealing with options is that such a vocabulary can readily subsume the major benefits of affluence, while making it clear that money is not the sole source of those benefits. Hence, if there were some simple equation between the abundance of options and the quality of life, we could both put affluence in perspective and establish optimistic links between societal growth and life quality at the same stroke.

Now, at the very simplest of logical levels, it is hard to see how the sheer addition of new options to a situation could diminish the quality of the situation from the point of view of the actor. Of course, if such an addition entailed the discarding of some older and preferred options, then one could imagine the change being experienced as a diminution or deterioration. But if to a situation where conventional options are A, B, and C, and we merely add to these options D, E, and F, it would seem that the situation could in no way be diminished, and would likely be enriched. It would be a case of nothing to lose and conceivably something to gain, since for those uninterested in any of the new options, no latitude has been lost; and in the measure that some might prefer the new options, the quality of the situation is necessarily improved, at least from a subjective point of view.

While such logical analysis is not without its point, it leaves out several problems. Far and away the most important of these is the possibility that one or more of the added options are hidden noxious ones, or options which, though they may be chosen by some actors, will have unexpected noxious consequences either for the actor farther down the road, or more broadly in a second-order sense for the social group of which he is a part. This is not to say that one or more of the original options A, B, and C may not have hidden defects as well; but the fact that they are by construction familiar and long-exercised ones reduces the probability that there are major, but as yet unknown, noxious outcomes lurking in the wings.

We do not have to look far these days for examples of new options with hidden noxious consequences. The realm of new drug creations has in recent decades provided any number of exemplars. So has the proliferation of options associated with increasing pressure on exhaustible energy resources.

Even with hidden noxious options ruled out, serious questions of other kinds can be and have been raised about the unequivocal attractiveness of new proliferations of options. These doubts run a wide gamut, from the elegance of argument presented by Eric Fromm in his *Escape from Freedom*, to the vernacular complaint "Decisions, decisions!" as the waitress runs the customer through the litany of choices. How compelling these doubts are may well vary from observer to observer. I do not think that I find them overwhelming, but they may deserve brief recognition.

It is surely true that choice often brings psychological conflict, and this conflict can be unpleasant even when the stakes involved are rather petty. For more basic decisions over the life span, the stakes are by definition high and the possibilities for long-term regret at "the roads not taken" are lively indeed. Furthermore, where decisions of this magnitude are concerned, information seems oppresively inadequate and almost impossible to come by. Will I, ten years from now, be the kind of person in the kind of position such that I will be glad to have started a family now? Ironically, the more the options, the more information that is needed. There is little wonder that many might prefer to be swept along through clear-cut social channels "free" of major choices, as may be more nearly the case in societies of limited technologies and restrictive mores: Then at least one need not suffer personal guilt or blame if at a later point things go wrong.

Expansions of options can have unpleasant overtones for others beyond the individuals obliged to select among them. A set of parallel complaints can be developed from the point of view of third parties who find the exercise of certain types of options by other persons to be highly threatening. To some degree the concerns registered by third parties may reflect judgments, in some cases quite informed, that the new options being exercised are hidden noxious ones. But even beyond such grounds, social groups demand some minimum of conformity, and conformity is in the most direct way a restriction of options.

Obviously, the exercise of new options is more threatening in this sense for some domains than others. Now and again, for example, groups have resisted new technologies, but in general the expansion of technological options is not too problematic. In domains where moral judgments are more central, however, the growth of new options can be the source of profound resentment and malaise.

Indeed, one of the things going on in the later 1960s and early 1970s, in addition to a considerable growth in affluence and its attendant options, was a proliferation of other kinds of options as to basic "life style." It is at this level that new options seem most threatening to third parties who would not themselves dream of exercising them. Now, I do not intend to imply that new life styles were the sole source of the public disenchantment registering in this period despite advancing affluence. After all, a significant portion of that disenchantment was expressed for other reasons by those who were pushing to broaden life-style options, not those who were discomfited by their broadening. But it would seem that such a reaction against broadened options did make some contribution to these trends. Undoubtedly the new options were feared in part because of suspicion that they might involve noxious consequences. But in some degree they seem to have been resented more simply because they endangered the cake of custom.

To summarize, then, the expansion of options associated with societal growth appears on its face to be a benign trend. However, the relationship between the expansion of options and the general quality of life is rather less than certain. This is true on the one hand because of the possibility that some of the seductive new options have hidden noxious consequences. It is true on the other hand because of a variety of psychological mechanisms that surround the increase of choice, including personal conflict, apprehension about responsibility, and concern over the threat to social conformity.

I have taken pains to lay out this summary in a form which helps to emphasize that the links between expanding options and the goodness of life are not straightforward *whichever* mode of definition of life quality we prefer, be it the objective or the subjective. That is, the various types of anxiety which can surround the expansion of options are quintessentially the elements likely to register in subjective measures of the quality of life, and likely to escape detection where measurement is purely objective. However, the possibility of hidden noxious consequences—that people may prefer options which, if the truth were known, are not good for them—is exactly the reason why we need to pay parallel attention to objective definitions of life quality.

In neither currency, then, can any simple links between the expansion of options and the quality of life be established, at least at the high level of abstraction at which we are trying to operate here. But I would offer a few closing observations which may suggest the directions in which more compelling conclusions can be sought. These observations have less to do with the fact of change in options than with questions of their timing and the rate of change.

Our logical scenario constructed to show that more options must in principle be better than fewer foundered on the reef that options are not all equal with respect to their outcomes: Some, if the truth be known, will be on balance self-defeating. And in particular, it is the newly added and hence scarcely tried options which have the greatest likelihood of hidden noxious consequences. This is not to say that old and long-used options can have no noxious consequences; they may in fact have some which will only become alarmingly apparent a century or two down the road. But usage over a long period of time has greatly reduced the likelihood that dramatic noxious consequences will become associated with them, short of vast changes in the environment of their exercise.

What this means in turn is that it is manifestly important to take a time dimension into account in talking of the expansion of options. Let us imagine once again that to conventional options A, B, and C we add at a point in time options D, E, and F. As we have seen, the apparent gain may be illusory because some of the new options may in fact turn out in a longer run to have disastrous hidden consequences. But let us cycle ahead a generation or two, or however long it may take for the most troublesome hidden consequences to make their presence felt. Conceivably by such a time, one or two of the added options D, E, and F will have become discredited. But if so much as one of the options has survived, and hence become essentially as time-tested as the original options A, B, and C, then the logic of our original scenario pertains, and we would likely admit that there had been a net advance, at least in the specific domain covered by these options.

For reasons laid out much earlier, time is also crucial where the subjective experience of the quality of life is concerned. Call it "future shock" or what you like, it is probable that an absolute deluge of expanding options will be experienced with some pain in the short and intermediate term. On the other hand, there is sufficient adaptability in the organism that in the kind of time scale over which at least some of the introduced options become tried and true, it is likely that the option set, expanded by comparison with the experience of earlier generations, will come to be taken for granted as an integral part of expectations.

As such an integral part, there may be little subjective accounting that the quality of life has improved as a consequence. Given this equilibrating property of expectations, the chief test of the value added to life by the expanded set of options, as registered in subjective evaluations, would be the nature of response if the more recent options were forcibly removed, stripping back the option set to that experienced by earlier generations. This kind of test is nothing that one organizes out of whim or, for that matter, mere scientific curiosity. And since in the current epoch we are largely surrounded by growth and its attendant steady expansion of options, there are rather few natural tests available. Perhaps the last major test in which there was a large-scale natural constriction of options occurred in the world-wide depression of the early 1930s, since the most obvious recent competitor, World War II, presents something of a mixed case. If some of the more bleak projections as to the speed with which expanding energy demands are overtaking developable conventional resources are true, then we may be facing a still sterner test at some time in the next couple of decades.

It is in part because of these bleak perspectives, along with bleak perspectives of other types that have become salient from time to time, that the notion of perpetual progress has fallen out of fashion. If progress is taken to mean, as it might in our vocabulary, a continuing and benign increase in alternatives, there is surely no reason to believe it is guaranteed to go forever steadily upward. Among other things, societal growth itself, while the general rule, has not avoided reversal in some times and places. If localized reversals of growth are possible, then so are constrictions of option sets. It is something of an ultimate irony that we may have difficulty being certain that a large option set is indeed a positive contribution to the quality of life, except as we witness an actual constriction.

# III

# The Future of Societal Growth

15

# Introduction

*Amos H. Hawley*

IT IS OBVIOUS that growth in scale of a social system cannot continue indefinitely. The limits would be reached in a world system encompassing all localities and regions. Immanuel Wallerstein and others have shown that we have already advanced far along the path to that end. It is possible, however, that a world system might never be more than a gossamer of linkages among a small number of large, tightly knit subsystems. On the other hand, granted that physical limits might be attained, growth of complexity might continue for some time thereafter until all components of the system are fully extended and no interstices for organizational ramification remain. Still another possibility, of course, is that growth may shift its locus from one sector of a world system to another. In that event, some centers of growth would have to decline to make room for the expansion of others. These are large issues, and their treatment in the chapters of this section is more oblique than direct. More attention is given to the penultimate question, that is: What are probable short-term outcomes of the growth process now in operation?

Wallerstein's view of the world system as a historic outcome of the expansion of capitalism from core states over peripheral areas held in a dependent status is well known. Here he examines the thrust of the political interplay among factions in core states and in peripheral areas. In that interaction the world view of the bourgeoisie is pitted against the nationalism of the working classes with the result that both parties are moved from state capitalism toward a universal socialism. At that point presumably an unstable equilibrium will prevail.

Irving Horowitz, who also acknowledges the existence of a world system, argues that the course of change has been conceived too much in ideological terms. He prefers a developmental conception of change, in contrast to either a modernization notion, which is expressive of an ethnocentric perspective, or a dependency interpretation derived largely from a Marxian position. From a developmental standpoint the least developed parts of the world are entering into a fuller partnership with the developed nations by adapting the institutional forms of advanced nations to their own cultural traditions. Cultural convergence in a capitalist economy would seem to be the expected outcome.

The era in which the state served as the prime mover of societal change ended with the close of the nineteenth century, according to Joseph Gusfield. Since then the trend has been toward a decentralization of the locus of change. Internal expansion, i.e., increasing complexity, resulting from mass education, universal literacy, and mass communications has shifted the locus of change from the legislative halls of states to the social institutions produced in social movements. Gusfield speaks of the "normalization" of change, a circumstance in which individual participation in the change process is maximized. Whether that will bring cumulative change or growth to its upper asymptote is left to speculation.

Writing on the discontinuities in growth, Scott Greer observes that despite the obsolescence of the simple, informal institutions of the past, the norms which governed their operations have persisted anachronistically into a period of large-scale organization. Contrary to Gusfield, Greer sees a trend toward increasing centralization. The difference, however, may be more semantic than substantive; that is, centralization may be more characteristic of the economic, voluntary, and welfare institutions than of the administrative agencies of the state. In any case, with growth in scale have come various integrative devices to serve as surrogates for the family and local community, such as reinforcements of the citizen's role, mass communication, and bureaucratic organization, each with its own peculiar ambiguities. The future of society would seem to be marked, therefore, by a continuing instability.

Finally we come back in Kenneth Boulding's chapter to an evolutionary perspective on societal growth, but one which appears to be more catholic than is Lenski's. Evolution is a creation of potential, while growth is the development of potential. Growth runs its course and encounters its limits in the filling of all available niches. Potential is renewable, however, though its resurgence is unpredictable. Renewability, the ever-present possibility of "mutations," is to Boulding a source of optimism for the future of humankind. Yet the elimination of isolated societies in the course of the formation of the world system increases the risks of evolutionary failure.

16

# World Networks and the Politics of the World-Economy

*Immanuel Wallerstein*

THE ANTINOMY BETWEEN STATE AND SOCIETY is often asserted to be a defining characteristic of the modern world. Some argue that the contradictions deriving from this antinomy following the French Revolution underlie the contrasting ideologies that arose in the nineteenth century, and that sociology itself as an intellectual discipline represents an attempt to analyze and resolve this antinomy. The concepts "state" and "society" refer usually to two structures that presumably coexist within a single set of boundaries (ultimately juridical boundaries). These structures are thought to be organizations of collective energy—one formal, one not, but both real—that operate on and are operated by the same set of individuals. If one starts with such an assumption, which has been widespread, indeed dominant, in Western, indeed world, thought since the French Revolution, then one can pose questions about the degree of fit between the values of the state and of the society, and seek to explain why the fit is far from perfect. In terms of policy, one can prescribe what one prefers to make the fit more perfect. This set of categories then becomes the basis of "comparative political sociology."[1]

The lack of value fit was perceived by many to be a lack of boundary fit. It followed that if the boundaries of the state were changed—diminished, enlarged, or redrawn—thus creating different juridical units, the fit would become greater. This is where the concept of nation and its allied terminology have fit in. "Nation" refers in the last analysis to a "society" that has a

[1]This is made very explicit in the well-known reader edited by Reinhard Bendix et al. (1968).

state to itself, or has the moral right to have a state to itself (the so-called right to self-determination). Since there has been considerable difference of views over the past 200 years as to which were the essences which had these moral rights to existence, there has been as we know enormous and often violent conflict about these issues.

But the very fact that there has been endless, passionate debate about which "entities" constitute which concrete "societies" throws fundamental doubt, it seems to me, on the utility of the concept "societies" as a starting point for analysis. States are at least visible, functioning organisms. There exist also visible, functioning collectivities of collective identification—call them nations or ethnic groups or what you will—whose boundaries may be constantly changing, but whose existence at any given point in time can in fact be empirically measured. But where can we find "societies" other than in the minds of the analysts, or of the orators? Social science would, in my view, make a great leap forward if it dispensed entirely with the term.[2]

For one thing, we would all then have to justify our unit of analysis instead of assuming it (and indeed frequently assuming it in the vaguest of all manners, such that the boundaries are totally unspecified). My own unit of analysis is based on the measurable social reality of interdependent productive activities, what may be called an "effective social division of labor" or, in code language, an "economy." In modern history, the dominant effective boundaries have expanded steadily from its origins in the sixteenth century, such that today it encompasses the earth.[3]

The actual measurement of the boundaries of the world-economy is both theoretically tricky and technically virtually unexplored, but logically poses no great problems. It is sufficient at this point to indicate the factors that would have to be measured. A world-economy is constituted by a cross-cutting network of interlinked productive processes which we may call "commodity chains," such that for any production process in the chain there are a number of "backward and forward linkages," on which the particular process (and the persons involved in it) are dependent. These various production processes usually require physical transportation of commodities between them, and frequently the transfers of "rights" to commodities in a chain are made by autonomous organizations, in which case we talk of the existence of "commerce." Commerce is frequent, but far from universal, as the mode of linkage, and is in no way essential to the functioning of a commodity chain, except at the very end when the final consumable product is sold to the final consumer. Both the great merchant companies of the seventeenth and eighteenth centuries and the contemporary multinational

[2] In the last twenty-five years, Western Marxists have substituted the term "social formation" for "society." This is just flimflam. It changes nothing. Everything one can say about the ontological vacuity of "society" applies equally to the concept "social formation."

[3] An elaboration of my position is to be found in Wallerstein, 1976*a*:343–52.

corporation have been structures that eliminated much (though seldom all) of the commerce in the interstices of given commodity chains.

Production for this cross-cutting set of integrated commodity chains is based on the capitalist principle of maximizing capital accumulation. It is based on this principle not because all persons share a value consensus that this is a desirable principle on which to make production decisions. Many, perhaps most, do not. Production is based on this principle because, in the absence of a single overarching political structure that could control production decisions at all points in this world-economy, the existence of world market alternatives for what is supplied by any particular production unit constrains producers to obey the law of accumulation (reduce costs to the maximum feasible, expand sales price to the maximum feasible), or pay grievous economic penalties (ultimately bankruptcy, which removes the nonconforming producer from the economy, at least in the role he had been playing).

The primary tool in the reduction of costs is force applied to the direct producer, reducing his income to a minimum and allowing someone else to appropriate the remaining "value" he has produced. The mechanisms of such appropriation are multiple, but they take three main forms. One is forced labor, in which the direct producer receives from the legal "proprietor" part or all of his income in kind. A second is wage labor, in which the direct producer receives from the legal "proprietor" part or all of his income in money. A third is petty proprietorship, in which the direct producer is indirectly forced, often through debt mechanisms, to sell his product at below the market value. In each of these forms, which in turn have a large number of variants, the legal system of contractual property rights is an essential element, and the role of the state machinery in ensuring the coercion of unequal contract is central to the functioning of the system.

The primary tool in the expansion of sales price is the creation of a monopoly, or at least a quasi monopoly, which reduces the alternatives of adjacent actors in the commodity chain. No absolute monopolies can exist in the absence once again of an overarching political structure for the whole world-economy. But quasi monopolies are not merely possible; they are constant and recurring, and this has been so at all points in the history of the capitalist world-economy. Quasi monopolies are only possible by the utilization of state power to constrain potential "competitors" of the holder of the putative monopoly.

Let us review the picture thus far. Production is organized in commodity chains, which should be visualized as a process to which there are multiple product entry points. For example, to oversimplify, there is a commodity chain that goes from cotton production to thread production to textile production to clothing production. At each of these production points there is an input of other productive materials (each of which has to be traced backward) and of labor (which had to be both produced and maintained, and hence there are further elements of the chain, as traced backward). Almost all commodity chains will cross state boundaries at some point, and many (even most) will cross them at many points. At each point that there is a laborer, there is state pressure on the laborer's income. At each point that there is an "exchange" of product, there is state pressure on the "price."

The first kind of state pressure, that on the laborer, governs the relationship between bourgeois and proletarian. The second kind of state pressure, that on exchange, governs the relationship among bourgeois. In a capitalist world-economy, the states are expressions of power. States enforce appropriation of value by the bourgeois from the proletarian, to the extent they are not restrained by organized resistance of direct producers. States favor appropriation of value by some bourgeois from other bourgeois, but not necessarily always the same ones. Thus there are two kinds of politics in the modern world-system: the class struggle between bourgeois and proletarian, and the political struggles among different bourgeois. Insofar as these different groups of bourgeois may control different state structures within a single world-economy, such intrabourgeois political struggle takes the form of interstate struggle.

The states are not givens. They are created institutions, and are constantly changing—in form, in strength, in boundaries—through the interplay of the interstate system. Just as the world-economy has expanded over time, its political expression—the interstate system—has expanded. As the commodity chains have become longer and more complex, and have involved more and more machinery, there has been a constant pressure by the strong against the weak. This pressure has concentrated more and more of the processes in the chains that are easiest to "monopolize" in a few areas—"core" processes in "core" areas—and more and more of the processes that require less skilled and more extensive manpower that is easiest to keep at a low-income level in other areas—"peripheral" processes in "peripheral" areas. Parallel to this economic polarization has been a political polarization between stronger states in core areas and weaker states in peripheral areas, the "political" process of "imperialism" being what makes possible the "economic" process of "unequal exchange."

The strength of states has to be understood within this context. A strong state does not mean an authoritarian state. Indeed, the correlation may almost be inverse. A state is stronger than another state to the extent that it can maximize the conditions for profit making by its enterprises (including state corporations) within the world-economy. For most states, this means creating and enforcing quasi monopoly situations, or restraining others from doing the same to its disadvantage. The strength of the very strongest state, however, under the exceptional situation of true hegemony, is measured by its ability to minimize *all* quasi monopolies, that is, to enforce the doctrine of free trade. If hegemony is defined as a situation in which a single core power has demonstrable advantages of efficiency *simultaneously* in production, commerce, and finance, it follows that a maximally free market would be likely to ensure maximal profit to the enterprises located in such a hegemonic power.

It is no accident therefore that, at the moment of Dutch accession to hegemony in the seventeenth century, Hugo Grotius published that "classic" of international law, *Mare Liberum*, in which he argued that "Every nation is free to travel to every other nation, and to trade with it," because "the act of exchange is a completion of independence which Nature requires" (Grotius, 1916).[4] This ideology was revived under British auspices in the mid-nineteenth century and American auspices in the mid-twentieth. In each case, the ideology was practiced only to the extent that—and as long as—the core power who promulgated it was truly hegemonic. But moments of true hegemony are rare, and intercore rivalry is the normal state of the world-system. Hence the doctrine of free trade seldom prevailed over the innumerable quasi monopolies instituted by or with the assistance of state structures.

It has been the case over the history of the capitalist world-economy that the system's growth or "development" has not been constant, but has occurred in wavelike spurts of expansion and contraction.[5] This is observable empirically, and theoretically it is not hard to discern the basic explanation. As production is expanded in the individual search for accumulation, there regularly come points where the amounts produced throughout the world-economy exceed the effective demand resulting from the existing distribution of world income (as fixed by the resolutions of prior acute sociopolitical conflicts). The consequent periods of stagnation both reduce overall production and lead to class struggles which force a redistribution of world income to lower strata within the world-economy. This redistribution expands the market, at least in the core zones, and this can be most effectively compensated for, in terms of the interest of the upper strata, by the incorporation of new zones within the world-economy, adding a new component of ultralow-income-receiving direct producers.

[4]The work was first published in 1608. The subtitle is "The right which belongs to the Dutch to take part in the East Indian Trade." The Portuguese and the Spanish, the ostensible objects of the treatise, were declining in any case. The Dutch view was even more hurtful to their rivals, the English (and the French). In 1617 John Selden, an Englishman, wrote a response, *Mare Clausum*.

Free trade is a pragmatic matter, as Sir George Downing, England's great diplomatist, observed with acerbity in 1663 about the Dutch, who by that time had supplanted the Portuguese in the East: "It is *mare liberum* in the British seas but *mare clausum* on the coast of Africa and in the East-Indies." Cited in Pieter Geyl, 1964:p.85.

[5]There are waves of varying lengths. For a review of the state of our knowledge, and an assessment of the relationships between different kinds of waves, see Research Group on Cycles and Trends, Fernand Braudel Center, "Cyclical Rhythms and Secular Trends of the Capitalist World Economy: Some Premises, Hypotheses, and Questions," *Review* II, 4 (Spring 1979): 483–500.

It is important here to see that the link between "politics" and "economics" operates in two opposite directions. The cyclical difficulties in capital accumulation lead to acute class conflict within core countries which over time in fact strengthens the political claims of workers in these countries and accounts for the clear pattern of relatively rising standards of living. But since, at the same time, new lower strata are incorporated into the system, it is unlikely that the world-economy–wide distribution of income is significantly changed; indeed, the opposite is probably true. Nonetheless, expansion serves as a spur to production, and hence renews expansion.

In the course of the periods of stagnation, the system undergoes a shakedown, in which producers of weaker efficiency are eliminated. This is what accounts for the musical chairs game at the top. The "old" dominant enterprises (and the states in which they are located) find their costs steadily rising, because of the costs of amortizing "older" capital investment, combined with rising labor costs resulting from the growing strength of workers' organization. "Newer" enterprises (and the states in which they are located) thus constantly overtake "older" enterprises in the quasi-monopolistic world market, and this "overtaking" is most likely to occur in periods of stagnation.

The game of musical chairs is not restricted to states at the top. It is also played by other states. There always are—indeed there must be—states somewhere in between on various criteria. We may call them semiperipheral states. The enterprises located within them are divided between those engaged in "corelike" processes and others engaged in "peripheral" processes. In moments of expansion of the world-economy, these states find themselves attached as satellites to one or another core power and serve to some extent as economic transmission belts and political agents of an imperial power.

The periodic difficulties of world capital accumulation present *a few* semiperipheral states with their opportunity. For one thing, the world squeeze on profit intensifies competition among core powers and weakens their hold on given semiperipheral states, who are freer to play among the rivals and erect new quasi-monopolistic constraints. However, the other side of this coin is that the semiperipheral states are cut off from some of the normal sources of income, of capital and technology transfer, etc. Those that are too weak eventually succumb and return to the imperial fold chastened. A few, one or two at the most, are strong enough to impose themselves as new core powers, usually displacing over time some falling core power.[6]

The key thing to notice about the game of musical chairs, as played at the top or in the middle, is that even though who plays what role may change, the distribution of the roles (how many in each role: i.e., core,

[6] My arguments for these propositions on semiperipheral states are to be found in Wallerstein, 1976*b*:461–83.

semiperiphery, periphery) has remained remarkably constant, proportionally, over the history of the world-economy.

In an interstate system, states are clearly in some sense actors. But states are themselves organizations, and we must discern who in fact does the acting. The state machineries of course reflect the pressures of the multiple enterprises whose ability to survive in a capitalist world-economy depends in very large part on the degree to which they can get these organizations, the states, to represent their interests. By and large, the enterprises have been remarkably successful in their efforts, or at least some of the enterprises—those that have flourished. But direct producers can also attempt to assert political strength, either by resisting the state machinery or seeking to seize it and use it for their own ends.

Thus, we cannot meaningfully discuss the politics of the interstate system without analyzing the ways in which populations are grouped for political purposes. It is here that the Weberian trinity of class, status group, and party can serve as a preliminary mode of classification.

I shall put forward some very schematic propositions about classes, status groups, and parties, forgoing elaboration or even justification, in order to relate group conflict to the existence of an interstate system as the political framework of the capitalist world-economy.

Classes are usefully defined as groups that have a common relationship to the economy. But if the effective "economy" (in the sense of a long-term, relatively integrated set of production processes, that is, a social division of labor) is in fact a world-economy, and if we accept the argument that the existence of "national economies" has been more rhetoric than reality, then it follows that classes—classes *an sich*—are classes of the world-economy and not of states. Since, however, class consciousness—classes *für sich*—is a *political* phenomenon, and since the most efficacious political structures are the sovereign states (or the sovereign units whose creation is sought by strong, organized movements/parties), it follows that class consciousness operates largely on a state level, which per se intrudes a constant element of false consciousness into most expressions of class consciousness.

This is the structural basis of the confusion between, the contradiction between, class consciousness and national/ethnic/race consciousness, a confusion/contradiction that is both pervasive in the modern world and pervasively discussed and debated. It may well be that under certain conditions, and at certain moments, national/ethnic/race consciousness is an expression—even the most realistic expression—of class consciousness, and at other moments of historical evolution, it is precisely the opposite. And such moments may be successive in time, running one into the other without any easy demarcation lines.

Indeed, because of the axial division of production processes in the capitalist world-economy, the core-periphery relations that reproduce themselves constantly and everywhere, the antimony of class—*an sich* in a world-economy, but *für sich* in the states—forces *most* expressions of consciousness to take a national/ethnic/race form. Nationalism is the "modern Janus," as Tom Nairn (1975: 17) calls it: "[A]ll nationalism is both healthy and morbid. Both progress and regress are inscribed in its genetic code from the start." But what do we conclude from this? Do we conclude, with Régis Debray (1977:41), that "to discard nationalism along with its oppressive aspects means courting disaster."? Or should we conclude, with Eric Hobsbawm (1977:17), that "The temptation to discover that [nationalism] can or must be [a detour on the way to revolution] is great, but so also is the danger that the detour will become the journey."

Should, however, the question be put primarily in voluntaristic terms? It is more to the point, it seems to me, to look at the factors which have made capitalism so durable as a system. Capitalism, overall, has been more exploitative (that is, extractive of surplus labor) and destructive of life and land, for the vast majority of persons located within the boundaries of the world-economy, than any previous mode of production in world history. (I know this will evoke howls of dismay among many as it seems to go against the grain of the "obvious" expansion of human well-being in the last two centuries. But this expansion of well-being has seemed to be obvious because it has been true of a highly visible minority, largely located in the core countries, and the perception of this rise in well-being has left out of account the populations that have been decimated and pauperized, largely in peripheral zones.)

When one wonders about the durability of a system so obviously detrimental to the vast majority, is not one of the explanations to be found in the unclarity (the social "veil") that is involved in a system whose economic parameters are world-wide but whose political organization is largely channeled into competitions for control of state structures, and into inter*state* conflicts?

Nor is this the only unclarity. Since there is a game of geographical musical chairs, there is hope for "mobility" despite "polarization"—mobility for states as well as for individuals. What is usually omitted from the analysis is that, in a stratified system, upward mobility for one unit is downward mobility for another. The wonder is not that there is so little class consciousness, but that there is so much.[7]

This brings us to the question of parties. The interstate system has steadily crystallized a process that started with the development of strong monarchies in Europe, beginning in the late fifteenth century, and has spread ever outward, the so-called rise of nationalism in the nineteenth and twentieth centuries—always in peripheral and semiperipheral zones, be it noted (including new peripheral zones located inside the old core states).

[7] I have discussed in much more detail the relations of class and status group in several essays, which are reprinted in Wallerstein, 1979: chaps. 10, 14, 18.

Parallel to this process has been a spreading realization by class forces that political efforts were more meaningfully directed to gaining control of state machineries than smaller, less structured, entities within these states.

While the multiple political organizational expressions of the world bourgeoisie—controlling as they did de facto most state structures—could navigate with relative ease the waters of murky geographical identity, it was precisely the world's workers' movements that felt obliged to create national, that is statewide, structures, whose clear boundaries would define and limit organizational efforts. If one wants to conquer state power, one has to create organizations geared to this objective. Thus, while the world bourgeoisie has, when all is said and done, always organized in relationship to the world-economy (which accounts for all of the "strange alliances," from those of the Thirty Years' War to those of the Second World War), the proletarian forces—despite the internationalist rhetoric—have been far more nationalist than they claimed or than their ideology permitted. The marriage of socialism and nationalism in the national liberation movements of the twentieth century is not an anomaly. These movements could never have been truly "socialist" were they not "nationalist," not truly "nationalist" had they not been "socialist."

And yet these *parties* not only claim to be, but are indeed, a reflection of a world *class* struggle. This is a contradiction, to be sure, but how can proponents of a Marxist world view, like the parties in power in many peripheral and semiperipheral areas of the world, doubt that the contradictions of a capitalist world-economy would find expression in their own actions (just as much as in the actions of other social actors)?

We arrive therefore at the point. The world-system has experienced "growth" in a host of ways over five centuries of existence. Like all social structures, its contradictions both sustain it and undermine it. This is a temporally discrete process, the slow but eventual transformation of quantity into quality. A system is born, not suddenly but at some point decisively. It then lives and grows, surmounting its ongoing difficulties—the moments of "stagnation"—by mechanisms which restore its forward movement—the moments of "expansion." But some of these mechanisms of reinvigoration approach their asymptote. For example, new peripheries are created, until we come near the end of new spaces to incorporate in the system. Or semiproletarian, low-cost labor is fully proletarianized, expanding effective demand but raising the real cost of labor, which sustains the system until it comes near the end of new compensatory processes of peripherization.

In the directly political arena, there is a slow process of increased awareness. Workers' movements become politicized, seek state power, and then learn the limitations of state power, especially state power in peripheral and semiperipheral zones. There is only so much the state machineries of such peripheral and semiperipheral states can do effectively to alter the unequal exchange mechanisms of a capitalist world-economy. Workers' movements are thus being forced beyond their nationalism to world-wide organization. This last process is in a very early stage, as these movements are caught in a dilemma. They can reinforce their state power, with the advantage of holding on to a foothold in the interstate system, but they face the risk of making the detour the journey, in Hobsbawm's phrase. Or they can move to organize transnationally, at the great risk of losing any firm base, and at the risk of internecine struggle, but it may be that power is only truly available at the world level.

The world bourgeoisie is not without its multiple divisions, to be sure. But their weakness lies less in these divisions than in the growing inability to maintain the world social veil. This decline of the facade was attributed by Marx to the effects of the steady growth of the forces of production, and by Schumpeter to the self-destructive "antifeudalism" of the bourgeoisie which destroyed the political "protective strata" in order to further the interests of accumulation.

It doesn't really matter whether Marx or Schumpeter was right. Quite probably, they both were. The point is that either analysis is a mode of accounting for the world transition from capitalism to socialism through which we are now living and which will take easily another century to complete.

As social scientists, we can interpret human history and we can project where social forces are heading. But we are not gods, and nothing, however probable, is inevitable. The reality of the world is too complex, and offers too many alternative solutions at minor and major turning points, to efface what has been romantically called throughout history "free will."

Free will, however, is not anarchic option. It is simply the reflection of complexity. Social science is one political mode of treating this complexity. It can clarify it or obscure it. Social science was born out of the interstate system, and social scientists have been historically, despite their rhetoric, closely tied to nationalism and to state structures. This is inevitable for "professions," and we all know the steady trend to professionalization of all the branches of knowledge.

But social reality is centered in the workings of the world-economy, and we will not be able to analyze intelligently any social phenomenon, however "micro" it may seem, without placing it as an element constrained by the real system in which it finds itself.

As, however, world parties emerge, slowly substituting themselves for national/ethnic/race structures as the real expression of class divisions, the logic of professionalization will break down, and social science as we know it may undergo a sea change as great as its earlier separation from philosophy. Indeed, as is obvious, we are in fact living in the midst of this sea change, whose evolutions parallels and reflects the world-wide transition from capitalism to socialism.

17

# The Sociology of Development and the Ideology of Sociology

*Irving Louis Horowitz*

THIS PRESENTATION IS INTENDED to be neither celebratory nor condemnatory of the role of sociology with respect to the study of international development and social change.[1] I will be content with both a description and explanation of what that role has been in recent years. What makes the study of sociological inputs to the field of international development so difficult is the overlapping constituencies that are involved. The field of international development was pioneered first by historians under the rubric of dynastic change; then came the economists, who formalized the study of social transformation in large-scale systems; next came the anthropologists, who saw the processes of development in relativistic "then and now" terms, but nonetheless gave development studies broad cultural dimensions lacking in the pre–World War II period. The field was then enriched by political scientists, whose profound understanding of the role of state power, policy mak-

[1] The dual purpose of this brief statement is to indicate the coexistence of three alternative models for the analysis of development, and to briefly note the contributions of American sociology to this paradigmatic mosaic. As a result, I am eschewing conventional references. Instead, I will submit in due course three central sociological works and one major article illustrative of each of the major theoretical frameworks discussed in my statement. It would be an absence of frankness not to admit that in many instances the work done by economists, psychologists, anthropologists, and political scientists is at least equal to, if not considerably superior to, the efforts of sociologists. Indeed, in certain instances, where an antecedent contribution has been cross-disciplinary, and with clear implications for current sociological research, the nonsociological reference has been used. With similar candor, I would have to say that contributions by social scientists outside the United States are also equal to, if not superior, to the domestic product. But again, to make such citations would clearly exceed the boundaries of this admittedly frail effort.

ing, and authority showed beyond a shadow of doubt that the study of international development is not simply a matter of inexorable economic trends or social tendencies, but represents decisions arrived at in local, national, and international exchanges.

## The Contributions of Sociology to the Study of International Development

The contribution of sociologists, and here one must be frank, has not been so much to enrich empirical studies as it has been to develop the theoretical dimensions of development. Empirical work, especially in the post–World War II era, involved attitude studies and motivational studies transplanted from American to overseas contexts, utilizing scales and measures largely developed by social and clinical psychology. While attitudinal and motivational studies were of profound importance in giving sociologists input into the analysis of international development, the transformation of these psychological studies into general sociological theory is the concern of this statement.

This is not to diminish or denigrate the empirical contributions of sociology to the field of international development. Those contributions have been substantial and real. But again, they have been primarily at the level of explanation, and this can well be understood. The classics of sociology are filled with broad theoretical jumps from the data: the explanation by Marx of the stages of development in terms of class formation and reformation; the explanation by Durkheim of the movement from organic to contractual foundations for establishing social solidarity; and, of course, Weber's emphasis on the role of religion and culture in creating a set of values that permit sustained growth. These classical formulations provide the background to current attitudes and orientations about international development.

For example, Lipset's entrepreneurial thesis, in which a "deviant" class of entrepreneurs creates the foundation for new values permitting capitalism to form in Latin America, is a direct descendant of the Weber hypothesis. At the other end of the spectrum, Frank's dependency theory, in which the underdevelopment of the Third World is explained by the overdevelopment of the First World, has clear roots, if not in Marxism directly, then certainly in Leninism and its theory of imperialism. To the extent that sociology, more than any other discipline in social science, has inherited a broad nineteenth-century tradition of social theory, to that degree there is an unbroken line of theorizing about the processes of social change and international development.

Sociologists have played a profound and central role in the creation of three orientations toward the study of development: the modernization, developmental, and dependency theses. These, in turn, can be examined in terms of the personnel involved, the publications produced, the places where the work is primarily located, and above all, the intellectual positions adduced. It might be best to start with this last element, since better than any other focus, the general ideology of development outlooks explains what sociology has meant and done.

1. The *modernization* school (Hoselitz, 1960; Lipset, 1968; Lerner, 1964; Shils, 1960) is perhaps sociologist's oldest and most highly evolved position. Basically, it holds that modernization is the central source of development, just as traditionalism is the main source of stagnation, or nondevelopment. There are near-infinite variations on this theme, but above all, each involves an assumption that the historical transition is from tradition to modernity and that the motor force in this transition is the infusion or injection of highly sophisticated mechanisms of communication and transportation. As these permeate and percolate, the values of the society shift, and demands for participation in modern world systems accelerate.

The modernization thesis is basically informed by Keynesian economics, by a notion of mixed economies of public and private sectors bargaining for the latest and best equipment, and the highest forms with which to express the impulse toward modernized systems and behavior. Generally, too, the modernization thesis sees the central change as one involving a shift from feudal, landed agrarian economies to urban-based industrial economies. The policy consequences of this position are a higher form of bargaining, and the examination of class in terms of leverage factors contained by each class or group, or what might be called the reforming impulse. Modernization comes to be perceived as a way to achieve change without the destructive potential of revolution or reaction. A great deal of the modernization literature assumes the standpoint that the higher the degree of social mobility, physical mobility, or diffusion of information, the greater the degree of democratization of the social system. Hence, there is a strong implication that modernity is the fundamental expression of democratization.

The model for modernization is the advanced Western powers, largely those who won World War II, and stabilized capitalist democracy. Modernization clearly reflected the rise of an American century: consumer-oriented values, communication universals, and cultural relativisms. It further reflected the export of democratic individualism: the highest form of achievement-oriented societies. The actual, continued stratification gaps, class, race, ethnic, and sexual disparities, military definitions of world realities, these somehow were magically filtered out of consideration. By definition, agencies for change were held to be gradual and commercial. The entrepreneurial approach was exported to nations where entrepreneurs exhibited little instinct for risk investments or technological innovation. A mechanistic transvaluation of class values took place, with little appreciation of the exaggerations involved in creating international systems based on the actions of powerful donor nations and the reactions of recipient nations. In retrospect, what is so remarkable is how long the modernization position held unquestioned sway in American social science. It was so patently and transparently based on only one set of political and economical experiences that what requires explanation is why such a position remained impervious to any sense of inner strain, and took even longer to respond to external intellectual pressures.

2. Perhaps because of this assumed correlation, because of the implication that modernity implied and even entailed democratic values, the shocking emergence of all kinds of authoritarian, totalitarian, and military regimes in the Third World, no less than the military practices in East-West cold war politics, led to a reconsideration of modernization theory as such. A younger generation of theorists, who might best be labeled *developmentalists* (Horowitz, 1972; Huntington, 1968; Furtado, 1964; Portes, 1973), perceived a breakdown in the isomorphism between modernity and freedom. For this group, interest theory rather than value theory was central. That is to say, the relative position of any state or society, or different sectors, classes, and subclasses within state and society, determines outcomes more than values, instincts, and attitudes. In a sense, this was simply a long overdue shift from psychologism to sociologism; an emphasis on structural factors over and against personality factors.

For the most part, historical evolution was seen no longer as being from traditional societies to modern societies, but rather from colonialism to independence, and a shift away from Europe and America to an appreciation of Asia, Africa, and Latin America. There was also a sense that the developmental process was triangular in character: with economic classes preeminent in the formation of capitalism, political classes central to the formation of socialism, and military classes preeminent in the evolution and development of the Third World. In this frame of reference, policy became even more important an aspect of development since questions of capitalism or socialism, democracy or authoritarianism, were matters of choices for the new nations rather than historical inevitabilities. At the same time, decisions concerning reform and/or revolution were determined by strategies and tactics, and not models of social change imported from European systems of the past.

The model for developmentalism was clearly Third World nations as a whole, those which were largely successful in achieving independence after World War II. The revolutions of a nationalist type were registered not by disregarding either the First or Second worlds, but by amalgamating what were held to be the most feasible structural components of each. The developmentalist position took note of the fact of the strong Third World/new nation political commitment to one-party rule, extensive military leveraging of the social order, and the emergence of a bureaucratic sector having a specific set of planning and developmental tasks. However, the Third

World took its economic cues from Western society, specifically the Keynesian revolution in marketing, exchange, and circulation of capital. As a result, consumer-oriented values and the instinct to commodity acquisitions, far from being crushed in these Third World states, emerged to full flowering. The Third World, which first appeared on the scene of history as a unicorn, a strange eclectic amalgam of communist politics and capitalist economics, gradually evolved its own symmetries as well as its own structures. The developmentalist perspective was clearly a response to the stability and durability of this new situation, to a rejection of the idea that the Third World was simply a transitional phase marching toward modernization or, for that matter, toward socialism. The new nations were indeed marching, but to a beat generated by their own leadership drummers. It was the close analysis of this new beat, this new turn, that gave substance to the developmentalist frame of reference.

3. More recently, the *dependency* school (Wallerstein, 1974; Cockroft et al., 1972; Baran, 1957; Weaver, 1976) has come about in an effort to restore a sense of holism and hegemony to the study of development. Here, the emphasis is more on power theory than either value theory or interest theory. Underwriting the assumption of the dependency school is that the state of backwardness of most Third World countries is not simply a consequence of variations in historical evolution, but the conscious manipulation of the advanced First World of a dominated Third World. The idea of imperialism became central for the dependency school, replacing the idea of class for the developmental school, and the idea of nation in the modernizing school.

The world was seen to be not so much tripartite (First, Second, and Third worlds) as in the developmentalist school, or bifurcated between modern and traditional sectors as in the modernization school, but rather a unified world system that could best be understood in terms of placement either in the core, semiperiphery, or periphery of power and dominion. Hence, the dependency group was less interested in policy making for the Third World than in the need to make revolution as a precondition for any policy transformation anywhere in the world.

The dependency model clearly took its cue from Lenin's theory of imperialism, from the notion that what accounted for cultural backwardness and economic deprivation were not merely the natural histories of Third World countries, but the excessive power in international terms of advanced capitalist nations. If Leninism was Marxism in the era of imperialism, then it might be said that dependency theory was Leninism in the era of postindustrialism. What gave practical impulse to dependency theory was the realities of adventurous American foreign policy in Latin America ranging from the use of troops or conduits in nations such as Guatemala, the Dominican Republic, Cuba, Brazil, and Nicaragua, to the indirect participation in the management and manipulation of nearly every other regime in the Western hemisphere. It is largely for this reason too that the dependency school of sociology was so clearly rooted in United States/Latin American relationships. But if hemispheric politics provided the context, the Vietnam war provided the trigger mechanism for a general reconsideration of sociological standpoints. The conflict in Southeast Asia provided a seemingly overwhelming illustration of the United States' intervention in the affairs of dependent and small nations.

But the bandwagon effect of the dependency school, buoyed by American "defeats" in Vietnam and Cuba, turned out to be Pyrrhic. The dissolution of the dependency school came slowly. The defeats of the United States in the Vietnam war, the growing independence of Latin American nations, the expanding economic management of energy affairs by the Middle East OPEC nations, these seeming defeats for international capitalism were in effect defeats for the excesses of American capitalism. The systemic properties of capitalism showed signs of being strengthened rather than weakened by new developments. Vietnam and Cambodia became proxies and client states for their larger masters, the Soviet Union and China, respectively. Latin America developed a strong sense of national independence, military rule, and capitalist entrepreneurship. The OPEC nations developed their own notion of sharing profits, and that meant investment in, rather than destruction of, capitalist bastions of power. Taken as a whole, the globalization of capitalism changed the ratio of power within the system, but left the system as such unperturbed. Some dependency advocates actually saw the Soviet Union falling under the sway of capitalist blandishments and multinational offerings. Still, the dependency model provided a sensitizing agency to the realities of imbalance in world power. It furthermore displayed a dazzling theoretical paradigm for the analysis of such imbalances. The dependency theorists globalized the notion of equity; egalitarianism was made into a world-wide policy stance; it was understood that the rights of individuals and collectivities must be adhered to quite beyond the boundaries of any one given nation or economy.

## Sociological Schools of Thought and Their Ideological Institutionalization

All three of these schools have been described in the broadest possible terms, and the degree of overlap between them is almost as great as the sense of integration within each of these three schools. Yet clear lines do exist. Some of the leading figures in the modernization school are Bert Hoselitz, Alex Inkeles, Wilbur Schramm, S. M. Lipset, Kingsley Davis, Edward Shils, and Daniel Lerner. One can see immediately that there is an age group involved. Most of these people did their primary field researches in the fifties, although most of them are still quite active and vigorous at this point. *Economic Development and Cultural Change* is probably the foremost journal for giving expression to the modernizing school for the past twenty five years. If, over time, there has been a tendency to mute the more obvious ideological assumption that modernization and Americanism are one, there is nonetheless a continuing and clear persuasion that national development, to make sense, has to employ modernization in all its parts: capital-intensive industry, bureaucratic politics, and mass society. That means changes in attitudes no less than growth in industrial output. The modernization school, because it was developed early in time, and because it had the full weight of authority of sociological tradition, is perhaps strongest at the Ivy League schools such as Harvard and Princeton, and also at Stanford and Chicago. These institutions often also contain important institutes for the study of world communism and European politics, which fit directly into the modernizing thesis that often indicated overlapping orientations toward the developing areas. Involved, too, was a confrontation in ideology no less than policy with Soviet power in the Third World. The modernization school, sometimes consciously, other times covertly, became part of a world struggle perceived as taking place between a democratic West and a totalitarian East. There really is no way to disengage these two aspects of modernization theory since sociological theory and political sentiments both served to underwrite this point of view.

The second tendency of developmentalism, involving people such as myself, Alejandro Portes, Allan Schnaiberg, Charles Moskos, Denis Goulet, Gino Germani, Pablo Gonzalez Casanova, Fernando Henrique Cardoso, Luis Ratinoff, was much more a phenomenon of the sixties than of the fifties. No doubt, this in part reflected a thaw in the cold war and a termination of the Dulles era in the United States and the Stalin era in the Soviet Union. But it also signified a much higher level of participation by scholars from the Third World, especially the advanced countries of Latin America, in fashioning their own theories. It, too, developed its own publication framework, primarily around *Studies in Comparative International Development* which began as a monograph series fifteen years ago and has since evolved into a quarterly journal, and *Comparative Politics*, now a decade old. As one might expect, some of those institutions such as Michigan, Northwestern, Rutgers, Syracuse, State University of New York, and Pittsburgh, which came into prominence in the 1960s as graduate education in sociology rapidly expanded, were also centers for the developmental approach in this country. The growth of the developmental model also implied an increased sensitivity to problems of policy and the bargaining aspects of power relations: seeing the Third World as a series of choices, decisions, and options, rather than the inexorable tendencies from tradition to modernization or, as was later to be the case with the dependency model, from feudalism to socialism. There was also a much deeper penetration of the structural variables in each of these societies by the developmental school, an emphasis on how the processes of electrification and energy allocation shaped behaviors and demands of masses for migration and participation.

There is a time series aspect to the development literature: Just as the fifties gave rise to modernization, and the sixties to developmentalism, the re-emergence of Marxism as a respectable university framework gave impetus to dependency theory, to a belief that the problem of international development was one that could be best understood and examined primarily in the bowels of multinational corporations and Western capitals rather than in backward peripheral societies. A new periodical issued by the Fernand Braudel Center (*Review*) is probably the best exemplar of this newest tendency, with publications such as *Perspectives on Latin America, Insurgent Sociologist*, and *Kapitalistate*, earlier harbingers of a similar, albeit more strident, point of view. Again, the personnel that are carrying the torch in this vision tend to be younger people, led perhaps by Immanuel Wallerstein and including Richard Rubinson, Terrence Hopkins, Gabriel Kolko, Dale Johnson, Andre Gunder Frank, and Susanne J. Bodenheimer, among others.

One problem which has most recently cropped up in the dependency trend is the unified world view that leads to an analysis of dependency only as a United States phenomenon, with scant attention to the Soviet Union. Hence, dependency is seen only as economic rather than as political in character. Other problems have also arisen. The dependency school sometimes appears as the reverse side of the modernization school, emphasizing unifying global factors, but with a strong critical posture toward the U.S.A. rather than the earlier critical emphasis on the U.S.S.R. There is also an ideological substitution of public enterprise for private enterprise as a mechanism for solving developmental problems, without much attention to the problems of incentive, corruption, and innovation that are commonplace in socialist-type economies. These and other problems remain to be worked out.

## The Sociology of Development and the Development of Sociology

One ultimately is left with a serious problem in the sociology of knowledge. Are we dealing with a sequence of serial events, moving from modernization to developmentalism to dependency, as one moves from the fifties to the sixties to the seventies? Or is there in fact a possibility of making decisions about these three positions as alternative strategies in the pursuit of scientific prediction and explanation? For surely, if sociological participation in developmental studies is subject simply to a genetic explanation, all we could possibly hope for is a more interesting theory for the 1980s. I suspect this is not the case: that, in fact, the three postwar decades have outlined and issued into three alternatives, each of which is to be tested in the crucible of real history in the years ahead.

It might be the case that modifications in each position will be forthcoming, made imperative by certain methodological refinements. On the other hand, it is equally feasible and plausible that one of these three positions will triumph intellectually because it better explains the way the world functions. It is not necessarily the case that that which comes last, in terms of evolution, will be intellectually triumphant. From my own point of view—having been central to the developmental thesis, and with a confirmed and convinced belief that this represents the mainstream of sociological good sense and, at the same time, alone holds open the possibility of a Third World perspective on itself and for itself—it would be foolish to simply relativize the properties of these three schools of thought. I have discussed these matters elsewhere and at great length, so it suffices to point out that I have a position without unduly burdening this survey and overview.

Developmental studies provide an important case in the sociology of knowledge, and also an equally interesting case in the knowledge of sociology. For the development of different sociological contributions to the study of international development have closely followed professional tendencies in sociology and, at the same time, political tendencies in the world at large. The question of the chicken or the egg, of how much any one discipline provides in the way of leadership or how much it is simply following trends, will have to be worked out in the future and with the greatest amount of care. Whatever the results are, it is quite apparent that sociology has made a serious and sustained contribution to the study of international development, albeit one that has provided a deeper sense of the problems rather than a truer response to the need for solutions.

After years in the field of development studies one becomes acutely aware of the limits of interpretation and integration. Even if we achieve agreement that some rough correlations are possible between conservatism and modernization, liberalism and developmentalism, and radicalism and dependency theory—and I would strongly demur from such a sociology-of-knowledge persuasion—we are still left with the scientific decision on the most satisfactory and efficacious mode of analysis. By the same token, if we shift our orientation to satisfy contemporary fashion—i.e., which particular paradigm is most prevalent among specialists at any given period in time—we must still confront the matter of truth. This is considerably beyond the problem in paradigm formation in the history of science, but is an attempt to create an isomorphism between reality and experience.

After the most careful review of the literature published in journals and monographs alike, I remain convinced that the developmentalist perspective is the most balanced; it is productive of useful results. Developmentalism uniquely accounts for external pressures and internal dynamics in the growth process. It combines the best and most advanced techniques of qualitative and quantitative research procedures. It insists upon exact attention to ethnographic, linguistic, and national characteristics of those peoples and processes under investigation. To be sure, developmentalism leaves open the question of the fundamental construction of social reality; in this it is like the best of sociology generally. It makes the fewest a priori assumptions as to whether economic, political, social, or military factors are central in terms of their explanatory power. More, developmentalism also leaves open the possibility that priorities for big items may shift in a nation. Policy making, evaluation studies, and reshuffling social indicators may change the very structure of the development process. The future, no less than the past, must be appreciated, and developmentalism is uniquely situated to make such adjustments. The risks of eclecticism in such a viewpoint are real enough, and have been duly noted by the opponents of the developmental perspective. Yet what are the alternatives?

To ask this question is to confront the intellectual bankruptcy of fanaticisms, left and right. Modernization offers a furtive "model of models," in which the measurement of development becomes the productive techniques of advanced industrial countries; their commodity fetishes, and the behavior and attitudes of the citizenry of these nonrandomly selected nations. Hence, the measurement of modernization beomes inescapably linked to the celebration of Western capitalism. Such a viewpoint is extrinsic to, and often alien to, the self-discovered needs of the developing areas themselves. Dependency theory offers a reverse side of this model of models in which the measurement of development becomes the productive techniques of advanced socialist countries, the social organization of these societies, and the behavior and attitudes of the leaders of these countries. The measurement of moving beyond dependency becomes inexorably linked to the celebration of, or at least participation in, Soviet communism. Such a viewpoint is also extrinsic to and alien from the grounded growth needs of developing areas.

The long and short of the situation is that developmentalism as a standpoint and an ideology offers the closest approximation to the structure of the social scientific community, and to the needs of the Third World for an autonomic standpoint for assessing its own achievements and limitations. Developmentalism is the only standpoint that does not presume that the Third World is somewhere in limbo—magically and mysteriously "on the road" to either modernization or socialization. Indeed, it is "the road" that for the most part eludes analysis based on ideological assumptions. Developmentalism as a perspective takes seriously the contours of the national and regional requirements of developing regions as such. For these hopefully objective reasons, I am led to conclude that developmentalism has emerged as the master paradigm of social science research and political policy goals.

But there is also a significant but quite subjective distinction between modernization *and* dependency theories on one side, and development theory on the other—the level of intensity brought to bear on the goals of a society. Modernization advocates, armed with functionalism, just *know* that the United States and the OECD nations represent the model of models and the future of the future. Dependency advocates, armed with historicism, know with equal fervor that American imperialism is the source of all evil for the developmental process. They are perhaps somewhat less certain about which form of socialism provides total cure for total sin, but they are not above advocating a course of action leading to utopian socialist goals. The developmentalists, lacking any variety of the synthetic a priori, are reduced to levels of uncertainty and intellectual hedging that hardly makes for firm adherents or clear-eyed emancipators. Indeed, the situation might best be characterized by Yeats's words: "the best lack all conviction, while the worst are full of passionate intensity." But in the world of social science, insofar as it takes the science part seriously, fanaticism is a dubious distinction, while caution and doubt have their own merits. The point is simply that modernists and *dependistas*, by disallowing the present to alter their vision of the future, inevitably lead the independent researcher to inquire about hidden agendas and private motives; and not without good reason. That the developmentalist perspective has not been etched on the sociological conscience with the unmistakable clarity of their adversaries is, hence, less a consequence of confusion or eclecticism; than a condition for the performance of social science as an act of a courage born of direct investigation.

18

# The Modernity of Social Movements: Public Roles and Private Parts

*Joseph Gusfield*

THE THEME OF THE GREAT TRANSFORMATION to modern life is a major feature of theories of societal growth. In the usage of paired concepts of community and society, tradition and modernity, preindustrial and industrial, feudal and capitalistic, there is an underlying evolutionary assumption: The past is discarded as the present arises. The present too will wither and the future, like a phoenix, emerge from its ashes. My concern with societal growth in this chapter is with the interplay of the private and the public as minor themes in this narrative. It is a chapter about change, both about some aspects of the mechanisms of change and, reflexively, about how transformation is perceived and acted upon. My focus is on the emergence of public institutions of change in the form of social movements and on their relationship to the transformation of institutions and persons.

The growth that constitutes the subject of this chapter is both societal and personal. It represents some change in what have been my own past views, but also much continuity. Earlier in my own work I have been sharply critical of evolutionary models of change, especially as embodied in modernization theory (Gusfield, 1967, 1975, 1976). Similarly I have attacked the utility for political analysis of the concept of modern society as a "mass society" (Gusfield, 1962). In both cases the same message was clear. There is much consistency between seemingly inconsistent social forms, more continuity between the old and the new than is implied in evolutionary models and modernization theory. Traditional relationships and institutions do not die quick deaths as new forms are born. Community is not displaced by Society, tradition defeated by modernity, group life dispersed by mass activities. Social change is not a drama of the chambered nautilus that leaves the old shell behind as it builds a new one. The richest mine for sociological gold is in understanding the interplay of past and present. It lies in seeing how they sometimes conflict, sometimes reinforce, sometimes are indifferent to each other.

While I will continue that perspective in this discussion, I also hope to correct some imbalances, to emphasize some sharp transformations between past and present in advanced, industrial societies. The emergence of aggregates of people conceived as members of a common society and engaged in action in public arenas is the focus of my attention. The development of deliberate attempts to change that society through collective actions, social movements, and shared invocations to change is both a major new civil institution and part of the experience of other civil institutions in modern societies. The paradox of the institution of change is a significant feature of modern as distinguished from traditional or premodern life. Such organizations and associations occupy a large space on the landscape of modernity.

But I am not recanting my emphasis on continuity and duality. The "mass culture" theme calls attention to the new and distinct relation between persons, localities, and provincial groups on the one hand and public events on the other. It does so in this chapter, however, as an interplay between such events and its observers, between public acts as observed events and publics as participants, as spectators, and as audiences. To see public action as theater is to emphasize the problematic character of the relation between the public level of staged, reported, and observed events and the day-do-day levels of routine and private actions by individuals, groups, and institutions.

It is not significant that modern societies are societies in transformation. Most contemporary societies are. What is unique is both societal and cultural. It is societal in that a structure of organization and association has emerged which is the expected way to produce and define change—forms of collective action and social movements. It is cultural in that people reflect upon and think about change as an aspect of life, that they self-consciously go about deciding in what ways to accept and reject what has become possible. "[T]he dominant culture," writes Zygmunt Bauman, " consists of transforming everything which is not inevitable into the improbable" (1976:123). As public events, as theater, collective actions and social movements are constantly creating new meanings, new claims to possibility.

## The Emergence of Society and the Public

A profound part of the drama of sociology is embedded in the imagery of a lost world of "little communities" and the found world of complex, modern society. It was said of the European peasant of the past centuries that he was oblivious to the wars, the politics, and the grand events that made up historical accounts. Unconcerned and unaware, he tilled the soil no matter who won the battles. This portrait of a world of self-sufficient, autonomous local settlements has been painted over with a vision of centralized national states, interdependent markets, homogeneous cultures, and nationalistic identities that bind large territories into a unity and draw peripheries into contact with and awareness of a center (Tilly, 1975; Shils, 1961; Bendix, 1964: chaps. 2, 3).

Here I call attention to three aspects of that transformation from a world of multiple communities to one of a single centralized society. The first is the expansion of society as a structural fact—the growth of institutions through which disparate people and groups are made interdependent and homogeneous. The second is the expansion of society as a cultural fact—the ability to conceptualize the network of relationships as a society and to identify oneself, one's group, and one's locality as members of a larger society. The third aspect is again cultural. It is the development of society as an object of change—an object understood as a source of change and an object to be thought about, changed, or cherished.

## THE EXPANSION OF SOCIETY

The rise of modern nations is a saga of evolving integration and interdependence. Localisms and primordial identities, while not necessarily disappearing, are no longer the limits of the social world. Markets, communications systems, transportation, and nationalistic ideas are among key factors in expanding the size of the social universe within which people have come to live. Perhaps the most crucial development of the modern period is the growth and importance of the national state, the centralizing of political power over a wider territory and encompassing cultural, economic, and linguistically diverse groups.[1]

Both state and society have expanded in a vertical as well as a horizontal direction. As polity, as state, the modern world has involved the incorporation of classes and groups that have been "outside" society and state. The development of citizenship status, which accompanies participation and an ideology of civil and political rights, is one aspect of this (Bendix, 1964; Marshall, 1965). But it also has meant that what happens at the center of the society is a matter of concern and note throughout the territory. "The mass of society has become incorporated *into* society" (Shils, 1960:288). "Society" has ceased to be the exclusive province of elites. This fundamental democratization is a major change which modernization has brought with it (Lerner, 1958; Mannheim, 1940:44–49).

[1]Note how the Federalists defended the new Constitution by arguing for the value of a larger policy, in distinction from the conventional wisdom that democracy required a small society (Federalist Papers, nos. 9, 10). The same process of expanding the sphere within which primordial groups interact appears as well in new nations in the twentieth century (Geertz, 1963).

## THE CULTURAL REALITY OF SOCIETY AND THE EMERGENCE OF THE PUBLIC

"There are no masses", wrote Raymond Williams. "There are only ways of seeing people as masses"(1960:319). To "see" or imagine events, processes, and people as incorporated into a common unity, a "society," is the cultural side of the expansion of society. "American society," 'Western society," are terms which become invested with reality, objects capable of being thought about and acted toward. They imply the emergence of society as an object distinct from this or that specific class or group. It is this universalistic conception of society to which I refer as it forms a basis for modes of acting at societal levels. Bluntschli, writing in 1849, identified the emergence of the concept of society with the rise of the bourgeoisie; it signified parts of societal life outside of the court (quoted in Frankfort Institute for Social Research, 1973, pp. 17, 33).

As most of the late-nineteenth- and early-twentieth-century theorists recognized, the implications of the expansion of society as an object involve imagined interaction rather than the face-to-face relationships of communal groups. The inclusion of strangers, enemies, and celebrated persons into the same society represents a sphere of attention and activity that distinguishes between what is public and what is private in a salient and significant fashion. The discovery of society is an essential requisite to efforts to remake it. It is in the public sphere that such efforts have been most observable.

The emergence of the public is a part of the history of modern societies, a facet in the development of national states and middle-class societies. The word "public" owes its origins to the literary world, where it arose to describe the new and anonymous consumers of literature who came to replace the patronage of wealthy sponsors (Beljame, 1948:130; Auerbach, 1953: 499–500). It is this quality of accessibility to diverse groups and persons on a formal plane of equality which has been the hallmark of the modern public. As long as politics and society were the "property" of families of notables, the distinction between the private and the public remained blurred. As Alvin Gouldner has put it: "In contrast, however, a public sphere is in its modern sense a sphere open to all, or to all 'men with an *interest*,' and who have a measure of competence in the ordinary language spoken" (1976:72). The last phrase in Gouldner's concept of the public is important. It suggests the massive significance for societal expansion of the revolution in culture that mass education, universal literacy, and mass communication have brought about (Bendix, 1978).

I refer to three dimensions or components of "public" as important to my evolving argument. First, public events, in contrast to private ones, are events visible to audiences of diverse persons and groups. Public acts are "front stage," conducted where they are observable and accessible (Arendt,

1959:45–53; Gusfield, 1975*a*). It is in this sense that the "public" has a mass character to it. All can observe it, whether or not they stand in an organized and structured relation to the actors.

The second connotation of "public" is the attribution of collective societal values and interests. Here the word is used in its meaning of "the public interest," as distinguished from private interests. As society is expanded in structure and in thought, the terms of discourse about policy must be those of societal benefit. The assumption is sustained that there is some underlying social agreement about collective ends such that the conflicts of private and special interests and sentiments can be resolved. Thus Rawls's *Theory of Justice* rests upon the logical necessity of a public interest as a criterion for public discourse (1971: chap. 1). Gouldner (1976) has made a similar argument in asserting that ideology as a modern form of idea system is a product of the development of a public in which rational discourse is essential to justification and argument. Such modes of public discourse further presuppose and grant reality to "society" as an object.

Third, what is public is a common object of attention. Here, once again, the concept of a mass society has relevance. It points to a realm of events and activities which are experienced at a distance but as a common experience among otherwise disparate and diverse people (Blumer, 1939:241–47; Kornhauser, 1959:13–38). The public is not only the domain of those who are active in its events; it is also the domain of those who observe it and share it as common spectacle. "To live together in the world means essentially that a world of things is between those who have it in common, as a table is located between those who sit around it" (Arendt, 1959:48).

## THE IDEA OF THE FUTURE SOCIETY

The participation of the various classes, both as citizens and as spectators, is associated with the development of the idea that the present society is problematic, that it can possibly be other than it is. The English word "reform" once suggested restoration to an original state. It is in the seventeenth and eighteenth centuries that it came to assume a meaning connoting *newness* (Walzer, 1965:11; Williams, 1976:221–22). Similarly, the idea of revolution is a product of societies in which a centralized state is both imaginable and possible. The vision of a world transformed through political and social rather than religious conversions is a modern myth of Sorelian form (Walzer, 1965: chap. 1; Aron, 1962; Gusfield, 1973; Williams, 1976:229).

Earlier historical periods had, of course, experienced rebellions, revolts, and protest actions. As Rude and Hobsbawm have both pointed out, even the protests of the seventeenth and eighteenth centuries in Europe generally backed a programmatic focus on changing the rules of society. They were specific responses to specific grievances, more often aimed at restoration of a particular situation than at changing relationships (Rude, 1959, 1964; Hobsbawm, 1959). What the premodern period lacked was a widespread conception of societal change as a constant, pervasive, and tangible possibility.

To speak of social movements as a regularized feature of modern societies is to point out that the widespread imagination of the future society as different and as shapable by our actions is a unique event in human history. This reflexive awareness of social change and of ourselves as possible authors of it is what is so distinctive to the modern period. William Irwin Thompson, in his study of the impact of literature on the Easter (1916) rebellion in Ireland, described the process eloquently:

> History is, in fact, a process by which a private imagination becomes a public event but any study which restricted itself to the public would have to ignore the fact that history is also the process by which public events become private imaginations. (1967:235)

## The Modernity of Movements

Conscious efforts to design, control, and produce societal change are *not* ubiquitous features of human life. They are historically specific to the modern world of industrialized and industrializing societies. Both interest groups, specifically oriented toward the self-defined interests of members, and "causes," directed toward some principle and action in the interests of others, are products of the modern period (Banks, 1972; Gusfield, 1978; Schlesinger, Sr., 1950). In studying movements, sociologists are studying one way in which social change is instituted in the modern period. The associational character of movements is not universal; it is instead a product of modern life (Tilly, 1969:4–45).

Organized efforts to promote social change are, in some respects, institutionalized forms of activity in modern society. They constitute a characteristic, widely understood, and anticipated way in which change can be pursued. They are associated with the rise of popular governments, the division of labor, a centralized political nationalism and the growing literacy, education, and standard of living of large segments of populations. Proactive movements, as distinguished from reactive ones, assert new claims not previously asserted, and such collective action, as Tilly (1978:147) maintains, has been proliferating in the past two centuries in European societies. The political acceptance of movements is also revealed in the substitution of the word "movement" for "mob," a revised way of thinking about collective behavior and social movements (P. Wilkinson, 1971:11–14; Hovard, 1977).

A digression from the major theme of societal growth and change is necessary to my argument at this point. Having placed social movements within historical context, I need to discuss the ways in which sociologists study such phenomena. Tilly's analysis of theories and methods for research on collective action is useful. He emphasizes the way in which groups and events are mobilized around interests as the subject matter of the field (Tilly, 1978:8–10, chap. 2). In doing so he specifically turns away from the concept of "social movements" as groups attached to a set of beliefs. "The fact that population, belief and action do not always change together causes serious problems for the student of social movements" (1978:10).

It is imperative to recognize the difference between studying collective action and studying social movements. In the first case, what is to be studied is the activity of an association of people organized around goals and programs. Much of the study of what is called "social movements" is of this nature. What is studied are the Black Muslims, the Church of Scientology, or the Women's Christian Temperance Union. The second case, closer to what Tilly labels "social movements," is focused on the changes in meanings that occur both inside and outside associations of active partisans. It studies abolitionism, civil rights, temperance, or the movement against the war in Vietnam. The distinction is of course drawn too sharply, yet it's significant. Each draws attention to different corners, defines appropriate areas of study in diverse fashion, and, above all, locates the boundaries of study at different points on the social landscape.

In the remainder of this chapter I shall argue the importance of perceiving movements as self-consciously understood demands for changes in the meanings of actions at both public and private levels. The emphasis on the study of associations and organizations directs our attention to the public realm of collective goals, to ideologies and discourse, to purposes and activities, membership and followership. My argument is that this perspective concentrates on what happens in the public sphere and, as a result, overstates the importance of the public and understates the significance of the private, local, and routine areas of life and the interplay of the two in developing and directing societal change. Put in terms of an older distinction, it glorifies State at the expense of Society. The cost of this is to overlook crucial processes of cultural changes, especially those probably more emergent in recent chapters of the history of industrial societies. "[I]t is short-sighted," writes Paul Wilkinson, "to focus all our attention on what might be called primary-level politicization among social movements" (1971:53).

The prominence that sociologists have given to the dramatic—to civil disorder, pressure-group actions, and revolts—is a large part of the politicization of change. The transformation of public agencies, in government and the economy, is the arena of primary conflict in this drama. The transformation of persons and situations plays a secondary part.

Both of these distinctions—between associations and meanings, and between institutional and personal transformation—are hardly unrecognized by sociologists. Most make some distinction between movements or collective actions which seek to transform social institutions and those which gain their significance through tranforming persons (Wilson, 1973: chap. 1). Most make some distinction between movements which affect general and diffuse change, such as humanitarianism, and those seeking specific and bounded changes, such as the child labor movement. Blumer's (1939) distinction between "general" and "specific" movements and Smelser's (1962) between norm-oriented and value-oriented are cases in point.

These typologies of movements can be rephrased as components of movements, aspects which inhere in many transformational processes. The dimension of institutional-personal transformation is what I am referring to in the public and private dichotomy. Here the movement "exists" in its public form as observable, reportable actions. It happens to those who strike public roles—as adherents, enemies, detached analysts. The activity of a civil rights march, the lobbying of the National Organization For Women, the public meetings, parades, and literature of gay rights and opposing organizations—all these are instances of movements in pursuit of fixed goals.

At another level movements also "exist" in the ways in which transformation is perceived as socially shared, as an aspect of the society in a given historical period. The quality of interpersonal interaction, of decisions in situated moments, in day-to-day actions, is the focus here. The movement is to be found in the housewife considering entry into the labor force, the relations of blacks and whites in ambiguous situations, the response of parents to knowledge of a child's homosexuality, the decision of a Polish- or Italian- or Mexican-American to retain an ethnic name or not.

What distinguishes this component of change from unrecognized, slowly developing social and cultural change (what Sumner called crescive change) is the reflection of participants on the shared nature of transformation, on belief in the existence of the movement. Movement implies momentum, change in process. It signifies that a form of action has become possible, thinkable, a matter at least of conflict in the society. An area of life is in motion, in flux and ambiguity. It has ceased to be either the accepted, unchallenged definition of reality and morality or the unchallenged definition of impossible or idiosyncratic. To be gay in 1978 is not socially the same as in 1948. To expect that an employer recognize union representation was not the same in 1935 as it was in 1900. Movements are not necessarily, nor even entirely, associations. They are also meanings which construe social behavior as "in motion." They create choices where choices did not exist as possibilities.

Preoccupation with the sense of transformation is the unifying theme in the study of social movements. To talk about the existence of a "movement'' is then a way of referring to the quickening of change and its status as a matter of advocacy and rejection in public and/or private arenas. In our time they run the gamut—general and specific, interest-oriented and cause-oriented, organized and unorganized. What is signified is that new forms of society are imaginable and possible. They are in motion in areas ranging from art, as imagination, to history, as action. When the individual acts in a world of movements, he or she (a phrase I wouldn't have used ten years ago) does so societally, self-consciously as one of a number and not as an isolated person.

## The Interplay of the Public and the Private

This reflexivity of movements is at the center of my argumental wheel. Movements are not only objects of attention for members or partisans; they are also objects for nonmembers, the "general public." As such the existence of a movement is a public fact about the society. It signifies that some aspect of the social environment is in motion, in process of possible change. An alternative arrangement is now available to the structure of thought. What has been unthinkable or impossible can now be thought about and even perceived as possible. The recent tax-relief movement generated in California makes many people and officials in many other states suddenly conscious of possible political responses. It makes the matter of taxation an issue in a different manner than it was prior to the recognition of the movement. The pro-abortion movement signifies not only the effort to achieve certain legislation; its existence now indicates that abortion has become publicly admissible, societally at issue and thus en route to legitimacy. The impact of movements *is* not only in their intended and stated goals. It is also in what they signify by being. In this sense they have audiences as well as adherents.

The belief that social order is a fact, that others neither doubt the legitimacy of institutions nor fail to carry out their roles, is not itself a stable piece of social reality. It, too, has to be constructed and is capable as well of being destroyed. Acts of deviance, defiance, and alienation, as Durkheim realized, subvert order beyond the immediate effects. Events, processes, and persons that disturb belief in the facticity of an orderly society make it apparent that the hold of norms, values, and beliefs on the population is more tenuous than had been imagined. "Creative disturbance" disturbs. It makes the orderly account of events and expectations problematic and no longer taken for granted. The "crazies," the impetuous "left-wing adventurers," the proponents of "revolution for the hell of it" have recognized this by attempts to carry out the absurd and in this way to make it possible to imagine the social order as different (Hoffman, 1968).

## THE DRAMATIC CHARACTER OF PUBLIC ACTIONS

In the large, diverse, and extended societies of modern-day life, personal experience of a direct kind cannot be depended upon to monitor the society, to convey the most general of generalized others. Much of the objectlike character of society, and the sense of social change, emerges in the public arena. The newspaper, the magazine, television, and mass education, including sociology, provide a monitoring of society. Relatively unorganized movements owe much to such media in the construction of belief in a shared demand for change. The Senator Joseph McCarthy movement, as one example, became an object of reality and power in part through the attribution of a powerful movement as a means of explaining fragmented and otherwise unrelated events which might have been construed otherwise (Spinrad, 1970: chap. 7). As John McCarthy and Mayer Zald (1973) have suggested, the classic pattern of an organized movement with members, leaders, and followers is often an inappropriate model for contemporary societies.

The monitoring of society is a crucial part of the process by which movements are constructed in modern life. The reporting, analysis, and debate over social and cultural changes accentuate attention but also present particular actions as shared over a wide area, publicly statable and adequately described as a "movement." Not only is this the case with relatively organized segments of movements—Right-to-Life, for example—but it is especially pertinent where "movements" are unorganized. The "hippie" movement and the sexual revolution are two cases in point.

I call this process "dramatic" as a way of pointing to several characteristics of how movements emerge in modern societies. The first aspect is that organized and unorganized movements become observable to audiences. They have a presentational as well as a purposive dimension. Secondly, the presentation of movements as spectacles often involves a heightened excitement and interest conveyed by styles which make the actions more interesting, more attention-getting for audiences, more stimulating and engrossing for members. This is what is meant by "dramatizing the news." Thirdly, dramatizing also involves an abstract selecting and filtering process which changes the events through interpretation (Lang and Lang, 1968:291).

In becoming observable and dramatically interesting, the events and activities construed as movements become signposts of the societal. They convey what is now undergoing change and what is being resisted. The scenarios of conflict, antagonists, and protagonists, of events moving toward climax and resolution are the stuff of the careers of movements. As they symbolize the character of society, they take on symbolic attributes as well as more direct and instrumental purposes. The movement to limit marijuana usage is an instance of an issue containing symbolic conflicts over issues of youth culture and adult power (Gusfield, 1975*a*). Even the tax revolt in California in 1978 won the votes of many non-property owners and suggests actions which symbolize opposition to government and government spending as well as narrower and specifically interest-oriented politics.

## NORMALIZATION AND SOCIAL CHANGE

The very concept "movement" indicates that something is in motion, undergoing possible change and transformation. What is occurring through the public arena is that actions, beliefs, and ideas that have been outside the realm of the normal are now portrayed as undergoing the possibility of being transformed into the normal. What has appeared as just, natural, or unquestioned within the public and the society is now posed as an issue, potentially unjust, unnatural, and questioned. A new perspective is offered toward old relations, actions, or ideas. In the past decade homosexuality has been publicly transformed from behavior seen as deviant and abnormal to behavior now in the public realm of conflict. In the view of the society now emerging in public, homosexuality, in the sense that the term was once used, ceases to be "queer."

The implications of this normalization of previously abnormalized beliefs, actions, and ideas is to change the structure of consciousness. The labor movement made unionization less absurd, unthinkable, or "crazy." The women's movement has raised such consciousness-producing implications to deliberate and organized action. The arguments over terminology (*chairman, chairwoman, chairperson, chair*) are dramatized instances in which the unequal position of women is brought to attention and new claims are given support. They are also instances of changing cultural meanings for events, changes which provide new linguistic designations less connoting or supporting of male dominion.

The public character of the normalization process is what I am stressing. The once-dissident act, the previously unexpected alternative, the resolution of tensions through new outcomes are, as they become publicy observable acts or advocacies, no longer individual, idiosyncratic, and bizarre. In one form, the public arena not only reflects the society; it also refracts. It provides definition, explanation, elaboration, and program. It gives value, diffuse, and unspoken thoughts "a local habitation and a name."

## THE INTERPLAY OF THE PUBLIC AND THE PRIVATE

One of the implications of growth of centralized states and national societies has been the evolution of the welfare of the citizen as a rightful obligation of the society. Many problems that were once dealt with at the level of the family are in contemporary societies viewed as public woes (Weinberg, 1974).

One of the major areas of interplay between the public and the private is simply the extent and depth with which private issues become public ones. Certainly some of the most poignant sources of human concern are even today outside the realm of public attitudes, discussion, or remedy. No movement of welfare for unrequited love or surcease for parental disappointment has yet emerged. Yet the list of private woes made into public worries is lengthening. Movements of personal identity, of ethnic and racial status, add to the transformations of person implied in life-style movements and religious transformations. Some are public in that they call for state action, as in the pro- and anti-abortion movements. Some are less state-directed but involve public attitudes and discussion, as in sexual codes. Areas of life left outside of the public realm may move into them or, as in the case of many past religious conflicts, move outside and into the private.

In much of this chapter I have stressed the way in which public and publicly constructed movements impinge upon and affect private areas. In this dimension, "the movement" is to be found in its microsocial arenas, through the realization that areas of life are "in motion." The housewife who decides to enter the labor force or seeks to reformulate her relationship with her husband, insofar as the recognition of male-female relations as undergoing transformation is part of her awareness, does so with a sense that her behavior is shared, her claims are not bizarre. Ibsen's *A Doll's House* is part of a process of recognition that an individual feeling of protest is socially shared. It matters very much whether or not the individual acts alone or with a recognition of being "with history." These transformations are profound and are not registered in the collective goals achieved through organization, in bits of legislation or new institutional regulations. They are deeply implicated in the accommodations by which human beings in modern societies frequently respond to the recognition of a changing society. They make change a more conscious and deliberate act even at individual and situational levels.

In another form, the private interacts with the public in being the source of that which the public arena monitors. I have already called attention to this in discussing how it is that public media, including education, turn private acts into movements by defining and portraying them. Thus a recent study, based on survey research data, found the existence of profeminist attitudes before the advent of women's rights organizations, although the organized movement appears to have accentuated them.

The public, mass character of movements in the modernization of societies should not deceive us into the belief that what occurs in the public arena is either the most significant way or exhausts the ways in which social change happens in a self-conscious fashion. The modernization of society into an object available to the multitude of citizens does not mean the disappearance of continuity, of a separate and semi-autonomous realm of the traditional and the private. In my focus on the evolution of the public I do not mean to turn away from the dualities of community *and* society, tradition *and* modernity, state *and* society, the public *and* the private. The emphasis on social change through organized movements, political goals, and interest-oriented groups hides the cultural sources of change, and, especially, the most recent transformations of contemporary life.

## The Overpoliticization of Society in Modern Sociology

A number of years ago, Dennis Wrong (1961) attacked the conformist stereotype of human beings in the sociology of that period. His paper had as its title "The Over-socialized Conception of Man in Modern Sociology." I have paraphrased that as the title of this final section.

The study of deliberate and self-conscious change has emphasized two aspects of collective action and social movements. One is the role of the state and the importance of political power in defining the goals and impacts of movements. The other is the importance of organized associational forms as the mechanisms for achieving social and cultural change. In both aspects the study of social movements has overstated the degree to which modern societies are unified and centralized entities and exaggerated the extent and significance of political power. In a third failing, the model of social movements as organized efforts to achieve public changes is less adequate for an understanding of transformations occurring in contemporary modernized societies under the impetus of universal education, mass communications, and "middle-class" standards of living. The increase in incomes, the added leisure, and the growth of awareness and imagination have produced a situation in which "all of us have become, simultaneously, workers and aristocrats" (Plath, 1964:3).

To be sure, there is a spectrum of movements and change-oriented associations. The narrow-interest group, appealing to a specific constituency through a highly organized association, is more likely to find its impact in particular and well-defined purposes which governmental and institutional power can control. Here the interest group, exemplified in the International Longshoremen's Association, the Dairymen's League, and the League of American Wheelmen (Bicyclists), fits the model well. Others appeal to a public morality more directly and "disinterested." Less susceptible to Olsen's "free rider" analysis, organizations like the National Urban League, the American Anti-Slavery Society, the Church Peace Union, and the National Union for Social Justice represent "causes" less than they do interest groups. More diffuse and less organized movements, like the "hippies" or the women's movement, are involved in transformations at levels and arenas outside, in addition to, or alternatively to the public. The spectrum fades into highly general movements almost too amorphous to be represented in any organization or particular event. Here the movement toward narcissism in human relations is an example (Sennett, 1978:4).[2]

A distinction between state and society is a frequent starting point in the analyses of political sociology (Hintze, 1968:154–69). The relations between the two, their mutual dependence, their independence, and the dominion of one over the other have been the starting point for controversy. One tradition, deep in orthodox Marxism and in political behaviorism, has been to see the state as largely a creation of society. Political institutions and events are then traceable to the interests and "needs" of major economic and social groups and classes (Lipset, 1960; Mills, 1956; O'Connor, 1973). Other sociological traditions have stressed a "neutral" role for the state, as in pluralist formulations (Rose, 1967; Dharendorf, 1959) or a more significant yet independent role as a source of power in the modern world (Bendix, 1964, 1978).

In many respects, the problems of gaining entry into state power were *the* crucial issues of conflict and change in the nineteenth century in Europe and America (Tilly, 1969; Bendix, 1964). Acquiring position in state and in institutional life in society were major sources of collective violence. The state, I am asserting, is less vital as the arena of contemporary movements in contemporary modern societies. The civil rights movement may be the last major movement of the nineteenth-century type.

## THE FAILURE OF STATE POWER

We are today, in my judgment, in a period of retreat from the public arena as the most significant site of social and cultural change. Whether this portends a general shift in modern societies or is a transient, ephemeral trend is not clear. However, in many respects it builds on the structural changes which have made twentieth-century populations in modernized countries more like the middle classes of the nineteenth century. It is accentuated by the educational spread and the public media of mass communications which report the society to itself and turn individual actions into shared ones. The theatrical character of the public arena is also indicative of its weak role as direct and instrumental. Many of the crucial movements of

[2]The specific organizations mentioned in this paragraph are taken from the fifty-three used by William Gamson in his study *The Strategy of Social Protest* (Gamson, 1975). Using this description of the groups given by Gamson, I classify twenty-four as being directed to a special interest-group constituency and twenty-eight toward a more causelike general constituency. (One is unclassifiable.) Concerned primarily with the public and political arena, Gamson's sample contains no movements that are involved in the transformation of the person. Protest is confined to the public arena.

our times have their locus outside of the political and institutional areas of life, at the level of interpersonal encounters, of routine daily life. Although centralized power and legal institutions are utilized to affect them, the power of such agencies is highly limited. In searching for transformation outside of the public realm, in society rather than in state, the contemporary world may be moving away from some of the centralizing trends of the past two centuries into what I have elsewhere called "the privatization of Utopia" (Gusfield, 1973:31).

One aspect of this is the weakness of government to effectuate its edicts. In the literature of social movements and collective action the story usually ends with "victory" or "defeat" in the halls of the legislatures, the appearance of new agencies, legal decisions, or electoral success. Whether such events are followed by the behavior sought through them is problematic. The capacity of the local area, the organization or industry, or the lone individual to distort and evade public edicts is an old theme in political science and sociology. Murray Edelman (1964) has portrayed much of the drama and language of public, political movements as achieving a "symbolic quiescence" leading the audience of spectators and adherents to believe that a situation has been remedied when, in point of fact, little further effective action occurs. Similarly, studies of the implementation of programs point to the considerable difficulties in making reforms into effective impacts on daily, routine behavior (Pressman and Wildalsky, 1973). The cooptation of regulatory agencies by those they were inaugurated to regulate is a persistent theme.

Sociologists, political scientists, and lawyers have for long discussed the difficulties in using legal decisions as effective means to produce reform behavior. In his forthcoming analyses of thirty-eight cases involving four major social movements, Joel Handler (forthcoming) found it difficult to achieve tangible results from the reforming of the law. The bureaucratic contingencies involved in implementing decisions were particularly impediments. The literature on deterrence and punishment and on deterrence by use of law similarly does not reach sanguine conclusions about attempts to control criminal or other behavior through laws against crimes (Zimring and Hawkins, 1973; Gibbs, 1975).

Nor does the state appear, in many modern societies, to be as effective an agent of repression as hoped or feared. Despite the actions of the CIA and the FBI, the anti–Vietnam war movement was neither extinguished nor greatly weakened. The ability of determined American males to avoid compulsory military service in the 1960s was considerable. Despite the intensive processes of centralization and nationalization in Europe during the past 200 years, the local nationalisms of Spain, the United Kingdom, Belgium, and the Soviet Union remain persistent issues of national integration (Hechter, 1975; Zilborg, 1974). They are not so distant from the linguistic, religious, and tribal schisms of less "advanced" countries such as India and Nigeria.

Like the impact of the public on the private, the effects of the state on the society are problematic eventualities rather than deducible conclusions. It is not that state action has *no* impact on social institutions or human relationships. I am suggesting that the effects of state power and the centralized unity of societies in the modern period are less effective and less significant than has been accepted. My emphasis on the dramatic or symbolic character of political events is also a way of calling attention to the ways in which political conflicts are staging areas for clashes between adherents and enemies that have their significance in the private and routine parts of life. The current conflict over government obligations to provide medical expenses for abortions is one such ground on which the public legitimacy of abortion is being tested.

## THE PRIVATIZATION OF SOCIAL MOVEMENTS

Perhaps the more salient consideration in my theme of the overpoliticization of society in contemporary sociology is the widening areas of change that are less organized than the prevailing models of collective action and social movements encompass, that reflect the growing concern of populations with the transformation of the self in human encounters, in religious experience and in the styles of work and leisure. Although the public arena serves to dramatize and communicate such movements, they represent a turning away from the importance of the public as the focal point of change. They are movements with a locus closer to the private and the self than to the public and the institution. "The insides are where it's at," wrote a student in 1969; ". . . the current revolution is not an external affair to be determined by political, military and economic means. Primarily it's an internal affair to be engaged in as a learning experience" (quoted in Gusfield, 1973:30–31).

The retreat from the public and the political is a growing theme in contemporary American intellectual life. Recently several writers—Ralph Turner, Richard Sennett, and Lionel Trilling—have made it, in one way or another, a central point in their work. Turner (1969, 1976) finds the problem of personal alienation, of self and group identity, among the major issues of contemporary movements. Sennett (1978), after an examination of European public life in past centuries, asserts the growing privatization of life and the trend away from public interactions and public norms as loci of activity and criteria of behavior. Trilling sums up much of this shifting focus of emphasis on self rather than role in his belief that modern societies are witnessing a transition from glorification of sincerity—the fit between the self and role—to authenticity—the expression of the self in opposition to role. There is in all three of these writers a supposition that the profoundest problems of modern life are seen as those of expressiveness—of the place that impulse, narcissism, and personal feeling have in the context of social controls and social roles. Not Marx but Freud appears as the patron saint of the twentieth century.

These cultural changes are themselves a movement, a "cultural drift," to use Herbert Blumer's term (1939:286). They are not without historical analogues in the romantic and youth movements of upper-middle-class European society in the nineteenth and early twentieth centuries (Grana, 1964: part 3; Becker, 1946). They bear resemblance to aristocratic attitudes and suggest the nature of social and cultural changes. Populations of "middle-class" character can now focus their attention upon other than material issues.

In the stress on styles of life, on the importance of personal emotions and feelings, in the reassessment of values of ambition and accomplishment, the rationalistic emphasis of an industrial and capitalistic society is undergoing potential deep transformation (Bell, 1976). The major political movements of the nineteenth and twentieth centuries, though often anticapitalistic, were themselves wedded to the same rationalism and scientific culture that characterized the bourgeois society they sought to transform (Gusfield, 1973; Bauman, 1976). The organizational form of movements and their quest for political and economic transformations mirror this as well. Writing in 1969 and commenting on the cultural revolution of the 1960s, Carl Oglesby took issue with the description of the May 1968 Paris uprisings by a Marxist theoretician. Andre Glucksmann had written that the student actions were a revolt *of* the forces of production. Wrote Oglesby, "Quite on the contrary. . . . [It] is a revolt *against* the forces of production" (quoted in Gusfield, 1973:31).

Many of the most strident conflicts of contemporary modern societies are *not* issues of class and material welfare. Social and cultural movements that are transforming society and human life are visible not only in organized demands for new social structure. They appear as well in the perceived and shared questioning of older values and styles of life as they occur in individual and situational areas. Moral and spiritual questions reflect the movements of change that occur at the level of private life but mirrored in the public reports of societal happenings. The world of public institutions, of politics and economics, of organized associational efforts, is itself a focus of criticism and indifference.

Organized protest and reform have been the institutional mechanisms of change in modernized societies. As a facet of societal growth, social movements and collective action, as we sociologists have defined and depicted them, have represented the accepted, understood, and organized mechanism for social change. Mass collective action, less organized and associational, does not fit easily into our models of change. The shared search for personal salvation and transformation, the generation of new moralities and meanings, is not caught in the nets of understanding that have worked for the nineteenth and early twentieth centuries' obsession with the state. Politicians squirm and wriggle when confronted by issues of abortion, pornography, sexuality, religion. They lack the institutional ways to treat them as political concerns. Sociologists find mass movements and mass change hard to study. But that is one mark of change—that it catches us unprepared for it. When I was a college freshman, I was impressed by a quotation from John Dewey on the first page of my social science syllabus: "Change is the fundamental fact in the social sciences as motion is in physical science." I have grown more skeptical about any such sweeping statement. Nevertheless it suggests one important attribute of the modern. We are ourselves both party to change and affected by it in what and how we study change. If history does not package our materials in the containers we have laid out, it becomes necessary to revise our art and construct new ones.

19

# Discontinuities and Fragmentation in Societal Growth

*Scott Greer*

THE SUBJECT IS AT ONCE so enormous, vague, and amorphous that, at the risk of becoming tedious, some limits in the form of definition must be set in place. I shall try to think seriously about the notion of societal growth and the notion of societal discontinuities.

It is certain that we have to be clear about what aspects of a society are growing. Even if we settle for quantitative increase, we have the spectacle of California and India, the latter increasing biogically by numbers that are, annually, equal to a large fraction of California's total population, while the twenty million Californios operate an economy which is about as rich in terms of dollar-valued product as that of the subcontinent.

One concept that resolves this problem is Fred Cottrell's (1955) image of a society as an energy-transforming system. Growth would then be the increase in the total amount of human and nonhuman energy transformed to human purposes. Thus with E. Adamson Hoebel (1949), we could compare the number of horsepower hours available to a band of hunting and gathering Shoshones to that of a comparable number of average contemporary citizens of Utah. The difference is, of course, astronomical.

Further, having so described societal growth, we have some bounds for the society: It is a system, and a system is characterized by the interdependence of parts. Thus, in principle we could delineate the bounds of the relevant society by comparing within-group/between-group dependency. And it is clear that, for some purposes, much of contemporary society must be seen as a global system, however discrepant the political structures may be from the energy interdependencies.

Growth, then, is not to be confused with progress; the latter being, in Wilbert Moore's (1968) terms, valued change. Instead it is change in one direction, however evaluated. For, while all societies change, all societies do not grow. While the United States as a society has grown enormously, such areas of rural New England and Appalachia have in recent times declined relatively or, in some cases, absolutely. They are examples of societal shrinkage, as the brush and forest reclaims the farmstead, field, and village. Seen from one perspective, according to I. J. Singer's (1936) view of the birth and growth of Lodz, or Daniel Boorstin's (1973) view of this country, the speed of growth, change, decline, and death are almost cinematic. Such speed of societal growth and decline is obviously one generator of "discontinuities and fragmentation."

The most obvious way to conceive of discontinuities which precede or result from societal growth is to focus on momentous growth in a relatively short period. One is conquest and incorporation in a larger and more productive system; an example far from home is Japanese conquest of Taiwan and Korea, still today among the high-energy systems in the Orient, along with their mentor. Another possibility of discontinuity producing growth, though it certainly does not guarantee it, is internal revolutions which release energies previously bound or unused, and coordinates them in societal tasks leading to growth. Such therapeutic revolutions (if one likes growth) usually signalize the cooptation of neglected but powerful human energies into the process of government and the distribution of prestige.

A more common type of discontinuity is produced by rapid change in technology, social and material. The change of the United States from a horse- and steam-drawn population to one propelled by internal combustion engine and electric car took place in a mere decade, from 1920 to the 1930s. Indeed the history of transportation in this country is filled with systems abandoned before completion because of new modes of getting about —from canal systems to railways to cars, trucks, and planes. In each case whole labor forces were unemployed or disorganized, and the distribution of population was rearranged in dramatic ways.

And, following such rapid shifts in technologies of the material sort are shifts in social technology. The increasing exploitation of coal and machinery was complemented by the creation of the modern factory, corporation, and labor union. All were inventions needed to organize and diffuse the exploitation of new energy transformers and resources. Such social technologies continue to emerge and evolve, and frequently they fit poorly with much of the context in which they flourish

This brings me to another sense of discontinuity—that discontinuity across the society at a given point in time. Following W. F. Ogburn (1950), we may say this results from rapid growth in one section and lag in interdependent sections of the society. Cottrell discusses the effects of a labor-intensive, agrarian society with a high mortality rate on the norms with respect for human life. It is valued, if not absolutely, at least highly, and both birth and perpetuation of the individual come close to core values. However, in a capital-intensive, urban society with infant mortality rates approaching the biological minimum, the norms and sanctions appropriate to earlier worlds make little sense: Both abortion and the considered termination of life-support systems begin to seem reasonable, yet they violate some of the most emotionally held beliefs of a substantial part of the population (Cottrell, 1975).

When our health services were developed, they depended upon medical capitalism for the prosperous, medical charity for the poor. In such a context doctors were educated, hospitals were built, and socially supported medicine was confined to the armed forces, sailors, Amerinds, and epidemic prevention. Now the practitioners of such health services are faced with a 180-degree turn; they learn that the organization of American medical services is evil in a society which believes that every citizen has a right to medical services. And it *is* inappropriate, for it was never meant to serve such a purpose. Very basic assumptions have been changed, and the physician moves from culture hero to delinquent in a few years. Such discontinuities are broad shifts in cultural definitions, and when they result in basic changes in power, as with the creation of Medicare and Medicaid, an entire institutional area of the society is up for criticism and revision (Greer, 1975).

Thus, we retain profoundly conservative norms from our long past: All fertilized eggs should come to birth; all lives should be prolonged if possible. At the same time we have developed a medical technology which allows both easy birth control and life support for the critically damaged. In the process we have lost the fatalism which made life and death bearable in our rural past.

With the norm of equal health care for all it is possible for the entire energy surplus to be spent on medical services. But it is not likely; there are always counterforces and conflicting demands. The late Howard Becker's (1945) geological metaphor seems appropriate; the present we move in is a topography produced by a long past, and it is never entirely fixed. Societies which change slowly in a stable physical environment may shape themselves, over many generations, to a certain coherence and form of culture, and a way of organization that does not often contradict itself and its cultural norms. This is not the situation in which we find ourselves. There has been too much and too rapid change in the past, while most of that change consists in reshaping the environment itself. Indeed, the fantastic increase in the rate of change is one of the most striking discontinuities produced by societal growth. As late as 140 years ago, Stendahl could say, "How slow the life of man, how rapid the life of men."

At this point we should ask how much continuity, integration, a society must have to persist. If we return to the image of society as an energy-transforming system, we can say it needs sufficient integration and continuity to coordinate the actions of people for the purpose of maintaining that system. This requires organized and dependable inputs of energy resources, human and nonhuman; an inner order which transforms that energy into humanly valuable terms; an output from each cycle adequate to supply the input necessary for the next. For growth, the society must (1) increase the energy resources available, or (2) improve the efficiency of its energy transformers, or (3) improve the terms of trade between output and the source of input. Individuals must be motivated to accept the necessary rules, do the necessary jobs, and improve their performance.

Sometimes growth may alter the preconditions for further growth, or even prevent it altogether. For the past two centuries we have seen such growth in energy transformation and organizational scale that we have tended to assume it is a constant. It may even be a necessity for some societies (as someone said of the Southern California economy, "It stays erect only by falling forward"). Nevertheless, such growth is unprecedented and so, in all likelihood, are the discontinuities and fragmentation which result.

Norton Long (1962) has argued that the individualistic or atomistic view of humanity which became common in the nineteenth century represents a dangerous distortion of the facts. It assumes that solidarity, trust, community commitment, and a degree of altruism are "free givens," as air to breathe was once believed by economists to be. The truth is that the growth of the last century and a half depended upon the social support and virtues nurtured in small-town society, Polish *shtetls*, Italian villages. And the processes of growth gravely eroded the societal bases for these civic virtues.

With the displacement of its functions to large-scale formal organization, kinship was weakened as a bond. Even the nuclear family was harmed as a socializing device; the home without one or more parents, with little functional use for children, competed for influence with the large public institution which absorbed the child's best hours from an early age on and, today, of course, with electronic advertising media.

The local area as community suffered a similar weakening, persisting longest in isolated rural areas and ethnic enclaves of the city. Even so, in most important matters it is increasingly controlled by bureaucracies, public and private, with little concern for the quality of local life. In the weakening of the local community the churches lost moral authority; with increasing affluence the doctrine of "hard work" and "self-denial" gave way to that of "entitlement." Long sees this loss of community authority as the root cause of the desolated inner city.

And there is the other side of it. The relaxing of constraints has meant increasing social choice for those with the time and money. And, with the doctrine of entitlement, even the bottom dogs do get fed—some of us can remember times in the 1930s when even that became highly problematical.

The abuse of public welfare by right and left, client and official, often obscures the *fact* of welfare—and the nature of the alternative. It is a salutary experience to visit a society where there is no welfare system at all.

Perhaps the most important long-run effect of the weakening of the local system and the growth of the central government has been the extension of citizenship to large segments of the population previously unenfranchised. Politically, economically, and educationally, American blacks are moving from a servile status at an impressive rate. Perhaps with fuller participation in the labor force, educational equality, and the vote, women will also take their place in the hierarchies of power. Such repressed groups as Hispanic-Americans, Vietnamese, and Samoans are given a reception considerably different than would have occurred a century ago.

The great change in the position of blacks results from the economic growth only indirectly; a more direct result is their movement into the urban labor force. Discontinuity with their southern, agrarian life, in the form of inapplicable economic skills, together with continuity in the form of racism, moved them into the lower-paid jobs in the labor force and the poorest housing in the city. The greater opportunities of the urban economy, however, has allowed the gradual emergence of a substantial black middle class. One cannot automatically assume a single black interest.

The improved status of blacks created many abrupt discontinuities for whites, particularly in the South and among those who interacted with blacks. Nevertheless, it is a near-miracle that a change of such magnitude could have occurred so rapidly and with so little physical violence. Here we must see economic growth as an important factor, for in a growth economy all may gain together.

Meanwhile there are other counterforces and surrogates. Perhaps the most important counterforce is the continuing reinforcement of the role of citizen. And here it is clear that protecting that role requires the weakening of the arbitrary power of family, local community, church, and state. The continuing movement to open up opportunities to the hitherto excluded increases the value of the citizen's role; whether it increases the sense of duty which should accompany rights in a reasonable group is another matter. Indeed, the chief danger in the doctrine of entitlement is just here: With union labor, civil service positions, tenured professors, one envisages an entirely tenured society given over to struggle between variously entitled groups.

Other surrogates for the integrating institutions of the past include the mass media, consumerism, and the memo culture of bureaucracy. With respect to the mass media, financed by advertisement and searching for the widest audience, we can say that usually it integrates only at the price of trivializing. One takes such a medium seriously, not for the quality and depth of its content, but because it absorbs a large proportion of the consciousness of a large population which in other days would have devoted the time to cultivating turnips and grain.

Consumerism is, of course, the active form of what is essentially passive with the mass media. While I believe Daniel Boorstin (1973) exaggerates the importance of consumer communities, I suspect that the fetishism of commodities has never been in better health than today. Those who can't get ahead get things; those who can, display the varieties of snobbery depicted by Tom Wolfe and arbitrated by the *New Yorker, Bazaar*, and the like.

Perhaps the most important surrogate for older integrative institutions is the bureaucracy. Whether in the public domain or the private, such organizations have preempted the heart of the American economy and a large share of its day-to-day governance. This is not because they represent the most efficient way of doing the world's work, or governing it, though that may sometimes be. More to the point are two interrelated aspects of private economic organizations: Those which are successful grow large, and those which grow large have proportionate power to control the source of supplies and to determine the terms of trade with the market for their output. They can preempt a field and be, at an extreme, the only game in town. In the public sector, bureaucracies grow in budget and personnel because they *are*, typically, the only game in town.

No, bureaucracies are not necessarily efficient as productive units. They are, however, fairly efficient as control systems. Such control may be in the interests of stockholder or citizens, but many suspect there is always an element of self-interest in it. And, when bureaucracy is combined with tenure, it clearly slips toward the least efficient way to do business. This is particularly apt to occur in those governmental bureaus where there is no "bottom line" of profit or loss. Private not-for-profit corporations are an interesting hybrid; frequently the effort to ape business without a genuine profit line simply results in concentration on cost containment, with little attention to the question of whether or not the agency is getting done what it purports to do.

Indeed, one of the most frustrating aspects of the bureaucracies in the human services is the difficulty of demonstrating any output. Evaluation, in the absence of any market, tends to rely upon such matters as the number of people with specified certificates of training, or the kinds of procedures that are carried out in what numbers on whom. But in the absence of hard data on the relationships of these measures to desired outcomes, they are not really evaluations at all. They measure procedure, not achievement.

However, the bureaucracy is an integrative institution, a surrogate for extended kin, village, and in some cases church. It is an orderly world with its own, frequently clear-cut rank order. It develops its own argot, heavily loaded with acronymns, nicknames, and "family" jokes. It usually provides a quite secure position to those below executive rank in private corporations, political rank in government agencies. Security is greater in the public agency; not only civil service, but also the lack of specifiable output, usually protects the worker from competition. Meanwhile the extended network of those who have appointed each other gives a distinct impression of kinfolk.

At the same time that bureaucracies integrate the behavior of millions of people, they exclude other millions. Since the latter are paying the salaries of the former, there is an understandable resentment on their part, sometimes aggravated by the suspicion that the agency really has no outcome at all. This is, of course, most likely in respect to public agencies, yet it did seem that many people were more pleased than sad when the Penn-Central railway went bankrupt.

The rapid shift from a society organized for production by farm and shop to these huge organizations is one of the most striking discontinuities in American history. In the individual life it is a shift from a childhood and youth in a nuclear family that is increasingly nonauthoritarian, where social distance across age and sex is minimized, to a structure that is in principle hierarchical, ordered by formal rules, impersonal, and efficient. No wonder Max Weber's ideal type seems so very idealistic in the United States. A society used to underplaying formal authority, and implying equality, would seem a poor candidate for bureaucratization. And, in the view of at least one critic, the trouble with our complex organizations is that they aren't bureaucratized enough.

Of course there have always been bureaucracies wherever civilizations occur. But bureaucracies in the past were a small part of the total labor force, relatively elite, and directly contacting few of the citizens who supported them. Our bureaucracy is nearly pandemic, including or affecting everyone. At the same time it is, as Norton Long (1962) has pointed out, the most democratic of our three branches of government, rather faithfully reflecting the demographic composition of the labor force. This circumstance, combined with bureaucracy's bad press, has greatly increased the number of its critics. It has also greatly increased the number of supporters.

This is dramatized in the politics of our great cities. One result of extending the role of citizen and mass education, both fostered by societal growth (if not required by it), was the decline of the ethnic neighborhood and, with it, the political machine. With the latter went the ability of the local branches of the national parties to control the vote, and hence the government, of the city (Chicago, as always, excepted). Thus the structure of urban politics came unglued just at the time that public services were expanding—reflecting growing wealth and rising norms, as well as the redistribution of federal and state funds to the cities. The result was the growth of public service bureaucracies at a great speed to great size.

Heavily endowed with wealth and legitimacy, these bureaucratic structures moved toward self-government. This was achieved in many cases, most spectacularly by the Port of New York Authority. It occurred more generally in humdrum agencies (schools, police) whose purposes and processes became so complex and of such a scale as to baffle the ordinary elected official, and much more the voters. With the agencies grew the public services workers' unions, those shadow governments which help make a great deal of policy for the agencies and, directly or indirectly, the city government.

In the private sector we are governed by corporate bureaucracies. They in turn are governed by boards of directors who, operating under the fiction that they are dealing with small-scale nineteenth-century enterprises, face matters of such complexity that they are unable to direct. They delegate to experts, whom they may on occasion fire—thus the representatives of the stockholders. In the public sector we have legislative bodies in a similar situation, delegating to staff experts and to the bureaucratic agencies the formation of policies they judge; if they find them good and pass a law, its implementation is delegated to the appropriate agency to implement. It is an old Washington saw: "*You* write the law and let *me* write the regulations"—thus the representatives of the citizens.

The rapid growth of modern society is made possible by the increase in societal scale. That involves an increase in the radius of networks of interdependence and communication with a consequent ordering of behavior adequate to see that the basic norms are honored and, from this, that the jobs get done. It is possible that we are faced with the Durkheim dilemma. Increasing interdependence requires more cultural integration than we can manage; growth itself has undermined the cultural support system. While bureaucratization may increase order within a segment of the society, what is to guarantee order among segments? While universal public education creates some commonality in belief systems and values among most citizens, is it adequate to a society so problematic, so filled with alternatives? The mass media are doubled-edged, as President Nixon found out. While we have undoubtedly had presidents equally devious in the past (and elections more suspect), they were far away in Washington, and "it's a big country," and government was not of so vital an interest to so many. Television amplifies the image and the slipping mask. The leader becomes all things to all factions, and not much to any. Given the jobs of dealing with such continual rough waters as the business cycle or international violence, such a situation is not conducive to confidence in the unconditional value of cultural integration via the mass media.

Ralph Linton (1936:284) wrote, some forty years ago:

> In modern civilizations . . . the core of the culture is being progressively reduced. Our own civilization, as it presents itself to the individual, is mainly an assortment of alternatives between which he may or frequently must choose. We are rapidly approaching the point where there will no longer be enough items on which all members of the society agree to provide the culture with form and pattern.

Or a government legitimated by a common commitment. However, it may be that the fragmentation accompanying the discontinuities of societal growth may be accommodated in one working system through symbiosis, *not* cultural integration. We would then think in terms of trading partners, controlled markets, formal and informal cooptation. Given the increasing number of role players who do not "know their place," from white working-class men to black college-educated women, such a system will take an awful lot of work by leaders, middlemen, and fixers, as well as some luck.

The faith of those who identify themselves and their fellow citizens as American is a faith in our ability to develop and sustain a universal concept of humanity. (Its *function* internally would be the same as the Russian effort to create the New Soviet Man.) The truth is that the only times we have approximated such a consensus were during the economic disaster of the 1930s and the international horror of World War II. Nietzsche was a good sociologist, and war is the health of the state—though apparently the right war at the right time.

Contemplating the problem in an earlier and simpler time, Ralph Linton (1936) goes on to say:

> That our own culture and society will eventually stabilize and reintegrate can hardly be doubted, but two things will have to happen first. We shall have to develop some sort of social unit which can take the place of the old local groupings as a bearer and transmitter of culture and insure a similar high degree of individual participation. There must also be some diminution in the flood of new elements which are being poured into our culture from the laboratories of the scientists and technologists. The breakdown of our present economic system would solve both problems. The descendants of those who survived would be forced to return, for the most part, to life as peasants in small communities, while research would cease through lack of the economic surplus and trained personnel which it requires.

Linton wrote in a more propitious time, ten years before Hiroshima.

20

# The Limits to Societal Growth

*Kenneth F. Boulding*

THE UNIVERSE IS A SYSTEM of interrelated subsystems, and where one subsystem ends and another begins is not always easy to say, except perhaps in astronomy. Even at this level, the earth, the moon, and the sun form a system which affects very substantially the subsystem of the earth, but it is very slightly affected by the other planets. Geologically, the earth seems to be a single system of plate tectonics, with local variations due to rainfall, climate, and so on. The biosphere is an extraordinary complex cluster of moderately separated habitats, each of which contains an ecosystem, though the migration of species from one habitat to another has been a very important factor in the evolutionary process. Once Adam and Eve appeared on the scene, evolution went into a new gear with the enormous production of human artifacts. There are two evolutionary processes that might be called genetic. The first is *biogenetic* evolution, in which genetic information or know-how is transmitted in the genes from one generation to the next and develops by mutation, and then the selection of mutants which produces phenotypes that occupy a niche in an ecosystem, a niche being an equilibrium population of the phenotype. Production is a process by which the know-how of the genotype is able to capture energy to transport and transform materials into the improbable structures of the phenotype; that is, the structure that the genotype "knows how" to make.

Long before the advent of the human race another genetic process, which I have called *noogenetics*, comes into play. It is the development of learned structures in nervous systems or their equivalent which are then transmitted from one generation to the next by a learning process. The biogenetic know-how produces only the potential for these learning structures in the brains (or whatever it is) of the phenotypes, but this potential has to be realized by a process again of mutation, that is, new structures, and again selection if the phenotypes for these new structures have a niche that they can occupy. For all I know this begins in the amoeba. It is present in snails, and possibly in worms; it is certainly present in birds and mammals.

Noogenetic evolution becomes dominant with the development of the human race, with the enormous potential of its biogenetically produced brains for immensely elaborate structures of images, know-what, and know-how. Noogenetic evolution takes place by mutations in the knowledge structure, that is, new ideas which are derived from its internal communication system of the brain, and then by selection if these new structures can be transmitted from one generation to the next in forms which permit the possessors of these structures to occupy a niche in the total system. The early *Homo* and *Mulier sapiens* had the noogenetic potential for Beethoven and Einstein, but they took fifty or a hundred thousand years of noogenetic evolution to realize that potential. We still do not know what the ultimate noogenetic potential of the human organism may be. It may be very large or we may be approaching its limits; it is impossible to say. One interesting thing that we are discovering is that other animals, such as the chimpanzee, also have noogenetic potential which has been previously unrealized, and the capacity of the human race for realizing noogenetic potential in other animals may be extremely important in the next epoch. Noogenetic evolution is, of course, Lamarckian, in the sense that the experience of the phenotype is transmitted to the next generation of phenotypes. Biogenetic evolution is strictly Mendelian; the experience of the phenotype affects its gene structure very little, unless, for instance, it is exposed to radiation or other mutagens. Even then, it is not the experience that is transmitted but the effects of this on the genes.

Scholars have a strong conviction, which it is a little hard to pin down, that the evolutionary process on the earth has had a direction to it, that is, a "time's arrow," at least in the direction of increasing complexity. Just why this should be so is not wholly clear. The most plausible explanation seems to be that in every ecosystem there are empty niches for organisms of higher complexity than those which already exist, and there are less likely to be empty niches for organisms of lower complexity, simply because these are likely to have been occupied in the past. This gives a kind of ratchet effect to the mutation-selection process in that at least a small proportion of mutations in the direction of complexity, even if these are random, are likely to survive because their corresponding phenotypes find empty niches.

At any one time there is a limit, of course, to how many empty niches there are. There are not likely to be empty niches for organisms at a much higher level of complexity than those existing. Mammals, for instance, would almost certainly not have survived, even if they had been produced, before the advent of plants which they could eat. There are limits also on the power of mutation to make changes at any one time. Small changes are much more probable than large ones, although in the evolutionary process the occurrence of rare events is a very important principle because of the irreversibility which it introduces into the process. A hundred-year flood by human standards is a fairly rare event with a one percent per annum probability, but the probability of its happening sometime within a thousand years is 99.995 percent, so that it is virtually certain. We could say, therefore, that in the ten billion years of the universe, a billion-year flood has happened. One has an uneasy feeling that it may have been us! The evolutionary history of the human race in the last two million years seems to have been a succession of extraordinarily improbable mutations, and even of luck and selection; otherwise, how did an organ as redundant as the human brain ever come to grow in a series of successive mutations when it was so little used?

One consequence of continually increasing complexity is that the evolutionary process passes over thresholds with the development of new evolutionary potential, in which the evolutionary process itself changes and usually accelerates. We can distinguish a number of such "gear changes." The largest, of course, was the development of DNA and of life itself. Another was the development of the cell and the oxygen-using organisms which developed after the original anerobic organisms polluted the atmosphere with oxygen, which killed most of them off. Another important development was the many-celled organism. Another was the invention of sex; another, the development of the vertebrate skeleton, and so on. The development of the human race is one of a long series of such evolutionary watersheds and perhaps represents a fundamental transition from biogenetic to noogenetic evolution.

The relation between development and growth is a tricky question. Growth is simply something getting bigger according to some measure. Development can perhaps best be defined as fulfilling some kind of potential. Development may or may not involve growth; the potential may be for greater complexity or higher values in smaller quantitities, whatever growth is measured in. It is not clear, for instance, that evolution has produced any sustained expansion of the total biomass, that is, the mass of living matter on the earth. This may well have been larger indeed in the days of the original ocean soup. One suspects that at some stages in particular evolutionary processes the total mass of evolving species grows as, for instance, the growth of complexity permits the use of new resources, new materials, new sources of energy.

We see this exemplified best perhaps in the history of the human race. *Homo sapiens* starts off with a niche of perhaps ten million people in the early Paleolithic. The evolution of human artifacts and the growth of human know-how, which has permitted constant increase in the types, materials, and sources of energy available to the human race, have undoubtedly resulted in its expansion in simple numerical terms. Almost every increase in human knowledge has increased the niche of the human race. Thus, the development of agriculture increased it to several hundred million, through the more efficient utilization of solar energy with crops and livestock, and the acquisition of new materials in the form of textiles, metals, clay and pottery, and so on. The development of civilization in cities represents a mutation in organizational artifacts, following perhaps from metallurgy and the invention of swords, and chariots, and especially the use of the horse as a transformer of solar energy.

With the mutation into science comes an enormous expansion of energy sources in terms of fossil fuel, nuclear energy, even increased utilization of solar energy to improve agricultural yields, plus a large expansion of available materials—aluminum, titanium, plastics, and so on. All this has tremendously expanded the "sociomass," that is, the total mass of human artifacts including human beings, as well as creating a spectacular rise in the human population itself. In the last 10,000 years the human population may have increased 400 times and the per capita mass of human artifacts may well have increased another 400 times, from the arrowheads, caves, and perhaps tents of 10,000 years ago, to the automobiles, power stations, and cities of today.

In social systems we think of development not only in terms of complexity and very simple measures of quantity such as mass, but in terms of some structure of human valuation. In human terms, growth is something getting bigger and development is something getting better. We cannot even identify complexity with "goodness." Increasing complexity can be perverse and even lead to extinction, as we see occasionally in the history of biological organisms, where one of the signs of the exhaustion of a particular line of evolutionary potential is the development of unnecessary and perverse complexity. We may be running into something of this in social systems today. It is a real question, for instance, whether the growth of scientific knowledge into an immense complexity of learned structures and their derived artifacts does not ultimately threaten the human race in the form, for instance, of nuclear war, or, perhaps even more devastatingly, biological and genetic warfare, which could well reduce the niche of the human race to zero.

It is quite legitimate, however, to regard development in terms of "human betterment" according to some structure of human evaluations. People have fairly strong judgments about this. They can usually assess whether they themselves are better or worse off than they were at this time last year. They have some idea of whether their own society or the whole world is better or worse off than it was at this time last year or this time ten or a hundred years ago. We run into the profound difficulty here that different people make different valuations and these different valuations must be coordinated in some way in the processes of society. These coordinations, however, constantly take place by a number of different processes. Elsewhere I have suggested that there are three major groups of these, which I have called the "three P's": prices, policemen, and preachments. "Prices" is the market mechanism which coordinates individual preferences for economic goods and bads into the dynamic system of price and advantage structures and distribution of resources and income. "Policemen" stands for the political system of legitimated threat by which governments collect taxes and decide how to spend them, and make laws and regulations and establish sanctions for noncompliance, and so on. "Preachments" is shorthand for the moral order by which communications of many kinds, from the raised eyebrow to the thundering sermon, change people's preference structures and personal valuations toward the ethos of the group, which ethos in turn continually changes through mutations and selection in the moral economy.

There is a constant complex process of feedback between perceptions of the state of the world, its evaluation, and action designed to change it. There is indeed what I have called the "paradox of decision." All decisions are for the best, that is, a decision is a selection of an image of the future which is perceived at the time to be better than the alternatives. Nevertheless, in retrospect, there is a great deal of regret, in the sense that things have often gone from bad to worse instead of from bad to better as the decision proposed. There are many complex reasons for this which are part of the study of what I have called "normative science": such things as market failure, externalities, Parkinson's laws and Peter principles, organizational pathologies, tragedies of the commons, perverse dynamics like arms races, the instabilities of legitimacies, dynamic processes of increasingly unacceptable inequality, and so on. Part of the learning process of the human race, particularly in the social sciences, is the study and understanding of these processes and the development of institutions which, in part at least, can deal with them.

In regard to human betterment, there is at least modest grounds for optimism, grounded in the enormous evolutionary potential of the human brain, which is still very far from having been exhausted, and in the asymmetry of the human learning process in which error can be detected and truth cannot. An erroneous image is much more likely to change than a realistic one under conditions of testing and challenge. A similar process goes on in human valuations. Preferences and values, ethical systems, and so on, which turn out to be dissappointing face challenges that will change them. Those which turn out to be less disappointing have less challenge and are less likely to change. Change, of course, is not always in the right direction. But if it is in the wrong direction, it faces a further challenge. This is the principle of selection.

Following the previous principle of increasing complexity, we might say that in social systems there are more likely to be empty niches for the better than for the worse species which emerge out of new mutations, under the various criteria of coordinated human values. On the other hand. the possibility of long, perverse processes in which things go from bad to worse is certainly very apparent in human history, though even darkest ages have had something of a silver lining. It was the fall of Rome, for instance, which set off a long process of technological improvement in Europe which led eventually to the rise of science. Catastrophe is sometimes, though not always, the creator of evolutionary potential, especially if it destroys previous perverse dynamic processes for low-level equilibria. We suspect this even in our very imperfect record of biological evolution. The end of one geologic age and the beginning of another often seems to have been punctuated by catastrophe, perhaps a climatic change, an active movement of plate tectonics, magnetic reversals, or solar flares—these events are rare and often leave very imperfect traces, but their result seems to have been widespread extinction of the old species and the beginning of a new era in which there was a very rapid rate of development into species of a different kind, usually at a higher level of complexity.

We can trace somewhat the same "catastrophe principle" in human history. There are many examples besides the fall of Rome. The Black Death of the fourteenth century, for instance, destroyed an old price structure and perhaps set in motion forces which led to the replacement of the relatively stable medieval consensus, with science and an expanding economy. Even in the twentieth century the defeat of Germany and Japan in World War II seems to have released an enormous outburst of economic development, whereas the victorious nations developed much more slowly. Even in personal life a dramatic failure sometimes leads into a reorganization of the person and the development of new potential for a richer and higher-valued future. On the other hand, there have been catastrophes which have been fatal, for instance, the extinction of the Mayan civilization or the cultural collapse of many American Indian societies in the face of the advance of a scientific civilization. Toynbee's proposition that the challenge has to be "just right"—neither too great nor too small (I have sometimes called this "Goldilock's principle")—undoubtedly operates, although it is very hard to identify exactly what is "just right."

Several propositions of importance for social systems emerge from the above framework: The growth of any subsystem results from some development of potential, whether biological, evolutionary, or societal. Thus, the growth of a single organism, such as a human being, originates in the formation of biological genetic potential in the form of a fertilized egg which has the know-how to "plan" the growth, maturation, and eventual decline and death of the person. The creation of evolutionary potential, as we have seen, sets in motion expansions of population and processes of various kinds. Similarly, in society an entrepreneur may create evolutionary potential for a business organization; a prophet for a church; a founding father for a nation; a conqueror for an empire; and so on.

There is a tricky problem here in regard to the laws of conservation. The general law of conservation is a truism or identity, that if there is a fixed quantity of anything, it can only be pushed around among subsystems, so that growth in one subsystem must involve decline in all the others taken together. The empirical question, of course, is what in any particular situation is in fixed quantity and can be transformed one into the other? Conservation principles crop up in evolutionary history, especially in the concept of the "carrying capacity" of a particular habitat, particularly where species are competitive one with another, so that the more of one the less of the other. On the earth, however, this principle is very loose and it is continually being modified by the evolution of genetic know-how in both biological and social systems, which results sometimes in general niche expansion through more efficient utilization of existing inputs or resources or the discovery of new ones.

The second principle is that the potential which produces growth in any system is itself exhausted by the growth itself, so that in no system does exponential growth at a constant rate go on for very long, for no potentials are infinite. Thus, the human fertilized egg grows very rapidly at first into a fetus, the baby, the child, the adolescent. Physical growth virtually ceases at maturity and may be followed by decline in old age and eventually death. All this is programmed in the original "plan" of the fertilized egg, although it may be modified by the events, environments, and experiences that happen along the way. This indeed is an example of what might be called the generalized second law—that if anything happens, it is because there is a potential for its happening, and after it has happened, that potential has been used up.

This, however, leads to the third principle—that potential can be re-created, and this indeed is the key to the whole evolutionary process. Simple forms of potential, like thermodynamic potential (negentropy, or negative entropy), do not seem to be re-created in the universe as a whole, although we cannot be sure of this. It certainly must have been created in the beginning in the "big bang." In subsystems, of course, thermodynamic potential is re-created all the time. This happens when we fill up an automobile with gasoline at a gas station. As we move into evolutionary systems, the concept of potential becomes both complex and mysterious. We really do not understand the formation of evolutionary potential, though it is very clear that it happens. The key here is that evolutionary systems are dominated by information and know-how structures, and information is not conserved, as everyone who teaches a class knows. At the end of the class, frequently the students know more and so does the teacher. DNA (sometimes called the first three-dimensional Xerox machine) is a prize example of the ability of information structures to reproduce themselves almost indefinitely.

Another principle is that evolutionary systems have considerable irreducible unpredictability, simply because they are based on information, know-how, and knowledge. Information has to be surprising or it is not information, and there is the famous principle that we cannot predict the future of knowledge or we would know it now. Predictability is only possible in systems where the parameters do not change, as in celestial mechanics, that is, in equilibrium systems. We can only predict if nothing is happening to something. Evolutionary systems, while they exhibit some stability which enables us to predict hesitantly and with caution, are subject to unpredictable parametric change. Hence, the model of celestial mechanics does not apply.

The development of capacity to migrate, that is, geographical mobility, is a crucial element in the interaction of subsystems, especially on the ecological scale, and as migration capacity increases, the individual ecosystems become larger until finally the earth becomes a single ecosystem. The situation is complicated because some species have a larger capacity for migration than others. The various systems are bound together by the migrant species and differentiated by the stay-at-homes. The migrants create new niches and destroy old ones in previous systems. There may still be niches for stay-at-homes, though not necessarily the same group.

The degree to which ecosystems are isolated has an important impact on the general pattern of evolution, simply because niches may exist in isolated systems which would not exist in larger systems, and if these isolated niches are significant from the point of view of general development, the destruction of isolation could very well impede, or at least change, the larger patterns of evolutionary development. Darwin's finches would not have developed so many subspecies if the islands of the Galápagos Archipelago had not been somewhat isolated. They would also not have developed if the islands had been completely isolated from each other. This is a very tricky problem and hard to reduce to simple form. It is of great importance, not only for biological but also for societal evolution. It is significant, for instance, that the sea, in which migration is relatively easy and isolated systems are hard to sustain except through temperature and pressure gradients, did not develop mammals. Only the rise of relatively isolated land areas seems to have permitted that development. Presumably whales are the descendants of land mammals that went back to the sea, which could never itself have produced them.

In the evolution of social systems both isolation and migration have been of enormous importance. On many occasions in human history isolated societies have developed an evolutionary process in terms of artifacts, ideas, or forms of organization, which have then led to their expansion into areas which have not produced these changes and in which there was, therefore, an empty niche for the more "advanced" society. One thinks of the expansion of the ancestors of the American Indians from Asia into the American continents some 11,000 or 12,000 years ago, across the Bering land bridge; the expansion of Aryan language cultures in India and into

Europe from their presumed origin in what is now western Russia; the expansion of the Chinese culture into South China; of Japanese culture from Kansei into the whole Japanese archipelago; and, of course, the migration which has dominated the last 500 years, the expansion of European cultures, and particularly science-based culture, into the whole world.

The initial creation of potential which leads to these expansive cultures is still very puzzling. Some of it may have to do with the discovery of new sources of energy or of food, especially, for instance, of protein. One is tempted at times to develop a protein theory of history—but in each case the circumstances are very different and it is hard to find a common pattern. Something which might be called "niche pressure" is what we are looking for here. When an ecosystem is in equilibrium, each species in it has an equilibrium population in which the number of births and the number of deaths is equal. The species that is below the equilibrium population will have an excess of births and will grow; the species above the equilibrium population will have an excess of deaths and will decline. Suppose now we have a species in which mutation occurs—this could be either of biological or of social species—which is niche-expanding, that is, which creates a situation in which at the old equilibrium population there is an excess of births so that the population grows. This may be accommodated simply by a change in the equilibrium of the original system, in which other species contract to smaller niches and the favored species expands. If, however, the mutation involves an increase in mobility, the species may expand into other ecosystems, often with a large resulting change in the equilibrium structure, therein creating new niches and destroying old ones.

In conclusion, let us take a very brief look at the implications of evolutionary dynamics for the present position and possible future of the human race. Human history consists of the working out of the evolutionary potential, up to now almost entirely noogenetic, of the biogenetically produced human brain. Biogenetically, the human race has changed very little in the last 50,000 or 100,000 years. Noogenetically, it has transformed the whole face of the earth, creating cities, transportation networks, libraries, and computer banks; replacing prairies with wheat fields; in some places creating deserts; establishing organizations of great size and complexity; shifting populations and cultures from one part of the world to another; and so on. As a result we have now developed a world superculture, the culture of skyscrapers, automobiles, airplanes, telephones, television, machines, complex educational systems, international corporations, and centrally planned economies, which might be described as national corporations.

This superculture originated primarily in Europe; why is by no means clear. Indeed the random factors in this process may be very large. If Constantine had not seen something in the sky; if Christianity had not become the established religion in Europe with its strange working-class origins, legitimating both work and the material world; if the Mongols had not destroyed Baghdad, perhaps at a point of takeoff into science; if China had not been dominated by Confucianism; if the pace of development in Mesoamerica had been faster . . . these *if's* of history are fascinating, frustrating, and unanswerable. In any case, the record is fairly clear. The European peninsula experienced slow, cumulative, and steady technical improvement from about the fifth century on, reacted to the challenge of Islam, produced the Renaissance, mutated—perhaps accidently—into science, an unusual subculture which valued curiosity and veracity and hence produced an enormous expansion of human knowledge and know-how. It was prescientific expansion of technology that increased the mobility of Europeans, especially in ships, and to certain improvements in agriculture which led to expanding internal food supplies and populations, and internal niche expansion. This then led to mobility and the settlement of the Americas, Australasia, South Africa, and Siberia by European populations with a technology of what might be called "dawn science," from 1500 to 1860.

Then, from about 1860 on, comes the major impact of the science-based technical upsurge that produced cheap steel skyscrapers, railroads, automobiles, telephones, electric power, scientific agriculture, computers, automation, and so on. The bulk of this change took place between about 1860 and 1930, that is, my grandfather's lifetime. It walked on two legs. The first was the development of organized research and especially applied scientific research. The second was the discovery of new sources of stored energy, and to a lesser extent of new materials, particularly, of course, oil and gas stemming from Titusville in 1859. Had it not been for science and the rise of science-based technology, the world would still look very much as it did in 1800 or even 1860. If it had not been for the existence of fossil fuels, which are in a sense an accident of plate tectonics, again the world would look much more like what it looked like in 1860.

Within the immensely mobile and uniform species of the superculture (for instance, skyscrapers, automobiles, and university graduates), local immobile species remain, but their niches have profoundly changed. Hereditary constitutional monarchy survives in northern Europe, tatami in Japan, walk abouts in Australia, kachina dolls in Arizona, kilts in Scotland, muezzins (with electronic amplifiers) in Kuwait, Marxism in Moscow, and so on. The interaction of the superculture with the local cultural and biological ecosystems is very large, very complex, very diverse.

What of the stability of the superculture? This is a matter of its unexhausted potential and to some extent, luck, for the random factor in the realization of potential is always present. Part of the potential in terms of fossil fuels and concentrated ores and the capacity of the world system to absorb pollution, that is, the production of "bads" that goes along with goods, is being exhausted rather rapidly. The know-how potential, however, can still lead to niche expansion; for instance, in space colonies, in the utilization of nuclear and solar energy, in the development of new materials. There are also profound dangers. The current international system has a positive probability of nuclear war; if it continues long enough, it will happen. There are subtle psychological species connected with such phenomena as the loss of nerve which we understand very little. There are perverse dynamic processes that might ruin us. There is a danger, furthermore, due to the lack of isolation. All systems face eventual catastrophe, that is, death. The evolutionary process has survived the death of innumerable individuals and species because of isolation and diversity, but a single world system might face universal and irretrievable catastrophe. One world could lead to no world. The one source for hope is the unexhausted potential of the human mind and the unexhausted potential of the evolutionary process itself. Any species, the human race not excepted, from an evolutionary point of view is a transmitter of the process of increasing complexity. When its work is done, it passes from the scene. How long the human race will last, we do not know. At the rate at which we have speeded up the evolutionary process, the life span of all species may be diminishing markedly. We may not have long to go. If we produce our evolutionary successor, however, we will not have been wasted.

# References


ADAM, HERIBERT

**1971*a*** Modernizing Racial Domination: South Africa's Political Dynamics. Berkeley: University of California Press.

**1971*b*** "The South African power-elite: A survey of ideological commitment." Pp. 73–102 in Heribert Adam (ed.), South Africa: Sociological Perspectives. London: Oxford University Press.

*Africa Today*

**1970** "Apartheid and imperialism: A study of U.S. corporate involvement in South Africa." 17(5): 1–39.

AFRICAN NATIONAL CONGRESS

**1971** The South African Trade Union Movement. London: Publicity and Information Bureau of the African National Congress.

AMERICAN BAR ASSOCIATION

**1977** A Review of Legal Education in the United States. Section of Legal Education and Admissions to the Bar.

ARENDT, HANNAH

**1959** The Human Condition. Garden City, N.Y.: Anchor/ Doubleday.

ARIÈS, PHILIPPE

**1962** Centuries of Childhood: A Social History of Family Life. Translated by Robert Baldick. London: Cape.

ARON, RAYMOND

**1962** Opium of the Intellectuals. New York: W. W. Norton.

ARRIGHI, GIOVANNI, AND JOHN S. SAUL
**1973** "Nationalism and revolution in sub-Saharan Africa." Pp. 44–104 in Giovanni Arrighi and John S. Saul (eds.), Essays on the Political Economy of Africa. New York: Monthly Review Press.

AUERBACH, ERICH
**1953** **1968** Mimesis. Princeton: Princeton University Press. (1st ed. 1953.)

BABCOCK, GEORGE D.
**1918** The Taylor System in Franklin Management, 2nd ed. New York: Engineering Magazine Company.

BANKS, J. A.
**1972** The Sociology of Social Movements. London: Macmillan Press.

BARAN, PAUL
**1957** The Political Economy of Growth. New York: Monthly Review Press.

BARAN, P. A., AND P. M. SWEEZY
**1966** Monopoly Capital. New York: Monthly Review Press.

BARBERA, HENRY
**1978** "The international mosaic: Contact, conflict and cooperation in world society." In Louis Kriesberg (ed.), Research in Social Movements, Conflicts and Change. Greenwich, Conn.: JAI Press.

BARNO, TIBOR (ed.)
**1967** Structural Interdependence and Economic Development. London: Macmillan.

BARTHOLOMEW, D. J.
**1972** Stochastic Models for Social Processes, 2nd ed. New York: Wiley.

BAUMAN, Z.
**1974** "Officialdom and class: Bases of inequality in Socialist society." In F. Parkin (ed.), The Social Analysis of Class Structure. London: Tavistock.

**1976** Socialism: The Active Utopia. New York: Holmes & Meier.

BEALE, CALVIN L.
**1975** "The revival of population growth in nonmetropolitan America." Economic Development Division, Department of Agriculture, ERS 650 (June).

BEALE, CALVIN L., AND GLENN V. FUGUITT
**1975** "The new pattern of nonmetropolitan population change." Madison, Wisc.: Center for Demography and Ecology, University of Wisconsin. Center Paper 75–22.

BEATTIE, CHRISTOPHER

**1974** Minority Men in a Majority Setting: Francophones and Anglophones. New York: McClellan and Stewart.

BECKER, G. S.

**1960** "An economic analysis of fertility." Pp. 209–213 in Demographic and Economic Change in Developed Countries. Universities–National Conference Bureau Series, 11. Princeton: Princeton University Press.

**1977** The Economic Approach to Human Behavior. Chicago: University of Chicago Press.

BECKER, HOWARD

**1940** "Historical sociology." In Harry Elmore Barnes, Howard Becker, and Frances Bennett Becker (eds.), Contemporary Social Theory. New York: Appleton-Century-Crofts.

**1946** German Youth: Bond or Free. New York: Oxford University Press.

BECKMAN, M.

**1958** "City hierarchies and the distribution of city size." Economic Development and Cultural Change 6:243–48.

BELJAME, ALEXANDRE

**1948** Men of Letters and the English Public in the Eighteenth Century. London: Kegan Paul, Trench, Trubner & Company.

BELL, DANIEL

**1968** "The measurement of knowledge and technology." In E. B. Sheldon and W. Moore (eds.), Indicators of Social Change. New York: Russell Sage Foundation.

**1972** "On meritocracy and equality." The Public Interest 29 (Fall):29–68.

**1973** The Coming of Post-Industrial Society. A Venture in Social Forecasting. New York: Basic Books.

**1976** The Cultural Contradictions of Capitalism. New York: Basic Books.

BEN-DAVID, JOSEPH, AND AWRAHAM ZLOCZOWER

**1962** "Universities and academic systems in modern societies." European Journal of Sociology 3(1):45–85.

BENDIX, REINHARD

**1960** Max Weber: An Intellectual Portrait. New York: Doubleday.

**1964** National-Building and Citizenship. New York: Wiley.

**1978** Kings or People. Berkeley and Los Angeles: University of California Press.

BENDIX, REINHARD, AND BENNETT BERGER

**1959** "Images of society and problems of concept-formation in sociology." Pp. 92–120 in Llewellyn Gross (ed.), Symposium on Sociological Theory. New York: Harper and Row.

BENDIX, REINHARD, ET AL. (eds.)

**1968** State and Society: A Reader in Comparative Political Sociology. Boston: Little, Brown.

BENSMAN, JOSEPH

**1973** "American youth and the class structure." Pp. 62–82 in Harry Silverstein (ed.), The Sociology of Youth: Evolution and Revolution. New York: Macmillan.

BERG, IVAR

**1970** Education and Jobs: The Great Training Robbery. New York: Praeger.

BERG, IVAR, MARCIA FREEDMAN, AND MICHAEL FREEMAN

**1978** Managers and Work Reform: A Limited Engagement. New York: Free Press.

BERGMAN, LESLIE F.

**1968** "Technological change in South African manufacturing industry, 1955-64." South African Journal of Economics 36(1):3–12.

BERKNER, LUTZ

**1972** "The stem family and the developmental cycle of the peasant household." American Historical Review 77(2): 398–418.

**1975** "The use and misuse of census data for the historical analysis of family structure." Journal of Interdisciplinary History 5(4):721–38.

BERKOV, BETH, AND JUNE SKLAR

**1972** "Does illegitimacy make a difference?" Population and Development Review 2(June):201–17.

**1975** "Methodological options in measuring illegitimacy and the difference they make." Social Biology 22 (Winter):356–71.

BERNARD, JESSIE

**1961** "Teen-age culture: An overview." Annals of the American Academy of Political and Social Science 338 (November):2–12.

BERREMAN, G. D.

**1978** "Scale and social relations." Current Anthropology 19(2): 225–45.

BERRILL, N. J.

**1966** Biology in Action: A Beginning College Textbook. New York: Dodd, Mead.

BERRY, BRIAN J. L.

**1961** "City size distributions and economic development." Economic Development and Cultural Change 9:573–88.

BERRY, BRIAN J. L., AND JOHN D. KASARDA

**1977** Contemporary Urban Ecology. New York: Macmillan.

BISH, ROBERT L., AND VINCENT OSTRUM

**1973** Understanding Urban Government: Metropolitan Reform Reconsidered. Washington, D.C.: American Enterprise Institute for Public Policy Research.

BIXBY, LENORE F.

**1970** "Income of people aged 65 and older: Overview from 1968 survey of the aged." Social Security Bulletin (April):3–27.

BLAKE, JUDITH

**1961** Family Structure in Jamaica: The Social Context of Reproduction. New York: Free Press.

**1965** "Parental control, delayed marriage, and population policy." Pp. 132–36 in Proceedings of the World Population Conference, Belgrade, 1965. Vol. 2.

**1974** "The changing status of women in developed countries." Scientific American 231 (September):137–47.

**1975** "The family and fertility control: A discussion of some central issues in the Symposium on Population and the Family." Pp. 343–46 in Vol. 2, Papers of the World Population Conference, The Population Debate: Dimensions and Perspectives. New York: United Nations.

**1979** "Is zero preferred? American attitudes toward childlessness in the 1970's." Journal of Marriage and the Family (May).

BLAU, PETER, AND OTIS DUDLEY DUNCAN

**1967** The American Occupational Structure. New York: Wiley.

BLAU, P. M., AND R. SCOTT

**1962** Formal Organizations. San Francisco: Chandler.

BLUMBERG, RAE LESSER, AND ROBERT WINCH

**1972** "Societal complexity and familial complexity: Evidence for the curvilinear hypothesis." American Journal of Sociology 77:898–920.

BLUMER, HERBERT

**1939** "Collective behavior." In Robert Park (ed.), An Outline of the Principles of Sociology. New York: Barnes and Noble.

BOGGS, ROBERT K., JR.

**1978** "Dynamics of bureaucratic change in a traditional polity: The case of Nepal." Unpublished dissertation, University of California, Berkeley.

BÖHNING, W. R.
**1972** The Migration of Workers in the United Kingdom and the European Community. Oxford: Oxford University Press.

BOORSTIN, DANIEL
**1973** The Americans, the National Experience. New York: Random House.

BORING, E. G., H. S. LANGFELD, AND H. P. WELD
**1939** Introduction to Psychology. New York: Wiley.

BORTS, G. H.
**1957** "Comment on Frank Hanna, 'Analysis of interstate income differentials: Theory and practice.' " In Regional Income ("Studies in Income and Wealth," Vol. XXI. A Report of the National Bureau of Economic Research). Princeton: Princeton University Press.

BOUDON, R.
**1974** Education, Opportunity and Social Inequality, Changing Prospects in Western Society. New York: Wiley.

BOULDING, KENNETH
**1953** "Toward a general theory of growth." Canadian Journal of Economics and Political Science XIX:326–40.
**1965** The Meaning of the Twentieth Century. New York: Harper & Row.
**1969** "Technology and the changing social order." Pp. 126–40 in David Popenoe (ed.), The Urban Industrial Frontier. New Brunswick, N.J.: Rutgers University Press.
**1970** A Primer on Social Dynamics. History as Dialectics and Development. New York: Free Press.

BRADLEY, DONALD S.
**1977** "Neighborhood transition: Middle-class home buying in an innter-city, deteriorating community." Paper presented at the annual meeting of the American Sociological Association, Chicago.

BRAUDEL, FERNAND
**1966** The Mediterranean and the Mediterranean World in the Age of Philip II. New York: Harper & Row.

BRAVERMAN, HARRY
**1974** Labor and Monopoly Capital. New York: Monthly Review Press.

BRAYFIELD, A. H., C. E. KENNEDY, JR., AND W. E. KENDALL
**1954** "Social status of industries." Journal of Applied Psychology 38:213–15.

BROOM, LEONARD, AND ROBERT G. CUSHING

**1977** "A modest test of an immodest theory: The functional theory of stratification." American Sociological Review 42:157–69.

BURAWOY, MICHAEL

**1976** "The functions and reproduction of migrant labor: Comparative material from Southern Africa and the United States." American Journal of Sociology 81(5):1050–87.

BURGESS, ERNEST

**1924** Publications of the American Sociological Society, Vol. 18.

BURNHAM, JAMES

**1941** The Managerial Revolution: What Is Happening in the World. New York: John Day.

BURNS, JOHN

**1978** "South Africa's penal system, descended from Calvinism, falls hardest on blacks." New York Times, July 21, p. A2.

BURT, RONALD S.

**1975** Corporate Society: A Time Series Analysis of Network Structure. Chicago: National Opinion Research Center.

BURTON, M.

**1972** "Semantic dimensions of occupation names." In A. K. Romney, R. N. Shepard, and S. B. Nerlove (eds.), Multidimensional Scaling: Theory and Applications in the Behavioral Sciences, vol. 2, Applications. New York: Seminar.

*Business Week*

**1977** "Doing business with a blacker South Africa." February 14, pp. 64–80.

BUTZ, WILLIAM P., AND MICHAEL WARD

**1977** The Emergence of Countercyclical U.S. Fertility. Monograph No. R-1605-NIH. Santa Monica, Calif.: Rand Corporation.

CALLINICOS, ALEX, AND JOHN ROGERS

**1977** Southern Africa after Soweto. London: Pluto Press.

CAMPBELL, DONALD

**1965** "Variation and selective retention in socio-cultural evolution." P. 30 in H. Barringer, G. I. Blankston, and Ray Mack (eds.), Social Change in Developing Areas. Cambridge, Mass.: Schlenkman.

CAMPBELL, R. E.

**1960** "The prestige of industries." Journal of Applied Psychology 44:1–5.

CARLSSON, GÖSTER
1968 "Change, growth and irreversibility." American Journal of Sociology 73:706–14.

CARNOY, MARTIN
1977 "Education and economic development: The first generation." Economic Development and Cultural Change 25 (1977 Supplement):428–448.

CARTER, A. P., AND A. BRODY
1970 Contributions to Input-Output Analysis. Amsterdam: North Holland.

CARTER, GWENDOLYN M., THOMAS KARIS, AND NEWELL M. STULTZ
1967 South Africa's Transkei: The Politics of Domestic Colonialism. Evanston, Ill.: Northwestern University Press.

CENTERS, R.
1953 "Social class, occupation, and imputed belief." American Journal of Sociology 58:543–55.

CHAFE, WILLIAM
1972 The American Woman. New York: Oxford University Press.

CHANDLER, ALFRED D.
1977 The Visible Hand: The Managerial Revolution in American Business. Cambridge, Mass.: Harvard University Press.

CHODAK, SZYMON
1973 Societal Development. New York: Oxford University Press.

CHOUCRI, NAZLI, AND ROBERT C. NORTH
1974 Nations in Conflict: National Growth and International Conflict. San Francisco: W. H. Freeman.

CHRISTALLER, W.
1966 Central Places in Southern Germany. Englewood Cliffs, N.J.: Prentice-Hall. Originally published in 1933 as Die Zentralenen Orte in Suddeutschland.

CICOUREL AARON L., AND JOHN L. KITUSE
1963 The Educational Decision-Makers. Indianapolis: Bobbs-Merrill.

CLAGUE, ALICE J., AND STEPHANIE J. VENTURA
1968 Trends in Illegitimacy. U. S. Department of Health, Education, and Welfare, National Center for Health Statistics Series Number 21, Publ. Number 15. Washington, D.C.: Government Printing Office.

CLARK, BURTON R.
1977 The Distinctive College: Antioch, Reed, and Swarthmore. Chicago: Aldine.

CLARK, BURTON R., PAUL HEIST, T. R. MCCONNELL, MARTIN A. TROW, AND GEORGE YONGE

**1972** Students and Colleges: Interaction and Change. Berkeley, Calif.: Center for Research and Development in Higher Education, University of California, Berkeley.

COALE, ANSLEY J.

**1973** "The demographic transition." Pp. 53–72 in International Union for the Scientific Study of Population, International Population Conference, Liège. Vol. 1.

COCKROFT, JAMES D., ANDRE GUNDER FRANK, AND DALE L. JOHNSON

**1972** Dependence and Underdevelopment. Garden City, N.Y.: Doubleday.

COHEN, JULIUS, REGINALD A. H. ROBSON, AND ALAN BATES

**1958** Parental Authority: The Community and the Law. New Brunswick, N.J.: Rutgers University Press.

COHEN, MALCOLM S.

**1971** "Sex differences in compensation." Journal of Human Resources 6(Fall): 434–47.

**1973** "Economic problems of women." Hearings before the Joint Economic Committee, Congress of the United States. July 10–12, 24–26, and 30.

COHEN, Y.

**1969** "Social boundary systems." Current Anthropology 10(1).

COLE, SONIA

**1965** The Prehistory of East Africa. New York: Mentor.

COLEMAN, JAMES S.

**1972** "The children have outgrown the schools." Psychology Today 5 (February):72–75, 82.

**1974** Youth: Transition to Adulthood. Chicago: University of Chicago Press.

COLLINS, RANDALL

**1971** "Functional and conflict theories of educational stratification." American Sociological Review, 36(6):1002–19.

CONVERSE, PHILIP

**1973** "Prototype state-of-the region report for Los Angeles county." School of Architecture and Urban Planning, University of California, Los Angeles, pp. 272–89.

COONEY, ROSEMARY SANTANA

**1978** "A comparative study of work opportunities for women." Industrial Relations 17(1):64–74.

COSER, ROSE LAUB, AND LEWIS A. COSER

**1973** "The principle of legitimacy and its patterned infringement in social revolutions." Pp. 119–30 in Marvin B. Sussman and Betty E. Cogswell (eds.), Cross-National Family Research. Leiden, the Netherlands: Brill.

COTTRELL, FRED

**1955** Energy and Society. New York: McGraw-Hill.

**1975** "Discussion of Freidson." In Proceedings: Conference on Professional Self-Regulation. Washington, D.C.: Health Services Administration, Public Health Service.

CROZIER, MICHAEL

**1964** The Bureaucratic Phenomenon. Chicago: University of Chicago Press.

CUTRIGHT, PHILLIPS

**1963** "National political development." American Sociological Review 28:253–64.

**1965** "Political structure, economic development, and national social security programs." American Journal of Sociology 70:537–50.

DAHRENDORF, ROLF

**1959** Class and Class Conflict in Industrial Society. Stanford, Calif.: Stanford University Press.

DALTON, MELVILLE

**1959** Men Who Manage: Fusions of Feeling and Theory in Administration. New York: Wiley.

DAVIES, J. C.

**1962** "Toward a theory of revolution." American Sociological Review 27 (February): 5–18.

DAVIS, KINGSLEY

**1937** "The sociology of prostitution." American Sociological Review 2 (October): 744–55.

**1942** "A conceptual analysis of stratification." American Sociological Review 7(3):309–21.

**1949** Human Society. New York: Macmillan.

**1971** World Urbanization, 1950–1970. Vol. I: Basic Data for Cities, Countries, and Regions (revised edition). Vol. II: Analysis of Trends, Relationships, and Development (revised edition). Berkeley, Calif.: University of California, Institute of International Studies, Population Monograph Series, Nos. 4 and 9. Reprinted in 1976 by the Greenwood Press, Westport, Conn., in one volume.

**1976** "Sexual behavior." Pp. 219–61 in Robert K. Merton and Robert Nisbet (eds.), Contemporary Social Problems. New York: Harcourt Brace Jovanovich.

**1977** "The theory of teenage pregnancy in the United States." International Population and Urban Research, Preliminary Paper No. 10 (March 1977). University of California, Berkeley: Institute of International Studies.

DAVIS, KINGSLEY, AND JUDITH BLAKE

**1956** "Social structure and fertility: An analytic framework." Economic Development and Cultural Change 4 (April): 211–35.

DAVIS, KINGSLEY, AND WILBERT E. MOORE

**1945** "Some principles of stratification." American Sociological Review 10:242–49.

DEBRAY, RÉGIS

**1977** "Marxism and the national question." P. 41 in New Left Review 105 (September–October).

DELACROIX, JACQUES, AND CHARLES RAGIN

**1978** "Modernizing institutions, mobilization, and Third World development: A cross-national study." American Journal of Sociology 84(1):123–50.

DELAMOTTE, Y.

**1972** "British productivity agreements, German rationalization agreements, and French employment security agreements." International Institute of Labour Studies Bulletin 9, pp. 30–44.

DEMENY, PAUL

**1968** "Early fertility decline in Austria-Hungary: A lesson in demographic transition." Daedalus 97 (Spring):502–22.

DJILAS, M.

**1957** The New Class. New York: Praeger.

DONOVAN, MARJORIE

**1977** "And let who must achieve: High school education and white collar work in nineteenth century America." Ph.D. dissertation, University of California at Davis.

DOWNS, ANTHONY

**1973** Opening Up the Suburbs: An Urban Strategy for America. New Haven: Yale University Press.

DOXEY, G. V.

**1961** The Industrial Colour Bar in South Africa. London: Oxford University Press.

DUMOND, DON E.

**1975** "The limitation of human population: A natural history." Science 187: 713–21.

DUNCAN, BEVERLY, AND OTIS DUDLEY DUNCAN

**1968** "Minorities and the process of stratification." American Sociological Review 33:356–64.

DUNCAN, OTIS DUDLEY

**1957** "Community size and the rural-urban continuum." In Paul K. Hatt and Albert J. Reiss (eds.), Cities and Societies. New York: Free Press.

**1959** "Residential segregation and social differentiation." Proceedings of the International Population Conference, Vienna.

**1961*a*** "A socioeconomic index for all occupations." In A. J. Reiss, Jr., et al., Occupations and Social Status. New York: Free Press of Glencoe.

**1961*b*** "Properties and characteristics of the socioeconomic index." In A. J. Reiss, Jr., et al., Occupations and Social Status. New York: Free Press of Glencoe.

**1964** "Social organization and the eco-system." In R. E. L. Faris (ed.), Handbook of Modern Sociology. Chicago: Rand-McNally.

**1968** "Social stratification and mobility: Problems in the measurement of trend." In E. B. Sheldon and W. E. Moore (eds.), Indicators of Social Change: Concepts and Measurements. New York: Russell Sage Foundation.

**1969*a*** "Inheritance of poverty or inheritance of race?" Pp. 85–110 in Daniel P. Moynihan (ed.), On Understanding Poverty: Perspectives from the Social Sciences. New York: Basic Books.

**1969*b*** Toward Social Reporting: Next Steps. New York: Russell Sage Foundation.

**1975** "Measuring social change via replication of surveys." In K. C. Land and S. Spilerman (eds.), Social Indicator Models. New York: Russell Sage Foundation.

DUNCAN, OTIS DUDLEY, AND A. J. REISS, JR.

**1956** Social Characteristics of Urban and Rural Communities, 1950. New York: Wiley.

DUNCAN, OTIS DUDLEY, R. P. CUZZORT, AND B. DUNCAN

**1961** Statistical Geography: Problems in Analyzing Areal Data. Glencoe, Ill.: Free Press.

DUNCAN, OTIS DUDLEY, D. L. FEATHERMAN, AND B. DUNCAN

**1972** Socioeconomic Background and Achievement. New York: Seminar.

DURKHEIM, EMILE
[1922] 1956 Education and Sociology. Glencoe, Ill.: Free Press.
1938 The Rules of Sociological Method. Glencoe, Ill.: Free Press.

EASTERLIN, R. A.
1967 "Effects of population growth on the economic growth of developing countries." Annals of the American Academy of Political and Social Science (January).

EDELMAN, MURRAY
1964 The Symbolic Uses of Politics. Urbana: University of Illinois Press.

EDELSTEIN, MELVILLE LEONARD
1972 What Do Young Africans Think? Johannesburg: South African Institute of Race Relations.

EHRLICH, P.
1968 The Population Bomb. New York: Ballantine.

EISENSTADT, S. N.
1963 The Political Systems of Empires. Glencoe, Ill.: Free Press.
1964 "Social change, differentiation and evolution." American Sociological Review 29:375.
1970*a* "Breakdowns in modernization." In S. N. Eisenstadt (ed.), Readings in Social Evolution and Development. London: Pergamon Press.
1970*b* "Introduction social change and development." In S. N. Eisenstadt (ed.) Readings in Social Evolution and Development. London: Pergamon Press.
1971 Social Differentiation and Stratification. Glenview, Ill.: Scott, Foresman.
1976 "Prestige, participation and strata formation." In J. A. Jackson (ed.), Social Stratification. Cambridge: Cambridge University Press.

EISENSTADT, S. N., AND M. CURELARU
1976 The Forms of Sociology: Paradigms and Crises. New York: Wiley.

ELGIN, DUANE S., AND R. A. BUSHNELL
1977 "The limits to complexity." The Futurist 11:337–49.

ELVIN, MARK
1973 The Pattern of the Chinese Past. Stanford, Calif.: Stanford University Press.

EMERY, F. E., AND E. L. TRIST
1972 Towards a Social Ecology. London: Plenum Press.

EMMONS, DAVID

**1978** "Saul Alinsky and Chicago's citizens action program." Working paper, Workshop in Community and Society, Department of Sociology, University of Chicago.

EPSTEIN, CYNTHIA FUCHS

**1970** Woman's Place: Options and Limits in Professional Careers. Berkeley: University of California Press.

**Forthcoming** Woman Lawyers. Unpublished ms.

FARLEY, REYNOLDS

**1970** "The changing distribution of Negroes within metropolitan areas: The emergence of black suburbs." American Journal of Sociology 75 (January).

**1976** "Components of suburban population growth." In Barry Schwartz (ed.), The Changing Face of the Suburbs. Chicago: University of Chicago Press.

FARLEY, REYNOLDS, ET AL.

**1977** "Chocolate city, vanilla suburb: Will the trend toward racially separate communities continue?" A paper of the Population Studies Center, University of Michigan.

FEATHERMAN, D. L., AND R. M. HANSEN

**1978** Opportunity and Change. New York: Academic Press.

FEATHERMAN, D. L., AND R. M. HAUSER

**1976** "Prestige or socioeconomic scales in the study of occupational achievement?" Sociological Methods and Research 4:403–22.

FEDERALIST, PAPERS

**[1787–1788]** Federalist Papers. New York: The Morgan Library, n. d.

FEIT, EDWARD, AND RANDALL G. STOKES

**1976** "Racial prejudice and economic pragmatism: A South African case study." Journal of Modern African Studies 14(3):487–506.

FELDMAN, K. A., AND THEODORE M. NEWCOMB

**1969** The Impact of College on Students. San Francisco: Jossey-Bass.

FIRST, RUTH, JONATHAN STEELE, AND CHRISTABEL GURNEY

**1973** The South African Connection: Western Investment in Apartheid. Harmondswoth: Penguin Books.

FISCHER, CLAUDE

**1976** The Urban experience. New York: Harcourt Brace Jovanovich.

FISCHER, PAUL
**1978** "The Social Security crisis: An international dilemma." Aging and Work: Journal on Age, Work and Retirement (formerly Industrial Gerontology) 1(1):1–14.

FLAUGHER, RONALD L.
**1978** "The many definitions of test bias." American Psychologist 33(7):671–79.

FORSTALL, R. C.
**1975** "Trends in metropolitan and non-metropolitan population growth since 1970." Washington, D.C.: Population Division, Bureau of the Census.

FRANKFORT INSTITUTE FOR SOCIAL RESEARCH
**1973** Aspects of Sociology. London: Heinemann Educational Books.

FREEDMAN, R., ET AL.
**1972** "Trends in family size preferences and practice of family planning: Taiwan, 1965–1970." Studies in Family Planning 3:281–96.

FREEMAN, RICHARD B.
**1973** "Changes in the labor market for black Americans, 1948–72." Brookings Papers on Economic Activity 3:67–120.
**1976** The Over-Educated American. New York: Academic Press.

FRIEDAN, BERNARD J.
**1964** The Future of Old Neighborhoods. Cambridge, Mass.: MIT Press.

FRIEDAN, BETTY
**1963** The Feminine Mystique. New York: Dell.

FRIEDENBERG, EDGAR Z.
**1959** The Vanishing Adolescent. Boston: Beacon.

FRIEDMAN, JULIAN R.
**1974** Basic Facts on the Republic of South Africa and the Policy of Apartheid. New York: United Nations, Unit of Apartheid, Department of Political and Security Council Affairs.

FRISBIE, PARKER, AND CLIFFORD CLARKE
**1979** "Technology in evolutionary and ecological perspective: Theory and measurement at the societal level." Social Forces 59(2)(December).

FRITZ, ROBERT J.
**1977** "Judging the status of the illegitimate child in various Western legal systems." Loyola Law Review 23(1):1–58.

FUCHS, VICTOR
**1971** "Differences in hourly earnings between men and women." Monthly Labor Review (May):9–15.

1974 "Recent trends and long-run prospects for female earnings." American Economic Association 64(May):236–42.

FURTADO, CELSO
1964 Development and Underdevelopment. Berkeley and Los Angeles: University of California Press.

GALBRAITH, JOHN KENNETH
1968 The New Industrial State. New York: New American Library.

GALLE, O. R.
1963 "Occupational composition and the metropolitan hierarchy: The inter-intra-metropolitan division of labor." American Journal of Sociology 69:260–69.

GAMSON, WILLIAM
1975 The Strategy of Social Protest. Homewood, Ill.: Dorsey.

GANS, HERBERT J.
1962 The Urban Villagers: Group and Class in the Life of Italian-Americans. New York: Free Press.

GATES, MARGARET J.
1976 "Occupational segregation and the law." Pp. 61–74 in Martha Blaxall and Barbara Reagan (eds.), Women and the Workplace. Chicago and London: University of Chicago Press.

1977 "Homemakers into widows and divorcees." Pp. 215–32 in Jane Roberts Chapman and Margaret Gates (eds.), Women into Wives. Beverly Hills, Calif.: Sage.

GEERTZ, CLIFFORD
1963 "Primordial sentiments and civil politics in the new states." In Clifford Geertz (ed.), Old Societies and New States. Glencoe, Ill.: Free Press.

GENERAL SOCIAL SURVEY
1972 National Data Program for the Social Sciences. Chicago: National Opinion Research Center, University of Chicago.

GERVASI, SEAN
1970 Industrialization, Foreign Capital, and Forced Labor in South Africa. New York: United Nations Unit on Apartheid, Department of Political and Security Council Affairs.

GEYL, PIETER
1964 The Netherlands in the Seventeenth Century. Part Two: 1648–1715. London: Ernest Benn.

GIBBS, JACK
1975 Crime, Punishment and Deterrence. New York: Elsevier.

GIDDENS, A.

**1972** "Elites in the British class structure." Sociological Review 20(3):345

**1973** The Class Structure of the Advanced Societies. New York: Harper & Row.

GLAZER, NATHAN

**1971** "Blacks and ethnic groups: The difference, and the political difference it makes." Social Problems 18:444–61.

GLAZER, NATHAN, AND DANIEL PATRICK MOYNIHAN

**1963** Beyond the Melting Pot: The Negroes, Puerto Ricans, Jews, Italians, and Irish of New York City. Cambridge, Mass.: MIT Press.

GLENDON, MARY ANN

**1975** "Power and authority in the family: New legal patterns as reflections of changing ideologies." American Journal of Comparative Law 23 (Winter): 1–33.

GLICK, PAUL C., AND ARTHUR J. NORTON

**1977** "Marrying, divorcing, and living together in the U.S. today." Population Bulletin 32 (October):1–39.

GOLD, NEIL N.

**1972** "The mismatch of jobs and low-income people in metropolitan areas and its implications for the central-city poor." In Sara Mill Mazie (ed.), U.S. Commission on Population Growth and the American Future, Vol. 5. Washington, D.C.: Government Printing Office.

GOLDENWEISER, A.

**1942** Anthropology: An Introduction to Primitive Culture. New York: F. S. Crofts.

GOODE, WILLIAM J.

**1960** "A deviant case: Illegitimacy in the Caribbean." American Sociological Review 25 (February):21–30.

**1963** World Revolution and Family Patterns. New York: Free Press.

**1967** "Protection of the inept." American Sociological Review 32(1):5–19.

GOODY, JACK

**1972** "The evolution of the family." Pp. 103–24 in Peter Laslett and Richard Wall (eds.), Household and Family in Past Time. Cambridge: Cambridge University Press.

GORDON, MARGARET S., AND MARGARET THAL-LARSEN

**1969** Employer Policies in a Changing Labor Market: Report of the San Francisco Bay Area Employer Policy Survey.

Berkeley: Institute of Industrial Relations, University of California

GOUBERT, PIERRE
**1977** "Family and province: A contribution to the knowledge of family structures in early modern France." Journal of Family History 2 (Fall):179–95.

GOUGH, KATHERINE
**1955** "The social structure of a Tanjore village." Pp. 36–52 in McKim Marriott (ed.), Village India. Chicago: University of Chicago Press.

GOULDNER, ALVIN
**1976** The Dialectic of Ideology and Technology. New York: Seabury Press.

GRANA, CESAR
**1964** Modernity and Its Discontents. New York: Basic Books.

GRANT, GERALD, AND DAVID RIESMAN
**1978** The Perpetual Dream: Reform and Experiment in the American College. Chicago: University of Chicago Press.

GRAS, N. S. B.
**1922** An Introduction to Economic History. New York: Harper Brothers.

GRAUMAN, JOHN
**1968** "Population growth." International Encyclopedia of the Social Sciences 12:376–81. New York: Macmillan and The Free Press.

GREELEY, ANDREW M.
**1974** Ethnicity in the United States: A Preliminary Reconnaisance. New York: Wiley.

GREEN, BERT F., JR.
**1978** "In defense of measurement." American Psychologist 33(7):664–70.

GREER, SCOTT
**1962** The Emerging City: Myth and Reality. New York: Free Press.

**1975** "Professional self-regulation in the public interest: The intellectual politics of PSRO." In Proceedings: Conference on Professional Self-Regulation. Washington, D.C.: Health Resources Administration, Public Health Service.

GRIER, GEORGE
**1975** Reported in "Black rise by 100,000 in suburbs." Washington Post, May 18, 1975.

GRIFFITHS, MARTHA W.

**1976** "Can we still afford occupational segregation? Some remarks." Pp. 7–14 in Martha Blaxall and Barbara Reagan (eds.), Women and the Workplace. Chicago and London: University of Chicago Press.

GROSS, EDWARD

**1968** "Plus ça change . . . ? The sexual structure of occupations over time." Social Problems 16(2):198–208.

GROSSMAN, NAAVA BINDER

**1974** A Study of the Relative Participation of Persons and Corporate Actors in Court Cases. Chicago: National Opinion Research Center. Mimeo.

GROTIUS, HUGO

**1916** The Freedom of the Seas. New York: Oxford University Press. (1st ed. 1608.)

GURR, T. R.

**1970** Why Men Rebel. Princeton: Princeton University Press.

GUSFIELD, JOSEPH

**1962** "Mass society and extremist politics." American Sociological Review 27 (February):19–30.

**1967** "Tradition and modernity: Misplaced polarities in the study of social change." American Journal of Sociology 72 (January):351–62.

**1973** Utopian Myths and Movements in Modern Societies. (Module) Morristown, N.J.: General Learning Press.

**1975*a*** "The (f)utility of knowledge? The relation of social science to public policy toward drugs." Annals of the American Academy of Political and Social Sciences (January):1–15.

**1975*b*** Community: A Critical Response. New York: Harper & Row.

**1976** "Becoming modern: Review essay of Inkeles and Smith, Becoming Modern." American Journal of Sociology 82 (September):443–48.

**1978** "Historical problematics and sociological fields: American liberalism and the study of social movements." In Robert A. Jones (ed.), Research in Sociology of Knowledge, Sciences and Art, Vol. 1. Greenwich, Conn.: JAI Press.

GUTKIND, FREDERICK

**1953** The Expanding Environment: The End of Cities and the Rise of Communities. London: Freedom Press.

HAGGARD, ERNEST A.

**1954** "Social-status and intelligence: An experimental study of certain cultural determinants of measured intelligence." Genetic Psychology Monographs 49:141–86.

HAGGERTY, LEE J.

**1971** "Another look at the Burgess hypothesis: Time as an important variable." American Journal of Sociology 76 (May): 1084–93.

HAJNAL, JOHN

**1965** "European marriage patterns in perspective." Pp. 101–43 in D. V. Glass and D. E. C. Eversley (eds.), Population in History. Chicago: Aldine.

HALL, R.

**1972** Organizations: Structure and Process. Englewood Cliffs, N.J.: Prentice-Hall.

HALL, ROBERT E., AND RICHARD A. KASTEN

**1973** "The relative occupational success of blacks and whites." Brookings Papers on Economic Activity 3:781–98.

HALSEY, A. H., AND MARTIN A. TROW

**1971** The British Academics. Cambridge: Mass.: Harvard University Press.

HANDLER, JOEL

**Forthcoming** Social Movements and Legal System. Madison, Wis.: Insti-

HARRIS, MARVIN

**1968** The Rise of Anthropoligical Theory. New York: Crowell.

HARRISON, BENNET

**1974** Urban Economic Development. Washington, D.C.: Urban Institute.

HARTMAN, M.

**1975** "The gradings of occupations by sociologists." Paper presented at the annual meetings of the Israeli Sociological Association (in Hebrew).

*Harvard Law Review* (editorial—Case Comments)

**1977** "Property rights upon termination of unmarried cohabitation: Marvin vs. Marvin." Harvard Law Review 90: 1708–20.

HAUSER, PHILIP M.

**1960** Population Perspectives. New Brunswick, N.J.: Rutgers University Press.

**1963** "Statistics and society." Journal of the American Statistical Association 58(1):1–12.

**1969** "The chaotic society: Product of the social morphological revolution." American Sociological Review 34(1):1–19.

**1977** "Chicago-urban crisis exemplar." In J. John Palen (ed.), City Scenes. Boston: Little, Brown.

HAUSER ALBERT M., ET AL.

**1975*a*** "Temporal change in occupational mobility: Evidence for men in the United States." Amerian Sociological Review 40(3):279–97.

**1975*b*** "Structural changes in occupational mobility among men in the United States." American Sociological Review 40(5): 585–98.

HAUSER, R. M., AND D. L. FEATHERMAN

**1977** The Process of Stratification. New York: Academic Press.

HAWLEY, AMOS H.

**1950** Human Ecology. A Theory of Community Structure. New York: Ronald Press.

**1971** Urban Society: An Ecological Approach. New York: Ronald Press.

HAWLEY, AMOS H., AND VINCENT P. ROCK (eds.)

**1975** Metropolitan America in Contemporary Perspective. Beverly Hills, Calif.: Sage.

HEBERLE, R.

**1948** "Social consequences of the industrialization of Southern cities." Social Forces 27:29–37.

HECHTER, MICHAEL

**1975** Internal Colonialsim. Berkeley: University of California Press.

HEDGES, J. N.

**1970** "Women workers and manpower demands of the 1970's." Monthly Labor Review 93(6):19–29.

HEERS, JACQUES

**1968** "Les limites des méthodes statistiques pour les recherches de démographie médiévale." Annales de Démographie Historique 23:43–72.

**1974** Le Clan familial au moyen age: Etude sur les structures politiques et sociales des milieux urbains. Paris: Presses Universitaires de France.

HEILBRONER, ROBERT L.

**1974** An Inquiry into the Human Prospect. New York: Norton.

HERMAN, EDWARD, AND RICHARD DUBOFF

**1977** "The urban fiscal crisis: A short term manifestation of institutional decline." In J. John Palen (ed.), City Scenes. Boston: Little, Brown.

HERNES, GUDMUND

**1976** "Structural changes in social processes." American Journal of Sociology 82:513–47.

HINTZE, OTTO

**1968** "The state in historical perspective." In Reinhard Bendix et al., State and Society. Boston: Little, Brown.

HIRSCH, F.

**1976** Social Limits to Growth. Cambridge, Mass.: Harvard University Press.

HOBSBAWM, ERIC

**1959** Primitive Rebels. Manchester: Manchester University Press.

**1977** "Some reflections on 'the break-up of Britain.' " P. 17 in New Left Review 105 (September–October).

HODGE, R. W.

**1962** "The status consistency of occupational groups." American Sociological Review 27:336–43.

HODGE, R. W., AND R. KLORMAN

**1975** "An econometric model of American society." Paper presented at the annual meeting of the American Sociological Association, San Francisco.

HODGE, R. W., P. M. SIEGEL, AND P. H. ROSSI

**1964** "Occupational prestige in the United States, 1925–1963." American Journal of Sociology 70:286–302.

HOEBEL, E. ADAMSON

**1949** Man in the Primitive World. New York: McGraw-Hill.

HOFFMAN, ABBIE

**1968** Revolution for the Hell of It. New York: Dial Press.

HOMANS, GEORGE C.

**1941** English Villagers of the Thirteenth Century. Cambridge, Mass.: Harvard University Press.

**1964** "Bringing man back in." American Sociological Review 29:809–18.

HORNER, J. A.

**1972** Black Pay and Productivity in South Africa. Johannesburg: South African Institute of Race Relations.

HOROWITZ, IRVING LOUIS

**1972** Three Worlds of Development: The Theory and Practice of International Development. New York and London: Oxford University Press. (1st ed. 1966.)

HORRELL, MURIEL

**1973** The African Homelands of South Africa. Johannesburg: South African Institute of Race Relations.

**1976** A Survey of Race Relations in South Africa 1975. Johannesburg: South African Institute of Race Relations.

**1977** A Survey of Race Relations in South Africa 1976. Johannesburg: South African Institute of Race Relations.

HORWITZ, RALPH

**1967** The Political Economy of South Africa. London: Weidenfeld and Nicolson.

HOSELITZ, BERT F.

**1960** Sociological Aspects of Economic Growth. New York: Macmillan and The Free Press.

HOUGHTON, D. HOBART

**1967** The South African Economy, 2nd ed. Cape Town: Oxford University Press.

**1971** "Economic development 1865–1965." Pp. 1–48 in Monica Wilson and Leonard Thompson (eds.), The Oxford History of South Africa, Vol. 2. London: Oxford University Press.

HOVARD, RICHARD

**1977** "The interactionist paradigm: The collective behavior and pluralist conception of politics and society." Paper presented at the annual meeting of the American Sociological Association, Chicago.

HUDSON, JAMES R

**1978** "Changing land-use patterns in SoHo: Residential invasion of industrial areas." Unpublished paper.

HUGHES, EVERETT

**1943** French Canada in Transition. Chicago: University of Chicago Press.

**1946** "The Knitting of Racial Groups in Industry." American Sociological Review 11: 512–19.

**1961** "Ethnocentric sociology." Social Forces 40:1–4.

HUMPHREY, CRAIG, AND RALPH SELL

**1975** "The impact of controlled access highways on population growth in Pennsylvania and non-metropolitan communities, 1940–1970." Rural Sociology 40 (Fall):332–43.

HUMPHREY, MELVIN

**1977** Black Experiences versus Black Expectations: A Case for Fair Share Employment. Equal Employment Opportunity Commission. Research Report no. 53.

HUNTER, ALBERT

**1974** Symbolic Communities: The Persistence and Change of Chicago's Local Communites. Chicago: University of Chicago Press.

**1975** "The loss of community: An empirical test through replication." American Sociological Review 40:537–52.

HUNTINGTON, SAMUEL P.
**1968** Political Order in Changing Societies. New Haven: Yale University Press.

HURD, R.
**1903** Principles of City Land Values. New York: Record and Guide.

HUTCHINSON E. P.
**1956** Immigrants and their Children, 1850–1950. A Volume in the Census Monograph Series. New York: Wiley.

HUTT, W. H.
**1964** The Economics of the Colour Bar. London: André Deutsch.

HYMAN, HERBERT, CHARLES R. WRIGHT, AND JOHN SHELTON REED
**1975** The Enduring Effects of Education. Chicago: University of Chicago Press.

INKELES, ALEX, AND DAVID H. SMITH
**1974** Becoming Modern: Individual Change in Six Developing Countries. Cambridge, Mass.: Harvard University Press.

INTERNATIONAL LABOUR OFFICE
**1974*a*** Tenth Special Report of the Director General on the Application of the Declaration Concerning Apartheid in the Republic of South Africa. Geneva: International Labour Office.

**1974*b*** Termination of Employment: General Study by the Committee of Experts on the Application of Conventions and Recommendations. International Labour Conference, 59th Session, Report III (Part 4B). Geneva: International Labour Office.

**1976** Twelfth Special Report of the Director General on the Application of the Declaration Concerning Apartheid in the Republic of South Africa. Geneva: International Labour Office.

JACKSON, E. F., AND R. F. CURTIS
**1972** "Effects of vertical mobility and status inconsistency: A body of negative evidence." American Sociological Review 37:701–13.

JACOB, FRANCOIS
**1977** "Evolution and tinkering." Science 196:1161–66.

JACOBS, JANE
**1961** The Death and Life of Great American Cities. New York: Random House.

JAIN, S.

**1975** Size Distribution of Income: A Compilation of Data. Baltimore: Johns Hopkins University Press.

JANOWITZ, MORRIS

**1967** The Community Press in an Urban Setting, 2nd ed. Chicago: University of Chicago Press.

JENCKS, CHRISTOPHER, AND DAVID RIESMAN

**1968** The Academic Revolution. Garden City, N.Y.: Doubleday.

JOHNSTONE, FREDERICK A.

**1970** "White prosperity and white supremacy in South Africa today." African Affairs 69:124–40.

**1976** Class, Race, and Gold. London: Routledge, Kegan, and Paul.

JUSENIUS, C. L., AND L. C. LEDEBUR

**1976** A Myth in the Making: The Southern Economic Challenge and Northern Economic Decline. Washington, D.C.: Economic Development Administration, Department of Commerce (November).

KANOWITZ, LEO

**1969** Women and the Law: The Unfinished Revolution. Albuquerque: University of New Mexico Press.

KANTER, ROSABETH MOSS

**1972** Commitment and Community: Communes and Utopias in Sociological Perspective. Cambridge, Mass.: Harvard University Press.

KASARDA, JOHN

**1976** "The changing occupational structure of the American metropolis: Apropos the urban problem." In Barry Schwartz (ed.), The Changing Face of the Suburbs. Chicago: University of Chicago Press.

**1978** "Industry, community, and the metropolitan problem." In David Street (ed.), Handbook of Urban Life. New York: Jossey-Bass.

KASARDA, JOHN, AND MORRIS JANOWITZ

**1974** "Community attachment in mass society." American Sociological Review 39:328–38.

KASARDA, JOHN, AND G. REDFEARN

**1975** "Differential patterns of urban and suburban growth in the United States." Journal of Urban History 2.

KATZ, SANFORD H., WILLIAM A. SCHROEDER, AND LAWRENCE R. SIDMAN

**1973** "Emancipating our children—coming of legal age in America." Family Law Quarterly 7:211–41.

KAY, HERMA H.
**1969** "The outside substitute for the family." Pp. 261–69 in John N. Edwards (ed.), The Family and Change. New York: Knopf.

KAY, HERMA, AND CAROL AMYX
**1977** "Marvin vs. Marvin: Preserving the options." California Law Review 65:937–77.

KELLER, SUZANNE
**1968** The Urban Neighborhood. New York: Random House.

KELLEY A. C.
**1972** "Demographic changes and American economic development: Past, present and future." Economic Aspects of Population Change U.S. Commission on Population Growth and the American Future, Research Papers, Vol. 2. Washington, D.C.: Government Printing Office.

KESSEL, DUDLEY
**1972** "Non-white wage increases and inflation in South Africa." South African Journal of Economics 40(4):361–76.

KINSLEY, SUSAN
**1977** "Women's dependency and federal programs." Pp. 79–91 in Jane Roberts Chapman and Margaret Gates (eds.), Women into wives. Beverly Hills, Calif.: Sage.

KITAGAWA, E. M., AND P. M. HAUSER
**1973** Differential Mortality in the United States: A Study in Socioeconomic Epidemiology. Cambridge, Mass.: Harvard University Press.

KLATSKY, SHEILA R.
**1972** Patterns of Contact with Relatives. Washington, D.C.: Rose Monographs, American Sociological Association.

KORNBLUM WILLIAM
**1974** Blue Collar Community. Chicago: University of Chicago Press.

KORNHAUSER, WILLIAM
**1959** The Politics of Mass Society. Glencoe, Ill.: Free Press.

KRAUS, V.
**1976** "Social gradings of occupations." Unpublished Ph.D. dissertation (in Hebrew with English summary), Hebrew University, Jerusalem.

KRAUS, V., E. O. SCHILD, AND R. W. HODGE
**1978** "Occupational prestige in the collective conscience." Social Forces 56:900–918.

KRAUSKOPF, JOAN M.
**1977** "Partnership marriage: Legal reforms needed." Pp. 93–121

in Jane Roberts Chapman and Margaret Gates (eds.), Women into Wives. Beverly Hills, Calif.: Sage.

KREPS, JUANITA

**1965** "The economics of intergenerational relationships." Pp. 267–88 in Ethel Shanas and Gordon F. Streib (eds.), Social Structure and the Family: Generational Relations. Englewood Cliffs, N.J.: Prentice-Hall.

**1971** Sex in the Marketplace. Baltimore and London: Johns Hopkins Press.

LADINSKY, JACK

**1967** "Higher education and work achievement among lawyers." Sociological Quarterly 8:222–32.

LAND, K. C.

**1975** "Social indicator models: An overview." In K. C. Land and S. Spilerman (eds.), Social Indicator Models. New York: Russell Sage Foundation.

LANDERS, DAVID

**1966** "Technological change and development in western Europe, 1750–1914." P. 464 in M. M. Postan and H. J. Babakkuk (eds.), The Cambridge Economic History of Europe. Cambridge: Cambridge University Press.

LANE, E.

**1971** The End of Inequality? Stratification Under State Socialism. London: Penguin Books.

LANG, KURT, AND GLADYS LANG

**1968** Politics and Television. Chicago: Quadrangle Books.

LASCH, CHRISTOPHER

**1965** The New Radicalism in America. New York: Vintage.

**1975*a*** "The emotions of family life." New York Review of Books 22 (November):37–42.

**1975*b*** "What the doctor ordered." New York Review of Books 22 (December):50–54.

LASLETT, PETER

**1970** The World We Have Lost, 2nd ed. London: Methuen.

**1972** "Introduction: The history of the family." Pp. 1–89 in Peter Laslett and Richard Wall (eds.), Household and Family in Past Time. Cambridge: Cambridge University Press.

**1977** "Characteristics of the Western family considered over time." Pp. 12–49 in Peter Laslett (ed.), Family Life and Illicit Love in Earlier Generations. Cambridge: Cambridge University Press.

LAUMANN, E. O.

**1973** Bonds of Pluralism. New York: Wiley-Interscience.

LAUMANN, E. O., AND F. U. PAPPI
**1976** Networks of Collective Action. A Perspective on Community Influence Systems. New York: Academic Press.

LAWRENCE, ANNE T.
**1977** "Industrialization and ascription in modern society: The South African case." Unpublished ms., University of California, Berkeley.

LAWRENCE, PAUL R., AND J. W. LORSCH
**1967** Organization and Environment. Boston: Harvard Business School.

LAZARSFELD, PAUL F., AND WAGNER THIELENS, JR.
**1958** The Academic Mind: Social Scientists in a Time of Crisis. Glencoe, Ill.: Free Press.

LEE, R. D. (ed.)
**1977** Population Patterns in the Past. New York: Academic Press.

LEGASSICK, MARTIN
**1974** "Capital accumulation and violence in South Africa." Economy and Society 3(3):253–91.

LEIBENSTEIN, H.
**1967** Economic Backwardness and Economic Growth. New York: Wiley.

LENSKI, GERHARD E.
**1966** Power and Privilege: A Theory of Social Stratification. New York: McGraw-Hill

**1970** Human Societies. New York: McGraw-Hill.

LENSKI, GERHARD E., AND JEAN LENSKI
**1978** Human Societies: A Macrolevel Introduction to Sociology, 3rd ed. New York: McGraw-Hill.

LERNER, DANIEL
**1958** The Passing of Traditional Society. Glencoe, Ill.: Free Press.

**1964** The Passing of Traditional Society. New York: Macmillan and The Free Press.

LESLIE, G. R.
**1973** The Family in Social Context, 2nd ed. New York: Oxford University Press.

LESSER, ALEXANDER
**1961** "Social fields and the evolution of society." Southwestern Journal of Anthropology 17:40–48.

LESTER, RICHARD A.
**1966** Manpower Planning in a Free Society. Princeton: Princeton University Press.

LEVY, MARION J.

**1949** The Family Revolution in Modern China. Cambridge, Mass.: Harvard University Press.

**1952** "Some sources of the vulnerability of the structures of relatively nonindustrialized societies to those of highly industrialized societies." Pp. 113–25 in Bert F. Hoselitz (ed.), The Progress of Underdeveloped Areas. Chicago: University of Chicago Press.

LEVY, MARION J., JR.

**1952** The Structure of Society. Princeton: Princeton University Press.

LIEBOW, ELLIOT

**1967** Tally's Corner: A Study of Negro Streetcorner Men. Boston: Little, Brown.

LIGHT, IVAN H.

**1972** Ethnic Enterprise in America: Business and Welfare Among Chinese, Japanese, and Blacks. Berkeley: University of California Press.

LINTON, RALPH

**1936** The Study of Man. New York: Appleton-Century.

LIPSET, SEYMOUR MARTIN

**1960** Political Man. Garden City, N.Y.: Doubleday.

**1968** Revolution and Counterrevolution: Change and Persistence in Social Structures. New York: Basic Books.

**1972** "Social mobility and equal opportunity." The Public Interest 29 (Fall): 90–108.

LITVAK, LAWRENCE, ROBERT DEGRASSE, AND KATHLEEN MCTIGUE

**1977** United States Investment in South Africa. A publication of the South Africa Catalyst Project. Palo Alto, Calif.: UP Press.

LITWAK, EUGENE

**1965** "Extended kin relations in industrial democratic society." Pp. 290–323 in Ethel Shanas and Gordon F. Streib (eds.), Social Structure and the Family: Generational Relations. Englewood Cliffs, N.J.: Prentice-Hall.

LIVI–BACCI, MASSIMO

**1968** "Fertility and population growth in Spain in the eighteenth and nineteenth centuries." Daedalus 97 (Spring):523–35.

LONG, CLARENCE D.

**1958** The Labor Force under Changing Income and Employment. Princeton: Princeton University Press.

LONG, NORTON

**1962** The Polity. Glenview, Ill.: Rand-McNally.

LOPREATO, JOSEPH, AND LIONEL S. LEWIS

**1963** "An analysis of variables in the functional theory of stratification." Sociological Quarterly 4:301–10.

LÖSCH, A.

**1954** The Economics of Location. Translated by William H. Woglom, with assistance of Wolfgang F. Stolger. New Haven: Yale University Press.

LOTKA, ALFRED J.

**1924** Elements of Mathematical Biology. Baltimore: Wilkins and Wilkins.

LOWI, THEODORE J.

**1969** The End of Liberalism. New York: Norton

MCCARTHY, JOHN, AND MAYER ZALD

**1973** The Trend in Social Movements in America: Professionalization and Resource Mobilization. (Module) Morristown, N.J.: General Learning Press.

MCCARTHY, KEVIN F., AND PETER A. MORRISON

**1978** "The changing demographic and economic structure of nonmetropolitan areas in the 1970's." Santa Monica, Calif.: Rand Corporation.

MCKAY, HENRY

**1967** "Juvenile delinquency and youth crime." Department of Justice, The Presidential Task Force Report. Washington, D.C.: Government Printing Office.

MCKENZIE, RODERICK D.

**1933** The Metropolitan Community. New York: McGraw-Hill.

**1934** "Industrial expansion and the interrelations of peoples." Chap. 2 in E. B. Reuter (ed.), Race and Culture Contacts. New York: McGraw-Hill.

MALINOWSKI, BRONISLAW

**1930** "Parenthood, the basis of social structure." Pp. 113–68 in V. F. Calverton and S. D. Schmalhausen (eds.), The New Generation. New York: Macauley.

MANNERS, GERALD

**1974** "The office in a metropolis: An opportunity for shaping metropolitan America." Economic Geography 50:93–110.

MANNHEIM, KARL

**1940** Man and Society in an Age of Reconstruction. London: Routledge and Kegan Paul.

MARCH, JAMES G., AND HERBERT A. SIMON

**1959** Organizations. New York: Wiley.

MARQUARD, LEO

**1969** The Peoples and Politics of South Africa. London: Oxford University Press.

MARSHALL, T. H.

**1965** Class, Citizenship and Social Development. Garden City, N.Y.: Anchor/Doubleday.

MATRAS, JUDAH

**1975** Social Inequality, Stratification and Mobility. Englewood Cliffs, N.J.: Prentice-Hall.

**1977** Introduction to Population. A Sociological Approach. Englewood Cliffs, N.J.: Prentice-Hall.

MAULDIN, W. P. AND B. BERELSON

**1978** "Conditions of fertility decline in developing countries, 1965–75." Studies in Family Planning 9(5):89–147.

MAYER, KURT

**1972** "Postwar immigration and Switzerland's demographic and social structure." Pp. 241–55 in William Petersen (ed.), Readings in Population. New York: Macmillan.

MAYER PHILIP

**1975** "Class, status, and ethnicity as perceived by Johannesburg Africans." Pp. 138–67. in Leonard Thompson and Jeffrey Butler (eds.), Change in Contemporary South Africa. Berkeley: University of California Press.

MAYHEW, LEON

**1968** "Ascription in modern societies." Sociological Inquiry 38(2):105–20.

MEADOWS, D. H.

**1972** The Limits to Growth. A Report on the Club of Rome's Project on the Predicament of Mankind. New York: Universe.

MEYER, G.

**1978** "Sex and marriage of raters in the evaluation of occupations." Social Science Research (December): 366–80.

MILKMAN, RUTH

**1977** "Apartheid, economic growth, and U.S. foreign policy in South Africa." Berkeley Journal of Sociology 22:45–100.

MILLER, SEYMOUR M.

**1967** "The credential society." Transaction 5(2):2.

MILLS, C. WRIGHT

**1956** The Power Elite. New York: Oxford University Press.

MISHAN, E. J.

**1977** The Economic Growth Debate: An Assessment. London: George Allen and Unwin.

MOLOTCH, HARVEY

**1973** Managed Integration: Dilemmas of Doing Good in the City. Berkeley: University of California Press.

MOORE, BARRINGTON

**1958** Political Power and Social Theory. Cambridge, Mass.: Harvard University Press.

MOORE, WILBERT E.

**1951** Industrialization and Labor: Social Aspects of Economic Development. New York: Cornell University Press.

**1960** "A reconsideration of theories of social change." American Sociological Review 25(6):810–18.

**1962** The Conduct of the Corporation. New York: Random House.

**1963** Social Change. Englewood Cliffs, N.J.: Prentice-Hall.

**1968** "Social change." Pp. 365–75 in International Encyclopedia of Social Science, Vol. 14. New York: Macmillan and The Free Press.

MOSKOS, CHARLES C., JR.

**1966** "Racial integration in the armed forces." American Journal of Sociology 72(2):132–48.

MUELLER, HANS-EBERHARD

**1974** "Bureaucracy and education: Civil service reforms in Prussia and England as strategies of monopolization." Ph.D. dissertation, University of California, Berkeley.

MURDOCK, GEORGE P.

**1957** "World ethnographic sample." American Anthropologist 59:664–87.

MYERS, DESAIX B., III

**1976** "Labor practices of U.S. corporations in South Africa." Special Report 1976-A. Washington, D.C.: Investor Responsibility Research Center.

MYRDAL, ALVA, AND VIOLA KLEIN

**1956** Women's Two Roles. London: Routledge and Kegan Paul.

NAIRN, TOM

**1975** "Marxism and the modern Janus." P. 17 in New Left Review 95 (November–December).

NATIONAL OPINION RESEARCH CENTER (NORC)

**1947** "Jobs and occupations: A population evaluation." Opinion News 9:3–13.

**1972** "National data program for the social sciences." General Social Survey, NORC. University of Chicago.

NATIONAL RESOURCES COMMITTEE

**1937** Our Cities: Their Role in the National Economy. Washington, D.C.: Government Printing Office.

NATIONAL URBAN COALITION

**1978** Displacement: City Neighborhoods in Transition. Washington, D.C.: Urban Coalition.

NATTRASS, JILL

**1976** "Migrant labour and South African economic development." South African Journal of Economics 44(1):65–83.

NELSON, DANIEL

**1975** Managers and Workers. Madison: University of Wisconsin Press.

NEWCOMB, T. M., K. E. KOENIG, R. FLACKS, AND D. P. NARWICK

**1967** Persistence and Change: Bennington College and Its Students after Twenty-Five Years. New York: Wiley.

NIMKOFF, M. F., AND RUSSELL MIDDLETON

**1960** "Types of family and types of economy." American Journal of Sociology 66 (November):215–25.

NISBET, ROBERT A.

**1969** Social Change and History. London: Oxford University Press.

NORR, JAMES L., AND K. L. NORR

**1977** "Societal complexity or production techniques." American Journal of Sociology 82:845–53.

O'CONNELL, MARTIN

**1978** "A cohort analysis of teenage fertility in the U.S. since the Depression." Paper read at the 1978 annual meeting of the Population Association of America, Atlanta.

O'CONNOR, JAMES

**1973** The Fiscal Crisis of the State. New York: St. Martin's Press.

OGBURN, WILLIAM F.

**1922** Social Change. New York: Huebsch.

**1950** Social Change with Respect to Culture and Original Nature. New York: Viking.

OLSEN, MARVIN

**1968** "Multivariate analysis of national political development." American Sociological Review 33:699–712.

OPPENHEIMER, VALERIE KINCADE

**1970** The Female Labor Force in the United States: Demographic and Economic Factors Governing Its Growth and Changing Composition. Berkeley: Institute of International Studies, University of California.

1974 "The sociology of women's economic role in the family: Parsons revisited and revised." Paper read at the annual meeting of the American Sociological Association.

OWEN, WILFRED

1964 Strategy for Mobility. Washington, D.C.: Brookings Institution.

PAMPEL, F. C., K. C. LAND, AND M. FELSON

1977 "A social indicator model of changes in the occupational structure of the United States: 1947–1974." American Sociological Review (December):951–64.

PARKIN, F.

1971 Class Inequality and Political Order. London: MacGibbon & Kee.

PARSONS, TALCOTT

1942 "Age and sex in the social structure." American Sociological Review 7 (October):604–16.

1943 "The kinship system of the contemporary United States." American Anthropologist 45 (January–March):22–28.

1949 Essays in Sociological Theory Pure and Applied. Glencoe, Ill.: Free Press.

1951 The Social System. New York: Free Press.

1955 "The American family: Its relations to personality and the social structure." Pp. 3–21 in Talcott Parsons and Robert F. Bales (eds.), Family Specialization and Interaction Process. New York: Free Press.

1965 "The normal American family." Pp. 31–50 in S. M. Farber, P. Mustacchi, and R. H. L. Wilson (eds.), Man and Civilization: The Family's Search for Survival. New York: McGraw-Hill.

1966 Societies, Evolutionary and Comparative Perspectives. Englewood Cliffs, N.J.: Prentice-Hall.

1971 "Kinship and the associational aspect of social structure." Pp. 409–38 in F. L. K. Hsu (ed.), Kinship and Culture. Chicago: Aldine.

PARSONS, TALCOTT, AND N. J. SMELSER

1956 Economy and Society: A Study in the Integration of Economics and Social Theory. Glencoe, Ill.: Free Press.

PARSONS, TALCOTT, ROBERT BALES, AND EDWARD SHILS

1953 Working Papers in the Theory of Action. New York: Free Press.

PEASLEE, ALEXANDER L.

1969 "Education's role in development." Economic Development and Cultural Change 17 (April): 293–317.

PERROW, CHARLES
**1972** Complex Organizations: A Critical Essay. Glenview, Ill.: Scott, Foresman.

PETERSEN, W.
**1970** The Politics of Population. Gloucester, Mass.: Peter Smith.

PFEIFFER, JOHN E.
**1972** The Emergence of Man. New York: Harper & Row.

PLATERIS, ALEXANDER A.
**1978** Divorces and Divorce Rates, United States. Vital and Health Statistics Series No. 21, U.S. Department of Health, Education, and Welfare Publication No. (PHS) 78-1907 (March 1978). Washington, D.C.: Government Printing Office.

PLATH, DAVID
**1964** The After Hours: Modern Japan and the Search for Enjoyment. Berkeley and Los Angeles: University of California Press.

PLUMB, J. H.
**1972** "The great change in children." Intellectual Digest 2 (April):82–84.

POLANYI, MICHAEL
**1959** The Study of Man. London: Routledge and Kegan Paul.

PORTER, PAUL R.
**1976** The Recovery of American Cities. New York: Two Continents Publishing Group.

PORTES, ALEJANDRO
**1973** "Modernity and development: A critique." Studies in Comparative International Development 8(3):247–79.

PRED, ALLEN
**1977** City-Systems in Advanced Economies. New York: Wiley (Halsted Press).

PRESSMAN, JEFFREY, AND AARON WILDALSKY
**1973** Implementation. Berkeley and Los Angeles: University of California Press.

PRESTON, S. H., AND A. T. RICHARDS
**1975** "The influence of women's work opportunities on marriage rates." Demography 12:209–22.

PRICE, DANIEL O.
**1969** Changing Characteristics of the Negro Population. A 1960 Census Monograph. Washington, D.C.: Government Printing Office.

QUIGLEY, CARROLL
**1961** The Evolution of Civilizations. New York: Macmillan.

RAO, M. S. A.

**1970** Urbanization and Social Change: A Study of a Rural Community on a Metropolitan Fringe. New Delhi: Orient Longman's.

RAWLS, JOHN

**1971** A Theory of Justice. Cambridge, Mass.: Harvard University Press.

REISS, A. J., JR., ET AL.

**1961** Occupations and Social Status. New York: Free Press of Glencoe.

REPUBLIC OF SOUTH AFRICA

**1976*a*** Population Census 1970, Vol. 16, "Occupations." Pretoria: Government Printer.

**1976*b*** South Africa 1975: Official Yearbook of the Republic of South Africa. Johannesburg: Perskor Printers.

**1978** Bulletin of Statistics. Department of Statistics, Vol. 12, no. 1. Pretoria: Government Printer.

REUBENS, BEATRICE G.

**1970** The Hard-to-Employ: European Programs. New York: Columbia University Press.

RIESMAN, DAVID, JOSEPH GUSFIELD, AND ZELDA GAMSON

**1971** Academic Values and Mass Education: The Early Years of Oakland and Monteith. Garden City, N.Y.: Anchor/Doubleday.

RILEY, MATILDA, AND ANNE FONER

**1968** Aging and Society. Vol. 1: An Inventory of Research Findings. New York: Russell Sage Foundation.

RIVLIN, ALICE M.

**1972** "Child care." Pp. 252–90 in Charles L. Schultze, Edward R. Fried, Alice M. Rivlin, and Nancy H. Teeters (eds.), Setting National Priorities: The 1973 Budget. Washington, D.C.: Brookings Institution.

ROGERS, BARBARA

**1976*a*** Divide and Rule: South Africa's Bantustans. London: International Defence and Aid Fund.

**1976*b*** White Wealth and Black Poverty: American Investments in Southern Africa. Westport, Conn.: Greenwood Press.

ROGOFF, NATALIE

**1953** Recent Trends in Social Mobility. Glencoe, Ill.: Free Press.

ROSE, ARNOLD

**1967** The Power Structure. New York: Oxford University Press.

ROSE, RICHARD
**1971** Governing without Consensus: An Irish Perspective. Boston: Beacon Press.

ROSENBERG, G. S., AND D. I. ANSPACH
**1973** Working Class Kinship. Lexington, Mass.: Heath.

ROSSI, ALICE S.
**1964** "Equality between the sexes: An immodest proposal." Daedalus 93 (Spring):98–143.
**1977** "A biosocial perspective on parenting." Daedalus 106(2): 1–31.

ROSSI, PETER
**1978** "Some issues in the evaluation of human services delivery." Pp. 235–61 in Rosemary Sarry and Ezekial Yeheskel (eds.), The Management of Human Services. New York: Columbia University Press.

ROTHMAN, SHEILA M.
**1973** "Other people's children: The day-care experience in America." The Public Interest 30 (Winter):11–27.

ROUTH, G.
**1965** Occupation and Pay in Great Britain: 1906–60. Cambridge: Cambridge University Press.

RUDÉ, GEORGE
**1959** The Crowd in the French Revolution. Oxford: Oxford University Press.
**1964** The Crowd in History. New York: Wiley.

SCHEINER, PHILIP
**1977** "The occupational mobility of black workers in the Witwatersrand building industry 1960–1976." South African Labour Bulletin 3 (10):32–44.

SCHILLER, BRADLEY, R.
**1971** "Class discrimination vs. racial discrimination." Review of Economics and Statistics 53:263–69.

SCHLESINGER, ARTHUR, SR.
**1950** The American as Reformer. Cambridge, Mass.: Harvard University Press.

SCHMANDT-BESSERAT, DENISE
**1978** "The earliest precursor of writing." Scientific American 238(6):50–59.

SCHMIDT, FRANK L., AND JOHN E. HUNTER
**1974** "Racial and ethnic bias in psychological tests: Divergent implications of test bias." American Psychologist 29:1–8.

SCHNORE, LEO F.

**1957** "Satellites and suburbs." Social Forces 36 (December).

**1965** The Urban Scene. New York: Free Press.

SCHNORE, LEO F., AND J. K. O. JONES

**1969** "The evolution of city-suburban types in the course of a decade." Urban Affairs Quarterly (June) 4:421–22.

SCHNORE, LEO F., CAROLYN D. ANDRE, AND HARRY SHARP

**1976** "Black suburbanization 1930–1970." In Barry Schwartz (ed.), The Changing Face of the Suburbs. Chicago: University of Chicago Press.

SCHULTZ, T. W.

**1973** "The value of children: An economic perspective." Journal of Political Economy 81:S2–S13.

SCHUMPETER, JOSEPH

**1942** Capitalism, Socialism, and Democracy. New York: Harper & Row.

**1951** Imperialism and Social Classes. New York: Augustus M. Kelley.

SCOTT, W. R.

**1965** "Field methods in the study of organizations." In J. G. March (ed.), Handbook of Organizations. Chicago: Rand McNally.

SELZNICK, PHILIP

**1957** Leadership in Administration: A Sociological Interpretation. Evanston, Ill.: Row, Peterson & Co.

SEMYONOV, M., R. W. HODGE, AND A. TYREE

**1978** "Gaps and glissandos: Inequality, economic development, and social mobility in 24 countries." Unpublished ms., State University of New York, Department of Sociology, Stony Brook, N.Y.

SENNETT, RICHARD

**1978** The Fall of Public Man. New York: Vintage.

SERVAN-SCHREIBER, J. J.

**1968** The American Challenge. New York: Atheneum.

SEWELL, WILLIAM H., AND ROBERT M. HAUSER

**1974** Education, Occupation, and Earnings: Achievement in the Early Career. New York: Academic Press.

SHELDON, E. B., AND W. MOORE (eds.)

**1968** Indicators of Social Change. New York: Russell Sage Foundation.

SHEPPARD, HAROLD L., AND A. HARVEY BELITSKY

**1966** The Job Hunt: Jobseeking Behavior of Unemployed

Workers in a Local Economy. Upjohn Institute for Employment Research. Baltimore: Johns Hopkins Press.

SHI CHANG WU
**1974** Distribution of Economic Resources in the United States. Chicago: National Opinion Research Center. Mimeo.

SHILS, EDWARD
**1960*a*** "Mass society and its critics." Daedalus 89 (Spring): 288–314.
**1960*b*** "Intellectuals in the political development of the new states." World Politics 12(3):329–68.

SHILS, EDWARD (ed.)
**1961** "Centre and periphery." In The Logic of Personal Knowledge: Essays Presented to Michael Polanyi. London: Routledge and Kegan Paul.

SHORTER, EDWARD
**1975** The Making of the Modern Family. New York: Basic Books.

SIEGEL, P. M.
**1970** "Occupational prestige in the Negro subculture." In E. O. Laumann (ed.), Social Stratification: Research and Theory for the 1970s. Indianapolis: Bobbs-Merrill.
**1971** "Prestige in the American occupational structure." Unpublished Ph.D. dissertation, University of Chicago Library.

SIMON, JULIAN
**1977** The Economics of Population Growth. Princeton: Princeton University Press.

SIMPSON, G. G.
**1967** The Meaning of Evolution. New Haven: Yale University Press.

SINGER, I. J.
**1963** The Brothers Askenazi. Columbus, Ohio: World Publishing.

SLOMCZYNSKI, KAZIMIERZ M., AND WLODZIMIERZ WESOLOWSKI
**1978** "Theoretical orientations in the study of class structure in Poland, 1945–1975." Pp. 7–31, in Polish Sociological Association, Social Structure.

SMELSER, NEIL
**1962** Theory of Collective Behavior. New York: Free Press.
**1968*a*** "Sociological history: The industrial revolution and the British working-class family." Pp. 76–91 in Neil Smelser (ed.), Essays in Sociological Explanation. Englewood Cliffs, N.J.: Prentice-Hall.

**1968*b*** "Toward a theory of modernization." Pp. 125–46 in Neil Smelser (ed.), Essays in Sociological Explanation. Englewood Cliffs, N.J.: Prentice-Hall.

SMELSER, NEIL (ed.)

**1968*c*** Essays in Sociological Explanation. Englewood Cliffs, N.J.: Prentice-Hall.

SMITH, ADAM

**[1789] 1937** An Inquiry into the Nature and Causes of the Wealth of Nations. New York: Random House, Modern Library.

SMITH, JOEL

**1968** "Transportation: Social aspects." Pp. 128–34 in Vol. 16 of International Encyclopedia of the Social Sciences. New York: Macmillan.

**1970** "Another look at socioeconomic status distributions in urbanized areas." Urban Affairs Quarterly (June) 5:423–53.

SMITH, MICHAEL G.

**1966** "Pre-industrial stratification systems." Pp. 141–76 in Neil J. Smelser and Seymour Martin Lipset (eds.), Social Structure and Mobility in Economic Development. Chicago: Aldine.

SMUTS, ROBERT W.

**1959** Women and Work in America. New York: Columbia University Press.

SORENSEN, A., K. TAEUBER, AND L. HOLLINGSWORTH, JR.

**1975** "Indexes of residential segregation for 109 cities in the United States, 1940–1970." Sociological Focus 8.

SOROKIN, PITIRIM A.

**1927** Social Mobility. New York: Harper.

SPENCER, HERBERT

**1880** First Principles. New York: A. L. Burt.

SPINRAD, WILLIAM

**1970** Civil Liberties. Chicago: Quadrangle Books.

SPRO-CAS (STUDY PROJECT ON CHRISTIANITY IN APARTHEID SOCIETY)

**1973** Power, Privilege, and Poverty. Report of the Economics Commission. Johannesburg: Ravan Press.

STANLEY, JULIAN C.

**1971** "Predicting college success of the educationally disadvantaged." Science 171 (3972):640–47.

STATE OF SOUTH AFRICA

**1978** Economic, Financial, and Statistical Yearbook for the Republic of South Africa. Johannesburg: Da Gama Publishers.

STEENKAMP, W. F. J.

**1971** "Labour policies for growth during the seventies: In the established industrial areas." South African Journal of Economics 39(2):97–111.

**1973** "Labour and management in manufacturing development." South African Journal of Economics 41(4):438–51.

STEINER, GILBERT Y.

**1971** The State of Welfare. Washington, D.C.: Brookings Institution.

STEINMETZ, S. K., AND MURRAY A. STRAUS (eds.)

**1974** Violence in the Family. New York: Harper & Row.

STERNLIEB, GEORGE

**1971** "The city as sandbox." The Public Interest 25 (Fall):14–21.

**1975** "Aging suburbs and black homeownership." Annals of the American Academy of Political and Social Science 422 (November).

STEWARD, JULIAN H.

**1955** Theory of Culture Change. Urbana, Ill.: University of Illinois Press.

STIGLER GEORGE

**1947** "An academic episode." American Association of University Professors Bulletin 33 (4):661–65.

STINCHCOMBE, ARTHUR L.

**1963** "Some empirical consequences of the Davis-Moore theory of stratification." American Sociological Review 28 (5): 805–8.

**1965** "Social structure and organizations." In J. G. March (ed.), Handbook of Organizations. Chicago: Rand McNally.

STONE, R.

**1971** Demographic Accounting and Model Building. Paris: Organization for Economic Cooperation and Development.

**1975** "Transition and admission models in social indicator analysis." In K. C. Land and S. Spilerman (eds.), Social Indicator Models. New York: Russell Sage Foundation.

STRAUS, MURRAY A.

**1977** "Sexual inequality, cultural norms, and wife-beating." Pp. 59–77 in Jane Roberts Chapman and Margaret Gates (eds.), Women into Wives. Beverly Hills, Calif.: Sage.

STRUMPEL, B. (ed.)

**1974** Subjective Elements of Well-Being. Paris: Organization for Economic Cooperation and Development.

SUBCOMMITTEE ON INTERGOVERNMENTAL RELATIONS

**1973** Confidence and Concern: Citizens View American Government. Washington, D.C.: Government Printing Office.

SUSSMAN, MARVIN B.

**1959** "The isolated nuclear family: Fact or fiction?" Social Problems 6 (Spring):333–39.

**1965** "Relationships of adult children with their parents." Pp. 62–92 in Ethel Shanas and Gordon F. Streib (eds.), Social Structure and the Family: Generational Relations. Englewood Cliffs, N.J.: Prentice-Hall.

SUTTLES, GERALD D.

**1968** The Social Order of the Slum: Ethnicity and Territory in the Inner City. Chicago: University of Chicago Press.

**1972** The Social Construction of Communities. Chicago: University of Chicago Press.

SVALASTOGA, K.

**1959** Prestige, Class, and Mobility. Copenhagen: Gyldendal.

**1965** "Social mobility: The Western European model." Acta Sociologica 9:175–82.

SWANSON, G. E.

**1971** Social Change. Glenview, Ill.: Scott, Foresman.

SWEDISH LABOUR MARKET BOARD

**1978** "Compulsory notification of vacancies." Labour Market Seminar.

TAEUBER, CONRAD (ed.)

**1978** "America in the seventies: Some social indicators." Annals of the American Academy of Political and Social Science 435 (January).

TAEUBER, KARL E.

**1975** "Racial segregation: The persisting dilemma." Annals of the American Academy of Political and Social Science (November);87–96.

TAYLOR, FREDERICK W.

**1911** Shop Management. New York: Harper.

TAYLOR, GEORGE R., AND IRENE O. NEU

**1956** The American Railroad Network: 1861–1890. Cambridge, Mass.: Harvard University Press.

THOMPSON, D'ARCY

**1943** On Growth and Form, 2nd ed. Cambridge: Cambridge University Press.

THOMPSON, J. L. P.

**1978** "Dual incorporation and the bases of ethnic resurgence in

Northern Ireland: An empirical test." Unpublished paper, June. University of California, Berkeley.

THOMPSON, LEONARD M.

**1966** Politics in the Republic of South Africa. Boston: Little, Brown.

THOMPSON, WILLIAM IRWIN

**1967** The Imagination of Insurrection: Dublin, Easter 1916. New York: Harper & Row.

THUROW, LESTER C.

**1975** Generating Inequality: Mechanisms of Distribution in the U.S. Economy. New York: Basic Books.

TILLY, CHARLES

**1969** "Collective violence in European perspective." In Hugh D. Graham and Ted Gurr (eds.), The History of Violence in America. New York: Bantam Books.

**1975** "Reflections on the history of European state-making." In Charles Tilly (ed), The Formation of National States in Western Europe. Princeton: Princeton University Press.

**1978** From Mobilization to Revolution. New York: Addison-Wesley.

TILLY, CHARLES (ed.)

**1978** Historical Studies of Changing Fertility. Princeton: Princeton University Press.

TIRYAKIAN, E. A.

**1958** "The prestige evaluation of occupations in an underdeveloped country: The Philippines." American Journal of Sociology 63:390–99.

TRAPIDO, STANLEY

**1971** "South Africa in a comparative study of industrialization." Journal of Development Studies 7 (3):309–20.

TREIMAN, D. J.

**1977** Occupational Prestige in Comparative Perspective. New York: Academic Press.

TRILLING, LIONEL

**1972** Sincerity and Authenticity. Cambridge, Mass.: Harvard University Press.

TROST, JAN

**1976** "Married and unmarried cohabitation: The case of Sweden, with some comparisons." Pp. 189–204 in Luis Lenero-Otero (ed.), Beyond the Nuclear Family Model: Cross-Cultural Perspectives. Beverly Hill, Calif.: Sage.

TROW, MARTIN

**1972** The Expansion and Transformation of Higher Education. Morristown, N.J.: General Learning Press.

**1974*a*** "Higher education and moral development." Working paper no. 16, Graduate School of Public Policy, University of California, Berkeley.

**1974*b*** "Problems in the transition from elite to mass education." Pp. 51–101 in Politics for Higher Education: General Report. Paris: OECD.

TUMIN, MELVIN M.

**1953** "Some principles of stratification: A critical analysis." American Sociological Review 18 (4):387–93.

TURNER, RALPH

**1941** The Great Cultural Traditions. New York: McGraw-Hill.

**1969** "The theme of contemporary social movements." British Journal of Sociology 20 (December):390–405.

**1976** "The real self: From institution to impulse." American Journal of Sociology 81 (March):989–1016.

TYREE, A., AND B. G. SMITH

**1978** "Occupational hierarchy in the United States: 1789–1969." Social Forces 56:881–99.

UDY, STANLEY H., JR.

**1959** Organization of Work. New Haven, Conn.: Hraf Press.

**1970** Work in Traditional and Modern Society. Englewood Cliffs, N.J.: Prentice-Hall.

UHLENBERG, PETER

**1974** "Cohort variations in family life cycle experiences of U.S. females." Journal of Marriage and the Family 36 (May): 284–92.

UNITED NATIONS

**1968** "Urbanization: Development policies and planning." P. 30 in International Social Development Review, No. 1.

**1977** Statistical Yearbook 1976. New York: United Nations.

**1978** "Distribution of income: Trends and policies." New York: United Nations Economic and Social Council. E/1978/29. Mimeo.

UNITED STATES BUREAU OF THE CENSUS

**1974** "Mobility of the population of the U.S., March 1970–March 1974." Current Population Reports. Washington, D.C.: Government Printing Office.

**1976** "Daytime care of children: October 1974 and February 1975." Current Population Reports. Series P-20, No. 298. Washington, D.C.: Government Printing Office.

**1977*a*** "Fertility of American women: June 1976." Current Population Reports. Series P-20, No. 308. Washington, D.C.: Government Printing Office.

**1977*b*** "Population profile of the United States." Current Population Reports. Series P-20, No. 324. Washington, D.C.: Government Printing Office.

**1977*c*** "Estimate of the population of the U.S., by age, sex, and race, July 1, 1974 to 1976." Current Population Reports, Series P-24, No. 643. Washington, D.C.: Government Printing Office.

**1977*d*** "School enrollment: Social and economic characteristics of students, October, 1976." Bureau of the Census, Series P-20, No. 309. Washington, D.C.: Government Printing Office.

**1977*e*** Statistical Abstract of the United States, 98th ed. Washington, D.C.: Government Printing Office.

**1978*a*** Geographical Mobility, March 1975 to March 1977. Washington, D.C.: Government Printing Office.

**1978*b*** "Population profile of the United States: 1977." Current Population Reports. Washington, D.C.: Government Printing Offiice.

UNITED STATES DEPARTMENT OF AGRICULTURE

**1974** PA-1. Washington, D.C.: Government Printing Office.

UNITED STATES DEPARTMENT OF COMMERCE, OFFICE OF FEDERAL STATISTICAL POLICY AND STANDARDS

**1977** Social Indicators 1976. Washington, D.C.: Government Printing Office.

UNITED STATES DEPARTMENT OF HEALTH, EDUCATION, AND WELFARE

**1969** Toward a Social Report. Washington, D.C.: Government Printing Office.

UNITED STATES DEPARTMENT OF HEALTH, EDUCATION, AND WELFARE, NATIONAL CENTER FOR HEALTH STATISTICS

**1972** Vital Statistics of the United States, 1972. Volume 1: Natality. Washington, D.C.: Government Printing Office.

**1978** Final Natality Statistics, 1978. Washington, D.C.: Government Printing Office.

UNITED STATES DEPARTMENT OF LABOR, BUREAU OF LABOR STATISTICS

**1975*a*** Jobseeking Methods Used by American Workers. Bulletin 1886. Washington, D.C.: Government Printing Office.

**1975*b*** "Educational attainment of workers." Special Labor Force Report 186 (March). Washington, D.C.: Government Printing Office.

**1975*c*** Handbook of Labor Statistics 1975. Washington, D.C.: Government Printing Office.

**1976** Data presented in *U.S. News and World Report*, April 5, p. 51.

**1977*a*** Handbook of Labor Statistics 1977. Washington, D.C.: Government Printing Office.

**1977*b*** Work Experience of the Population in 1976. Special Labor Force Report 201. Washington, D.C.: Government Printing Office.

UNITED STATES SENATE

**1978** "U.S. corporate interests in South Africa." Report to the Committee on Foreign Relations. Washington, D.C.: Government Printing Office.

U.S.A. STATISTICAL ABSTRACT 1976

**1976** Washington, D.C.: Government Printing Office.

VAN DE WALLE, ETIENNE

**1968** "Marriage and marital fertility." Daedalus 97 (Spring): 486–501.

VAN DEN BERGHE, PIERRE

**1967** South Africa: A Study in Conflict. Berkeley: University of California Press.

VAN DER HORST, SHEILA

**1965** "The effects of industrialization on race relations in South Africa." Pp. 97–140 in Guy Hunter (ed.), Industrialization and Race Relations. London: Oxford University Press.

VAN LAWICK-GOODALL, JANE

**1971** In the Shadow of Man. New York: Dell.

VEBLEN, THORSTEN

**1921** The Engineers and the Price System. New York: B. W. Huebsch.

VIDICH, ARTHUR, AND JOSEPH BENSMAN

**1960** Small Town and Mass Society. Garden City, N.Y.: Doubleday.

WAITE, L. J., AND R. M. STOLZENBERG

**1976** "Intended childbearing and labor force participation of young women: Insights from nonrecursive models." American Sociological Review 41:235–52.

WALBANK, F. W.

**1964** The Decline of the Roman Empire in the West. London: Cobbett Press.

WALLERSTEIN, IMMANUEL

**1974** The Modern World-System: Capitalist Agriculture and the Origins of the European World-Economy in the Sixteenth Century. New York and London: Academic Press.

**1976*a*** "Semi-peripheral countries and the contemporary world crisis." Theory and Society 3(4):461–83.

**1976*b*** "A world-system perspective on the social sciences." British Journal of Sociology 27(3):343–52.

**1979** "Social conflict in post-independence black Africa: The concepts of race and status-group reconsidered," "Class formation in the capitalist world-economy," and "Class conflict in the world-economy." Reprinted in the Capitalist World-Economy. London and New York: Cambridge University Press.

WALL STREET JOURNAL

**1978** "The bonus babies." May 15, p. 28.

WALSH, MARY ROTH

**1977** Doctors Wanted: No Women Need Apply. Sexual Barriers in the Medical Profession, 1835–1975. New Haven and London: Yale University Press.

WALZER, MICHAEL

**1969** The Revolution of the Saints. New York: Atheneum. (1st ed. 1965.)

WARNER, SAM BASS, JR.

**1962** Streetcar Suburbs: The Process of Growth in Boston, 1870–1900. Cambridge, Mass.: Harvard University Press.

WARREN, DONALD I.

**1975** Black Neighborhoods: An Assessment of Community Power. Ann Arbor: University of Michigan Press.

WASHBURN, SHERWOOD L.

**1978** "The evolution of man." Scientific American 239(3): 194–208.

WATKINS, J. W. H.

**1953** "Ideal types and historical explanation." Pp. 729–30 in Herbert Feigl and May Brodbeck (eds.), Readings in the Philosophy of Science. New York: Appleton-Century-Crofts.

WEAVER, FREDERICK STIRTON

**1976** "Capitalist development, empire, and Latin American underdevelopment." Latin American Perspectives 3(4): 17–53.

WEBER, MAX

**1968** Economy and Society. Vol. 3. New York: Bedminster Press.

WEINBERG, IAN

**1974** "Social problems are no more." In E. Smigel (ed.), Handbook of Social Problems. Chicago: Rand McNally.

WEITZMAN, LENORE J.

**1972** "Legal regulation of marriage: Tradition and change." California Law Review 62 (July–September):1169–1288.

WHITE, LESLIE A.

**1959** The Evolution of Culture. New York: McGraw-Hill.

WHYTE, WILLIAM H., JR.

**1956** The Organization Man. New York: Simon and Schuster.

WILENSKY, HAROLD L.

**1956** Intellectuals in Labor Unions: Organizational Pressures on Professional Roles. New York: Free Press–Macmillan.

**1960** "Work, careers, and social integration." International Social Science Journal 12 (4): 543–60.

**1964*a*** "Mass society and mass culture: Interdependence of independence?" American Sociological Review 29: 173–97.

**1964*b*** "Varieties of work experience." Pp. 124–54 in Henry Borow (ed.), Man in a World at Work. Boston: Houghton Mifflin.

**1965** "The problems and prospects of the welfare state." Pp. *v–lii* in H. L. Wilensky and C. N. Lebeaux, Industrial Society and Social Welfare. New York: Free Press–Macmillan. Enlarged paperbound edition.

**1966** "Work as a social problem." Pp. 117–66 in Howard S. Becker (ed.), Social Problems. New York: Wiley.

**1967** "Careers, counseling, and the curriculum." Journal of Human Resources 2 (Winter):19–40.

**1968** "Women's work: Economic growth, ideology, structure." Industrial Relations 7:235–48.

**1975** The Welfare State and Equality: Structural and Ideological Roots of Public Expenditures. Berkeley: University of California Press.

**1976** The 'New Corporatism,' Centralization, and the Welfare State. Beverly Hills: Sage Publications.

**1978** "The political economy of income distribution: Issues in the analysis of government approaches to the reduction of inequality." Pp. 87–108 in J. Milton Yinger and Stephen J. Cutler (eds.), Major Social Issues: A Multidisciplinary View. New York: Free Press.

WILENSKY, HAROLD L., AND JACK LADINSKY

**1967** "From religious community to occupational group: Structural assimilation among professors, lawyers, and engineers." American Sociological Review 32 (4):541–61.

WILENSKY, HAROLD L., AND CHARLES N. LEBEAUX

**1958** Industrial Society and Social Welfare. New York: Russell Sage Foundation.

WILKINSON, KENNETH P.

**1970** "The community as a social field." Social Forces 48:311–22.

WILKINSON, PAUL

**1971** Social Movement. New York: Praeger.

WILLIAMS, GREGORY

**1975** "A research note on trends in occupational differentiation by sex." Social Problems 22:543–47.

WILLIAMS, RAYMOND

**1960** Culture and Society. Garden City, N.Y.: Anchor/Doubleday.

**1976** Keywords: A Vocabulary of Culture and Society. New York: Oxford University Press.

WILLIAMS, ROBIN M., JR.

**1977** Mutual Accommodation: Ethnic Conflict and Cooperation. Minneapolis: University of Minnesota Press.

WILSON, E. O.

**1975** Sociobiology: The New Synthesis. Cambridge, Mass.: Harvard University Press.

WILSON, FRANCIS

**1975** "The political implications for blacks of economic changes now taking place in South Africa." Pp. 168–200 in Leonard Thompson and Jeffrey Butler (eds.), Change in Contemporary South Africa. Berkeley: University of California Press.

WILSON, GEOFFREY, AND MONICA WILSON

**1954** The Analysis of Social Change. Cambridge: Cambridge University Press.

WILSON, JOHN

**1973** Introduction to Social Movements. New York: Basic Books.

WILSON, WILLIAM J.

**1978** The Declining Significance of Race: Blacks and Changing American Institutions. Chicago: University of Chicago Press.

WINCH, ROBERT F., AND RAE LESSER BLUMBERG

**1968** "Societal complexity and familial organization." Pp. 70–92 in Robert F. Winch and Louis Goodman (eds.), Selected Studies in Marriage and the Family. New York: Holt, Rinehard & Winston.

WIRTH, LOUIS

**1928** The Ghetto. Chicago: University of Chicago Press.

1938 "Urbanism as a way of life." American Journal of Sociology 44 (July):1–24.

WIRTZ, WILLARD W.

1965 The Older American Worker: Age Discrimination in Employment. A report of the Secretary of Labor to the Congress under Section 715 of the Civil Rights Act of 1964. Washington, D.C.: Government Printing Office.

WOLPE, HAROLD

1970 "Industrialism and race in South Africa." Pp. 151–79 in S. Zubaida (ed.), Race and Racialism. London: Tavistock.

WOODRUFF, WILLIAM

1966 Impact of Western Man: A Study of Europe's Role in the World Economy, 1950–1960. New York: St. Martin's Press.

WOOLSEY, SUZANNE H.

1977 "Pied piper politics and the child-care debate." Daedalus 106 (Spring):127–45.

WRIGLEY, E. ANTHONY

1969 Population and History. New York: McGraw-Hill.

1977 "Reflections on the history of the family." Daedalus 106 (Spring):71–85.

WRONG, DENNIS

1961 "The over-socialized conception of man in modern sociology." American Sociological Review 26 (April):189–93.

YEMIN, EDWARD

1976 "Job security: Influence of ILO standards and recent trends." International Labour Review 113 (1):17–33.

ZABLOCKI, BENJAMIN

1971 The Joyful Community: An Account of the Bruderhof, a Communal Movement Now in Its Third Generation. Baltimore: Penguin.

ZIMMER, BASIL G.

1974 "The urban centrifugal drift." In Amos H. Hawley and Vincent Rock (eds.), Metropolitan America in Contemporary Perspective. Beverly Hills, Calif.: Sage.

1976 "Suburbanization and changing political structures." In Barry Schwartz (ed.), The Changing Face of the Suburbs. Chicago: University of Chicago Press.

ZIMRING, FRANKLIN, AND GORDON HAWKINS

1973 Deterrence. Chicago: University of Chicago Press.

ZILBORG, ARISTIDE R.

1974 "The making of Flemings and Walloons: Belgium, 1830–1910." Journal of Interdisciplinary History 5 (Fall):179–236.

# Name Index

# Subject Index

Such topics as national and international associations, foundations, and departments of the federal government are listed in the Name Index.